T0385686

LOEB CLASSICAL LIBRARY
FOUNDED BY JAMES LOEB 1911

EDITED BY
JEFFREY HENDERSON

SOPHOCLES

I

LCL 20

SOPHOCLES

AJAX · ELECTRA · OEDIPUS TYRANNUS

EDITED AND TRANSLATED BY

HUGH LLOYD-JONES

HARVARD UNIVERSITY PRESS
CAMBRIDGE, MASSACHUSETTS
LONDON, ENGLAND

First published 1994
Reprinted with corrections 1997

Library of Congress Cataloging-in-Publication Data
Sophocles.
(Loeb classical library; 20–21,483)
Includes bibliographical references.
1. Sophocles—Translations into English.
2. Greek drama (Tragedy)—Translations into English.
3. Mythology, Greek—Drama.
I. Lloyd-Jones, Hugh. II. Title. III. Series.
PA4414.A1L56 1992 882'.01—dc20 92–19295
ISBN 978-0-674-99557-4

Composed in ZephGreek and ZephText by
Technologies 'N Typography, Merrimac, Massachusetts.
Printed on acid-free paper and bound by
The Maple-Vail Book Manufacturing Group

CONTENTS

PREFACE

By kind permission of the Oxford University Press, the text of Sophocles printed in these volumes is virtually the same as that of the text edited by me in collaboration with N. G. Wilson, which was published as an Oxford Classical Text in 1990 and reprinted, with a few corrections, in 1992. It is virtually the same, and not quite the same, because in this edition I have sometimes put an emendation in the text where the Oxford text had a crux, and because in a few places I have changed my opinion.

My translation has no literary pretensions, being intended as an aid to those who wish to understand the Greek text that is printed opposite. At the same time as the Oxford text, Nigel Wilson and I brought out a book called *Sophoclea: Studies in the Text of Sophocles,* in which we explained the reasons for some of our editorial decisions.

I would like to thank the Editor and the Trustee of the Loeb Classical Library, Professors George Goold and Zeph Stewart, and also Margaretta Fulton, of the Harvard University Press, for the considerable assistance that I have received from them. Nigel Wilson has not only allowed our joint work to be utilised for this edition, but has added to my obligation to him by correcting the proofs.

Hugh Lloyd-Jones

Wellesley, Massachusetts
28 June 1993

NOTE TO SECOND PRINTING

The need for a new printing has enabled me to make a number of corrections as well as alterations, most of which the reader will find explained in H. Lloyd-Jones and N. G. Wilson, *Sophocles: Second Thoughts* (Hypomnemata 100), Vandenhoek und Ruprecht, Göttingen, 1997.

H. Ll.-J.

10 March 1997

INTRODUCTION

Many modern readers of Greek tragedy seem to feel a special affinity with Sophocles, and it is worth while to endeavor to account for this.

The notion that each tragedy has a single hero from whose standpoint the whole action should be viewed is a mistake. But each surviving Sophoclean tragedy contains at least one heroic figure, at least one character whose strength, courage, and intelligence exceed the human norm. In a dire crisis only such persons as these can protect common human beings; yet they suffer, to use a French expression, from the defects of their qualities, being proud, obstinate, and irascible. In each surviving play, such characters come into conflict with the order of the universe, and suffer in consequence. Some modern scholars insist that the divine government of the universe is necessarily just, and that the heroes must learn wisdom by suffering; others hold that the poet's sympathy is with the heroes as they defy unjust and arbitrary gods. R. P. Winnington-Ingram, in his excellent study of the complete plays, calls the former group "the pietists" and the latter "the hero-worshippers."

The Women of Trachis presents the end of the life on earth of the greatest of Greek heroes, Heracles. Although he is Heracles' father, Zeus punishes him for his ruthless behaviour towards the family and city of Eurytus, for whose daughter Iole he has conceived a fatal passion. The brutality of Heracles, and in particular his unfeeling conduct towards his wife Deianeira, who is portrayed with great delicacy and sympathy, is unsparingly presented (as is his greatness and his service to mankind); Zeus punishes him for it, yet his agonising death will be followed by apotheosis, as the text clearly indicates.

Antigone is another heroic character, skilfully contrasted with her sister Ismene, who without being heroic does not lack courage or affection. Antigone's defiance of Creon's edict forbidding the burial of her brother has never failed to win the admiration of audiences and readers. But Antigone, like Heracles, has the defects that go with her heroic qualities; her obstinate refusal to compromise and her fatal impetuosity make the final catastrophe worse than it need have been. We are several times reminded that the daughter of Oedipus lies under the curse upon the house of Laius.

The murderous and treacherous attack upon the Greek chieftains to which Ajax is impelled by the award of the arms of the dead Achilles to Odysseus is by no means extenuated by the poet, and the harshness of the hero's character is never minimised; he treats Tecmessa no more considerately than Heracles treats Deianeira. But the poet presents with deep sympathy the greatness of the hero and the clear-sighted courage with which he realises that he must kill himself if he is not to renounce the proud conception of honour which is central to his life. He is contrasted with Odysseus, a very different kind of hero, whose heroism Ajax himself is unable to appreciate. Ajax is confident that after his death his family will be protected by his brother Teucer. But though Teucer defends his dead brother and his family with unfailing loyalty and courage, his defence would have been unavailing without support from the very last quarter from which Ajax would have expected it. Still, at the end of the play the impression of the greatness of the hero, as well as that of the sadness of his fate, is most powerfully conveyed.

The Oedipus of the *Oedipus Tyrannus* is a hero more sympathetic than Heracles or Ajax, or even Electra and Antigone; his courage and intelligence and his unselfish determination to save the city from the plague are there for all to see. But he too to some extent shows the defects inseparable from his heroic qualities; witness the ferocity which accompanies his unjust suspicion of Tiresias and Creon. It is a mistake to suppose that he is accounted personally guilty because of the killing of Laius and his party; he had been provoked by persons unknown to him, and the lives of Heracles, Theseus, and other heroes were full of such incidents. More relevant to his sad fate is the curse upon his father Laius, well known in myth; if it is not stressed in the play, that is because the poet is for the moment concerned to show how, not why, Oedipus met with his catastrophe. As Ajax is contrasted with Odysseus, Oedipus is contrasted with Creon—not that Creon is presented as a sympathetic character; our impression of his self-righteous smugness in the final scenes must have been intended by the poet, who after all knew the stories about Creon used in his own *Antigone* and *Oedipus at Colonus*.

The courage and nobility with which Electra over many years defies her father's murderers establish her heroic status. Yet she herself is aware that she has become a monster of hatred and resentment, though she pleads that she has been made one by her situation and the oppression of her enemies. She is contrasted with Chrysothemis, who though she is no heroine is not the coward for whom her sister takes her. The horror of the matricide is by no means minimised; when she hears her mother cry out after Orestes' first blow, Electra exclaims, "Strike twice as hard!" As in the *Antigone*, the family curse has its importance in the play.

Philoctetes is a hero even more sympathetic than the first Oedipus; the courage with which he has supported his ordeal and the noble generosity revealed in his conversations with another true hero, Neoptolemus, clearly establish his heroic character. But he too has much of the hardness that goes with heroism; after his bow has been returned, he comes within a whisker of killing Odysseus, and nothing could have persuaded him to sail to Troy and take part in its capture but the miraculous appearance of the now deified Heracles.

The heroic nobility of the aged Oedipus is immediately recognised by Theseus, with whom he has an obvious affinity, and who sees at once the importance of securing for his city the protection which Oedipus as a defunct hero will be able to provide. But the devotion of Oedipus to his loyal daughters is equalled by his hatred for his disloyal sons, and his treatment of the sons will finally involve the daughters too in their destruction.

These tragedies can only be understood if one has some understanding of the religion that lies behind them; we must avoid the opposite mistakes of assuming that this religion resembled Christianity, or that since it did not resemble Christianity it was not really a religion. For the Olympian gods men are only a secondary consideration;

Greek religion thus avoids the problem of evil, which has perplexed many Christians. But they have certain human favourites, and the chief god, Zeus, punishes the crimes of men, although since the wicked often flourish it often happens that the punishment is not immediate, but falls only on the descendants of the criminal. Thus even the most admirable of men may be struck down in a moment for a crime committed by an ancestor; the most obvious example is the case of Oedipus. By showing the gods the honour that they demand, and by taking care to remember the limitations of mortality, it was possible for worshippers to remain on comparatively good terms with them; but often it was the bravest and most intelligent among men who like Heracles or Ajax were tempted to commit the offences which provoked divine resentment. Zeus would then punish them, but that punishment did not diminish their heroic status.

Before dismissing this religion as an outmoded superstition, one may well ask whether it has not certain merits. Neither the "pietists" nor the "hero-worshippers" are altogether right; the truth lies somewhere in between. The Greek gods stand for forces which we can see working in the world, and the things that happen in the world are more easily explained if the universe is ruled by powers like them than if it is controlled by an all-powerful and all-good divinity. Nietzsche, who at the age of twenty lost his Christian faith after reading Darwin's *Origin of Species*, started his career as a professor of Greek, and the influence of this outlook on his philosophy is readily apparent.[1] In a period in which he and writers influenced

[1] See the essay on Nietzsche in my book *Blood for the Ghosts*.

by him have attracted so much attention, it is easy to understand why Sophocles has aroused special interest.

Life

The ancient evidence for the life of Sophocles is conveniently collected by Stefan Radt, *Tragicorum Graecorum Fragmenta* IV: *Sophocles* (1977), 29–95; Radt's collection of Testimonia will be referred to by the symbol T.

The ancient life preserved in a number of manuscripts of the plays (see T 1) was dated by F. Leo, *Die griechisch-römische Biographie* (1901), 22, in the generation after Aristarchus (216–144 B.C.); that is likely enough, seeing that the latest author whom it quotes is Carystius of Pergamum, a writer of the last third of the second century B.C. Its author, who is something better than a mere compiler, cites several Hellenistic scholars, including three pupils of Callimachus: Satyrus, Hermippus, and Ister. Satyrus wrote a life of Sophocles of which we have considerable fragments (P.Oxy. 1176, fr. 39 = T 148); Duris of Samos wrote on Sophocles (FGrH 76 F 29 = T 150), and also on Euripides; and Ister evidently wrote an account of Sophocles (see T, section U). See Mary R. Lefkowitz, *The Lives of the Greek Poets* (1981) for a translation (pp. 160–163) and discussion (pp. 66–74) of the *Life*. The general conclusion of her study is that little material was available to the Hellenistic biographers but inferences from the poets' own works or mentions of them in comedy, often used uncritically; contemporary information about them like that given by Ion of Chios in his *Epidemiai* or in inscriptions giving the names of public officials or victors in the dramatic competitions is found only rarely.

Sophocles died in 406 B.C. (T, section B; see Jacoby on Apollodorus 244 FGrH 35). The Parian Marble (A 56) says that he won his first victory in 469/8 at the age of 28, which would make him born in 497/6; the date given by Apollodorus, 495/4, may have been obtained by assuming that he "flourished," that is, reached the age of forty, in 456/5, the year in which Aeschylus died and Euripides made his debut.

His father's name, Sophillus, is well attested; the author of the *Life* (T, section A) sensibly corrects authors who said his father was a carpenter or a sword maker by pointing out that he came from a rich and noble family, so that the notion may have arisen from his father's having had slaves who pursued these activities. His deme was Colonus, which he made the setting of his *Oedipus at Colonus*; that is Kolonos Hippios, so called to distinguish it from Kolonos Agoraios in the city, which was not a deme at all. The site of Kolonos Hippios now lies in an unpleasant part of modern Athens, near the railway station; in ancient times it was a rural deme, just north of the city.

The statement in the *Life* (7) that Sophocles was notable for his good looks, affability, and general popularity seems to be well supported. As a boy he is said to have excelled both in *mousike* and in *gymnastike*, not surprisingly in a young man of his social class and his attainments. His instructor in music is said to have been the poet Lamprus (*Life* 3); we are not obliged to believe this, or that Aeschylus taught him about tragedy, but whatever their personal relations may have been it is obvious that he learned a good deal from Aeschylus' work.

Sophocles is said to have won the tragic prize with the first trilogy he exhibited (T, section Hc); the conjecture, which goes back to Lessing's life of Sophocles, that the *Triptolemus* was part of the trilogy victorious on that occasion, cannot be substantiated, but neither can it be refuted. The *Life* (18) says that 130 plays were attributed to him, of which seventeen (or possibly seven) were thought to be spurious; the life of Sophocles in the Byzantine lexicon called the Suda (T 2) says 123, which yields the same total if the number of the spurious plays was seven. The official list of victors at the Dionysia credits him with eighteen victories; the Suda life says twenty-four, Carystius in *Life* 8 says twenty, and victories at the Lenaea may account for the difference. Not that his career was an unqualified success; Cratinus fr. 17 Kassel-Austin complains that an archon once refused him a chorus and gave one to the inferior poet Gnesippus, and Dicaearchus fr. 80 Wehrli (= T 39) recorded that the trilogy that contained the *Oedipus Tyrannus* was defeated by the tragedian Philocles. Still, according to the *Life*, he never won third prize.

Of the seven complete plays we have evidence for the dates of only two; *Philoctetes* was produced in 409 and *Oedipus at Colonus* in 401. The dates of the others are conjectural, and many scholars have underrated the difficulty of conjectural dating. Our material is limited, more so than in the case of Euripides, so that stylometric evidence must be viewed with caution; in any case, it is obvious that a poet might choose to treat different subjects in different fashions, so that even if we possessed all the works of Sophocles we could not be sure that stylometry would yield an accurate chronology. The story told in the

Life (4) that Sophocles was appointed general in 441 because of the success of the *Antigone* has surely little value for dating the play, like the story, also told in the *Life* on the authority of Satyrus, that he died while reading out *Antigone*. With great caution one may say that *The Women of Trachis* and *Antigone* seem to show a less advanced technique than the other plays, and may be conjectured to be comparatively early. Many scholars have believed *Ajax* to be an early work, alleging that it has elements of Aeschylean grandiloquence (ὄγκος); but if the passages bracketed in this text are indeed interpolated, this judgment has to be revised. To me *Ajax* seems to be a mature masterpiece, probably not much earlier than *Oedipus Tyrannus*. *Electra* is generally thought to show affinity with the two late plays of which we know the dates, and is presumably a late work also. One might, then, hazard the conjecture that *The Women of Trachis* and *Antigone* may belong to the fifties or the forties of the fifth century, *Ajax* and *Oedipus Tyrannus* to the thirties or the twenties, and *Electra* to the period between 420 and 410.

Aristotle, *Poetics* 1449 A 15, says that Sophocles introduced the third actor and also scene painting (T 95; see T, section R). We cannot be sure that the statement about the third actor is correct; Themistius 26, 316 D (T 96, doubtless following earlier authorities) says that the third actor was introduced by Aeschylus, who certainly used him to great advantage in his later works. The statement about scene painting apparently conflicts with the words of Vitruvius (VII, praef. 11) that the first scene painter was Agatharchus of Samos "Aeschylo docente"; but the date of Agatharchus is disputed.

Aristoxenus fr. 79 Wehrli (quoted in the *Life* 23) says that Sophocles introduced the Phrygian type of song into tragedy and also elements of the dithyrambic style; a Byzantine treatise on tragedy that may be by Psellus (eleventh century) says that he introduced not only the Phrygian but also the Lydian tone (T 99a). This means that besides the traditional Ionian and Dorian modes he used other modes believed to have come from Asia Minor; the Phrygian resembled the Dorian in being more austere, and the Lydian was more relaxed, like the Ionian. The *Life* (4) and the life in the Suda (T 2, 3) say that he increased the number of the chorus from twelve to fifteen; this is doubted by O. Taplin, *The Stagecraft of Aeschylus* (1977) 323n2, who can see little point in so small a change, but then how could the mistake have arisen? The life in the Suda (T 2, 4) appears to say that he was the first to present four independent plays instead of a tetralogy on a single theme. This is wrong, since Aeschylus sometimes presented independent plays, as in the case of his tetralogy of 472 B.C., which included the *Persae*, but what was characteristic of Sophocles was the development of the single independent play. Other alleged technical innovations (see T, section R) are of less significance.

The statement in the *Life* (6) that Sophocles organised a society (*θίασος*) of educated persons honouring the Muses is dubious. Aristophanes, *Thesm.* 41, says that a *θίασος Μουσῶν*, a company of the Muses, visits the house of the tragedian Agathon, and the notion may derive from a similar passage in a comedy; see Lefkowitz, *Hermes* 112 (1984), 147. The life in the Suda (T 2, 7) says that he wrote a prose treatise on the chorus in dispute with Thespis and Choerilus; but these tragedians were active during the last third of the sixth century, long before Sophocles, nor can they have left treatises to which he could have replied. In all likelihood the three were characters in a Hellenistic dialogue about tragedy. Such a dialogue may well have contained the account of his own development ascribed to Sophocles by Plutarch, *De profectibus in virtute* 7, 79 B (T 100): "having got through the stages of playing with Aeschylean grandiloquence and then with the displeasing and artificial element in my own manner of elaborating my theme, now in the third stage I am changing to the kind of style that is most expressive of character and the best."

As a young man he is alleged to have appeared in his own plays with success, triumphing as Nausicaa playing ball in *Nausicaa* and playing the lyre in *Thamyras* (T 1, 24f; 99b2). The former story may well have originated in a comic poet's joke, and the latter may have been invented because Thamyras was a poet who played and sang, but both stories attest the personal glamour which Sophocles obviously possessed. Several stories credit him with many erotic triumphs; see T, section N, "Amatoria." Thus Athenaeus 13, 603 E f preserves a long extract from the *Epidemiai* of Sophocles' contemporary Ion of Chios, telling how at a banquet which Sophocles attended when he was serving as a general at the time of the revolt of Samos he employed a stratagem to kiss a beautiful boy who was pouring wine for the guests. And a story is told by the Peripatetic Hieronymus (fr. 35 Wehrli) of how a boy whom Sophocles had taken out of the city in order to enjoy him managed to make off with the poet's cloak, leaving his own in its place. Plato in the first book of the

Republic (329 B) says that when Cephalus asked Sophocles, now an old man, if he were still capable of sexual intercourse, the poet replied that he was happy to have escaped from the power of an insane and cruel master, meaning the god of love.

Sophocles is the only one of the great tragedians who is known to have held public office in the Athenian democracy. An inscription (T 18 = tab. 12, 36; Meritt, Wade-Gery, McGregor, *The Athenian Tribute Lists* 2, p. 18) shows that in 443/2 he was one of the treasurers of Athena, a Hellenotamias, and several authorities tell us (T 19–25) that in 441/0 he was one of the ten generals and in that capacity took part in the suppression of the revolt of Samos. Ion of Chios, who met him and told stories of his conduct on that occasion, reports that "in political matters he was neither clever nor energetic, but like any Athenian nobleman," *τῶν χρηστῶν Ἀθηναίων* (T 75, 31–32) (surely the word "good," *χρηστῶν*, indicates a social class rather than a moral quality). The story that he was chosen as general because of the success of his *Antigone* (T 25, the first ancient summary of that play, attributed to Aristophanes of Byzantium) is most improbable. The story of a second generalship (see T 26) seems very dubious; see Radt's note on the subject on p. 45.

Aristotle, *Rhet.* 3, 18, 1419 A 25, says that when Pisander asked Sophocles whether he had agreed with the other *probouloi* (commissioners) when they voted to entrust the government to the Four Hundred, Sophocles said that he had, and when Pisander asked if he did not think this a bad decision, he replied, "Yes, it was because there was no other that was better." This is our only indication that Sophocles, who will have been eighty-six years old at the time, was one of the commissioners appointed in the crisis of 411 B.C. (Thucydides 8,1,3), but this may well have been the case. Thucydides describes the commission as ἀρχήν τινα πρεσβυτέρων ἀνδρῶν, and Hagnon, the only other person named as a commissioner, had been general in 440 and founder of Amphipolis in 437/6. Obviously old and respected persons were chosen, as in 1940 Marshal Pétain seemed to the French the safest choice.

The *Life* (11) says that Sophocles was the priest of a hero with powers of healing called Halon, and that in this capacity he was chosen to take care of the cult statue of Asclepius in his house when the cult was being introduced from Epidaurus and the *temenos* assigned to the god was not yet ready to receive him (see T, section M). A note in the ancient etymological lexica s.v. Dexion says that because of this the poet after his death was worshipped as a hero under the name Dexion, which suggests the word δέχεσθαι and therefore the notion of "receiving" the god. There was indeed a hero called Dexion, as inscriptions show (T 70 and 71 = IG II/III 1252–3), but some doubt attaches to this story; Lefkowitz (*Lives of the Greek Poets*, p. 84) remarks that "in actual cult practice adult heroes are worshipped under their own names and do not acquire new identities," and wonders if the plot of *Oedipus at Colonus* may not be responsible for the story. E. Kearns, "The Heroes of Attica," *Bulletin of the Institute of Classical Studies*, Suppl. 57 (1989), 154, who defends the tradition, fails to cite another instance of a change of name.

Oedipus at Colonus very probably played a part in the genesis of the story, told in the *Life* (13) and in several other places (see T, section O), that his son Iophon brought a legal action against him, claiming that he was out of his mind and incapable of managing his property. The *Life* quotes Satyrus as making him say "If I am Sophocles, I am not out of my mind; if I am out of my mind, I am not Sophocles," and then read out *Oedipus at Colonus*. Iophon, who himself wrote tragedies (see T, section L), was the son of the poet by his wife Nicostrate; but Sophocles had another son, Ariston, by a Sicyonian woman called Theoris. Legal marriage with a foreigner would have been impossible, so that the statement in a passage of Athenaeus (13, 592 A), containing gossip for which no authority is given, that she was an hetaira is likely to be true. But the story Athenaeus goes on to tell, that at the end of his life Sophocles became infatuated with another hetaira called Archippe and made her his heiress, seems improbable; against it one must set the anecdote about Cephalus related by Plato (T 80 a, and see above, p. 11). The author of the *Life* alleges that Iophon's action against his father was prompted by his jealousy of the partiality shown by the poet for Ariston's son, who was also named Sophocles. There can be little doubt that the whole story derives from a comedy; see Lefkowitz, *Lives of the Greek Poets*, 84–85.

Sophocles was generally thought to have been a most agreeable person. Aristophanes, who in his *Peace* of 421 had accused him of avarice (695–699), in his *Frogs* of 405, produced not long after the death of Sophocles, makes Heracles ask Dionysus why he does not wish to bring back from the dead Sophocles rather than Euripides (76f). Dionysus replies that he wants to see what Iophon can manage to write without his father, and that Euripides, being a villain, will readily agree to escape from Hades in his company, whereas Sophocles was easy-going in this world and will be easy-going in the next (ὁ δ' εὔκολος μὲν ἐνθάδ', εὔκολος δ' ἐκεῖ). Later in the play (759f), a slave in Hades tells the slave of Dionysus, Xanthias, how Euripides on his arrival has claimed for himself the throne of the greatest master of tragedy, hitherto occupied by Aeschylus. When Xanthias (786) asks why Sophocles did not claim the throne, the other slave tells him that when Sophocles arrived he kissed Aeschylus and clasped his hand. If Aeschylus prevails in his contest with Euripides, the slave explains, Sophocles will remain where he is; but if Euripides wins, then Sophocles will challenge him. When Aeschylus leaves Hades to return to earth with Dionysus (1515f), he asks Pluto to let Sophocles occupy the throne and keep it for him in case he ever returns. In another play Aristophanes speaks of Sophocles as being "anointed with honey" (fr. 598 Kassel-Austin; see their note ad loc.), and in his *Muses*, produced soon after Sophocles' death, the comic poet Phrynichus (fr. 32 Kassel-Austin) writes:

> *μάκαρ Σοφοκλέης, ὃς πολὺν χρόνον βιοὺς*
> *ἀπέθανεν, εὐδαίμων ἀνὴρ καὶ δεξιός·*
> *πολλὰς ποιήσας καὶ καλὰς τραγῳδίας*
> *καλῶς ἐτελεύτησ', οὐδὲν ὑπομείνας κακόν.*
> Fortunate Sophocles, who after a long life
> died, a happy and a gifted man;
> after writing many fine tragedies
> he made a good end, having endured no evil.

Only when a man was dead, according to the Greek way of thinking, could one pronounce him fortunate. So "he made a good end" is apposite; the various anecdotes about Sophocles' death—he choked on a grape pip (like the comic poet Philemon), he died reading aloud *Antigone*, he died of joy when that play won the prize—are, like many anecdotes about Greek poets, valueless (see T, section P, and Lefkowitz, *Lives of the Greek Poets*, 85–86).

History of the Text

During the fourth century the works of Sophocles were often revived. Dramatic texts are particularly subject to interpolation, abbreviation, and every kind of corruption, and the texts that circulated at that time are likely to have varied a great deal. Pseudo-Plutarch, *Vitae X Oratorum* 841 F (= Plutarch, *Vita Lycurgi* 15; T 156) states that the orator Lycurgus carried a decree ordering that an official copy of all the works of the three great tragedians be made and that all performances conform to this text; this will have happened between about 338 and 326 B.C. Early in the third century the Alexandrian Library was founded by Ptolemy I, and scholars began to collect, classify, and edit the works of the principal Greek poets. Galen, *In Hippocratis Epidemias* 3, 2, 4 (T 157), records that Ptolemy Euergetes—he obviously means Ptolemy Euergetes I, who reigned from 247 to 222—borrowed the official copy from Athens, leaving a deposit of fifteen talents of silver, a very large sum, to be forfeited in case it was not returned, and then kept it, forfeiting the fifteen talents. Doubtless this official copy formed the basis of the editions of the text of the three tragedians established by Aristophanes of Byzantium (c. 257–180

B.C.); but W. S. Barrett, *Euripides, Hippolytos* (1964) 47, points out that "it is likely to have been no more than an ordinary text of its day, carrying most of the modifications established by actors during the preceding century."

Other scholars continued to work on the text of Sophocles. A commentary on Sophocles is likely to have been written by the famous scholar Aristarchus (c. 216–144 B.C.); see R. Pfeiffer, *History of Classical Scholarship from the Beginnings to the End of the Hellenistic Age* (1968), 222–223. In Augustus' time Didymus, nicknamed Χαλκέντερος, "of brazen guts," produced a vast variorum edition, incorporating material from many different scholars; the scholia in our Byzantine manuscripts represent a severely abbreviated version of this work (see Pfeiffer, 277).

After the time of Didymus the ancient period of Greek learning continued for another six centuries, until the seventh century. The plays continued to be copied, and new commentaries to be composed, but these became more and more elementary. At a date which is extremely difficult to determine, but was probably not earlier, and perhaps later, than the third century A.D. (see Barrett, *Euripides, Hippolytos*, 53), someone made a selection of seven plays each of Aeschylus and Sophocles and ten plays of Euripides, and after that the other plays became very rare indeed.

During the dark age of Byzantine culture, between the seventh and the ninth centuries, few manuscripts are likely to have been copied, and Sophocles must have been very little studied. But in the ninth century at least one manuscript of the seven plays was translated from the old uncial writing into the newly created minuscule script (see L. D. Reynolds and N. G. Wilson, *Scribes and Scholars*, 3rd ed., 1991, 58f). Of the two hundred or so medieval manuscripts, by far the greater number contain only the three plays of a later selection, *Ajax*, *Electra*, and *Oedipus Tyrannus*; and only three of our manuscripts come from the first period of Byzantine scholarship, which began in the ninth century and came to an end with the conquest of Constantinople by the crusaders of the Fourth Crusade in 1204.

One of these is the famous Laurentianus 32. 9, preserved in the Laurentian Library in Florence, called M in editions of Aeschylus and L in Sophocles and Apollonius Rhodius; this and its twin in Leiden, BPG 60A, a palimpsest of which the greater part cannot be read, were probably written soon after the middle of the tenth century. Laurentianus 31. 10 (K) was written in the second half of the twelfth century. All other Byzantine manuscripts of Sophocles are later than the Crusader conquest. They can be arranged in several different groups, of which the most important are the Roman family (r) and the Paris family (a). In *Antigone, Women of Trachis, Philoctetes* and *Oedipus at Colonus* a family called z is occasionally useful; other manuscripts written during the Palaeologan period (c. 1261-c. 1350) are referred to by the symbol p.

Modern texts of the seven complete plays of Sophocles are based upon the medieval manuscripts; we possess as many as seventeen papyrus fragments of the complete plays, but only one of these is as early as the first century B.C., and they seldom offer a text superior to that of the medieval manuscripts. An exception is P.Oxy. 2180, a manuscript of the second century A.D., which W. S. Barrett has shown to contain several valuable new readings in the *Oedipus Tyrannus*.

For a fuller account of the manuscripts, see the preface to the Oxford Classical Text edition and literature there quoted.

Sophoclean Scholarship in Modern Times

The text of Sophocles was not printed before 1502, when a not very distinguished Aldine edition made its appearance (on Aldus Manutius, see N. G. Wilson, *From Byzantium to Italy*, 1992, 127f). The first notable edition was that of Adrianus Turnebus, published at Paris in 1552/3. Unfortunately Turnebus based his text on the manuscript Paris. gr. 2711, containing the recension of the fourteenth-century Byzantine scholar Demetrius Triclinius (on whom see N. G. Wilson, *Scholars of Byzantium*, 1983, 249f); but he did a good deal to improve the text. The edition of Henricus Stephanus (Paris, 1568) included a Latin version by the German scholar Joachim Camerarius which for a long time had far more readers than the original Greek. During the seventeenth century the Thirty Years' War had a disastrous effect on European culture, and no further important edition of Sophocles appeared till that of R. F. P. Brunck in 1786. Brunck based his text upon a manuscript in Paris, gr. 2712, written in about 1300, the leading representative of what is now called the a family, and a good deal superior to Triclinius for this purpose. After that editions followed rapidly on one another. That of C. G. A. Erfurdt (1802–1825) had valuable notes by Gottfried Hermann (1772–1848), who later brought out an edition of his own (1830–1855). Hermann has made a greater contribution to the establishment of the texts of the tragedians than any other scholar. Before he had begun to publish his own edition, the Englishman Peter Elmsley had collated the Laurentian manuscript L (see above) and had used it for an edition of *Oedipus at Colonus* (1823), and from then on the special value of this manuscript was generally appreciated. Indeed, enthusiasm for it was carried too far, for many scholars, including Wilhelm Dindorf, who brought out numerous editions between 1825 and 1867, wrongly supposed it to be the ancestor of all the other manuscripts.

Editions and collections of critical notes now appeared in rapid succession, and for a time scholars indulged excessively in radical emendation. Three radical emenders, however, made a valuable contribution to the improvement of the text. August Nauck, who in 1856 and again in 1886 brought out new editions of the useful brief edition by F. G. Schneidewin, made a number of brilliant conjectures; F. H. M. Blaydes, who brought out many editions between 1859 and 1903, and H. van Herwerden, in an edition of *Oedipus Tyrannus* (1866) and several collections of critical notes, were less successful than Nauck but were not without success.

A reaction against excessive emendation was evident in the work of Lewis Campbell (i, 2nd ed., 1879; ii, 1881), who though somewhat too conservative made a distinguished contribution, which was augmented by his small book *Paralipomena Sophoclea* (1907). In 1883 began the series of commentaries on the seven complete plays by Sir Richard Jebb, who although he fell short of many of his German contemporaries in learning had a fine feeling for Greek, wrote elegant English, and produced a work that is still indispensable. G. Kaibel, the friend of Wilamowitz, brought out a learned commentary on *Electra* (1896). A. C. Pearson rounded off Jebb's edition by editing the fragments, with commentary (1917), and followed this with an Oxford Classical Text of the seven complete plays that was replaced only in 1990. A. Turyn, following up important work by the Italian scholar V. de Marco, brought out a learned study of the manuscripts. His results were later improved on by R. D. Dawe, who in his *Studies in the Text of Sophocles* (i and ii, 1973; iii, 1978) and in his Teubner edition of the text (i, 2nd ed., 1984; ii, 1985) has done invaluable service by collating a number of manuscripts not previously examined. The Oxford Classical Text edited by H. Lloyd-Jones and N. G. Wilson appeared in 1990. It was accompanied by a book called *Sophoclea*, designed to explain the editors' choice of reading in a number of cases, and also containing matter intended to supplement the existing commentaries.

J. C. Kamerbeek in a series of commentaries on all seven complete plays (1953–84) has accumulated some valuable material, though his excessive conservatism in textual matters and his lack of interest in metre are grave disadvantages.

There are various modern commentaries on individual plays: W. B. Stanford's *Ajax* (1963), J. H. Kells' *Electra* (1974), R. D. Dawe's *Oedipus Tyrannus* (1982), Gerhard Müller's *Antigone* (1967), Andrew Brown's *Antigone* (1987), P. E. Easterling's *Trachiniae* (1982), M. Davies' *Trachiniae* (1991), T. B. L. Webster's *Philoctetes* (1970); Easterling is working at a commentary on *Oedipus at Colonus*. In spite of the advantage which their place in time gives them, none of these modern commentaries enables one altogether to dispense with Jebb. Richard Carden, *The Papyrus Fragments of Sophocles* (1974), usefully supplemented the work of Pearson; the *Ichneutae*, which Carden omitted, has been edited by E. V. Maltese (1982); and Stefan Radt, *Tragicorum Graecorum Fragmenta*, Vol. 4 (1977), has produced an authoritative edition of the fragments.

The *Lexicon Sophocleum* of F. Ellendt, revised by H. Genthe (1872), is of high quality; Radt has added to his edition of the fragments (pp. 659–682) a supplement which brings the Lexicon up to date.

For the greater part of the ancient scholia we must still use the edition of P. N. Papageorgiu (1888); but there are separate editions of the scholia on *Oedipus at Colonus* by V. de Marco (1952), of those on *Ajax* by G. A. Christodoulou (1982) and of the Byzantine scholia on the *Oedipus Tyrannus* by O. Longo (1971).

The ancient *hypotheseis*, or summaries of the plots of the plays, sometimes accompanied by didascalic notices and other information, may be found in Pearson's Oxford text, but not in Dawe's Teubner edition or the new Oxford text of Lloyd-Jones and Wilson, the editors of the two latter works having felt, perhaps mistakenly, that an edition of these should form part of an edition of the ancient scholia.

A. A. Long, *Language and Thought in Sophocles* (1968) is a very useful book; so is A. C. Moorhouse, *The Syntax of Sophocles* (1982), though Moorhouse is not sufficiently attentive to the textual problems which Sophocles' work presents.

Modern general interpretations of the work of Sophocles are very numerous. The modern period of interpretation starts with the posthumously published book on the poet's dramatic technique by Tycho von Wilamowitz-Moellendorff (1885–1914, the son of Ulrich von Wilamowitz-Moellendorff and the grandson of Theodor Mommsen), *Die dramatische Technik des Sophokles* (1917), who in reaction against the psychologising interpretations common at that time argued that the poet aimed above all else at securing a powerful effect for the actual scene he was composing. For a discussion of this book, see H. Lloyd-Jones, *Classical Quarterly* 22 (1972) 214–228 = *Academic Papers* I (1990) 401–418. This book stimulated Karl Reinhardt (1886–1958) to produce the most influential German work on Sophocles of its time, *Sophokles*, 1933, 3rd ed., 1947; English translation by Hazel and David Harvey, 1979. Reinhardt argued that, though not concerned with the psychological niceties beloved of believers in the naturalism of the *fin-de-siècle*, Sophocles presented his characters in sufficient depth to explain the actions they perform. Unfortunately Reinhardt did not discuss the choral odes, a grave oversight, since they are closely linked to the action.

The best general book on Sophocles in English that has appeared in modern times seems to me to be R. P. Winnington-Ingram's *Sophocles; an Interpretation* (1980).

Other useful works bearing on the general interpretation of Sophocles are:

Diller, H., "Göttliches und Menschliches Wissen bei Sophokles," 1950 = *Kleine Schriften* (1971), 255–271.

——— "Über das Selbstbewusstsein der sophokleischen Personen," *Wiener Studien* 69 (1956), 70–85 = *Kleine Schriften* (1971), 272–285.

——— "Menschendarstellung und Handlungsführung bei Sophokles," *Antike und Abendland* 6 (1957) 157–169 = *Kleine Schriften* (1971) 286–303.

Dodds, E. R., "On Misunderstanding the Oedipus Rex," *Greece and Rome* 13 (1966), 37–49 = *The Ancient Concept of Progress* (1973), 64–77.

Easterling, P. E., "Repetition in Sophocles," *Hermes* 101 (1973), 14–34.

——— "Character in Sophocles," *Greece and Rome* 24 (1977), 123–129 = *Oxford Readings in Greek Tragedy*, ed. E. Segal (1983), 138–145.

Ferrari, Franco, *Ricerche sul testo di Sofocle* (1983).

Friedländer, P., "Πολλὰ τὰ δεινά," *Hermes* 69 (1934), 56–63 = *Studien zu der antiken Literatur und Kunst* (1969), 183–192.

Friis Johansen, H., "Sophocles, 1939–59," *Lustrum* 7 (1962), 94–342.

Günther, H. C., *Exercitationes Sophocleae* (1996).

Jones, John, *On Aristotle and Greek Tragedy* (1962).

Knox, B. M. W., *The Heroic Temper: Studies in Sophoclean Tragedy* (1964).

Lesky, A., "Sophokles und das Humane" (1952) = *Gesammelte Schriften* (1966) 190–203.

Müller, Gerhard, "Chor und Handlung bei den griechischen Tragikern," in *Sophokles* (*Wege der Forschung* 95, 1967), 212–238.

Schadewaldt, W., *Sophokles und das Leid* (1944; 4th ed., 1948) = *Hellas und Hesperien* (2nd ed., 1970), I 385–401.

——— "Sophokles, Aias und Antigone," *Neue Wege zur Antike* 8 (1929), 61–117.

Taplin, O., *Greek Tragedy in Action* (1978).

Whitlock Blundell, M., *Helping Friends and Harming Enemies: a Study in Sophocles and Greek Ethics* (1989).

SIGLA

l	the common source of L (Laur. 32. 9) and Λ (Leiden, BPG 60A), and K (Laur. 31.10)
r	Roman family: G (Laur. CS 152), Q (Paris, supp. gr. 109) and R (Vat. gr. 2291)
P	two or more of the MSS (written between 1261 and 1350) known as *veteres*: C (Paris. gr. 2735), F (Laur. 28.25), H (Laur. 32.40), N (Matrit. gr. 4677), O (Lugd. Voss. gr. Q 6), P (Heidelberg Pal. gr. 40), Pa (Vat. gr. 904), S (Vat. Urb. gr. 141), V (Marc. gr. 468), Wa (Mediol. Ambros. E. 103 sup.)
a	two or more of the MSS of the Paris family: A (Paris gr. 2712), D (Neapol. II F.9), Xr (Vindobon. phil. gr. 161), Xs (Vindobon. supp. gr. 71), Zr (Marc. gr. 616)
t	Demetrius Triclinius, whose edition is preserved in Paris. gr. 2711 (T) and Marc. gr. 470 (Ta)
J	Jenensis, Bos. q. 7
Zc	Vat. gr. 1333
Greg.Cypr.	Escorial codex of Gregory of Cyprus (13th c.)

SIGLA

II 1	P.Oxy.1615, saec. iv
II 2	P.Oxy.2093, saec. ii-iii
II 3	P.Berol.21208, saec. v-vi
II 4	P.Colon.251, saec. ii
II 5	P.Antinoop.2, 72, saec. vi-vii
II 6	P.Oxy.693, saec. iii
II 7	P.Oxy.2180, saec. ii
II 8	P.S.I.1192,saec.ii
II 9	P.Oxy.22 + P.Lit.Lond.69, saec. iv-v
II 10	P.Oxy. 1369, saec. v-vi

Σ	scholium
γρ	*γράφεται*
ac	ante correctionem
pc	post correctionem
s.l.	supra lineam
cett.	ceteri

AJAX

ΤΑ ΤΟΥ ΔΡΑΜΑΤΟΣ ΠΡΟΣΩΠΑ

Ἀθηνᾶ
Ὀδυσσεύς
Αἴας
Χορὸς Σαλαμινίων ναυτῶν
Τέκμησσα
Ἄγγελος
Τεῦκρος
Μενέλαος
Ἀγαμέμνων

ΚΩΦΑ ΠΡΟΣΩΠΑ

Εὐρυσάκης
Παιδαγωγός
Κῆρυξ

DRAMATIS PERSONAE

Athena
Odysseus
Ajax
Chorus of Salaminian sailors
Tecmessa
Messenger
Teucer
Menelaus
Agamemnon

MUTES

Eurysaces
Slave
Herald

Scene: In front of the hut occupied by Ajax during the siege of Troy.

ΑΙΑΣ

ΑΘΗΝΑ

Ἀεὶ μέν, ὦ παῖ Λαρτίου, δέδορκά σε
πεῖράν τιν᾽ ἐχθρῶν ἁρπάσαι θηρώμενον·
καὶ νῦν ἐπὶ σκηναῖς σε ναυτικαῖς ὁρῶ
Αἴαντος, ἔνθα τάξιν ἐσχάτην ἔχει,
πάλαι κυνηγετοῦντα καὶ μετρούμενον
ἴχνη τὰ κείνου νεοχάραχθ᾽, ὅπως ἴδῃς
εἴτ᾽ ἔνδον εἴτ᾽ οὐκ ἔνδον. εὖ δέ σ᾽ ἐκφέρει
κυνὸς Λακαίνης ὥς τις εὔρινος βάσις.
ἔνδον γὰρ ἁνὴρ ἄρτι τυγχάνει, κάρα
στάζων ἱδρῶτι καὶ χέρας ξιφοκτόνους.
καί σ᾽ οὐδὲν εἴσω τῆσδε παπταίνειν πύλης
ἔτ᾽ ἔργον ἐστίν, ἐννέπειν δ᾽ ὅτου χάριν
σπουδὴν ἔθου τήνδ᾽, ὡς παρ᾽ εἰδυίας μάθῃς.

ΟΔΥΣΣΕΥΣ

ὦ φθέγμ᾽ Ἀθάνας, φιλτάτης ἐμοὶ θεῶν,
ὡς εὐμαθές σου, κἂν ἄποπτος ᾖς ὅμως,
φώνημ᾽ ἀκούω καὶ ξυναρπάζω φρενὶ
χαλκοστόμου κώδωνος ὡς Τυρσηνικῆς.
καὶ νῦν ἐπέγνως εὖ μ᾽ ἐπ᾽ ἀνδρὶ δυσμενεῖ
βάσιν κυκλοῦντ᾽, Αἴαντι τῷ σακεσφόρῳ.
κεῖνον γάρ, οὐδέν᾽ ἄλλον, ἰχνεύω πάλαι.

AJAX

The stage building represents the hut where Ajax has his quarters during the siege of Troy. Enter ODYSSEUS, *prowling about and looking closely at the ground; then comes* ATHENA, *who stands there quietly.*

ATHENA

Always, son of Laertes, my eye is on you as you prowl about to snatch some opportunity against your enemies; and now I see you by the hut of Ajax near the ships, where he occupies the last position, a long while on his trail and scanning his newly made footprints, to see whether he is inside or not; moving like a Spartan hound with keen scent, you travel quickly to your goal. Yes, the man is now inside, his face and hands that have slaughtered with the sword dripping with sweat. And now you no longer need to peer inside this gate, but you must tell me what is the reason for your efforts, so that you may learn from me who knows.

ODYSSEUS

Voice of Athena, dearest of the gods to me, how easily do I hear your words and grasp them with my mind, even if I cannot see you, as though a Tyrrhenian trumpet spoke with brazen mouth. And now you have rightly guessed that I am circling round on the trail of an enemy, Ajax the shieldbearer. For it is he and no other I have long been

νυκτὸς γὰρ ἡμᾶς τῆσδε πρᾶγος ἄσκοπον
ἔχει περάνας, εἴπερ εἴργασται τάδε·
ἴσμεν γὰρ οὐδὲν τρανές, ἀλλ᾽ ἀλώμεθα·
κἀγὼ ᾽θελοντὴς τῷδ᾽ ὑπεζύγην πόνῳ.
ἐφθαρμένας γὰρ ἀρτίως εὑρίσκομεν
λείας ἁπάσας καὶ κατηναρισμένας
ἐκ χειρὸς αὐτοῖς ποιμνίων ἐπιστάταις.
τήνδ᾽ οὖν ἐκείνῳ πᾶς τις αἰτίαν τρέπει.
καί μοί τις ὀπτὴρ αὐτὸν εἰσιδὼν μόνον
πηδῶντα πεδία σὺν νεορράντῳ ξίφει
φράζει τε κἀδήλωσεν· εὐθέως δ᾽ ἐγὼ
κατ᾽ ἴχνος ᾄσσω, καὶ τὰ μὲν σημαίνομαι,
τὰ δ᾽ ἐκπέπληγμαι, κοὐκ ἔχω μαθεῖν ὅπου.
καιρὸν δ᾽ ἐφήκεις· πάντα γὰρ τά τ᾽ οὖν πάρος
τά τ᾽ εἰσέπειτα σῇ κυβερνῶμαι χερί.

ΑΘΗΝΑ

ἔγνων, Ὀδυσσεῦ, καὶ πάλαι φύλαξ ἔβην
τῇ σῇ πρόθυμος εἰς ὁδὸν κυναγίᾳ.

ΟΔΥΣΣΕΥΣ

ἦ καί, φίλη δέσποινα, πρὸς καιρὸν πονῶ;

ΑΘΗΝΑ

ὡς ἔστιν ἀνδρὸς τοῦδε τἄργα ταῦτά σοι.

ΟΔΥΣΣΕΥΣ

καὶ πρὸς τί δυσλόγιστον ὧδ᾽ ᾖξεν χέρα;

ΑΘΗΝΑ

χόλῳ βαρυνθεὶς τῶν Ἀχιλλείων ὅπλων.

28 τρέπει Lp: νέμει rpa

tracking; because during last night he has perpetrated against us a thing appalling, if indeed he is its doer; we know nothing for certain, but we are at sea, and I have volunteered to undertake this work. Lately we found all the cattle we had plundered dead, slaughtered by some hand, with the guardians of the flocks. The guilt of this all men assign to him; a scout who had seen him rushing alone across the plain with dripping sword reported to me and revealed the matter, and at once I darted off on the trail. Some things I can make out, but by others I am thrown off course, and I cannot discover where he is. You have come opportunely; because as in the past, so in the future it is your hand that steers me.

ATHENA

I knew it, Odysseus, and some time ago set out on the way, eager to guide you in your hunt.

ODYSSEUS

Dear mistress, am I labouring to any purpose?

ATHENA

Know that these are the actions of that man!

ODYSSEUS

And why did he lash out so foolishly?

ATHENA

He was stung by anger on account of the arms of Achilles.[a]

[a] The armor of the dead Achilles has been awarded by a jury to Odysseus, and not to Ajax.

---

33 ὅπου L^{ac}Ka: ὅτου rpat

35 χερί] φρενί lemma in Σ L et γρ in N

ΟΔΥΣΣΕΥΣ

τί δῆτα ποίμναις τήνδ' ἐπεμπίπτει βάσιν;

ΑΘΗΝΑ

δοκῶν ἐν ὑμῖν χεῖρα χραίνεσθαι φόνῳ.

ΟΔΥΣΣΕΥΣ

ἦ καὶ τὸ βούλευμ' ὡς ἐπ' Ἀργείοις τόδ' ἦν;

ΑΘΗΝΑ

κἂν ἐξεπράξατ', εἰ κατημέλησ' ἐγώ.

ΟΔΥΣΣΕΥΣ

ποίαισι τόλμαις ταῖσδε καὶ φρενῶν θράσει;

ΑΘΗΝΑ

νύκτωρ ἐφ' ὑμᾶς δόλιος ὁρμᾶται μόνος.

ΟΔΥΣΣΕΥΣ

ἦ καὶ παρέστη κἀπὶ τέρμ' ἀφίκετο;

ΑΘΗΝΑ

καὶ δὴ 'πὶ δισσαῖς ἦν στρατηγίσιν πύλαις.

ΟΔΥΣΣΕΥΣ

καὶ πῶς ἐπέσχε χεῖρα μαιμῶσαν φόνου;

ΑΘΗΝΑ

ἐγώ σφ' ἀπείργω, δυσφόρους ἐπ' ὄμμασι
γνώμας βαλοῦσα, τῆς ἀνηκέστου χαρᾶς,
καὶ πρός τε ποίμνας ἐκτρέπω σύμμεικτά τε
λείας ἄδαστα βουκόλων φρουρήματα.

45 ἐξεπράξατ' L et ΣL: ἐξέπραξεν rpa
51 ἀπείργω Lpat ἀπεῖρξα rp, A s.l.

ODYSSEUS

Why did he launch this onslaught on the flocks?

ATHENA

He thought he was staining his hand with your blood.

ODYSSEUS

Was his plan aimed against the Argives?

ATHENA

Yes, and he would have accomplished it, had I been negligent.

ODYSSEUS

How could he dare such a thing? What gave him confidence?

ATHENA

He set out alone against you by night, in secret.

ODYSSEUS

Did he come near us? Did he reach his goal?

ATHENA

Indeed he was at the gates of the two commanders.

ODYSSEUS

And how did he come to hold back his eager arm from murder?

ATHENA

It was I that held him back from his irresistible delight, casting upon his eyes mistaken notions, and I diverted him against the herds and the various beasts guarded by the herdsmen and not yet distributed. Here he fell

ἔνθ᾽ ἐσπεσὼν ἔκειρε πολύκερων φόνον
κύκλῳ ῥαχίζων, κἀδόκει μὲν ἔσθ᾽ ὅτε
δισσοὺς Ἀτρείδας αὐτόχειρ κτείνειν ἔχων,
ὅτ᾽ ἄλλοτ᾽ ἄλλον ἐμπίτνων στρατηλατῶν.
ἐγὼ δὲ φοιτῶντ᾽ ἄνδρα μανιάσιν νόσοις
ὤτρυνον, εἰσέβαλλον εἰς ἕρκη κακά.
κἄπειτ᾽ ἐπειδὴ τοῦδ᾽ ἐλώφησεν πόνου,
τοὺς ζῶντας αὖ δεσμοῖσι συνδήσας βοῶν
ποίμνας τε πάσας ἐς δόμους κομίζεται,
ὡς ἄνδρας, οὐχ ὡς εὔκερων ἄγραν ἔχων.
καὶ νῦν κατ᾽ οἴκους συνδέτους αἰκίζεται.
δείξω δὲ καὶ σοὶ τήνδε περιφανῆ νόσον,
ὡς πᾶσιν Ἀργείοισιν εἰσιδὼν θροῇς.
θαρσῶν δὲ μίμνε, μηδὲ συμφορὰν δέχου,
τὸν ἄνδρ᾽· ἐγὼ γὰρ ὀμμάτων ἀποστρόφους
αὐγὰς ἀπείρξω σὴν πρόσοψιν εἰσιδεῖν.
οὗτος, σὲ τὸν τὰς αἰχμαλωτίδας χέρας
δεσμοῖς ἀπευθύνοντα προσμολεῖν καλῶ·
Αἴαντα φωνῶ· στεῖχε δωμάτων πάρος.

ΟΔΥΣΣΕΥΣ

τί δρᾷς, Ἀθάνα; μηδαμῶς σφ᾽ ἔξω κάλει.

ΑΘΗΝΑ

οὐ σῖγ᾽ ἀνέξῃ μηδὲ δειλίαν ἀρῇ;

ΟΔΥΣΣΕΥΣ

μὴ πρὸς θεῶν· ἀλλ᾽ ἔνδον ἀρκείτω μένων.

58 ἐμπίτνων Elmsley: ἐμπιτνῶν at: ἐμπίπτων LGQpZr
61 πόνου a: φόνου rpat

upon them and hacked the horned beasts to death, cleaving their spines all around him; and at one time he thought it was the two Atreidae whom he held and was killing with his own hand, at another that he was attacking now this chief, now that. And as the man wandered in the madness that afflicted him, I urged him on and drove him into a cruel trap. Then when he rested from this work he tied up those of the cattle that were still alive and all the sheep, and brought them home, thinking he had men there, and not the horned creatures that were his prey, and now he is torturing them, bound as they are, inside his dwelling.

And I will show this madness openly to you also, so that you may tell all the Argives what you have seen. Stay to meet the man with confidence, do not expect disaster; I shall divert the rays of his eyes so that he cannot see you.

You there, who are bending back with ropes the arms of your prisoners, I call you to come here! I speak to Ajax! Come out in front of the hut!

ODYSSEUS

What are you doing, Athena? By no means call him out!

ATHENA

Will you not be quiet, and not show yourself a coward?

ODYSSEUS

No, I beg you! Be content for him to stay there!

68–70 del. Reichard

70 ἀπείρξω] ἀπείργω L

75 ἀρῇ Hesych. s.v., in L add. librarius cod. A: ἀρεῖς at: ἄρης Lrp

ΑΘΗΝΑ

τί μὴ γένηται; πρόσθεν οὐκ ἀνὴρ ὅδ᾽ ἦν—

ΟΔΥΣΣΕΥΣ

ἐχθρός γε τῷδε τἀνδρὶ καὶ τανῦν ἔτι.

ΑΘΗΝΑ

οὔκουν γέλως ἥδιστος εἰς ἐχθροὺς γελᾶν;

ΟΔΥΣΣΕΥΣ

ἐμοὶ μὲν ἀρκεῖ τοῦτον ἐν δόμοις μένειν.

ΑΘΗΝΑ

μεμηνότ᾽ ἄνδρα περιφανῶς ὀκνεῖς ἰδεῖν;

ΟΔΥΣΣΕΥΣ

φρονοῦντά γ᾽ ἂν νιν οὐκ ἂν ἐξέστην ὄκνῳ.

ΑΘΗΝΑ

ἀλλ᾽ οὐδὲ νῦν σε μὴ παρόντ᾽ ἴδῃ πέλας.

ΟΔΥΣΣΕΥΣ

πῶς, εἴπερ ὀφθαλμοῖς γε τοῖς αὐτοῖς ὁρᾷ;

ΑΘΗΝΑ

ἐγὼ σκοτώσω βλέφαρα καὶ δεδορκότα.

ΟΔΥΣΣΕΥΣ

γένοιτο μέντἂν πᾶν θεοῦ τεχνωμένου.

ΑΘΗΝΑ

σίγα νυν ἑστὼς καὶ μέν᾽ ὡς κυρεῖς ἔχων.

79 οὔκουν Hermann: οὐκοῦν codd.
80 ἐν δόμοις a: εἰς δόμους Lrpt
82 γ᾽ ἂν Blaydes: γάρ νιν codd.: γάρ τἂν lemma in L

ATHENA

What are you afraid of? Was he not before a man . . .?

ODYSSEUS

Yes, an enemy to me, and he still is.

ATHENA

Is not laughing at one's enemies the most delightful kind of laughter?

ODYSSEUS

I am content for him to stay inside.

ATHENA

Are you afraid to see a man who is obviously mad?

ODYSSEUS

Why, when he was sane I would not have stood out of his way in fear!

ATHENA

But now he will not even see you near him.

ODYSSEUS

How so, if he is seeing with the same eyes?

ATHENA

I shall place his eyes in darkness, even though they see.

ODYSSEUS

Indeed anything can happen if a god contrives it.

ATHENA

Then stand in silence and remain as you are.

ΟΔΥΣΣΕΥΣ

μένοιμ᾽ ἄν· ἤθελον δ᾽ ἂν ἐκτὸς ὢν τυχεῖν.

ΑΘΗΝΑ

ὦ οὗτος, Αἴας, δεύτερόν σε προσκαλῶ.
τί βαιὸν οὕτως ἐντρέπῃ τῆς συμμάχου;

ΑΙΑΣ

ὦ χαῖρ᾽ Ἀθάνα, χαῖρε Διογενὲς τέκνον,
ὡς εὖ παρέστης· καί σε παγχρύσοις ἐγὼ
στέψω λαφύροις τῆσδε τῆς ἄγρας χάριν.

ΑΘΗΝΑ

καλῶς ἔλεξας. ἀλλ᾽ ἐκεῖνό μοι φράσον,
ἔβαψας ἔγχος εὖ πρὸς Ἀργείων στρατῷ;

ΑΙΑΣ

κόμπος πάρεστι κοὐκ ἀπαρνοῦμαι τὸ μή.

ΑΘΗΝΑ

ἦ καὶ πρὸς Ἀτρείδαισιν ᾔχμασας χέρα;

ΑΙΑΣ

ὥστ᾽ οὔποτ᾽ Αἴανθ᾽ οἵδ᾽ ἀτιμάσουσ᾽ ἔτι.

ΑΘΗΝΑ

τεθνᾶσιν ἄνδρες, ὡς τὸ σὸν ξυνῆκ᾽ ἐγώ.

ΑΙΑΣ

θανόντες ἤδη τἄμ᾽ ἀφαιρείσθων ὅπλα.

98 οἵδ᾽] οἶδ᾽ L

ODYSSEUS

I shall remain; but I wish I were not here.

ATHENA

You there, Ajax, I call you a second time! Why have you so little regard for your ally?

AJAX enters from the central door of the stage building that represents the hut.

AJAX

Hail, Athena! hail, daughter of Zeus! How loyally have you stood by me! Yes, I shall honour you with golden offerings from my booty to thank you for this catch.

ATHENA

I thank you; but tell me this, have you well stained your sword in the blood of the Argive army?

AJAX

I have a right to boast, and I shall not deny it!

ATHENA

Did you arm your hand against the sons of Atreus too?

AJAX

So that never again shall they refuse honour to Ajax.

ATHENA

The men are dead, if I understand your words.

AJAX

Let them try to deprive me of my arms, now that they are dead!

ΑΘΗΝΑ

εἶεν· τί γὰρ δὴ παῖς ὁ τοῦ Λαερτίου;
ποῦ σοι τύχης ἕστηκεν; ἦ πέφευγέ σε;

ΑΙΑΣ

ἦ τοὐπίτριπτον κίναδος ἐξήρου μ᾽ ὅπου;

ΑΘΗΝΑ

ἔγωγ᾽· Ὀδυσσέα τὸν σὸν ἐνστάτην λέγω.

ΑΙΑΣ

ἥδιστος, ὦ δέσποινα, δεσμώτης ἔσω
θακεῖ· θανεῖν γὰρ αὐτὸν οὔ τί πω θέλω.

ΑΘΗΝΑ

πρὶν ἂν τί δράσῃς ἢ τί κερδάνῃς πλέον;

ΑΙΑΣ

πρὶν ἂν δεθεὶς πρὸς κίον᾽ ἑρκείου στέγης—

ΑΘΗΝΑ

τί δῆτα τὸν δύστηνον ἐργάσῃ κακόν;

ΑΙΑΣ

μάστιγι πρῶτον νῶτα φοινιχθεὶς θάνῃ.

ΑΘΗΝΑ

μὴ δῆτα τὸν δύστηνον ὧδέ γ᾽ αἰκίσῃ.

ΑΙΑΣ

χαίρειν, Ἀθάνα, τἄλλ᾽ ἐγώ σ᾽ ἐφίεμαι,
κεῖνος δὲ τείσει τήνδε κοὐκ ἄλλην δίκην.

112 ἐγώ σ᾽ QRpa: ἔγωγέ σ᾽ LGp: ἔγωγ᾽ F. W. Schmidt

AJAX

ATHENA

So! But what of the son of Laertes, what is his situation? Did he escape you?

AJAX

Did you ask me where the cunning fox was?

ATHENA

I did; I mean your rival, Odysseus.

AJAX

Mistress, he sits inside, the most welcome of prisoners! I do not want him to die yet.

ATHENA

Before you have done what or have got what advantage?

AJAX

Before, bound to the pillar of the hut I live in . . .

ATHENA

You will have done what mischief to the wretched man?

AJAX

He has perished, after first having his back made bloody by my whip.

ATHENA

Do not so torture the poor man!

AJAX

In all other matters, Athena, I salute you; but that man shall pay this penalty and no other.

ΑΘΗΝΑ

σὺ δ' οὖν—ἐπειδὴ τέρψις ἥδ', <ἐν> σοὶ τὸ δρᾶν—
χρῶ χειρί, φείδου μηδὲν ὧνπερ ἐννοεῖς.

ΑΙΑΣ

χωρῶ πρὸς ἔργον· τοῦτο σοὶ δ' ἐφίεμαι,
τοιάνδ' ἀεί μοι σύμμαχον παρεστάναι.

ΑΘΗΝΑ

ὁρᾷς, Ὀδυσσεῦ, τὴν θεῶν ἰσχὺν ὅση;
τούτου τίς ἄν σοι τἀνδρὸς ἢ προνούστερος
ἢ δρᾶν ἀμείνων ηὑρέθη τὰ καίρια;

ΟΔΥΣΣΕΥΣ

ἐγὼ μὲν οὐδέν' οἶδ'· ἐποικτίρω δέ νιν
δύστηνον ἔμπας, καίπερ ὄντα δυσμενῆ,
ὁθούνεκ' ἄτῃ συγκατέζευκται κακῇ,
οὐδὲν τὸ τούτου μᾶλλον ἢ τοὐμὸν σκοπῶν.
ὁρῶ γὰρ ἡμᾶς οὐδὲν ὄντας ἄλλο πλὴν
εἴδωλ' ὅσοιπερ ζῶμεν ἢ κούφην σκιάν.

ΑΘΗΝΑ

τοιαῦτα τοίνυν εἰσορῶν ὑπέρκοπον
μηδέν ποτ' εἴπῃς αὐτὸς ἐς θεοὺς ἔπος,
μηδ' ὄγκον ἄρῃ μηδέν', εἴ τινος πλέον
ἢ χειρὶ βρίθεις ἢ μακροῦ πλούτου βάθει.
ὡς ἡμέρα κλίνει τε κἀνάγει πάλιν
ἅπαντα τἀνθρώπεια· τοὺς δὲ σώφρονας
θεοὶ φιλοῦσι καὶ στυγοῦσι τοὺς κακούς.

114 ἥδ', <ἐν> σοὶ Jackson: ἥδε σοὶ codd.

ATHENA

Well, since this is your pleasure, the action is in your power! Do not hold your hand, do not stop at anything you have in mind!

AJAX

I go to work! And this I say to you, always stand by me and fight with me thus!

AJAX returns into the hut.

ATHENA

Do you see, Odysseus, how great is the power of the gods? What man was found to be more farsighted than this one, or better at doing what the occasion required?

ODYSSEUS

I know of none, and I pity him in his misery, though he is my enemy, because he is bound fast by a cruel affliction, not thinking of his fate, but my own; because I see that all of us who live are nothing but ghosts, or a fleeting shadow.

ATHENA

Look, then, at such things, and never yourself utter an arrogant word against the gods, nor assume conceit because you outweigh another in strength or in profusion of great wealth. Know that a single day brings down or raises up again all mortal things, and the gods love those who think sensibly and detest offenders!

Exit ATHENA, then ODYSSEUS also leaves.

The Chorus, consisting of Ajax's sailors, enters the orchestra; their opening lines are chanted in recitative as they march in, and the lyrics of the parodos proper begin only at line 172.

ΧΟΡΟΣ

Τελαμώνιε παῖ, τῆς ἀμφιρύτου
Σαλαμῖνος ἔχων βάθρον ἀγχίαλον,
σὲ μὲν εὖ πράσσοντ᾽ ἐπιχαίρω·
σὲ δ᾽ ὅταν πληγὴ Διὸς ἢ ζαμενὴς
λόγος ἐκ Δαναῶν κακόθρους ἐπιβῇ,
μέγαν ὄκνον ἔχω καὶ πεφόβημαι
πτηνῆς ὡς ὄμμα πελείας.
ὡς καὶ τῆς νῦν φθιμένης νυκτὸς
μεγάλοι θόρυβοι κατέχουσ᾽ ἡμᾶς
ἐπὶ δυσκλείᾳ, σὲ τὸν ἱππομανῆ
λειμῶν᾽ ἐπιβάντ᾽ ὀλέσαι Δαναῶν
βοτὰ καὶ λείαν,
ἥπερ δορίληπτος ἔτ᾽ ἦν λοιπή,
κτείνοντ᾽ αἴθωνι σιδήρῳ.
τοιούσδε λόγους ψιθύρους πλάσσων
εἰς ὦτα φέρει πᾶσιν Ὀδυσσεύς,
καὶ σφόδρα πείθει. περὶ γὰρ σοῦ νῦν
εὔπειστα λέγει, καὶ πᾶς ὁ κλυὼν
τοῦ λέξαντος χαίρει μᾶλλον
τοῖς σοῖς ἄχεσιν καθυβρίζων.
τῶν γὰρ μεγάλων ψυχῶν ἱεὶς
οὐκ ἂν ἁμάρτοι· κατὰ δ᾽ ἄν τις ἐμοῦ
τοιαῦτα λέγων οὐκ ἂν πείθοι.
πρὸς γὰρ τὸν ἔχονθ᾽ ὁ φθόνος ἕρπει.
καίτοι σμικροὶ μεγάλων χωρὶς
σφαλερὸν πύργου ῥῦμα πέλονται·
μετὰ γὰρ μεγάλων βαιὸς ἄριστ᾽ ἂν

CHORUS

Son of Telamon, you who occupy the seagirt pedestal of Salamis, when you prosper I rejoice. But when the stroke of Zeus assails you, or a quick-spreading rumour voiced by evil tongues comes from the Danaans, I am greatly anxious and am fearful, like the troubled glance of the winged dove. As during the night that has now perished loud clamours beset us, tending to our discredit, that you entered the meadow where horses graze and destroyed the beasts that were the Danaans' booty, taken by the spear and not yet shared, killing them with flashing iron. Such are the whispered words which Odysseus is putting together and carrying to the ears of all, and he is most persuasive; for what he is now saying about you is plausible, and each hearer takes greater pleasure than the teller in your troubles, exulting over you. For when someone shoots at noble spirits, he will never miss, though if he were to say such things against me he would not win credence; for it is against him who has that envy marches. Yet small men without the aid of great men are unsafe guardians of a wall; for little men are best supported by

---

135 ἀγχίαλον H (coni. Bothe): ἀγχιάλου codd.

149 πᾶσιν rpat: πάντων Lp, quo recepto Ὀδυσεύς Nauck

151 κλυὼν secundi aoristi accentu notatum, ut *Aj.* 290, 1000, 1320, 1323: κλύων codd.

καὶ μέγας ὀρθοῖθ᾽ ὑπὸ μικροτέρων.
ἀλλ᾽ οὐ δυνατὸν τοὺς ἀνοήτους
τούτων γνώμας προδιδάσκειν.
ὑπὸ τοιούτων ἀνδρῶν θορυβῇ
χἠμεῖς οὐδὲν σθένομεν πρὸς ταῦτ᾽
ἀπαλέξασθαι σοῦ χωρίς, ἄναξ.
ἀλλ᾽ ὅτε γὰρ δὴ τὸ σὸν ὄμμ᾽ ἀπέδραν,
παταγοῦσιν ἅτε πτηνῶν ἀγέλαι·
μέγαν αἰγυπιὸν <δ᾽> ὑποδείσαντες
τάχ᾽ ἄν, ἐξαίφνης εἰ σὺ φανείης,
σιγῇ πτήξειαν ἄφωνοι.
ἦ ῥά σε Ταυροπόλα Διὸς Ἄρτεμις— στρ.
ὦ μεγάλα φάτις, ὦ
μᾶτερ αἰσχύνας ἐμᾶς—
ὥρμασε πανδάμους ἐπὶ βοῦς ἀγελαίας,
ἦ πού τινος νίκας ἀκαρπώτου χάριν,
ἦρα κλυτῶν ἐνάρων
ψευσθεῖσ᾽, ἀδώροις εἴτ᾽ ἐλαφαβολίαις
ἢ χαλκοθώραξ σοί τιν᾽ Ἐνυάλιος
μομφὰν ἔχων ξυνοῦ δορὸς ἐννυχίοις
μαχαναῖς ἐτείσατο λώβαν;
οὔποτε γὰρ φρενόθεν γ᾽ ἐπ᾽ ἀριστερά, ἀντ.
παῖ Τελαμῶνος, ἔβας
τόσσον ἐν ποίμναις πίτνων·
ἥκοι γὰρ ἂν θεία νόσος· ἀλλ᾽ ἀπερύκοι
καὶ Ζεὺς κακὰν καὶ Φοῖβος Ἀργείων φάτιν.
εἰ δ᾽ ὑποβαλλόμενοι
κλέπτουσι μύθους οἱ μεγάλοι βασιλῆς,

the great and the great by smaller men. But it is not possible to teach judgment in such matters to fools. Such are the men that clamour against you, and we have not the strength to defend ourselves against them without you, my lord. But when they have escaped your eye, they chatter like flocks of birds; yet were you suddenly to appear, they would take fright before the great vulture and cower in silence, voiceless.

Was it Artemis Tauropola, daughter of Zeus, O powerful rumour, you that are mother of the shame I feel, that sent him against the cattle of the people's flocks, perhaps on account of some victory for which he had made no offering, cheated of glorious spoils, or of her gift after the shooting of deer, or did Enyalios of the brazen corselet bear a grudge against you after some joint exploit and in darkness contrive to outrage you?

Never were you in your right mind when you went so far astray as to fall upon the flocks! No, a godsent sickness must have come upon you; but may Zeus and Phoebus avert the evil rumour of the Argives! But if the great kings and he of the worthless line of Sisyphus[a] are trumping

[a] There was a story that Odysseus was not really the son of Laertes but that the cunning king of Corinth, Sisyphus, was his real father, having seduced his mother Anticleia.

---

169 ‹δ'› Dawes
176 *ἀκαρπώτου* Johnson: *ἀκάρπωτον* codd.
177 *ἦρα* Hermann, Schaefer: *ἤ ῥα* codd.
179 *σοί* Reiske: *ἤ* codd.
182 *γὰρ*] *τἆν* Dawe: fort. *γ' ἆν*

χὠ τᾶς ἀσώτου Σισυφιδᾶν γενεᾶς,
μὴ μή, ἄναξ, ἔθ᾿ ὧδ᾿ ἐφάλοις κλισίαις
ἐμμένων κακὰν φάτιν ἄρῃ.
ἀλλ᾿ ἄνα ἐξ ἑδράνων ἐπ.
ὅπου μακραίωνι
στηρίζῃ ποτὲ τᾷδ᾿ ἀγωνίῳ σχολᾷ,
ἄταν οὐρανίαν φλέγων.
ἐχθρῶν δ᾿ ὕβρις ὧδ᾿ ἀτάρβηθ᾿
ὁρμᾶται ἐν εὐανέμοις βάσσαις,
πάντων βακχαζόντων
γλώσσαις βαρυάλγητ᾿·
ἐμοὶ δ᾿ ἄχος ἕστακεν.

ΤΕΚΜΗΣΣΑ

ναὸς ἀρωγοὶ τῆς Αἴαντος,
γενεᾶς χθονίων ἀπ᾿ Ἐρεχθειδᾶν,
ἔχομεν στοναχὰς οἱ κηδόμενοι
τοῦ Τελαμῶνος τηλόθεν οἴκου.
νῦν γὰρ ὁ δεινὸς μέγας ὠμοκρατὴς
Αἴας θολερῷ
κεῖται χειμῶνι νοσήσας.

ΧΟΡΟΣ

τί δ᾿ ἐνήλλακται τῆς ἡμερίας
νὺξ ἥδε βάρος;
παῖ τοῦ Φρυγίου Τελλεύταντος,
λέγ᾿, ἐπεί σε λέχος δουριάλωτον
στέρξας ἀνέχει θούριος Αἴας·
ὥστ᾿ οὐκ ἂν ἄιδρις ὑπείποις.

up charges and spreading false stories, do not, do not, my lord, remain thus in your huts by the sea and win an evil name!

Come, rise from the seat where you have been rooted to the spot in this long pause from battle, letting the flame of ruin flare up to heaven, while the insolence of your enemies rushes along fearlessly in the wind-swept glades, while they all run riot with their tongues in grievous fashion, and for me pain remains permanent!

Enter from the hut TECMESSA.

TECMESSA

Sailors of the ship of Ajax, from the race of the sons of Erechtheus sprung from earth, we who care for the house of Telamon from far away have cause for grief. For now the dread, the mighty Ajax, harsh in his might, lies low, stricken by a turbid storm of sickness.

CHORUS

And what is the grievous change from the fortune of the day brought by this night? Child of Phrygian Teleutas, tell us; for valiant Ajax has embraced you and maintains you as his spear-won bride, so that you would not answer without knowledge.

---

189 *χὠ τᾶς* Morstadt: *ἢ τᾶς* Lrpat
190 post *μὴ μή* add. *μ'* codd., del. Blaydes
191 *ἐμμένων* Reiske: *ὄμμ' ἔχων* codd.
196 *ἀτάρβηθ'* Lobeck: *ἀτάρβητα* Lrpat
198 *βακχαζόντων* L^ac r: *καγχαζόντων* pat
199 *βαρυάλγητ'* Nauck: *-τα* codd.
209 <*δυσφροσύνης πλέον*> post *νὺξ* suppl. Bruhn

ΤΕΚΜΗΣΣΑ

πῶς δῆτα λέγω λόγον ἄρρητον;
θανάτῳ γὰρ ἴσον πάθος ἐκπεύσῃ.
μανίᾳ γὰρ ἁλοὺς ἡμὶν ὁ κλεινὸς
νύκτερος Αἴας ἀπελωβήθη.
τοιαῦτ' ἂν ἴδοις σκηνῆς ἔνδον
χειροδάικτα σφάγι' αἱμοβαφῆ,
κείνου χρηστήρια τἀνδρός.

ΧΟΡΟΣ

οἵαν ἐδήλωσας ἀνδρὸς αἴθονος στρ.
ἀγγελίαν ἄτλατον οὐδὲ φευκτάν,
τῶν μελέων Δαναῶν ὕπο κληζομέναν,
τὰν ὁ μέγας μῦθος ἀέξει.
ὤμοι, φοβοῦμαι τὸ προσέρπον. περίφαντος ἁνὴρ
θανεῖται, παραπλήκτῳ χερὶ συγκατακτὰς
κελαινοῖς ξίφεσιν βοτὰ καὶ
βοτῆρας ἱππονώμας.

ΤΕΚΜΗΣΣΑ

ὤμοι· κεῖθεν κεῖθεν ἄρ' ἡμῖν
δεσμῶτιν ἄγων ἤλυθε ποίμναν·
ὧν τὰ μὲν εἴσω σφάζ' ἐπὶ γαίας,
τὰ δὲ πλευροκοπῶν δίχ' ἀνερρήγνυ.
δύο δ' ἀργίποδας κριοὺς ἀνελὼν
τοῦ μὲν κεφαλὴν καὶ γλῶσσαν ἄκραν
ῥιπτεῖ θερίσας, τὸν δ' ὀρθὸν ἄνω
κίονι δήσας
μέγαν ἱπποδέτην ῥυτῆρα λαβὼν
παίει λιγυρᾷ μάστιγι διπλῇ,

TECMESSA

How can I tell a tale that is unspeakable? For the disaster you shall learn of is as bad as death. During the night the glorious Ajax was overcome by madness and suffered outrage; such are the sacrifices, slaughtered by his hand and bathed in blood, that you will see within the hut, sacrifices of that man, ominous of the future.

CHORUS

What news regarding the valiant man have you revealed, not to be borne and not to be escaped, told by the miserable Danaans, a message which their loud rumour magnifies! Alas, I fear the future! Exposed to the sight of all, the man will perish, for his frenzied hand has slaughtered with dark blades the herds and the horse-guiding herdsmen.

TECMESSA

Alas! It was from there, from there that he came bringing the captive flock. Some of them he slaughtered indoors, on the ground, and the rest he tore apart, hacking at their sides. Taking two white-footed rams he slashed off and hurled away the head of one and the tip of its tongue, and bound the other, standing upright, to a pillar; then he took his great thong for tethering horses and lashed it

---

221 *ἀνδρὸς*] *ἀνέρος* Hermann (in v.245 *κρᾶτα* retento) | *αἴθονος* KN: *αἴθοπος* at: *αἴθωνος* rpa (L vix legitur)

224 *φευκτάν* rpa: *-όν* L[ac] ut videtur: *φερτάν* p

225 *μελέων* Ll.-J.: *μεγάλων* codd.

κακὰ δεννάζων ῥήμαθ᾽, ἃ δαίμων
κοὐδεὶς ἀνδρῶν ἐδίδαξεν.

ΧΟΡΟΣ

ὥρα τιν᾽ ἤδη κάρα καλύμμασι ἀντ.
κρυψάμενον ποδοῖν κλοπὰν ἀρέσθαι,
ἢ θοὸν εἰρεσίας ζυγὸν ἑζόμενον
ποντοπόρῳ ναῒ μεθεῖναι.
τοίας ἐρέσσουσιν ἀπειλὰς δικρατεῖς Ἀτρεῖδαι
καθ᾽ ἡμῶν· πεφόβημαι λιθόλευστον Ἄρη
ξυναλγεῖν μετὰ τοῦδε τυπείς,
τὸν αἶσ᾽ ἄπλατος ἴσχει.

ΤΕΚΜΗΣΣΑ

οὐκέτι· λαμπρᾶς γὰρ ἄτερ στεροπᾶς
ᾄξας ὀξὺς νότος ὣς λήγει,
καὶ νῦν φρόνιμος νέον ἄλγος ἔχει·
τὸ γὰρ ἐσλεύσσειν οἰκεῖα πάθη,
μηδενὸς ἄλλου παραπράξαντος,
μεγάλας ὀδύνας ὑποτείνει.

ΧΟΡΟΣ

ἀλλ᾽ εἰ πέπαυται, κάρτ᾽ ἂν εὐτυχεῖν δοκῶ·
φρούδου γὰρ ἤδη τοῦ κακοῦ μείων λόγος.

ΤΕΚΜΗΣΣΑ

πότερα δ᾽ ἄν, εἰ νέμοι τις αἵρεσιν, λάβοις,
φίλους ἀνιῶν αὐτὸς ἡδονὰς ἔχειν,
ἢ κοινὸς ἐν κοινοῖσι λυπεῖσθαι ξυνών;

with the whirring two-headed goad, uttering evil imprecations, which a god and none among men had taught him.

CHORUS

The hour now has come for me to veil my face with coverings and to steal away, or to take my seat upon the swiftly moving rowers' bench and give the sea-going ship her way! Such are the threats which the two royal sons of Atreus hurl against us! I am afraid of sharing the agony of the violence of stoning with him who is in the grasp of a fate unapproachable.

TECMESSA

No longer is it so; for like a south wind that rushes on without the bright flash of lightning his fury ceases, and now in his right mind he harbours a new pain; for to look upon one's own calamities, when no other has had a hand in them, lays before one grievous agonies.

CHORUS

Why, if it has ceased, I think he may indeed enjoy good fortune; for if the trouble is now departed, it counts for less.

TECMESSA

But if you were given a choice, would you prefer to grieve your friends but to enjoy happiness yourself, or to share pain with your companions?

---

245 τιν᾽ ἤδη pat: τιν᾽ ἤδη τοι rpa: fort. ᾽στὶν ἤδη vel ᾽στὶν ἁρμοῖ   κάρα t: κρᾶτα cett.

ΧΟΡΟΣ

τό τοι διπλάζον, ὦ γύναι, μεῖζον κακόν.

ΤΕΚΜΗΣΣΑ

ἡμεῖς ἄρ᾽ οὐ νοσοῦντος ἀτώμεσθα νῦν.

ΧΟΡΟΣ

πῶς τοῦτ᾽ ἔλεξας; οὐ κάτοιδ᾽ ὅπως λέγεις.

ΤΕΚΜΗΣΣΑ

ἀνὴρ ἐκεῖνος, ἡνίκ᾽ ἦν ἐν τῇ νόσῳ,
αὐτὸς μὲν ἥδεθ᾽ οἷσιν εἴχετ᾽ ἐν κακοῖς,
ἡμᾶς δὲ τοὺς φρονοῦντας ἠνία ξυνών·
νῦν δ᾽ ὡς ἔληξε κἀνέπνευσε τῆς νόσου,
κεῖνός τε λύπῃ πᾶς ἐλήλαται κακῇ
ἡμεῖς θ᾽ ὁμοίως οὐδὲν ἧσσον ἢ πάρος.
ἆρ᾽ ἐστὶ ταῦτα δὶς τόσ᾽ ἐξ ἁπλῶν κακά;

ΧΟΡΟΣ

ξύμφημι δή σοι καὶ δέδοικα μὴ ᾽κ θεοῦ
πληγή τις ἥκει. πῶς γάρ, εἰ πεπαυμένος
μηδέν τι μᾶλλον ἢ νοσῶν εὐφραίνεται;

ΤΕΚΜΗΣΣΑ

ὡς ὧδ᾽ ἐχόντων τῶνδ᾽ ἐπίστασθαί σε χρή.

ΧΟΡΟΣ

τίς γάρ ποτ᾽ ἀρχὴ τοῦ κακοῦ προσέπτατο;
δήλωσον ἡμῖν τοῖς ξυναλγοῦσιν τύχας.

269 νοσοῦντος Hermann: νοσοῦντες codd.

CHORUS

The double sorrow, lady, is the greater evil.

TECMESSA

Then now, when he is no longer sick, we are afflicted.

CHORUS

What do you mean? I do not understand what you are saying.

TECMESSA

That man, while he was sick, took pleasure in the troubles that possessed him, but to us who were sane caused grief by his proximity. But now that he has been relieved and has respite from his sickness, he is wholly racked by every kind of pain, and we are equally afflicted, no less than before. Is this not a double in place of a single sorrow?

CHORUS

I say the same, and am afraid some blow from a god has struck him; for how do things stand, if now that his sickness has ceased he is no happier than while it lasted?

TECMESSA

Since this is so, you have to know it.

CHORUS

What was the start of the trouble that came upon him? Tell us who share your grief what happened!

ΤΕΚΜΗΣΣΑ

ἅπαν μαθήσῃ τοὔργον, ὡς κοινωνὸς ὤν.
κεῖνος γὰρ ἄκρας νυκτός, ἡνίχ᾽ ἕσπεροι
λαμπτῆρες οὐκέτ᾽ ᾖθον, ἄμφηκες λαβὼν
ἐμαίετ᾽ ἔγχος ἐξόδους ἕρπειν κενάς.
κἀγὼ 'πιπλήσσω καὶ λέγω, "τί χρῆμα δρᾷς,
Αἴας; τί τήνδ᾽ ἄκλητος οὔθ᾽ ὑπ᾽ ἀγγέλων
κληθεὶς ἀφορμᾷς πεῖραν οὔτε του κλυὼν
σάλπιγγος; ἀλλὰ νῦν γε πᾶς εὕδει στρατός."
ὁ δ᾽ εἶπε πρός με βαί᾽, ἀεὶ δ᾽ ὑμνούμενα·
"γύναι, γυναιξὶ κόσμον ἡ σιγὴ φέρει."
κἀγὼ μαθοῦσ᾽ ἔληξ᾽, ὁ δ᾽ ἐσσύθη μόνος.
καὶ τὰς ἐκεῖ μὲν οὐκ ἔχω λέγειν πάθας·
εἴσω δ᾽ ἐσῆλθε συνδέτους ἄγων ὁμοῦ
ταύρους, κύνας βοτῆρας, εὔερόν τ᾽ ἄγραν.
καὶ τοὺς μὲν ηὐχένιζε, τοὺς δ᾽ ἄνω τρέπων
ἔσφαζε κἀρράχιζε, τοὺς δὲ δεσμίους
ᾐκίζεθ᾽ ὥστε φῶτας ἐν ποίμναις πίτνων.
τέλος δ᾽ ἀπᾴξας διὰ θυρῶν σκιᾷ τινι
λόγους ἀνέσπα, τοὺς μὲν Ἀτρειδῶν κάτα,
τοὺς δ᾽ ἀμφ᾽ Ὀδυσσεῖ, συντιθεὶς γέλων πολύν,
ὅσην κατ᾽ αὐτῶν ὕβριν ἐκτείσαιτ᾽ ἰών·
κἄπειτ᾽ ἐνᾴξας αὖθις ἐς δόμους πάλιν
ἔμφρων μόλις πως ξὺν χρόνῳ καθίσταται,
καὶ πλῆρες ἄτης ὡς διοπτεύει στέγος,
παίσας κάρα 'θώυξεν· ἐν δ᾽ ἐρειπίοις
νεκρῶν ἐρειφθεὶς ἕζετ᾽ ἀρνείου φόνου,
κόμην ἀπρὶξ ὄνυξι συλλαβὼν χερί.

TECMESSA

Since you have a share in it, you shall learn everything that happened. At dead of night, when the evening lamps no longer burned, he took his two-edged sword and made as though to start out, for no reason. And I objected, saying, "What are you doing, Ajax? Why are you starting on this expedition unbidden, when you have not been summoned by messengers nor heard any trumpet? Why, now all the army is asleep!" But the words he spoke to me were few and hackneyed: "Woman, silence makes a woman beautiful." Hearing this, I ceased, and he sped off alone. What happened there I cannot tell you; but he came in bringing with him bound bulls, herdsmen's dogs, and woolly prizes. Some he decapitated, others he turned upside down and cut their throats or clove their spines, and others he tortured while tied up, falling upon the beasts as though they had been men. At last he darted through the door and rapped out words addressed to some shadow, denouncing now the sons of Atreus, now Odysseus, laughing loudly at the thought of what violence he had inflicted in his raid. Then he rushed back into the hut and at last with difficulty came to his senses; and when he gazed at the room filled with ruin he struck his head and uttered a loud cry, then fell among the fallen corpses of the slaughtered sheep and sat there, grasping his hair and tearing it with his nails.

---

293 *γυναιξὶ* codd. et Π 2 s.l.: *γυναικὶ* Π 2, Ar., *Pol.* 1260 a 30
295 *λέγειν*] *φράζειν* J et Paris. gr. 2598
297 *εὔερόν* Schneidewin: *εὔκερων* codd.
305 *ἐνᾴξας* Π 2: *ἐπᾴξας* KGapt: *ἀπᾴξας* LpcQRp

καὶ τὸν μὲν ἧστο πλεῖστον ἄφθογγος χρόνον·
ἔπειτ᾽ ἐμοὶ τὰ δείν᾽ ἐπηπείλησ᾽ ἔπη,
εἰ μὴ φανοίην πᾶν τὸ συντυχὸν πάθος.
[κἀνήρετ᾽ ἐν τῷ πράγματος κυροῖ ποτε.]
κἀγώ, φίλοι, δείσασα τοὐξειργασμένον
ἔλεξα πᾶν ὅσονπερ ἐξηπιστάμην.
ὁ δ᾽ εὐθὺς ἐξῴμωξεν οἰμωγὰς λυγράς,
ἃς οὔποτ᾽ αὐτοῦ πρόσθεν εἰσήκουσ᾽ ἐγώ.
πρὸς γὰρ κακοῦ τε καὶ βαρυψύχου γόους
τοιούσδ᾽ ἀεί ποτ᾽ ἀνδρὸς ἐξηγεῖτ᾽ ἔχειν·
ἀλλ᾽ ἀψόφητος ὀξέων κωκυμάτων
ὑπεστέναζε ταῦρος ὣς βρυχώμενος.
νῦν δ᾽ ἐν τοιᾷδε κείμενος κακῇ τύχῃ
ἄσιτος ἁνήρ, ἄποτος, ἐν μέσοις βοτοῖς
σιδηροκμῆσιν ἥσυχος θακεῖ πεσών,
καὶ δῆλός ἐστιν ὥς τι δρασείων κακόν.
[τοιαῦτα γάρ πως καὶ λέγει κὠδύρεται.]
ἀλλ᾽, ὦ φίλοι, τούτων γὰρ οὕνεκ᾽ ἐστάλην,
ἀρήξατ᾽ εἰσελθόντες, εἰ δύνασθέ τι.
φίλων γὰρ οἱ τοιοίδε νικῶνται λόγοις.

ΧΟΡΟΣ

Τέκμησσα, δεινοῖς, παῖ Τελεύταντος, λέγεις
ἡμῖν τὸν ἄνδρα διαπεφοιβάσθαι κακοῖς.

ΑΙΑΣ

ἰώ μοί μοι.

ΤΕΚΜΗΣΣΑ

τάχ᾽, ὡς ἔοικε, μᾶλλον· ἢ οὐκ ἠκούσατε
Αἴαντος οἵαν τήνδε θωύσσει βοήν;

For most of the time he sat silent; but then he uttered awful threats against me if I should not reveal to him the whole disaster that had happened [and asked in what kind of plight he was]. I was afraid, my friends, and told him all that had been done, as well as I knew how. And he at once lamented with dreadful cries, such as I had never before heard from him. For he always used to teach that such weeping was the mark of a cowardly and spiritless man; but he would groan like a bellowing bull, with no sound of high-pitched wailings. And now, laid low by such an evil fortune, without food or drink, he sits quietly where he had fallen in the midst of the beasts slaughtered by the iron, and it is clear that he plans to do some evil [, for such are his words and such his lamentations].

Come, friends, for this is why I came, go in and help him, if you have any power to do so! For such men are won over by the words of friends.

CHORUS

Tecmessa, daughter of Teleutas, terrible are the evils by which you tell us that the man has been driven mad.

voice of AJAX *from the hut*

Ah me, ah me!

TECMESSA

Soon, it seems, he will be worse; did you not hear the cry that Ajax uttered?

---

313 φανοίην Xr: φανείην cett.
314 del. Nauck
327 del. Nauck
330 λόγοις Xs^{γρ} et Stobaeus: φίλοι cett.
331 δεινοῖς Bentley: δεινά codd.

ΑΙΑΣ

ἰώ μοί μοι.

ΧΟΡΟΣ

ἀνὴρ ἔοικεν ἢ νοσεῖν, ἢ τοῖς πάλαι
νοσήμασι ξυνοῦσι λυπεῖσθαι παρών.

ΑΙΑΣ

ἰὼ παῖ παῖ.

ΤΕΚΜΗΣΣΑ

ὤμοι τάλαιν'· Εὐρύσακες, ἀμφὶ σοὶ βοᾷ.
τί ποτε μενοινᾷ; ποῦ ποτ' εἶ; τάλαιν' ἐγώ.

ΑΙΑΣ

Τεῦκρον καλῶ. ποῦ Τεῦκρος; ἢ τὸν εἰσαεὶ
λεηλατήσει χρόνον, ἐγὼ δ' ἀπόλλυμαι;

ΧΟΡΟΣ

ἀνὴρ φρονεῖν ἔοικεν. ἀλλ' ἀνοίγετε.
τάχ' ἄν τιν' αἰδῶ κἀπ' ἐμοὶ βλέψας λάβοι.

ΤΕΚΜΗΣΣΑ

ἰδού, διοίγω· προσβλέπειν δ' ἔξεστί σοι
τὰ τοῦδε πράγη, καὐτὸς ὡς ἔχων κυρεῖ.

ΑΙΑΣ

ἰὼ στρ. α'
φίλοι ναυβάται, μόνοι ἐμῶν φίλων,
μόνοι ἔτ' ἐμμένοντες ὀρθῷ νόμῳ,
ἴδεσθέ μ' οἷον ἄρτι κῦ-
μα φοινίας ὑπὸ ζάλης
ἀμφίδρομον κυκλεῖται.

350 ἔτ' Hermann: τ' codd.

voice of AJAX

Ah me, ah me!

CHORUS

It seems that either he is sick, or he is grieved by the thought of the sickness that afflicted him before.

voice of AJAX

Ah, my son, my son!

TECMESSA

I am lost! Eurysaces,[a] it is for you he cries! What does he meditate? Where are you? I am lost!

voice of AJAX

It is Teucer[b] I am calling! Where is Teucer? Will he continue on his raid forever, while I am perishing?

CHORUS

The man seems to be sane! Come, open the door! Perhaps the sight of me will make him feel some shame.

TECMESSA

Look, I am opening the door, and you can see what he has done, and his own condition.

The door of the hut is opened, and AJAX *is revealed, sitting motionless among the slaughtered cattle.*

AJAX

Hail, dear sailors, the only ones among my friends who still abide by the rule of loyalty, see what kind of a wave, sent up by a deadly surge, circles rapidly about me!

[a] Her young son by Ajax.

[b] Teucer was Ajax's half-brother, being the son of Telamon by the captive Trojan princess Hesione.

ΧΟΡΟΣ

οἴμ᾽ ὡς ἔοικας ὀρθὰ μαρτυρεῖν ἄγαν.
δηλοῖ δὲ τοὔργον ὡς ἀφροντίστως ἔχει.

ΑΙΑΣ

ἰώ ἀντ. α´
γένος ναΐας ἀρωγὸν τέχνας,
ἅλιον ὃς ἐπέβας ἑλίσσων πλάταν,
σέ τοι σέ τοι μόνον δέδορ-
κα ποιμένων ἐπαρκέσοντ᾽.
ἀλλά με συνδάιξον.

ΧΟΡΟΣ

εὔφημα φώνει· μὴ κακὸν κακῷ διδοὺς
ἄκος πλέον τὸ πῆμα τῆς ἄτης τίθει.

ΑΙΑΣ

ὁρᾷς τὸν θρασύν, τὸν εὐκάρδιον, στρ. β´
τὸν ἐν δαΐοις ἄτρεστον μάχας,
ἐν ἀφόβοις με θηρσὶ δεινὸν χέρας;
οἴμοι γέλωτος· οἷον ὑβρίσθην ἄρα.

ΤΕΚΜΗΣΣΑ

μή, δέσποτ᾽ Αἴας, λίσσομαί σ᾽, αὔδα τάδε.

ΑΙΑΣ

οὐκ ἐκτός; οὐκ ἄψορρον ἐκνεμῇ πόδα;
αἰαῖ αἰαῖ.

CHORUS (TO TECMESSA)

Alas, you seem to be bearing witness all too truly! His action shows that he is beside himself.

AJAX

Hail, race helpful with the seaman's skill, you who came on board to ply the oar at sea, you, you are the only guardians I see who will help me! Come, kill me with the rest!

CHORUS

Speak no ill-omened words! Do not by trying to cure evil with evil make the pain worse than the plague that caused it!

AJAX

Do you see that I, the bold, the valiant, the one who never trembled in battle among enemies, have done mighty deeds among beasts that frightened no one? Ah, the mockery! What an insult I have suffered!

TECMESSA

Lord Ajax, do not, I beg you, say such things!

AJAX

Will you not leave? Will you not take yourself away! Ah, ah!

---

358 ἅλιον Hermann: ἁλίαν codd.
360 ποιμένων] πημονὰν Reiske
365 μάχας Blaydes: μάχαις codd.

ΤΕΚΜΗΣΣΑ

ὦ πρὸς θεῶν ὕπεικε καὶ φρόνησον εὖ.

ΑΙΑΣ

ὢ δύσμορος, ὃς χερὶ μὲν
μεθῆκα τοὺς ἀλάστορας,
ἐν δ' ἑλίκεσσι βουσὶ καὶ
κλυτοῖς πεσὼν αἰπολίοις
ἐρεμνὸν αἷμ' ἔδευσα.

ΧΟΡΟΣ

τί δῆτ' ἂν ἀλγοίης ἐπ' ἐξειργασμένοις;
οὐ γὰρ γένοιτ' ἂν ταῦθ' ὅπως οὐχ ὧδ' ἔχοι.

ΑΙΑΣ

ἰὼ πάνθ' ὁρῶν, ἅπαντ' ἀίων, ἀντ. β′
κακῶν ὄργανον, τέκνον Λαρτίου,
κακοπινέστατόν τ' ἄλημα στρατοῦ,
ἦ που πολὺν γέλωθ' ὑφ' ἡδονῆς ἄγεις.

ΧΟΡΟΣ

ξὺν τῷ θεῷ πᾶς καὶ γελᾷ κὠδύρεται.

ΑΙΑΣ

ἴδοιμι δή νιν, καίπερ ὧδ' ἀτώμενος—
ἰώ μοί μοι.

TECMESSA

I implore you, yield and be sensible!

AJAX

Wretched am I, who let the accursed ones slip through my hands, and fell upon horned oxen and noble flocks to shed black blood!

CHORUS

Why should you grieve over what is accomplished? It is impossible that things should be other than they are.

AJAX

Ah, you who see all things and hear all things, instrument of every crime, son of Laertes, filthiest trickster of the army, how you must be laughing in your delight!

CHORUS

Every man laughs or laments according as the god gives.

AJAX

If only I could see him, ruined though I am . . .! Ah me!

---

371 Tecmessae tribuit K. O. Müller, choro codd.

372 χερὶ μὲν Hermann (vid. ad 387): χερσὶ μὲν Lrpa: χεροῖν t

378 ἔχοι Herwerden: ἔχειν codd. plerique

379 ἄπαντ᾽ αἰῶν Ll.-J.: ἁπάντων τ᾽ αἰῶν p: ἁπάντων τ᾽ ἀεὶ cett.

ΧΟΡΟΣ

μηδὲν μέγ᾽ εἴπῃς· οὐχ ὁρᾷς ἵν᾽ εἶ κακοῦ;

ΑΙΑΣ

ὦ Ζεῦ προγόνων προπάτωρ,
πῶς ἂν τὸν αἱμυλώτατον,
ἐχθρὸν ἄλημα, τούς τε δισσ-
άρχας ὀλέσσας βασιλῆς,
τέλος θάνοιμι καὐτός;

ΤΕΚΜΗΣΣΑ

ὅταν κατεύχῃ ταῦθ᾽, ὁμοῦ κἀμοὶ θανεῖν
εὔχου· τί γὰρ δεῖ ζῆν με σοῦ τεθνηκότος;

ΑΙΑΣ

ἰώ στρ. γʹ
σκότος, ἐμὸν φάος,
ἔρεβος ὦ φαεννότατον, ὡς ἐμοί,
ἕλεσθ᾽ ἕλεσθέ μ᾽ οἰκήτορα,
ἕλεσθέ μ᾽· οὔτε γὰρ θεῶν γένος
οὔθ᾽ ἁμερίων ἔτ᾽ ἄξιος
βλέπειν τιν᾽ εἰς ὄνησιν ἀνθρώπων.
ἀλλά μ᾽ ἁ Διὸς
ἀλκίμα θεὸς
ὀλέθριον αἰκίζει.
ποῖ τις οὖν φύγῃ;
ποῖ μολὼν μενῶ;
εἰ τὰ μὲν φθίνει,
<–∪–> φίλοι,
τοῖσδ᾽ ὁμοῦ πέλας,

CHORUS

Speak no proud word! Do you not see what stage of misery you have reached?

AJAX

O Zeus, forebear of my ancestors, if only I could destroy the craftiest of all, the trickster that I detest, and the two brother kings, and at last die myself!

TECMESSA

When you pray for that, at the same time pray for death for me! Why must I live when you are dead?

AJAX

Ah, darkness that is my light, gloom that is most bright for me, take me, take me to dwell in you! For I am no longer worthy to look upon the race of gods nor upon that of mortal men to any profit. But the daughter of Zeus, the mighty goddess, tortures me to death! Where can one escape to? Where can I go and remain? If my great deeds perish, friends, near to these <slaughtered beasts>, and I have devoted myself to the pursuit of foolishly

---

387 *προπάτωρ*: *πάτερ* t
406 ex. gr. <*πτώμασιν*>, Ll.-J.

μώραις δ' ἄγραις προσκείμεθα,
πᾶς δὲ στρατὸς δίπαλτος ἄν
με χειρὶ φονεύοι.

ΤΕΚΜΗΣΣΑ

ὦ δυστάλαινα, τοιάδ' ἄνδρα χρήσιμον
φωνεῖν, ἃ πρόσθεν οὗτος οὐκ ἔτλη ποτ' ἄν.

ΑΙΑΣ

ἰὼ ἀντ. γ′
πόροι ἁλίρροθοι
πάραλά τ' ἄντρα καὶ νέμος ἐπάκτιον,
πολὺν πολύν με δαρόν τε δὴ
κατείχετ' ἀμφὶ Τροίαν χρόνον·
ἀλλ' οὐκέτι μ', οὐκέτ' ἀμπνοὰς
ἔχοντα· τοῦτό τις φρονῶν ἴστω.
ὦ Σκαμάνδριοι
γείτονες ῥοαὶ
κακόφρονες Ἀργείοις,
οὐκέτ' ἄνδρα μὴ
τόνδ' ἴδητ'—ἔπος
ἐξερῶ μέγα—
οἷον οὔτινα
Τρωία στρατοῦ
δέρχθη χθονὸς μολόντ' ἀπὸ
Ἑλλανίδος· τανῦν δ' ἄτι-
μος ὧδε πρόκειμαι.

ΧΟΡΟΣ

οὔτοι σ' ἀπείργειν οὔθ' ὅπως ἐῶ λέγειν
ἔχω, κακοῖς τοιοῖσδε συμπεπτωκότα.

chosen game, and the whole army may with sword grasped in both hands strike me dead!

TECMESSA

Wretched am I! That a strong man should speak such words, which in time past this man never would have spoken!

AJAX

Hail, surging straits of the sea, caves by the shore, and pastures of the coast! Long, long has been the time that you have detained me about Troy; but no more, no more shall I draw breath! Let any man who understands know that! O streams of Scamander near by, inimical to the Argives, no longer shall you look upon a man—I shall utter a mighty boast!—such as no other of the army that Troy has seen come from the land of Hellas! But now I lie here thus, deprived of honour.

CHORUS

I cannot restrain you, and I do not know how to let you speak, when you have encountered such woes as these.

---

418 *ὦ* t: *ἰὼ* cett.
420 *κακόφρονες* Ll.-J.: *εὔφρονες* codd.: *ἐύφρονες* Hermann
424 *Τρωία* Ll.-J.: *Τροία* codd.
428 *οὔθ'*] *οὐδ'* Elmsley

ΑΙΑΣ

αἰαῖ· τίς ἄν ποτ' ᾤεθ' ὧδ' ἐπώνυμον
τοὐμὸν ξυνοίσειν ὄνομα τοῖς ἐμοῖς κακοῖς;
νῦν γὰρ πάρεστι καὶ δὶς αἰάζειν ἐμοί,
[καὶ τρίς· τοιούτοις γὰρ κακοῖς ἐντυγχάνω·]
ὅτου πατὴρ μὲν τῆσδ' ἀπ' Ἰδαίας χθονὸς
τὰ πρῶτα καλλιστεῖ' ἀριστεύσας στρατοῦ
πρὸς οἶκον ἦλθε πᾶσαν εὔκλειαν φέρων·
ἐγὼ δ' ὁ κείνου παῖς, τὸν αὐτὸν ἐς τόπον
Τροίας ἐπελθὼν οὐκ ἐλάσσονι σθένει,
οὐδ' ἔργα μείω χειρὸς ἀρκέσας ἐμῆς,
ἄτιμος Ἀργείοισιν ὧδ' ἀπόλλυμαι.
καίτοι τοσοῦτόν γ' ἐξεπίστασθαι δοκῶ,
εἰ ζῶν Ἀχιλλεὺς τῶν ὅπλων τῶν ὧν πέρι
κρίνειν ἔμελλε κράτος ἀριστείας τινί,
οὐκ ἄν τις αὔτ' ἔμαρψεν ἄλλος ἀντ' ἐμοῦ.
νῦν δ' αὔτ' Ἀτρεῖδαι φωτὶ παντουργῷ φρένας
ἔπραξαν, ἀνδρὸς τοῦδ' ἀπώσαντες κράτη.
κεἰ μὴ τόδ' ὄμμα καὶ φρένες διάστροφοι
γνώμης ἀπῇξαν τῆς ἐμῆς, οὐκ ἄν ποτε
δίκην κατ' ἄλλου φωτὸς ὧδ' ἐψήφισαν.
νῦν δ' ἡ Διὸς γοργῶπις ἀδάματος θεὰ
ἤδη μ' ἐπ' αὐτοῖς χεῖρ' ἐπευθύνοντ' ἐμὴν
ἔσφηλεν ἐμβαλοῦσα λυσσώδη νόσον,
ὥστ' ἐν τοιοῖσδε χεῖρας αἱμάξαι βοτοῖς·
κεῖνοι δ' ἐπεγγελῶσιν ἐκπεφευγότες,

AJAX

Alas! Who ever would have thought that my name would come to harmonise with my sorrows? For now I can say "Alas" a second time [and a third; such are the sorrows I am encountering], I whose father came home from this land of Ida having won the army's first prize for valour, and bringing home every kind of fame. But I, his son, having come to the same place, Troy, with no less strong a force and having performed with my own hand no lesser deeds, am thus perishing, dishonoured by the Argives. Yet so much I think I well know, that if Achilles were alive and were to award the prize of valour in a contest for his own arms, no other would receive them but I. But now the sons of Atreus have made them over to an unscrupulous fellow, pushing aside this man's mighty deeds. And if my eye and mind had not been turned aside, swerving from my intention, they would not have lived to vote such a decision against another man. But as it is the fierce-eyed untamable goddess, daughter of Zeus, overthrew me, casting a plague of madness upon me just as I was stretching out my hand against them, so that I stained my hands with the blood of these beasts. And they have escaped and are laughing at me; the fault is not mine, but

---

433 del. Morstadt
446 ἔπραξαν] ἔπρασαν Hartung
450 ἀδάματος Elmsley: ἀδάμαστος codd.
451 ἐπευθύνοντ' lC: ἐπεντύνοντ' rpa

ἐμοῦ μὲν οὐχ ἑκόντος· εἰ δέ τις θεῶν
βλάπτοι, φύγοι τἂν χὡ κακὸς τὸν κρείσσονα.
καὶ νῦν τί χρὴ δρᾶν; ὅστις ἐμφανῶς θεοῖς
ἐχθαίρομαι, μισεῖ δέ μ᾽ Ἑλλήνων στρατός,
ἔχθει δὲ Τροία πᾶσα καὶ πεδία τάδε.
πότερα πρὸς οἴκους, ναυλόχους λιπὼν ἕδρας
μόνους τ᾽ Ἀτρείδας, πέλαγος Αἰγαῖον περῶ;
καὶ ποῖον ὄμμα πατρὶ δηλώσω φανεὶς
Τελαμῶνι; πῶς με τλήσεταί ποτ᾽ εἰσιδεῖν
γυμνὸν φανέντα τῶν ἀριστείων ἄτερ,
ὧν αὐτὸς ἔσχε στέφανον εὐκλείας μέγαν;
οὐκ ἔστι τοὔργον τλητόν. ἀλλὰ δῆτ᾽ ἰὼν
πρὸς ἔρυμα Τρώων, ξυμπεσὼν μόνος μόνοις
καὶ δρῶν τι χρηστόν, εἶτα λοίσθιον θάνω;
ἀλλ᾽ ὧδέ γ᾽ Ἀτρείδας ἂν εὐφράναιμί που.
οὐκ ἔστι ταῦτα. πεῖρά τις ζητητέα
τοιάδ᾽ ἀφ᾽ ἧς γέροντι δηλώσω πατρὶ
μή τοι φύσιν γ᾽ ἄσπλαγχνος ἐκ κείνου γεγώς.
αἰσχρὸν γὰρ ἄνδρα τοῦ μακροῦ χρῄζειν βίου,
κακοῖσιν ὅστις μηδὲν ἐξαλλάσσεται.
τί γὰρ παρ᾽ ἦμαρ ἡμέρα τέρπειν ἔχει
προσθεῖσα κἀναθεῖσα τοῦ γε κατθανεῖν;
οὐκ ἂν πριαίμην οὐδενὸς λόγου βροτὸν
ὅστις κεναῖσιν ἐλπίσιν θερμαίνεται.
ἀλλ᾽ ἢ καλῶς ζῆν ἢ καλῶς τεθνηκέναι
τὸν εὐγενῆ χρή. πάντ᾽ ἀκήκοας λόγον.

456 τἂν QC, coni. Elmsley: γ᾽ ἂν cett.

if one of the gods does harm, even the coward may escape the stronger man.

And now what must I do, I who patently am hated by the gods, and loathed by the army of the Greeks, and hated, too, by Troy and by these plains? Shall I cross the Aegean sea, leaving behind the station of the ships and the sons of Atreus, and go home? And what kind of face shall I show to my father Telamon when I appear? How ever shall he bring himself to look at me when I appear empty-handed, without the prize of victory, when he himself won a great crown of fame? The thing is not to be endured! But am I to go to the Trojan wall, challenge them all single-handed, achieve some feat, and at last perish? No, in that way I would give pleasure, I think, to the sons of Atreus. That cannot be! I must think of some action that will prove to my aged father that I his son was born no coward. When a man has no relief from troubles, it is shameful for him to desire long life. What pleasure comes from day following day, bringing us near to and taking us back from death? I would not set any value upon a man who is warmed by false hopes. The noble man must live with honour or be honourably dead; you have heard all I have to say.

ΧΟΡΟΣ

οὐδεὶς ἐρεῖ ποθ' ὡς ὑπόβλητον λόγον,
Αἴας, ἔλεξας, ἀλλὰ τῆς σαυτοῦ φρενός.
παῦσαί γε μέντοι καὶ δὸς ἀνδράσιν φίλοις
γνώμης κρατῆσαι, τάσδε φροντίδας μεθείς.

ΤΕΚΜΗΣΣΑ

ὦ δέσποτ' Αἴας, τῆς ἀναγκαίας τύχης
οὐκ ἔστιν οὐδὲν μεῖζον ἀνθρώποις κακόν.
ἐγὼ δ' ἐλευθέρου μὲν ἐξέφυν πατρός,
εἴπερ τινὸς σθένοντος ἐν πλούτῳ Φρυγῶν·
νῦν δ' εἰμὶ δούλη. θεοῖς γὰρ ὧδ' ἔδοξέ που
καὶ σῇ μάλιστα χειρί. τοιγαροῦν, ἐπεὶ
τὸ σὸν λέχος ξυνῆλθον, εὖ φρονῶ τὰ σά,
καί σ' ἀντιάζω πρός τ' ἐφεστίου Διὸς
εὐνῆς τε τῆς σῆς, ᾗ συνηλλάχθης ἐμοί,
μή μ' ἀξιώσῃς βάξιν ἀλγεινὴν λαβεῖν
τῶν σῶν ὑπ' ἐχθρῶν, χειρίαν ἐφείς τινι.
ᾗ γὰρ θάνῃς σὺ καὶ τελευτήσας ἀφῇς,
ταύτῃ νόμιζε κἀμὲ τῇ τόθ' ἡμέρᾳ
βίᾳ ξυναρπασθεῖσαν Ἀργείων ὕπο
ξὺν παιδὶ τῷ σῷ δουλίαν ἕξειν τροφήν.
καί τις πικρὸν πρόσφθεγμα δεσποτῶν ἐρεῖ
λόγοις ἰάπτων, "ἴδετε τὴν ὁμευνέτιν
Αἴαντος, ὃς μέγιστον ἴσχυσε στρατοῦ,
οἵας λατρείας ἀνθ' ὅσου ζήλου τρέφει."
τοιαῦτ' ἐρεῖ τις· κἀμὲ μὲν δαίμων ἐλᾷ,
σοὶ δ' αἰσχρὰ τἄπη ταῦτα καὶ τῷ σῷ γένει.

CHORUS

No one shall say that the words you have spoken are another's, Ajax; they come from your own mind. But give over, and allow your friends to rule your judgment, letting go these thoughts!

TECMESSA

Lord Ajax, there is no greater evil for men than the fate imposed by compulsion. I was born of a father who was free, greatest in wealth of all the Phrygians, and now I am a slave; that was the will of the gods, and in particular of your strength. Therefore, since I have come to share your bed, I wish you well; and I implore you by Zeus of the hearth and by your bed, in which you have been joined with me, do not think it right that I should suffer painful words from your enemies, abandoning me to one of them. For on the day when you perish and by your death abandon me, believe that on that day I shall be seized with violence by the Argives together with your son and shall have the treatment of a slave. And one of my masters shall let fall bitter words like these: "Look upon the concubine of Ajax, who was the army's mightiest man, and see what servitude she endures after being so envied!" So shall he speak, and I shall be the victim of my fate, and these words will be shameful for you and for your family.

495 ἐφείς LGpt: ἀφείς cett.
496 ᾗ Bothe: ἦν a: εἰ cett.

ἀλλ᾽ αἴδεσαι μὲν πατέρα τὸν σὸν ἐν λυγρῷ
γήρᾳ προλείπων, αἴδεσαι δὲ μητέρα
πολλῶν ἐτῶν κληροῦχον, ἥ σε πολλάκις
θεοῖς ἀρᾶται ζῶντα πρὸς δόμους μολεῖν·
οἴκτιρε δ᾽, ὦναξ, παῖδα τὸν σόν, εἰ νέας
τροφῆς στερηθεὶς σοῦ διοίσεται μόνος
ὑπ᾽ ὀρφανιστῶν μὴ φίλων, ὅσον κακὸν
κείνῳ τε κἀμοὶ τοῦθ᾽, ὅταν θάνῃς, νεμεῖς.
ἐμοὶ γὰρ οὐκέτ᾽ ἔστιν εἰς ὅ τι βλέπω
πλὴν σοῦ. σὺ γάρ μοι πατρίδ᾽ ᾔστωσας δορί,
καὶ μητέρ᾽ ἄλλη μοῖρα τὸν φύσαντά τε
καθεῖλεν Ἅιδου θανασίμους οἰκήτορας.
τίς δῆτ᾽ ἐμοὶ γένοιτ᾽ ἂν ἀντὶ σοῦ πατρίς;
τίς πλοῦτος; ἐν σοὶ πᾶσ᾽ ἔγωγε σῴζομαι.
ἀλλ᾽ ἴσχε κἀμοῦ μνῆστιν· ἀνδρί τοι χρεὼν
μνήμην προσεῖναι, τερπνὸν εἴ τί που πάθοι.
χάρις χάριν γάρ ἐστιν ἡ τίκτουσ᾽ ἀεί·
ὅτου δ᾽ ἀπορρεῖ μνῆστις εὖ πεπονθότος,
οὐκ ἂν γένοιτ᾽ ἔθ᾽ οὗτος εὐγενὴς ἀνήρ.

ΧΟΡΟΣ

Αἴας, ἔχειν σ᾽ ἂν οἶκτον ὡς κἀγὼ φρενὶ
θέλοιμ᾽ ἄν· αἰνοίης γὰρ ἂν τὰ τῆσδ᾽ ἔπη.

ΑΙΑΣ

καὶ κάρτ᾽ ἐπαίνου τεύξεται πρὸς γοῦν ἐμοῦ,
ἐὰν μόνον τὸ ταχθὲν εὖ τολμᾷ τελεῖν.

ΤΕΚΜΗΣΣΑ

ἀλλ᾽, ὦ φίλ᾽ Αἴας, πάντ᾽ ἔγωγε πείσομαι.

AJAX

Come, show regard for your father, whom you are deserting in bitter old age, and for your mother, heiress of many years, who often prays to the gods that you may return home alive. And pity your son, my lord, thinking how much harm you will cause to him and to me by your death, if he is robbed of his early sustenance and must live bereft of you, placed under unfriendly guardians! For I have nothing to look to except you; you devastated my country by violence, and another fate took my mother and my father in death to live in Hades. What country, what riches can there be for me but you? On you rests all my safety. Think of me also; a man should remember, should some pleasure come his way; for it is always one kindness that begets another, and if a man allows the memory of a kindness to slip away, he can no longer be accounted noble.

CHORUS

Ajax, I would wish you to have pity, as I do; yes, you should approve her words.

AJAX

She shall surely have my approval, if she will only take heart to do as she is ordered.

TECMESSA

Dear Ajax, I shall obey in all things!

ΑΙΑΣ

κόμιζέ νύν μοι παῖδα τὸν ἐμόν, ὡς ἴδω.

ΤΕΚΜΗΣΣΑ

καὶ μὴν φόβοισί γ' αὐτὸν ἐξελυσάμην.

ΑΙΑΣ

ἐν τοῖσδε τοῖς κακοῖσιν, ἢ τί μοι λέγεις;

ΤΕΚΜΗΣΣΑ

μὴ σοί γέ που δύστηνος ἀντήσας θάνοι.

ΑΙΑΣ

πρέπον γέ τἂν ἦν· δαίμονος τοὐμοῦ τόδε.

ΤΕΚΜΗΣΣΑ

ἀλλ' οὖν ἐγὼ 'φύλαξα τοῦτό γ' ἀρκέσαι.

ΑΙΑΣ

ἐπήνεσ' ἔργον καὶ πρόνοιαν ἣν ἔθου.

ΤΕΚΜΗΣΣΑ

τί δῆτ' ἂν ὡς ἐκ τῶνδ' ἂν ὠφελοῖμί σε;

ΑΙΑΣ

δός μοι προσειπεῖν αὐτὸν ἐμφανῆ τ' ἰδεῖν.

ΤΕΚΜΗΣΣΑ

καὶ μὴν πέλας γε προσπόλοις φυλάσσεται.

ΑΙΑΣ

τί δῆτα μέλλει μὴ οὐ παρουσίαν ἔχειν;

ΤΕΚΜΗΣΣΑ

ὦ παῖ, πατὴρ καλεῖ σε. δεῦρο προσπόλων
ἄγ' αὐτὸν ὅσπερ χερσὶν εὐθύνων κυρεῖς.

AJAX

Then bring me my son, so that I can see him!

TECMESSA

Why, I was afraid and sent him away.

AJAX

Because of these troubles, do you mean?

TECMESSA

I was afraid the poor boy might encounter you and die.

AJAX

That would have been fitting, and typical of my fortune!

TECMESSA

Well, I took precautions to avoid that, at least.

AJAX

I approve your action and the forethought that you showed.

TECMESSA

What can I do to help you as things stand now?

AJAX

Let me speak to him and see him face to face!

TECMESSA

Indeed, the servants are guarding him near by.

AJAX

Why am I kept waiting for his presence?

TECMESSA

My son, your father is calling you! Come, whichever of you attendants is guiding him, bring him here!

534 post ἦν interpunxit Jackson

ΑΙΑΣ

ἕρποντι φωνεῖς, ἢ λελειμμένῳ λόγου;

ΤΕΚΜΗΣΣΑ

καὶ δὴ κομίζει προσπόλων ὅδ' ἐγγύθεν.

ΑΙΑΣ

αἶρ' αὐτόν, αἶρε δεῦρο· ταρβήσει γὰρ οὔ,
νεοσφαγῆ τοῦτόν γε προσλεύσσων φόνον,
εἴπερ δικαίως ἔστ' ἐμὸς τὰ πατρόθεν.
ἀλλ' αὐτίκ' ὠμοῖς αὐτὸν ἐν νόμοις πατρὸς
δεῖ πωλοδαμνεῖν κἀξομοιοῦσθαι φύσιν.
ὦ παῖ, γένοιο πατρὸς εὐτυχέστερος,
τὰ δ' ἄλλ' ὁμοῖος· καὶ γένοι' ἂν οὐ κακός.
καίτοι σε καὶ νῦν τοῦτό γε ζηλοῦν ἔχω,
ὁθούνεκ' οὐδὲν τῶνδ' ἐπαισθάνῃ κακῶν.
ἐν τῷ φρονεῖν γὰρ μηδὲν ἥδιστος βίος,
ἕως τὸ χαίρειν καὶ τὸ λυπεῖσθαι μάθῃς.
ὅταν δ' ἵκῃ πρὸς τοῦτο, δεῖ σ' ὅπως πατρὸς
δείξεις ἐν ἐχθροῖς οἷος ἐξ οἵου 'τράφης.
τέως δὲ κούφοις πνεύμασιν βόσκου, νέαν
ψυχὴν ἀτάλλων, μητρὶ τῇδε χαρμονήν.
οὔτοι σ' Ἀχαιῶν, οἶδα, μή τις ὑβρίσῃ
στυγναῖσι λώβαις, οὐδὲ χωρὶς ὄντ' ἐμοῦ.
τοῖον πυλωρὸν φύλακα Τεῦκρον ἀμφί σοι
λείψω τροφῆς ἄοκνον ἔμπα κεἰ τανῦν
τηλωπὸς οἰχνεῖ, δυσμενῶν θήραν ἔχων.
ἀλλ', ἄνδρες ἀσπιστῆρες, ἐνάλιος λεώς,
ὑμῖν τε κοινὴν τήνδ' ἐπισκήπτω χάριν,

AJAX

Is the man you spoke to coming, or are your words lost on him?

TECMESSA

Already this attendant is close at hand, bringing him.

An attendant brings in EURYSACES.

AJAX

Lift him up, lift him up here! He will not be frightened to look on this newly spilt blood, if he is truly my son. You must begin now to break him in by his father's harsh rules and make his nature like mine.

Boy, may you be luckier than your father, but in all other ways resemble him! Then you will be no coward. Yet even now I can envy you at least for this, that you can sense nothing of these troubles; because the happiest life is lived while one understands nothing, before one learns delight or pain. But when you come to that, you will have to show in the presence of enemies what kind of son of what kind of father you are. But meanwhile be fed by the gentle breezes, nursing your young life, a delight to your mother here. None of the Achaeans, I know, shall insult you with hateful outrage, even though you are without me; such an intrepid watcher shall I leave to guard as you grow, Teucer, even if now he is far off, hunting his enemies.

But on you also, shield-bearing warriors, people of the sea, I lay this charge of gratitude, and do you report my

---

543 λόγου rpat: -ων l

554 post hunc versum τὸ μὴ φρονεῖν γὰρ κάρτ' ἀνώδυνον κακόν praebent codd. et Suda: om. Stobaeus: del. Valckenaer

κείνῳ τ' ἐμὴν ἀγγείλατ' ἐντολήν, ὅπως
τὸν παῖδα τόνδε πρὸς δόμους ἐμοὺς ἄγων
Τελαμῶνι δείξει μητρί τ', Ἐριβοίᾳ λέγω,
ὥς σφιν γένηται γηροβοσκὸς εἰσαεί,
[μέχρις οὗ μυχοὺς κίχωσι τοῦ κάτω θεοῦ,]
καὶ τἀμὰ τεύχη μήτ' ἀγωνάρχαι τινὲς
θήσουσ' Ἀχαιοῖς μήθ' ὁ λυμεὼν ἐμός.
ἀλλ' αὐτό μοι σύ, παῖ, λαβὼν τοὐπώνυμον,
Εὐρύσακες, ἴσχε διὰ πολυρράφου στρέφων
πόρπακος ἑπτάβοιον ἄρρηκτον σάκος·
τὰ δ' ἄλλα τεύχη κοίν' ἐμοὶ τεθάψεται.
ἀλλ' ὡς τάχος τὸν παῖδα τόνδ' ἤδη δέχου,
καὶ δῶμα πάκτου, μηδ' ἐπισκήνους γόους
δάκρυε. κάρτα τοι φιλοίκτιστον γυνή.
πύκαζε θᾶσσον. οὐ πρὸς ἰατροῦ σοφοῦ
θρηνεῖν ἐπῳδὰς πρὸς τομῶντι πήματι.

ΧΟΡΟΣ

δέδοικ' ἀκούων τήνδε τὴν προθυμίαν.
οὐ γάρ μ' ἀρέσκει γλῶσσά σου τεθηγμένη.

ΤΕΚΜΗΣΣΑ

ὦ δέσποτ' Αἴας, τί ποτε δρασείεις φρενί;

ΑΙΑΣ

μὴ κρῖνε, μὴ 'ξέταζε· σωφρονεῖν καλόν.

ΤΕΚΜΗΣΣΑ

οἴμ' ὡς ἀθυμῶ· καί σε πρὸς τοῦ σοῦ τέκνου
καὶ θεῶν ἱκνοῦμαι, μὴ προδοὺς ἡμᾶς γένῃ.

command to Teucer, that he may bring this boy to my home and show him to Telamon and to my mother, I mean Eriboea, that he may ever tend them in old age[, until they come to the dark regions of the god below]. And my arms shall not be set before the Achaeans by any umpire of contests, nor by him who has ruined me; but do you, boy, take the thing from which you take your name, Eurysaces, and carry it, wielding it by means of its well-sewn thong, my shield unbreakable, made of seven hides. But my other armour shall be buried in my grave.

Come, now speedily take the boy, and bar the doors, and make no weeping in front of the hut; surely women are prone to lamentation! Close the doors quickly! It is not the way of a clever doctor to chant incantations over a pain that needs surgery.

CHORUS

I am afraid when I hear you show this eagerness; I do not like the keen edge of your tongue!

TECMESSA

Lord Ajax, what have you in mind to do?

AJAX

Do not ask me, do not question me! It is best to show some sense!

TECMESSA

Ah, I feel despair! And I beg you for your son's sake and for that of the gods not to abandon us!

---

571 del. Elmsley

574 τοὐπώνυμον Fraenkel: ἐπώνυμον codd.

582 θρηνεῖν Lrpa: θροεῖν pat

ΑΙΑΣ

ἄγαν γε λυπεῖς. οὐ κάτοισθ᾽ ἐγὼ θεοῖς
ὡς οὐδὲν ἀρκεῖν εἴμ᾽ ὀφειλέτης ἔτι;

ΤΕΚΜΗΣΣΑ

εὔφημα φώνει.

ΑΙΑΣ

τοῖς ἀκούουσιν λέγε.

ΤΕΚΜΗΣΣΑ

σὺ δ᾽ οὐχὶ πείσῃ;

ΑΙΑΣ

πόλλ᾽ ἄγαν ἤδη θροεῖς.

ΤΕΚΜΗΣΣΑ

ταρβῶ γάρ, ὦναξ.

ΑΙΑΣ

οὐ ξυνέρξεθ᾽ ὡς τάχος;

ΤΕΚΜΗΣΣΑ

πρὸς θεῶν, μαλάσσου.

ΑΙΑΣ

μῶρά μοι δοκεῖς φρονεῖν,
εἰ τοὐμὸν ἦθος ἄρτι παιδεύειν νοεῖς.

ΧΟΡΟΣ

ὦ κλεινὰ Σαλαμίς, σὺ μέν που στρ. α´
ναίεις ἁλίπλακτος εὐδαίμων,
πᾶσιν περίφαντος αἰεί·
ἐγὼ δ᾽ ὁ τλάμων παλαιὸς ἀφ᾽ οὗ χρόνος

AJAX
You vex me in excess! Do you not know that I owe the gods no service any more?

TECMESSA
Speak no ill-omened words!

AJAX
Speak to those who will listen to you!

TECMESSA
Will you not comply?

AJAX
Already you have said too much!

TECMESSA
Because I am afraid, my lord.

AJAX
Close the doors at once!

TECMESSA
I beg you to relent!

AJAX
I think you are a fool if you mean now to try to educate my character.

Exit TECMESSA with EURYSACES; AJAX remains in the hut while the doors are fastened.

CHORUS
Famous Salamis, you lie lapped by the sea, blessed by the gods, ever famous in the sight of all; but long since have I,

†Ἰδαῖα μίμνων λειμωνίᾳ ποίᾳ† μη-
νῶν ἀνήριθμος αἰὲν εὐνῶμαι
χρόνῳ τρυχόμενος,
κακὰν ἐλπίδ᾽ ἔχων
ἔτι μέ ποτ᾽ ἀνύσειν τὸν ἀπότροπον ἀΐδηλον Ἅιδαν.
καί μοι δυσθεράπευτος Αἴας ἀντ. α΄
ξύνεστιν ἔφεδρος, ὤμοι μοι,
θείᾳ μανίᾳ ξύναυλος.
ὃν ἐξεπέμψω πρὶν δή ποτε θουρίῳ
κρατοῦντ᾽ ἐν Ἄρει· νῦν δ᾽ αὖ φρενὸς οἰοβώ-
τας φίλοις μέγα πένθος ηὕρηται,
τὰ πρὶν δ᾽ ἔργα χεροῖν
μεγίστας ἀρετᾶς
ἄφιλα παρ᾽ ἀφίλοις ἔπεσ᾽ ἔπεσε μελέοις
Ἀτρείδαις.
ἦ που παλαιᾷ μὲν σύντροφος ἁμέρᾳ, στρ. β΄
λευκῷ τε γήρᾳ μάτηρ νιν ὅταν νοσοῦν-
τα φρενοβόρως ἀκούσῃ,
αἴλινον αἴλινον
οὐδ᾽ οἰκτρᾶς γόον ὄρνιθος ἀηδοῦς
σχήσει δύσμορος, ἀλλ᾽ ὀξυτόνους μὲν ᾠδὰς
θρηνήσει, χερόπληκτοι δ᾽
ἐν στέρνοισι πεσοῦνται
δοῦποι καὶ πολιᾶς ἄμυγμα χαίτας.
κρείσσων γὰρ Ἅιδᾳ κεύθων ὁ νοσῶν
μάταν,
ὃς εἷς πατρῴας ἥκων γενεᾶς ἄρι- ἀντ. β΄

poor fellow, bivouacked for countless months in Ida's grassy meadows, worn by the passing of time, with the dark prospect of coming some day to the ruthless destroyer, Hades.

And as a companion I must reckon with Ajax, difficult to tend, alas, living with a godsent madness. In the past you sent him forth mighty in his valiant strength; but now he shepherds lonely thoughts, and has found deep mourning for his friends. And the deeds of greatest valour done earlier by his hands have been let drop, having won no friendship from men incapable of friendship, the miserable sons of Atreus!

Surely when his mother, dwelling with old age and white with the passage of time, hears that he is sick with a sickness that devours the mind, she will not abstain from mournful cries and from the lamentation of the piteous bird, the nightingale, but will sing the high-pitched notes of a dirge, and her hands will thud as they strike against her breast, and her white hair will be torn.

Yes, he who suffers a hopeless sickness is better when he lies in Hades; he who in respect of his lineage was the

---

601 ex. gr. *μίμνων ἀν' Ἴδαν λειμῶνι ποᾶντι* Pearson *μηνῶν* Hermann: *μήλων* codd.

622 *σύντροφος* Nauck: *ἔντροφος* codd.

625 *λευκῷ*] *λευκά* Schneidewin | *τε* Suda: *δὲ* codd.

626 *φρενοβόρως* Dindorf: *φρενομόρως* vel *-μώρως* codd.

629 *σχήσει* Reiske: *ἥσει* Lrpat

634 *ἄμυγμα* Bothe: *-ατα* codd.

635 *ὁ* Lobeck: *ἢ* codd.

636 *εἰς* Ll.-J.: *ἐκ* codd. *ἄριστα* Livineii 'V': *ἄριστος* t

στα πολυπόνων Ἀχαιῶν,
οὐκέτι συντρόφοις
ὀργαῖς ἔμπεδος, ἀλλ᾽ ἐκτὸς ὁμιλεῖ.
ὦ τλᾶμον πάτερ, οἵαν σε μένει πυθέσθαι
παιδὸς δύσφορον ἄταν,
ἃν οὔπω τις ἔθρεψεν
αἰὼν Αἰακιδᾶν ἄτερθε τοῦδε.

ΑΙΑΣ

ἅπανθ᾽ ὁ μακρὸς κἀναρίθμητος χρόνος
φύει τ᾽ ἄδηλα καὶ φανέντα κρύπτεται·
κοὐκ ἔστ᾽ ἄελπτον οὐδέν, ἀλλ᾽ ἁλίσκεται
χὠ δεινὸς ὅρκος χαἰ περισκελεῖς φρένες.
κἀγὼ γάρ, ὃς τὰ δείν᾽ ἐκαρτέρουν τότε,
βαφῇ σίδηρος ὣς ἐθηλύνθην στόμα
πρὸς τῆσδε τῆς γυναικός· οἰκτίρω δέ νιν
χήραν παρ᾽ ἐχθροῖς παῖδά τ᾽ ὀρφανὸν λιπεῖν.
ἀλλ᾽ εἶμι πρός τε λουτρὰ καὶ παρακτίους
λειμῶνας, ὡς ἂν λύμαθ᾽ ἁγνίσας ἐμὰ
μῆνιν βαρεῖαν ἐξαλύξωμαι θεᾶς·
μολών τε χῶρον ἔνθ᾽ ἂν ἀστιβῆ κίχω
κρύψω τόδ᾽ ἔγχος τοὐμόν, ἔχθιστον βελῶν,
γαίας ὀρύξας ἔνθα μή τις ὄψεται,
ἀλλ᾽ αὐτὸ νὺξ Ἅιδης τε σῳζόντων κάτω.
ἐγὼ γὰρ ἐξ οὗ χειρὶ τοῦτ᾽ ἐδεξάμην
παρ᾽ Ἕκτορος δώρημα δυσμενεστάτου,
οὔπω τι κεδνὸν ἔσχον Ἀργείων πάρα.
ἀλλ᾽ ἔστ᾽ ἀληθὴς ἡ βροτῶν παροιμία,

noblest of the much-enduring Achaeans stands no longer firm in the temper he grew up in, but lives outside it. Unhappy father, how hard to bear is the ruin of your son, which remains for you to hear, such as the lifetime of none of the sons of Aeacus has nurtured except for this one!

AJAX comes out of the hut, carrying a sword, followed by TECMESSA.

AJAX

All things long and countless time brings to birth in darkness and covers after they have been revealed! Nothing is beyond expectation; the dread oath and the unflinching purpose can be overcome. Why, even I, who earlier showed such hardness, like iron when it has been dipped, have had my words made soft by this woman; and I feel pity at leaving her a widow and my son an orphan near enemies. But I shall go to the meadows by the shore where I can wash myself, so that I can clean off the dirt upon me and escape the grievous anger of the goddess. I shall come to where I can find untrodden ground and conceal this sword of mine, most hated of all weapons, digging a hole in the ground where none can see it, but let the darkness of Hades guard it down below. For since I received this gift from Hector, the deadliest of my enemies, never have I had any good thing from the Argives. No, the saying of mortals is true, that the gifts of ene-

645 δίων Reiske
647 φύει: φαίνει Herwerden
649 χαὶ Musgrave: καὶ codd.
656 ἐξαλύξωμαι Hesych.: ἐξαλεύσωμαι codd.

ἐχθρῶν ἄδωρα δῶρα κοὐκ ὀνήσιμα.
τοιγὰρ τὸ λοιπὸν εἰσόμεσθα μὲν θεοῖς
εἴκειν, μαθησόμεσθα δ' Ἀτρείδας σέβειν.
ἄρχοντές εἰσιν, ὥσθ' ὑπεικτέον. τί μήν;
καὶ γὰρ τὰ δεινὰ καὶ τὰ καρτερώτατα
τιμαῖς ὑπείκει· τοῦτο μὲν νιφοστιβεῖς
χειμῶνες ἐκχωροῦσιν εὐκάρπῳ θέρει·
ἐξίσταται δὲ νυκτὸς αἰανὴς κύκλος
τῇ λευκοπώλῳ φέγγος ἡμέρᾳ φλέγειν·
δεινῶν δ' ἄημα πνευμάτων ἐκοίμισε
στένοντα πόντον· ἐν δ' ὁ παγκρατὴς Ὕπνος
λύει πεδήσας, οὐδ' ἀεὶ λαβὼν ἔχει·
ἡμεῖς δὲ πῶς οὐ γνωσόμεσθα σωφρονεῖν;
ἔγωγ'· ἐπίσταμαι γὰρ ἀρτίως ὅτι
ὅ τ' ἐχθρὸς ἡμῖν ἐς τοσόνδ' ἐχθαρτέος,
ὡς καὶ φιλήσων αὖθις, ἔς τε τὸν φίλον
τοσαῦθ' ὑπουργῶν ὠφελεῖν βουλήσομαι,
ὡς αἰὲν οὐ μενοῦντα. τοῖς πολλοῖσι γὰρ
βροτῶν ἄπιστός ἐσθ' ἑταιρείας λιμήν.
ἀλλ' ἀμφὶ μὲν τούτοισιν εὖ σχήσει· σὺ δὲ
ἔσω θεοῖς ἐλθοῦσα διὰ τέλους, γύναι,
εὔχου τελεῖσθαι τοὐμὸν ὧν ἐρᾷ κέαρ.
ὑμεῖς θ', ἑταῖροι, ταὐτὰ τῇδέ μοι τάδε
τιμᾶτε, Τεύκρῳ τ', ἢν μόλῃ, σημήνατε
μέλειν μὲν ἡμῶν, εὐνοεῖν δ' ὑμῖν ἅμα·
ἐγὼ γὰρ εἶμ' ἐκεῖσ' ὅποι πορευτέον,
ὑμεῖς δ' ἃ φράζω δρᾶτε, καὶ τάχ' ἄν μ' ἴσως
πύθοισθε, κεἰ νῦν δυστυχῶ, σεσωμένον.

mies are no gifts and bring no profit. Therefore for the future we shall learn to yield to the gods, and we shall learn to reverence the sons of Atreus. They are commanders, so that we must bow to them, how else? Why, the most formidable and the most powerful of things bow to office; winter's snowy storms make way before summer with its fruits, and night's dread circle moves aside for day drawn by white horses to make her lights blaze; and the blast of fearful winds lulls to rest the groaning sea, and all-powerful Sleep releases those whom he has bound, nor does he hold his prisoners forever. And how shall we not come to know how to be sensible? I, for one, shall; for I have lately learned that our enemy must be hated as one who will sometime become a friend, and in helping a friend I shall aim to assist him as one assists a man who will not remain a friend forever, since for most mortals the harbour of friendship cannot be trusted.

But as regards all this, things will turn out well; and do you go inside, woman, and pray to the gods that the things my heart longs for shall in all fullness be accomplished.

Exit TECMESSA.

And do you, my companions, honour my commands as she does, and when Teucer comes, tell him to have care for me, and to be loyal to you; for I must go the place I have to go to. And do you do what I tell you, and perhaps you shall learn that, even though now I am unfortunate, I have been preserved.

---

668 *τί μήν;* Linwood: *τί μή;* codd.
674 *δεινῶν* GQpat: *-ὸν* 1R | *δ'* Hermann: *τ'* codd.
678 *ἔγωγ'* Brunck: *ἐγὼ δ'* codd.
679 *ἡμῖν* K: *ἤμην* cett.

ΧΟΡΟΣ

ἔφριξ᾽ ἔρωτι, περιχαρὴς δ᾽ ἀνεπτάμαν. στρ.
ἰὼ ἰὼ Πὰν Πάν,
ὦ Πὰν Πὰν ἁλίπλαγκτε, Κυλ-
λανίας χιονοκτύπου
πετραίας ἀπὸ δειράδος φάνηθ᾽, ὦ
θεῶν χοροποί᾽ ἄναξ, ὅπως μοι
Μύσια Κνώσι᾽ ὀρ-
χήματ᾽ αὐτοδαῆ ξυνὼν ἰάψῃς.
νῦν γὰρ ἐμοὶ μέλει χορεῦσαι.
Ἰκαρίων δ᾽ ὑπὲρ κελεύθων
μολὼν ἄναξ Ἀπόλλων
ὁ Δάλιος εὔγνωστος
ἐμοὶ ξυνείη διὰ παντὸς εὔφρων.
ἔλυσεν αἰνὸν ἄχος ἀπ᾽ ὀμμάτων Ἄρης. ἀντ.
ἰὼ ἰώ, νῦν αὖ,
νῦν, ὦ Ζεῦ, πάρα λευκὸν εὐ-
άμερον πελάσαι φάος
θοᾶν ὠκυάλων νεῶν, ὅτ᾽ Αἴας
λαθίπονος πάλιν, θεῶν δ᾽ αὖ
πάνθυτα θέσμι᾽ ἐξ-
ήνυσ᾽ εὐνομίᾳ σέβων μεγίστᾳ.
πάνθ᾽ ὁ μέγας χρόνος μαραίνει·
κοὐδὲν ἀναύδητον φατίξαιμ᾽
ἄν, εὖτέ γ᾽ ἐξ ἀέλπτων
Αἴας μετανεγνώσθη
θυμῶν τ᾽ Ἀτρείδαις μεγάλων τε νεικέων.

Exit AJAX.

CHORUS

I thrill with longing, and leap up in my delight! Hail, hail, Pan, Pan! Pan, Pan, wandering over the sea, appear from the snow-beaten rocky ridge of Cyllene, lord who directs the dances of the gods, so that you can be with me and tread the Mysian and Cnosian measures that you have taught yourself! Now it is my wish to dance! And may Apollo, lord of Delos, come over the Icarian sea and be with me, forever kindly!

The war-god has removed dire grief from my eyes! Ah, ah, now once more, now, O Zeus, can the bright light of day shine upon the swift ships that glide over the sea, now that Ajax once more forgets his pain, and has fulfilled the ordinances of the gods with all their sacrifices, doing them reverence with all obedience. All things are withered by mighty time; and I would say that nothing was unpredictable, now that Ajax, beyond our hopes, has repented of his anger against the sons of Atreus and his great quarrel!

---

699 Μύσια Π 1 et Suda: Νύσια codd.

702 κελεύθων Ll.-J.: πελαγέων codd.

706 γὰρ post ἔλυσε(ν) habent codd., del. Elmsley

714 post μαραίνει add. τε καὶ φλέγει codd., del. Livineius

715 φατίσαιμ' Livineius

718 θυμῶν Gγρ, N s.l.: θυμὸν cett.: θυμοῦ Hermann

ΑΓΓΕΛΟΣ

ἄνδρες φίλοι, τὸ πρῶτον ἀγγεῖλαι θέλω,
Τεῦκρος πάρεστιν ἄρτι Μυσίων ἀπὸ
κρημνῶν· μέσον δὲ προσμολὼν στρατήγιον
κυδάζεται τοῖς πᾶσιν Ἀργείοις ὁμοῦ.
στείχοντα γὰρ πρόσωθεν αὐτὸν ἐν κύκλῳ
μαθόντες ἀμφέστησαν, εἶτ᾽ ὀνείδεσιν
ἤρασσον ἔνθεν κἄνθεν οὔτις ἔσθ᾽ ὃς οὔ,
τὸν τοῦ μανέντος κἀπιβουλευτοῦ στρατῷ
ξύναιμον ἀποκαλοῦντες, ὥς τ᾽ οὐκ ἀρκέσοι
τὸ μὴ οὐ πέτροισι πᾶς καταξανθεὶς θανεῖν.
ὥστ᾽ ἐς τοσοῦτον ἦλθον ὥστε καὶ χεροῖν
κολεῶν ἐρυστὰ διεπεραιώθη ξίφη.
λήγει δ᾽ ἔρις δραμοῦσα τοῦ προσωτάτω
ἀνδρῶν γερόντων ἐν ξυναλλαγῇ λόγου.
ἀλλ᾽ ἡμὶν Αἴας ποῦ ᾽στιν, ὡς φράσω τάδε;
τοῖς κυρίοις γὰρ πάντα χρὴ δηλοῦν λόγον.

ΧΟΡΟΣ

οὐκ ἔνδον, ἀλλὰ φροῦδος ἀρτίως, νέας
βουλὰς νέοισιν ἐγκαταζεύξας τρόποις.

ΑΓΓΕΛΟΣ

ἰοὺ ἰού.
βραδεῖαν ἡμᾶς ἆρ᾽ ὁ τήνδε τὴν ὁδὸν
πέμπων ἔπεμψεν, ἢ ᾽φάνην ἐγὼ βραδύς.

ΧΟΡΟΣ

τί δ᾽ ἐστὶ χρείας τῆσδ᾽ ὑπεσπανισμένον;

Enter MESSENGER

MESSENGER

My friends, I wish first to announce that Teucer is here, just back from the hills of Mysia; and when he came to the command post in mid camp, he was reviled by all the Argives at once. As he approached they saw him from a distance, and stood around him in a circle; then every single man of them assailed him with taunts this way and that, calling him the brother of the madman who had plotted against the army, and declaring that they would not be content till he was dead, mangled to death with stones. And so it came to such a pass that swords were drawn from their sheaths and passed into men's hands. The wish to quarrel had run to the furthest point before it was arrested by the seniors with conciliatory words. But tell me where Ajax is, so that I can make this known to him! One must report every piece of news to those who are responsible.

CHORUS

He is not in, but departed lately, with fresh counsels harnessed to a fresh mood.

MESSENGER

Ah, ah! Then he who sent me on this journey sent me too late, or else I am shown to have been too slow.

CHORUS

And what part of needed action has been neglected?

---

726 στρατῷ Schaefer: στρατοῦ codd.
738 βραδεῖαν] μάταιον Nauck

ΑΓΓΕΛΟΣ

τὸν ἄνδρ' ἀπηύδα Τεῦκρος ἔνδοθεν στέγης
μὴ 'ξω παρεῖναι, πρὶν παρὼν αὐτὸς τύχῃ.

ΧΟΡΟΣ

ἀλλ' οἴχεταί τοι, πρὸς τὸ κέρδιον τραπεὶς
γνώμης, θεοῖσιν ὡς καταλλαχθῇ χόλου.

ΑΓΓΕΛΟΣ

ταῦτ' ἐστὶ τἄπη μωρίας πολλῆς πλέα,
εἴπερ τι Κάλχας εὖ φρονῶν μαντεύεται.

ΧΟΡΟΣ

ποῖον; τί δ' εἰδὼς τοῦδε πράγματος πάρει;

ΑΓΓΕΛΟΣ

τοσοῦτον οἶδα καὶ παρὼν ἐτύγχανον.
ἐκ γὰρ συνέδρου καὶ τυραννικοῦ κύκλου
Κάλχας μεταστὰς οἶος Ἀτρειδῶν δίχα,
ἐς χεῖρα Τεύκρου δεξιὰν φιλοφρόνως
θεὶς εἶπε κἀπέσκηψε παντοίᾳ τέχνῃ
εἶρξαι κατ' ἦμαρ τοὐμφανὲς τὸ νῦν τόδε
Αἴανθ' ὑπὸ σκηναῖσι μηδ' ἀφέντ' ἐᾶν,
εἰ ζῶντ' ἐκεῖνον εἰσιδεῖν θέλοι ποτέ.
ἐλᾷ γὰρ αὐτὸν τήνδ' ἔθ' ἡμέραν μόνην
δίας Ἀθάνας μῆνις, ὡς ἔφη λέγων.

742 παρεῖναι Hartung: παρήκειν codd. plerique
743 κέρδιον K^{ac}, p: -ιστον Lrpat
747 πάρει Reiske: πέρι codd.
756 την δε θ]ημεραν μονην Π 1: τῇδέ θ' (τῇδ' ἔθ' Bothe) ἡμέρᾳ μόνῃ codd.

MESSENGER

Teucer said that you must not allow him to go out of the dwelling, until he himself should be there.

CHORUS

Why, he is gone; he had turned his thoughts in a more profitable direction, to be reconciled with the gods with whom he had been angry.

MESSENGER

These words are full of great folly, if Calchas is at all honest in his prophecy.

CHORUS

What is this? and what knowledge of this matter have you brought?

MESSENGER

So much as this I know, since I was there. Calchas moved away on his own from the group assembled around the commanders, apart from the sons of Atreus, placed his hand in Teucer's in friendly fashion, and spoke, charging him by every means to keep Ajax in the hut during this present day and not to let him out, if he wished ever to see him alive. For the anger of divine Athena shall pursue

τὰ γὰρ περισσὰ κἀνόνητα σώματα
πίπτειν βαρείαις πρὸς θεῶν δυσπραξίαις
ἔφασχ᾽ ὁ μάντις, ὅστις ἀνθρώπου φύσιν
βλαστὼν ἔπειτα μὴ κατ᾽ ἄνθρωπον φρονῇ.
κεῖνος δ᾽ ἀπ᾽ οἴκων εὐθὺς ἐξορμώμενος
ἄνους καλῶς λέγοντος ηὑρέθη πατρός.
ὁ μὲν γὰρ αὐτὸν ἐννέπει, "τέκνον, δορὶ
βούλου κρατεῖν μέν, σὺν θεῷ δ᾽ ἀεὶ κρατεῖν."
ὁ δ᾽ ὑψικόμπως κἀφρόνως ἠμείψατο,
"πάτερ, θεοῖς μὲν κἂν ὁ μηδὲν ὢν ὁμοῦ
κράτος κατακτήσαιτ᾽· ἐγὼ δὲ καὶ δίχα
κείνων πέποιθα τοῦτ᾽ ἐπισπάσειν κλέος."
τοσόνδ᾽ ἐκόμπει μῦθον. εἶτα δεύτερον
δίας Ἀθάνας, ἡνίκ᾽ ὀτρύνουσά νιν
ηὖδᾶτ᾽ ἐπ᾽ ἐχθροῖς χεῖρα φοινίαν τρέπειν,
τότ᾽ ἀντιφωνεῖ δεινὸν ἄρρητόν τ᾽ ἔπος·
"ἄνασσα, τοῖς ἄλλοισιν Ἀργείων πέλας
ἵστω, καθ᾽ ἡμᾶς δ᾽ οὔποτ᾽ ἐνρήξει μάχη."
τοιοῖσδέ τοι λόγοισιν ἀστεργῆ θεᾶς
ἐκτήσατ᾽ ὀργήν, οὐ κατ᾽ ἄνθρωπον φρονῶν.
ἀλλ᾽ εἴπερ ἔστι τῇδ᾽ ἔθ᾽ ἡμέρᾳ, τάχ᾽ ἂν
γενοίμεθ᾽ αὐτοῦ σὺν θεῷ σωτήριοι.
τοσαῦθ᾽ ὁ μάντις εἶφ᾽· ὁ δ᾽ εὐθὺς ἐξ ἕδρας
πέμπει μέ σοι φέροντα τάσδ᾽ ἐπιστολὰς
Τεῦκρος φυλάσσειν. εἰ δ᾽ ἀπεστερήμεθα,
οὐκ ἔστιν ἁνὴρ κεῖνος, εἰ Κάλχας σοφός.

him for this day only, so Calchas said. When men grow to a size too great to do good, the prophet said, they are brought down by cruel misfortunes sent by the gods, yes, each one who has human nature but refuses to think only human thoughts. But he from the moment of his leaving home was found to be foolish when his father spoke well. "My son," his father said to him, "wish for triumph in battle, but wish to triumph always with a god's aid!" And he replied boastfully and stupidly, "Father, together with the gods even one who amounts to nothing may win victory; but I am confident that I can grasp this glory even without them." Such a boast as that he uttered; and a second time, when divine Athena urged him on and told him to direct his bloody hand against the enemy, he made answer with these dreadful and unspeakable words, "Queen, stand by the other Argives; where I am the enemy shall never break through." By such words as these he brought on himself the unappeasable anger of the goddess, through his more than mortal pride. But if he is still alive this day, perhaps with a god's help we may preserve him. So much the prophet said, and at once Teucer rose and sent me to take to you these orders to observe. But if we are frustrated, that man is no more, if Calchas is a true prophet.

---

775 ἐνρήξει Ll.-J.: ἐκ- codd.
778 ἔθ' Lobeck: θ' Lrpat
782 ἆρ' ὑστερήμεθα Schenkl

ΧΟΡΟΣ

ὦ δαΐα Τέκμησσα, δυσμόρων γένος,
ὅρα μολοῦσα τόνδ' ὁποῖ' ἔπη θροεῖ.
ξυρεῖ γὰρ ἐν χρῷ τοῦτο μὴ χαίρειν τινά.

ΤΕΚΜΗΣΣΑ

τί μ' αὖ τάλαιναν, ἀρτίως πεπαυμένην
κακῶν ἀτρύτων, ἐξ ἕδρας ἀνίστατε;

ΧΟΡΟΣ

τοῦδ' εἰσάκουε τἀνδρός, ὡς ἥκει φέρων
Αἴαντος ἡμῖν πρᾶξιν ἣν ἤλγησ' ἐγώ.

ΤΕΚΜΗΣΣΑ

οἴμοι, τί φής, ἄνθρωπε; μῶν ὀλώλαμεν;

ΑΓΓΕΛΟΣ

οὐκ οἶδα τὴν σὴν πρᾶξιν, Αἴαντος δ' ὅτι,
θυραῖος εἴπερ ἐστίν, οὐ θαρσῶ πέρι.

ΤΕΚΜΗΣΣΑ

καὶ μὴν θυραῖος, ὥστε μ' ὠδίνειν τί φής.

ΑΓΓΕΛΟΣ

ἐκεῖνον εἴργειν Τεῦκρος ἐξεφίεται
σκηνῆς ὕπαυλον μηδ' ἀφιέναι μόνον.

ΤΕΚΜΗΣΣΑ

ποῦ δ' ἐστὶ Τεῦκρος, κἀπὶ τῷ λέγει τάδε;

ΑΓΓΕΛΟΣ

πάρεστ' ἐκεῖνος ἄρτι· τήνδε δ' ἔξοδον
<τὴν> ὀλεθρίαν Αἴαντος ἐλπίζει φέρειν.

784 δυσμόρων Paehler: δύσμορον codd.
794 θυραῖός <γ'> Elmsley 799 <τὴν> Ll.-J.

CHORUS

Unhappy Tecmessa, born of unfortunate parents, come and see what words this man is uttering! The razor's edge cuts close to misery for some!

TECMESSA enters from the hut with EURYSACES.

TECMESSA

Why do you get me up, when I had just got rest from sorrows inexhaustible?

CHORUS

Listen to this man, for he has come bringing news about Ajax that has caused me pain.

TECMESSA

Alas, what are you saying, fellow? Are we lost?

MESSENGER

I do not know what you mean by "news," but I know that about Ajax, if he is out of doors, I feel no confidence.

TECMESSA

Why, he is out of doors, so that I feel sharp pain as I wonder what you mean.

MESSENGER

Teucer gave orders that he be kept within the shelter of the hut and not allowed out alone.

TECMESSA

And where is Teucer, and what is his reason for saying this?

MESSENGER

He has lately come back. He believes that this departure seals the fate of Ajax.

ΤΕΚΜΗΣΣΑ

οἴμοι τάλαινα, τοῦ ποτ᾽ ἀνθρώπων μαθών;

ΑΓΓΕΛΟΣ

τοῦ Θεστορείου μάντεως, καθ᾽ ἡμέραν
τὴν νῦν ὃ τούτῳ θάνατον ἢ βίον φέρει.

ΤΕΚΜΗΣΣΑ

οἲ ᾽γώ, φίλοι, πρόστητ᾽ ἀναγκαίας τύχης,
καὶ σπεύσαθ᾽ οἱ μὲν Τεῦκρον ἐν τάχει μολεῖν,
οἱ δ᾽ ἑσπέρους ἀγκῶνας, οἱ δ᾽ ἀντηλίους
ζητεῖτ᾽ ἰόντες τἀνδρὸς ἔξοδον κακήν.
ἔγνωκα γὰρ δὴ φωτὸς ἠπατημένη
καὶ τῆς παλαιᾶς χάριτος ἐκβεβλημένη.
οἴμοι, τί δράσω, τέκνον; οὐχ ἱδρυτέον.
ἀλλ᾽ εἶμι κἀγὼ κεῖσ᾽ ὅποιπερ ἂν σθένω.
χωρῶμεν, ἐγκονῶμεν, οὐχ ἕδρας ἀκμή.
[σῴζειν θέλοντες ἄνδρα γ᾽ ὃς σπεύδῃ θανεῖν.]

ΧΟΡΟΣ

χωρεῖν ἑτοῖμος, κοὐ λόγῳ δείξω μόνον.
τάχος γὰρ ἔργου καὶ ποδῶν ἅμ᾽ ἕψεται.

802 ὃ τούτῳ Pearson: ὅτ᾽ αὐτῷ Lat
812 del. Dindorf

TECMESSA

Ah me, from what man did he learn this?

MESSENGER

From the prophet who is son of Thestor, a word that on this day brings death or life for him.

TECMESSA

Alas, my friends, guard me from the doom that fate threatens, and let some hasten Teucer's coming, and let others go to the western, others the eastern bends of the shore, and investigate the man's unfortunate departure! For I see that he has deceived me and cast me out from the favour I once enjoyed. Ah me, what shall I do, child? We must not sit here, but I too will go as far as my strength will let me. Let us go, let us make haste; this is no time to stay still [when we wish to save a man who is bent on death].

CHORUS

I am ready to go, and shall not show it by words alone; swift action and swift movement shall follow.

TECMESSA leaves by one of the side passages, leaving the child in the hut; the Chorus divides into two halves, and one leaves by the right-hand and the other by the left-hand passage. A pause follows, and the scene changes to a remote spot. Enter AJAX with his sword, which he fixes in the ground point uppermost; he does this presumably at the side of the stage, where a grove is indicated by painted panels or canvas, so that later he can fall upon the sword just out of sight of the audience.

ΑΙΑΣ

ὁ μὲν σφαγεὺς ἕστηκεν ᾗ τομώτατος
γένοιτ' ἄν, εἴ τῳ καὶ λογίζεσθαι σχολή,
δῶρον μὲν ἀνδρὸς Ἕκτορος ξένων ἐμοὶ
μάλιστα μισηθέντος, ἐχθίστου θ' ὁρᾶν.
πέπηγε δ' ἐν γῇ πολεμίᾳ τῇ Τρῳάδι,
σιδηροβρῶτι θηγάνῃ νεηκονής·
ἔπηξα δ' αὐτὸν εὖ περιστείλας ἐγώ,
εὐνούστατον τῷδ' ἀνδρὶ διὰ τάχους θανεῖν.
  οὕτω μὲν εὐσκευοῦμεν· ἐκ δὲ τῶνδέ μοι
σὺ πρῶτος, ὦ Ζεῦ, καὶ γὰρ εἰκός, ἄρκεσον.
αἰτήσομαι δέ σ' οὐ μακρὸν γέρας λαβεῖν.
πέμψον τιν' ἡμῖν ἄγγελον, κακὴν φάτιν
Τεύκρῳ φέροντα, πρῶτος ὥς με βαστάσῃ
πεπτῶτα τῷδε περὶ νεορράντῳ ξίφει,
καὶ μὴ πρὸς ἐχθρῶν του κατοπτευθεὶς πάρος
ῥιφθῶ κυσὶν πρόβλητος οἰωνοῖς θ' ἕλωρ.
τοσαῦτά σ', ὦ Ζεῦ, προστρέπω, καλῶ δ' ἅμα
πομπαῖον Ἑρμῆν χθόνιον εὖ με κοιμίσαι,
ξὺν ἀσφαδᾴστῳ καὶ ταχεῖ πηδήματι
πλευρὰν διαρρήξαντα τῷδε φασγάνῳ.
  καλῶ δ' ἀρωγοὺς τὰς ἀεί τε παρθένους
ἀεί θ' ὁρώσας πάντα τὰν βροτοῖς πάθη,
σεμνὰς Ἐρινῦς τανύποδας, μαθεῖν ἐμὲ
πρὸς τῶν Ἀτρειδῶν ὡς διόλλυμαι τάλας.
[καί σφας κακοὺς κάκιστα καὶ πανωλέθρους

839–42 del. Wesseling; alii alia secludunt

AJAX

The killer stands where it will be sharpest, if one has time to work it out, a gift of Hector, the acquaintance I most hated, and whose sight I most detested; it stands in the enemy soil of Troy, newly sharpened with a whetstone that cuts away the iron. And I have planted it there with care, so that it may loyally help me to a speedy death.

So I am well equipped; and after this, do you first, Zeus, help me, as is natural;[a] the favour I ask of you is not a great one. Send a messenger to bring the evil news to Teucer, so that he may be the first to handle me when I have fallen upon this sword, then newly bloodstained, and I shall not be seen first by some enemy and cast out as a prey for dogs and birds. So much, O Zeus, I ask of you, and at the same time I call on Hermes who escorts men below the earth to lull me fast to sleep, without writhing, with one rapid bound, when I have pierced my side with this sword.

And I call for help upon those who are ever maidens and see ever all the sufferings of mortals, the dread Erinyes with long stride, so that they witness my destruction at the hands of the sons of Atreus. [And may they snatch them up, with evil that befits their evil, and utterly

[a] Aeacus, father of Ajax's father Telamon, was a son of Zeus; cf. line 387.

ξυναρπάσειαν, ὥσπερ εἰσορῶσ᾿ ἐμὲ
αὐτοσφαγῆ πίπτοντα· τὼς αὐτοσφαγεῖς
πρὸς τῶν φιλίστων ἐκγόνων ὀλοίατο.]
ἴτ᾿, ὦ ταχεῖαι ποίνιμοί τ᾿ Ἐρινύες,
γεύεσθε, μὴ φείδεσθε πανδήμου στρατοῦ.
σὺ δ᾿, ὦ τὸν αἰπὺν οὐρανὸν διφρηλατῶν
Ἥλιε, πατρῴαν τὴν ἐμὴν ὅταν χθόνα
ἴδῃς, ἐπισχὼν χρυσόνωτον ἡνίαν
ἄγγειλον ἄτας τὰς ἐμὰς μόρον τ᾿ ἐμὸν
γέροντι πατρὶ τῇ τε δυστήνῳ τροφῷ.
ἦ που τάλαινα, τήνδ᾿ ὅταν κλύῃ φάτιν,
ἥσει μέγαν κωκυτὸν ἐν πάσῃ πόλει.
ἀλλ᾿ οὐδὲν ἔργον ταῦτα θρηνεῖσθαι μάτην·
ἀλλ᾿ ἀρκτέον τὸ πρᾶγμα σὺν τάχει τινί.
[ὦ θάνατε θάνατε, νῦν μ᾿ ἐπίσκεψαι μολών·
καίτοι σὲ μὲν κἀκεῖ προσαυδήσω ξυνών.
σὲ δ᾿ ὦ φαεννῆς ἡμέρας τὸ νῦν σέλας,
καὶ τὸν διφρευτὴν Ἥλιον προσεννέπω,
πανύστατον δὴ κοὔποτ᾿ αὖθις ὕστερον.]
ὦ φέγγος, ὦ γῆς ἱερὸν οἰκείας πέδον
Σαλαμῖνος, ὦ πατρῷον ἑστίας βάθρον,
κλειναί τ᾿ Ἀθῆναι, καὶ τὸ σύντροφον γένος,
κρῆναί τε ποταμοί θ᾿ οἵδε, καὶ τὰ Τρωικὰ
πεδία προσαυδῶ, χαίρετ᾿, ὦ τροφῆς ἐμοί·
τοῦθ᾿ ὑμὶν Αἴας τοὔπος ὕστατον θροεῖ,
τὰ δ᾿ ἄλλ᾿ ἐν Ἅιδου τοῖς κάτω μυθήσομαι.

854–58 del. Campe: 854–65 del. Zwierlein: alii alia secludunt

destroy them, as they see me fall by my own hand; even so may they perish by their own hands, through their most beloved offspring]. Come, Erinyes, swift to punish, take your fill, do not spare the host entire!

But do you who drive your chariot through high heaven, Sun, when you see my native land, check your golden rein and announce my ruin and my fate to my aged father and to the unhappy one who nursed me. Poor woman, when she hears this news she will utter loud wailing in all the city!

But no good is done by futile lamentation! I must begin the action with some speed! [Death, death, come now and look upon me! but to you I shall speak when I am with you. But you, light of this bright day, and you, Sun riding in your chariot, I call on for the last time, and never more!]

O light, O sacred plain of my own land of Salamis, O pedestal of my native hearth, and you glorious Athens, and the race that lives with you, streams and rivers here, and plains of Troy do I address; hail, you who have given me sustenance! This is the last word Ajax speaks to you; the rest I shall utter in Hades to those below.

AJAX falls upon his sword.

Enter from one of the passages one half of the Chorus, and then from the other passage the second half.

ΗΜΙΧΟΡΙΟΝ

πόνος πόνῳ πόνον φέρει.
πᾷ πᾷ
πᾷ γὰρ οὐκ ἔβαν ἐγώ;
κοὐδεὶς ἐπισπᾶταί με συμμαθεῖν τόπος.
ἰδοὺ ἰδού·
δοῦπον αὖ κλύω τινά.

ΗΜΙΧΟΡΙΟΝ

ἡμῶν γε ναὸς κοινόπλουν ὁμιλίαν.

ΗΜΙΧΟΡΙΟΝ

τί οὖν δή;

ΗΜΙΧΟΡΙΟΝ

πᾶν ἐστίβηται πλευρὸν ἕσπερον νεῶν.

ΗΜΙΧΟΡΙΟΝ

ἔχεις οὖν;

ΗΜΙΧΟΡΙΟΝ

πόνου γε πλῆθος κοὐδὲν εἰς ὄψιν πλέον.

ΗΜΙΧΟΡΙΟΝ

ἀλλ' οὐδὲ μὲν δὴ τὴν ἀφ' ἡλίου βολῶν
κέλευθον ἁνὴρ οὐδαμοῦ δηλοῖ φανείς.

ΧΟΡΟΣ

τίς ἂν δῆτά μοι, τίς ἂν φιλοπόνων στρ.
ἁλιαδᾶν ἔχων ἀΰπνους ἄγρας
ἢ τίς Ὀλυμπιάδων θεᾶν, ἢ ῥυτῶν
Βοσπορίων ποταμῶν,
τὸν ὠμόθυμον εἴ ποθι

1 CHORUS

Labour brings more labour through labour! Where, where, where have I not been? and no place draws me, so that I learn his whereabouts. Look, look! Now I hear a crash!

2 CHORUS

Yes, it is us your shipmates!

1 CHORUS

What news, then?

2 CHORUS

We have paced the whole ground west of the ships.

1 CHORUS

So have you found . . .?

2 CHORUS

Much trouble, but nothing we could see.

1 CHORUS

Neither has the man appeared coming by the eastern road.

CHORUS

If only some one of the industrious fishermen, sleepless in his hunting, or one of the nymphs of the Olympian heights,[a] or one of the flowing rivers of the Bosporus

[a] Mount Ida had four peaks, each of which was called an Olympus.

---

869 ἐπισπᾶταί Wecklein: ἐπίσταταί codd.
879 δῆτα Hermann: δή codd.
884 post ποταμῶν add. ἴδρις codd. praeter Mosqu. gr. 504

πλαζόμενον λεύσσων
ἀπύοι; σχέτλια γὰρ
ἐμέ γε τὸν μακρῶν ἀλάταν πόνων
οὐρίῳ μὴ πελάσαι δρόμῳ,
ἀλλ᾽ ἀμενηνὸν ἄνδρα μὴ λεύσσειν ὅπου.

ΤΕΚΜΗΣΣΑ

ἰώ μοί μοι.

ΧΟΡΟΣ

τίνος βοὴ πάραυλος ἐξέβη νάπους;

ΤΕΚΜΗΣΣΑ

ἰὼ τλήμων.

ΧΟΡΟΣ

τὴν δουρίληπτον δύσμορον νύμφην ὁρῶ
Τέκμησσαν, οἴκτῳ τῷδε συγκεκραμένην.

ΤΕΚΜΗΣΣΑ

οἴχωκ᾽, ὄλωλα, διαπεπόρθημαι, φίλοι.

ΧΟΡΟΣ

τί δ᾽ ἔστιν;

ΤΕΚΜΗΣΣΑ

Αἴας ὅδ᾽ ἡμῖν ἀρτίως νεοσφαγὴς
κεῖται, κρυφαίῳ φασγάνῳ περιπτυχής.

ΧΟΡΟΣ

ὤμοι ἐμῶν νόστων·
ὤμοι, κατέπεφνες, ἄναξ,
τόνδε συνναύταν, τάλας·
ὢ ταλαίφρων γυνή.

could descry him of the harsh temper where he wanders and call out to us! It is hard that I, who have long suffered as I strayed, should not draw near him, running to my goal, and that I should fail to discern the whereabouts of the stricken man.

From the side passage in which Ajax killed himself comes the

voice of TECMESSA

Ah me!

CHORUS

Whose cry came from the cover of the wood nearby?

voice of TECMESSA

Alas for me!

Enter TECMESSA.

CHORUS

I see the unhappy bride of the spear, Tecmessa, lost in that lament!

TECMESSA

I am gone, I am lost, I am utterly destroyed, my friends!

CHORUS

What is it?

TECMESSA

Here lies Ajax, lately killed, spitted upon a sword sunk deep into his body!

CHORUS

Alas for my homecoming! Alas, my lord, you have killed me your fellow sailor! O poor lady!

902 τάλας Hermann: ἰὼ τάλας codd. plerique
903 ὦ Dawe: ἰὼ codd. plerique

ΤΕΚΜΗΣΣΑ

ὡς ὧδε τοῦδ᾽ ἔχοντος αἰάζειν πάρα.

ΧΟΡΟΣ

τίνος ποτ᾽ ἆρ᾽ ἔπραξε χειρὶ δύσμορος;

ΤΕΚΜΗΣΣΑ

αὐτὸς πρὸς αὑτοῦ, δῆλον· ἐν γάρ οἱ χθονὶ
πηκτὸν τόδ᾽ ἔγχος περιπετοῦς κατηγορεῖ.

ΧΟΡΟΣ

ὤμοι ἐμᾶς ἄτας, οἶος ἄρ᾽ αἱμάχθης,
ἄφαρκτος φίλων·
ἐγὼ δ᾽ ὁ πάντα κωφός, ὁ πάντ᾽ ἄιδρις,
κατημέλησα. πᾷ πᾷ
κεῖται ὁ δυστράπελος
δυσώνυμος Αἴας;

ΤΕΚΜΗΣΣΑ

οὔτοι θεατός· ἀλλά νιν περιπτυχεῖ
φάρει καλύψω τῷδε παμπήδην, ἐπεὶ
οὐδεὶς ἂν ὅστις καὶ φίλος τλαίη βλέπειν
φυσῶντ᾽ ἄνω πρὸς ῥῖνας ἔκ τε φοινίας
πληγῆς μελανθὲν αἷμ᾽ ἀπ᾽ οἰκείας σφαγῆς.
οἴμοι, τί δράσω; τίς σε βαστάσει φίλων;
ποῦ Τεῦκρος; ὡς ἀκμαῖος ἂν βαίη μολὼν
πεπτῶτ᾽ ἀδελφὸν τόνδε συγκαθαρμόσαι.
ὦ δύσμορ᾽ Αἴας, οἷος ὢν οἵως ἔχεις,
ὡς καὶ παρ᾽ ἐχθροῖς ἄξιος θρήνων τυχεῖν.

TECMESSA

It is so with him, and we can only lament!

CHORUS

By whose hand did the unhappy man bring this about?

TECMESSA

By his own, it is clear; this sword planted in the ground proves that he fell upon it.

CHORUS

Alas for my ruin! How you were bathed in blood, with no protection from your friends! And I all deaf, all ignorant, took no care! Where, where lies the unmanageable Ajax of ill-omened name?

TECMESSA

He must not be looked upon! I shall cover him completely with this cloak folded about him, since none that was a friend could bear to look upon him spurting blood upwards to his nostrils, and the black gore from the deadly wound inflicted by self-slaughter.

Alas, what shall I do? Which of your friends shall lift you? Where is Teucer? How timely would be his coming, so that he could help to compose the body of his brother! Unhappy Ajax, what a man and what a fate, how deserving of lamentation even among enemies!

---

907 *περιπετοῦς* Musgrave: *-πετὲς* codd.
910 *ἄφαρκτος* Dindorf: *ἄφρακτος* codd.
921 *ἂν βαίη μολὼν* Pantazides: *εἰ βαίη μόλοι* codd.

ΧΟΡΟΣ

ἔμελλες, τάλας, ἔμελλες χρόνῳ ἀντ.
στερεόφρων ἄρ᾽ ἐξανύσσειν κακὰν
μοῖραν ἀπειρεσίων πόνων· τοῖά μοι
πάννυχα καὶ φαέθοντ᾽
ἀνεστέναζες ὠμόφρων
ἐχθοδόπ᾽ Ἀτρείδαις
οὐλίῳ σὺν πάθει.
μέγας ἄρ᾽ ἦν ἐκεῖνος ἄρχων χρόνος
πημάτων, ἦμος ἀριστόχειρ
<–∪∪–> ὅπλων ἔκειτ᾽ ἀγὼν πέρι.

ΤΕΚΜΗΣΣΑ

ἰώ μοί μοι.

ΧΟΡΟΣ

χωρεῖ πρὸς ἧπαρ, οἶδα, γενναία δύη.

ΤΕΚΜΗΣΣΑ

ἰώ μοί μοι.

ΧΟΡΟΣ

οὐδέν σ᾽ ἀπιστῶ καὶ δὶς οἰμῶξαι, γύναι,
τοιοῦδ᾽ ἀποβλαφθεῖσαν ἀρτίως φίλου.

ΤΕΚΜΗΣΣΑ

σοὶ μὲν δοκεῖν ταῦτ᾽ ἔστ᾽, ἐμοὶ δ᾽ ἄγαν φρονεῖν.

ΧΟΡΟΣ

ξυναυδῶ.

936 <χρυσοτύπων> ex. gr. suppl. Campbell

CHORUS

You were bound, unhappy man, you were bound in your obduracy to accomplish in the end an evil fate of troubles infinite! Such were the words, hostile to the sons of Atreus, which in the dark and in the light you groaned forth with grievous suffering. So that time was the beginning of great disasters, when the <golden> arms were made the prize in a contest of the greatest prowess!

TECMESSA

Ah me!

CHORUS

The anguish of a noble person pierces, I know, to the heart.

TECMESSA

Ah me!

CHORUS

I cannot feel surprise that you should cry out twice, lady, having just now been robbed of such a loved one.

TECMESSA

You can imagine this, but I can feel it all too well.

CHORUS

I must agree.

ΤΕΚΜΗΣΣΑ

οἴμοι, τέκνον, πρὸς οἷα δουλείας ζυγὰ
χωροῦμεν, οἷοι νῷν ἐφεστᾶσι σκοποί.

ΧΟΡΟΣ

ὤμοι, ἀναλγήτων
δισσῶν ἐθρόησας ἄναυδ'
ἔργ' Ἀτρειδᾶν τῷδ' ἄχει.
ἀλλ' ἀπείργοι θεός.

ΤΕΚΜΗΣΣΑ

οὐκ ἂν τάδ' ἔστη τῇδε μὴ θεῶν μέτα.

ΧΟΡΟΣ

ἄγαν ὑπερβριθές γε τἄχθος ἤνυσαν.

ΤΕΚΜΗΣΣΑ

τοιόνδε μέντοι Ζηνὸς ἡ δεινὴ θεὸς
Παλλὰς φυτεύει πῆμ' Ὀδυσσέως χάριν.

ΧΟΡΟΣ

ἦ ῥα κελαινώπᾳ θυμῷ ἐφυβρίζει
πολύτλας ἀνήρ,
γελᾷ δὲ τοῖσδε μαινομένοις ἄχεσιν
πολὺν γέλωτα, φεῦ φεῦ,
ξύν τε διπλοῖ βασιλῆς
κλύοντες Ἀτρεῖδαι.

947–48 ἄναυδ' ἔργ' Hermann: ἄναυδον ἔργον codd.
951 γε τἄχθος Blaydes: τε ἄχθος r: ἄχθος Lpat
955 κελαινώπᾳ θυμῷ Ll.-J.: -αν -ὸν Lrpat et Π 3, sed -ῶπα codd. pauci, Hesych., Eustath.
957 τοῖσδε Elmsley: τοῖσι t: τοῖς cett.

TECMESSA

Alas, my son, to what a yoke of slavery are we coming! Such are the masters that now stand over us.

CHORUS

Ah me, you named unspeakable actions of the ruthless twin sons of Atreus when you voiced this grief. But may a god avert it!

TECMESSA

Things would never have come to this but for the gods.

CHORUS

They have made the weight of our burden heavier than we can bear.

TECMESSA

Indeed the daughter of Zeus, the dread goddess, Pallas creates woe for the sake of Odysseus.

CHORUS

In truth the much-enduring man exults over us in his dark mind, and laughs loudly at our frenzied sorrows, and with him will laugh, when they hear the news, the two sons of Atreus.

ΤΕΚΜΗΣΣΑ

οἱ δ᾿ οὖν γελώντων κἀπιχαιρόντων κακοῖς
τοῖς τοῦδ᾿· ἴσως τοι, κεἰ βλέποντα μὴ ᾽πόθουν,
θανόντ᾿ ἂν οἰμώξειαν ἐν χρείᾳ δορός.
οἱ γὰρ κακοὶ γνώμαισι τἀγάθ᾿ ἐν χεροῖν
ἔχοντες οὐκ ἴσασι πρίν τις ἐκβάλῃ.
ἐμοὶ πικρὸς τέθνηκεν ἢ κείνοις γλυκύς,
αὑτῷ δὲ τερπνός· ὧν γὰρ ἠράσθη τυχεῖν
ἐκτήσαθ᾿ αὑτῷ, θάνατον ὅνπερ ἤθελεν.
[τί δῆτα τοῦδ᾿ ἐπεγγελῷεν ἂν κάτα;]
θεοῖς τέθνηκεν οὗτος, οὐ κείνοισιν, οὔ.
πρὸς ταῦτ᾿ Ὀδυσσεὺς ἐν κενοῖς ὑβριζέτω.
Αἴας γὰρ αὐτοῖς οὐκέτ᾿ ἐστίν, ἀλλ᾿ ἐμοὶ
λιπὼν ἀνίας καὶ γόους διοίχεται.

ΤΕΥΚΡΟΣ

ἰώ μοί μοι.

ΧΟΡΟΣ

σίγησον· αὐδὴν γὰρ δοκῶ Τεύκρου κλύειν
βοῶντος ἄτης τῆσδ᾿ ἐπίσκοπον μέλος.

ΤΕΥΚΡΟΣ

ὦ φίλτατ᾿ Αἴας, ὦ ξύναιμον ὄμμ᾿ ἐμοί,
ἆρ᾿ ἠμπόληκας ὥσπερ ἡ φάτις κρατεῖ;

ΧΟΡΟΣ

ὄλωλεν ἁνήρ, Τεῦκρε, τοῦτ᾿ ἐπίστασο.

TECMESSA

Well, let them laugh and rejoice at his sorrows! Even if they did not miss him while he lived, now that he is dead they may lament him in the urgency of battle. Men of evil mind do not know the good that they hold in their hands till they lose it.

For me his death is bitter as it is sweet to them, but to him it brought pleasure; for he got for himself what he longed for, the death he wished for. [How can they exult over him?] It is the gods that killed him, not they, no!

In the face of that let Odysseus insult us who are bereft! For they no more have Ajax, but he is gone, leaving pain and weeping for me.

From one of the side passages, the

voice of TEUCER

Ah me, ah me!

CHORUS

Be silent! for I think I hear the voice of Teucer, crying out in a strain that has regard to this disaster.

Enter TEUCER

TEUCER

O dearest Ajax, O brother who gave me comfort, have you in truth fared as the rumour said?

CHORUS

The man is dead, Teucer, be assured of that.

---

964 τἀγάθ' ἐν J, coni. Reiske: τἀγαθὸν codd. plerique
966 ᾗ Eustathius, coni. Schneidewin: ἢ codd.
969 del. Schneidewin

ΤΕΥΚΡΟΣ

ὤμοι βαρείας ἆρα τῆς ἐμῆς τύχης.

ΧΟΡΟΣ

ὡς ὧδ' ἐχόντων—

ΤΕΥΚΡΟΣ

ὢ τάλας ἐγώ, τάλας.

ΧΟΡΟΣ

πάρα στενάζειν.

ΤΕΥΚΡΟΣ

ὢ περισπερχὲς πάθος.

ΧΟΡΟΣ

ἄγαν γε, Τεῦκρε.

ΤΕΥΚΡΟΣ

φεῦ τάλας. τί γὰρ τέκνον
τὸ τοῦδε, ποῦ μοι γῆς κυρεῖ τῆς Τρῳάδος;

ΧΟΡΟΣ

μόνος παρὰ σκηναῖσιν.

ΤΕΥΚΡΟΣ

οὐχ ὅσον τάχος
δῆτ' αὐτὸν ἄξεις δεῦρο, μή τις ὡς κενῆς
σκύμνον λεαίνης δυσμενῶν ἀναρπάσῃ;
ἴθ', ἐγκόνει, σύγκαμνε. τοῖς θανοῦσί τοι
φιλοῦσι πάντες κειμένοις ἐπεγγελᾶν.

ΧΟΡΟΣ

καὶ μὴν ἔτι ζῶν, Τεῦκρε, τοῦδέ σοι μέλειν
ἐφίεθ' ἁνὴρ κεῖνος, ὥσπερ οὖν μέλει.

TEUCER

Alas, then, for my grievous fate!

CHORUS

This being the case —

TEUCER

Wretched, wretched am I!

CHORUS

We can lament!

TEUCER

O devastating blow!

CHORUS

Only too much so, Teucer!

TEUCER

Alas, unhappy one! What of his child, where in the Trojan land is he?

CHORUS

Alone by the hut.

TEUCER

Will you not bring him here at once, in case some enemy should snatch him up, like the cub of a lioness robbed of her mate? Go, make haste, assist us! All men like to mock the dead as they lie low.

Exit TECMESSA.

CHORUS

Why, that man while he still lived asked that you should take care of him, as you are now doing.

ΤΕΥΚΡΟΣ

ὦ τῶν ἁπάντων δὴ θεαμάτων ἐμοὶ
ἄλγιστον ὧν προσεῖδον ὀφθαλμοῖς ἐγώ,
ὁδός θ' ὁδῶν πασῶν ἀνιάσασα δὴ
μάλιστα τοὐμὸν σπλάγχνον, ἣν δὴ νῦν ἔβην,
ὦ φίλτατ' Αἴας, τὸν σὸν ὡς ἐπῃσθόμην
μόρον διώκων κἀξιχνοσκοπούμενος.
ὀξεῖα γάρ σου βάξις ὡς θεοῦ τινος
διῆλθ' Ἀχαιοὺς πάντας ὡς οἴχῃ θανών.
ἁγὼ κλυὼν δύστηνος ἐκποδὼν μὲν ὢν
ὑπεστέναζον, νῦν δ' ὁρῶν ἀπόλλυμαι.
οἴμοι.
ἴθ', ἐκκάλυψον, ὡς ἴδω τὸ πᾶν κακόν.
ὦ δυσθέατον ὄμμα καὶ τόλμης πικρᾶς,
ὅσας ἀνίας μοι κατασπείρας φθίνεις.
ποῖ γὰρ μολεῖν μοι δυνατόν, εἰς ποίους βροτούς,
τοῖς σοῖς ἀρήξαντ' ἐν πόνοισι μηδαμοῦ;
ἦ πού <με> Τελαμών, σὸς πατὴρ ἐμός θ' ἅμα,
δέξαιτ' ἂν εὐπρόσωπος ἵλεώς τ' ἰδὼν
χωροῦντ' ἄνευ σοῦ. πῶς γὰρ οὔχ; ὅτῳ πάρα
μηδ' εὐτυχοῦντι μηδὲν ἥδιον γελᾶν.
οὗτος τί κρύψει; ποῖον οὐκ ἐρεῖ κακὸν
τὸν ἐκ δορὸς γεγῶτα πολεμίου νόθον,
τὸν δειλίᾳ προδόντα καὶ κακανδρίᾳ
σέ, φίλτατ' Αἴας, ἢ δόλοισιν, ὡς τὰ σὰ
κράτη θανόντος καὶ δόμους νέμοιμι σούς.
τοιαῦτ' ἀνὴρ δύσοργος, ἐν γήρᾳ βαρύς,
ἐρεῖ, πρὸς οὐδὲν εἰς ἔριν θυμούμενος.

TEUCER

O most grievous of all the sights that my eyes have looked upon! O path that has pained my heart the most of all the paths that I have travelled, path that I trod just now, dearest Ajax, when I realised that I was pursuing and tracking down the manner of your death! Yes, a swift-moving rumour, as though the work of some god, went through all the Achaeans, that you were dead and gone; and when I heard it, poor fellow, I mourned quietly while I was still far off, but now that I can see I am stricken to death!

Alas! Come, uncover him, so that I may see the whole horror! O face dreadful to look on, face that reveals such bitter courage, what pains have you sown far and wide for me in your death! Where can I go, among what mortals, I who was not there to help you in your troubles? Smiling and kindly, I imagine, will be my welcome from Telamon, your father and also mine, when I come there without you! Of course, seeing that even when fortune is good it is not his way to smile more graciously! What will he keep back? What evil will he not speak of me, the bastard born of the prize he won in battle, the betrayer, in my cowardice and weakness, of you, dearest Ajax, or in my cunning, so that with you dead I might control your lordship and your house? Such words will be uttered by a man who is irascible, fierce in old age, and quick to quarrel

---

998 an ὡς ἐκ θεοῦ?

1008 suppl. Küster

1009 τ᾽ ἰδὼν Hermann: τ᾽ ἴσως codd. plerique: θ᾽ ἅμα p

τέλος δ' ἀπωστὸς γῆς ἀπορριφθήσομαι,
δοῦλος λόγοισιν ἀντ' ἐλευθέρου φανείς.
τοιαῦτα μὲν κατ' οἶκον· ἐν Τροίᾳ δέ μοι
πολλοὶ μὲν ἐχθροί, παῦρα δ' ὠφελήσιμα,
καὶ ταῦτ' ἄφαντα σοῦ θανόντος ηὑρόμην.
οἴμοι, τί δράσω; πῶς σ' ἀποσπάσω πικροῦ
τοῦδ' αἰόλου κνώδοντος; ὦ τάλας, ὑφ' οὗ
φονέως ἄρ' ἐξέπνευσας. εἶδες ὡς χρόνῳ
ἔμελλέ σ' Ἕκτωρ καὶ θανὼν ἀποφθίσειν;
[σκέψασθε, πρὸς θεῶν, τὴν τύχην δυοῖν βροτοῖν.
Ἕκτωρ μέν, ᾧ δὴ τοῦδ' ἐδωρήθη πάρα,
ζωστῆρι πρισθεὶς ἱππικῶν ἐξ ἀντύγων
ἐκνάπτετ' αἰέν, ἔστ' ἀπέψυξεν βίον·
οὗτος δ' ἐκείνου τήνδε δωρεὰν ἔχων
πρὸς τοῦδ' ὄλωλε θανασίμῳ πεσήματι.
ἆρ' οὐκ Ἐρινὺς τοῦτ' ἐχάλκευσε ξίφος
κἀκεῖνον Ἅιδης, δημιουργὸς ἄγριος;
ἐγὼ μὲν οὖν καὶ ταῦτα καὶ τὰ πάντ' ἀεὶ
φάσκοιμ' ἂν ἀνθρώποισι μηχανᾶν θεούς·
ὅτῳ δὲ μὴ τάδ' ἐστὶν ἐν γνώμῃ φίλα,
κεῖνός τ' ἐκεῖνα στεργέτω κἀγὼ τάδε.]

ΧΟΡΟΣ

μὴ τεῖνε μακράν, ἀλλ' ὅπως κρύψεις τάφῳ
φράζου τὸν ἄνδρα, χὤ τι μυθήσῃ τάχα.
βλέπω γὰρ ἐχθρὸν φῶτα, καὶ τάχ' ἂν κακοῖς
γελῶν ἃ δὴ κακοῦργος ἐξίκοιτ' ἀνήρ.

angrily over nothing. In the end I shall be rejected and cast out from the land, denounced as a slave, no longer a free man. That is what will happen at home; and at Troy I have many enemies and little to help me; and even that little I have found has vanished with your death. Alas, what can I do? How shall I tug you from the gleaming point of this cruel sword? What a killer has extinguished your life, wretched man! Do you see how in the end Hector even in death was to be your killer? [Consider, I beg you, the fates of two mortals! Hector was lashed to the chariot-rail with the belt that this man had given him and mangled till he breathed out his life; and this man, who had this gift from him, fell dead, perishing by this weapon. Was it not an Erinys that forged this sword, and Hades that made the belt, a cruel workman? I would say that these things, and all things at all times, are contrived for mortals by the gods, and whoever does not approve my judgment, let him cherish his opinion and me mine!]

CHORUS

Do not speak for long, but think how you are to bury the man, and what you are to say soon! For I see an enemy, and perhaps he has come to mock us in our troubles, like a villain.

1023 *ταῦτ' ἄφαντα* Jackson: *ταῦτα πάντα* Lrpat: *ταῦθ' ἅπαντα* p

1028–39 del. Morstadt

ΤΕΥΚΡΟΣ

τίς δ' ἐστὶν ὅντιν' ἄνδρα προσλεύσσεις στρατοῦ;

ΧΟΡΟΣ

Μενέλαος, ᾧ δὴ τόνδε πλοῦν ἐστείλαμεν.

ΤΕΥΚΡΟΣ

ὁρῶ· μαθεῖν γὰρ ἐγγὺς ὢν οὐ δυσπετής.

ΜΕΝΕΛΑΟΣ

οὗτος, σὲ φωνῶ τόνδε τὸν νεκρὸν χεροῖν
μὴ συγκομίζειν, ἀλλ' ἐᾶν ὅπως ἔχει.

ΤΕΥΚΡΟΣ

τίνος χάριν τοσόνδ' ἀνήλωσας λόγον;

ΜΕΝΕΛΑΟΣ

δοκοῦντ' ἐμοί, δοκοῦντα δ' ὃς κραίνει στρατοῦ.

ΤΕΥΚΡΟΣ

οὔκουν ἂν εἴποις ἥντιν' αἰτίαν προθείς;

ΜΕΝΕΛΑΟΣ

ὁθούνεκ' αὐτὸν ἐλπίσαντες οἴκοθεν
ἄγειν Ἀχαιοῖς ξύμμαχόν τε καὶ φίλον,
ἐξηύρομεν ξυνόντες ἐχθίω Φρυγῶν·
ὅστις στρατῷ ξύμπαντι βουλεύσας φόνον
νύκτωρ ἐπεστράτευσεν, ὡς ἕλοι δορί·
κεἰ μὴ θεῶν τις τήνδε πεῖραν ἔσβεσεν,
ἡμεῖς μὲν ἂν τῇδ' ἣν ὅδ' εἴληχεν τύχῃ
θανόντες ἂν προὐκείμεθ' αἰσχίστῳ μόρῳ,
οὗτος δ' ἂν ἔζη. νῦν δ' ἐνήλλαξεν θεὸς
τὴν τοῦδ' ὕβριν πρὸς μῆλα καὶ ποίμνας πεσεῖν.

1054 ξυνόντες Reiske: ζητοῦντες codd.: ξυνόντ' ἔτ' Günther

TEUCER

Who is the man from the army that you see?

CHORUS

Menelaus, for whom we launched this expedition.

TEUCER

I see him; now that he is near, he is not hard to recognise.

Enter MENELAUS, accompanied by a Herald.

MENELAUS

You there, I order you not to lift this body; leave it as it is!

TEUCER

For what purpose have you wasted so many words?

MENELAUS

It is my decision, and the decision of the ruler of the army.

TEUCER

Then will you tell us what reason you put forward?

MENELAUS

Because after thinking we had brought him from home as an ally and friend to the Achaeans, when we had him with us we found him more an enemy than the Phrygians—him who planned murder against the entire army and made his attack on us by night, to put us to the spear. And had not one of the gods frustrated his attempt, we by the fate which he has found would be lying there dead by a miserable death and he would be alive; but as things are, a god turned aside his violence so that it fell upon sheep and cattle.

1058 τῇδ' Kousis: τήνδ' codd. | τύχῃ Ll.-J.: τύχην codd.
1059 λαχόντες Helvetius

ὧν οὕνεκ᾽ αὐτὸν οὔτις ἔστ᾽ ἀνὴρ σθένων
τοσοῦτον ὥστε σῶμα τυμβεῦσαι τάφῳ,
ἀλλ᾽ ἀμφὶ χλωρὰν ψάμαθον ἐκβεβλημένος
ὄρνισι φορβὴ παραλίοις γενήσεται.
πρὸς ταῦτα μηδὲν δεινὸν ἐξάρῃς μένος.
εἰ γὰρ βλέποντος μὴ 'δυνήθημεν κρατεῖν,
πάντως θανόντος γ᾽ ἄρξομεν, κἂν μὴ θέλῃς,
χερσὶν παρευθύνοντες. οὐ γὰρ ἔσθ᾽ ὅπου
λόγων ἀκοῦσαι ζῶν ποτ᾽ ἠθέλησ᾽ ἐμῶν.
καίτοι κακοῦ πρὸς ἀνδρὸς ὄντα δημότην
μηδὲν δικαιοῦν τῶν ἐφεστώτων κλύειν.
οὐ γάρ ποτ᾽ οὔτ᾽ ἂν ἐν πόλει νόμοι καλῶς
φέροιντ᾽ ἄν, ἔνθα μὴ καθεστήκοι δέος,
οὔτ᾽ ἂν στρατός γε σωφρόνως ἄρχοιτ᾽ ἔτι,
μηδὲν φόβου πρόβλημα μηδ᾽ αἰδοῦς ἔχων.
ἀλλ᾽ ἄνδρα χρή, κἂν σῶμα γεννήσῃ μέγα,
δοκεῖν πεσεῖν ἂν κἂν ἀπὸ σμικροῦ κακοῦ.
δέος γὰρ ᾧ πρόσεστιν αἰσχύνη θ᾽ ὁμοῦ,
σωτηρίαν ἔχοντα τόνδ᾽ ἐπίστασο·
ὅπου δ᾽ ὑβρίζειν δρᾶν θ᾽ ἃ βούλεται παρῇ,
ταύτην νόμιζε τὴν πόλιν χρόνῳ ποτὲ
ἐξ οὐρίων δραμοῦσαν ἐς βυθὸν πεσεῖν.
ἀλλ᾽ ἑστάτω μοι καὶ δέος τι καίριον,
καὶ μὴ δοκῶμεν δρῶντες ἂν ἡδώμεθα
οὐκ ἀντιτείσειν αὖθις ἂν λυπώμεθα.
ἕρπει παραλλὰξ ταῦτα. πρόσθεν οὗτος ἦν
αἴθων ὑβριστής, νῦν δ᾽ ἐγὼ μέγ᾽ αὖ φρονῶ.
καί σοι προφωνῶ τόνδε μὴ θάπτειν, ὅπως
μὴ τόνδε θάπτων αὐτὸς ἐς ταφὰς πέσῃς.

For this reason there is no man mighty enough to bury this body, but he shall be cast out upon the pale sand and become prey for the birds along the coast. In the face of that raise up no fierce anger! Why, if we could not rule him while he was alive, at least we shall rule him now that he is dead, even if you do not wish it, controlling with our hands; for while he lived he would never listen to my words. Indeed it is the mark of a villain for a subordinate to refuse to obey those in authority. The laws of a city can never function well where no one is afraid, nor can an army be sensibly controlled, when it has not the protection of fear and respect. Even if a man has a mighty frame, he must remember that he can be brought down even by small mischief. Know that when a man feels fear and shame, then he is safe! But where he can be insolent and do as he pleases, believe that that city, though at first it has sailed along easily, will in time sink to the bottom! Let some terror be established where it is needed, and let us not suppose that if we act according to our pleasure we shall not in time pay for our actions with our pain. These things come by turns; formerly he was heated in his insolence, but now it is my hour of pride. I tell you not to bury him, lest in trying to bury him you yourself fall into the grave!

1071 ὄντα Reiske: ἄνδρα codd.

ΧΟΡΟΣ

Μενέλαε, μὴ γνώμας ὑποστήσας σοφὰς
εἶτ᾽ αὐτὸς ἐν θανοῦσιν ὑβριστὴς γένῃ.

ΤΕΥΚΡΟΣ

οὐκ ἄν ποτ᾽, ἄνδρες, ἄνδρα θαυμάσαιμ᾽ ἔτι,
ὃς μηδὲν ὢν γοναῖσιν εἶθ᾽ ἁμαρτάνει,
ὅθ᾽ οἱ δοκοῦντες εὐγενεῖς πεφυκέναι
τοιαῦθ᾽ ἁμαρτάνουσιν ἐν λόγοις ἔπη.
ἄγ᾽, εἴπ᾽ ἀπ᾽ ἀρχῆς αὖθις, ἦ σὺ φὴς ἄγειν
τόνδ᾽ ἄνδρ᾽ Ἀχαιοῖς δεῦρο σύμμαχον λαβών;
οὐκ αὐτὸς ἐξέπλευσεν ὡς αὑτοῦ κρατῶν;
ποῦ σὺ στρατηγεῖς τοῦδε; ποῦ δὲ σοὶ λεὼν
ἔξεστ᾽ ἀνάσσειν ὧν ὅδ᾽ ἤγετ᾽ οἴκοθεν;
Σπάρτης ἀνάσσων ἦλθες, οὐχ ἡμῶν κρατῶν·
οὐδ᾽ ἔσθ᾽ ὅπου σοὶ τόνδε κοσμῆσαι πλέον
ἀρχῆς ἔκειτο θεσμὸς ἢ καὶ τῷδε σέ.
[ὕπαρχος ἄλλων δεῦρ᾽ ἔπλευσας, οὐχ ὅλων
στρατηγός, ὥστ᾽ Αἴαντος ἡγεῖσθαί ποτε.]
ἀλλ᾽ ὧνπερ ἄρχεις ἄρχε, καὶ τὰ σέμν᾽ ἔπη
κόλαζ᾽ ἐκείνους· τόνδε δ᾽, εἴτε μὴ σὺ φὴς
εἴθ᾽ ἅτερος στρατηγός, ἐς ταφὰς ἐγὼ
θήσω δικαίως, οὐ τὸ σὸν δείσας στόμα.
οὐ γάρ τι τῆς σῆς οὕνεκ᾽ ἐστρατεύσατο
γυναικός, ὥσπερ οἱ πόνου πολλοῦ πλέῳ,
ἀλλ᾽ οὕνεχ᾽ ὅρκων οἷσιν ἦν ἐπώμοτος,
σοῦ δ᾽ οὐδέν· οὐ γὰρ ἠξίου τοὺς μηδένας.
πρὸς ταῦτα πλείους δεῦρο κήρυκας λαβὼν

CHORUS

Menelaus, after laying down wise judgments do not yourself commit outrage against the dead!

TEUCER

I could never again wonder at a man's doing wrong who was nothing on account of birth, when they who are thought to be nobly born go wrong in talk by uttering words like these. Come, tell me over again, do you say you brought this man here as an ally for the Achaeans? Did he not sail out as his own master? In what way are you his commander? What right have you to command the people whom he brought from home? You came as king of Sparta, not as ruler over us; no rule of command entitles you to admonish him any more than one entitles him to admonish you. [You sailed as the subordinate of others, not as commander of us all, so that you could command Ajax.] No, rule over your own subjects, and rebuke them with your pompous words; and him will I bury, as I have a right to, even though you or the other generals say no, with no fear of your verbiage. For he did not go to war for the sake of your wife, like those who are weighed down with heavy labour, but because of the oaths that bound him, not because of you; for he did not value nobodies. In the face of that come here bringing more

---

1101 ἤγετ' anon.: ἡγεῖτ' codd.

1105–6 del. Schneidewin

1111–17 del. Reichard, 1111–14 del. Wecklein

1113 ἐπώμοτος Krpat: ἐν- Lpc

καὶ τὸν στρατηγὸν ἧκε· τοῦ δὲ σοῦ ψόφου
οὐκ ἂν στραφείην, ἕως ἂν ᾖς οἷός περ εἶ.

ΧΟΡΟΣ

οὐδ᾽ αὖ τοιαύτην γλῶσσαν ἐν κακοῖς φιλῶ·
τὰ σκληρὰ γάρ τοι, κἂν ὑπέρδικ᾽ ᾖ, δάκνει.

ΜΕΝΕΛΑΟΣ

ὁ τοξότης ἔοικεν οὐ σμικρὸν φρονεῖν.

ΤΕΥΚΡΟΣ

οὐ γὰρ βάναυσον τὴν τέχνην ἐκτησάμην.

ΜΕΝΕΛΑΟΣ

μέγ᾽ ἄν τι κομπάσειας, ἀσπίδ᾽ εἰ λάβοις.

ΤΕΥΚΡΟΣ

κἂν ψιλὸς ἀρκέσαιμι σοί γ᾽ ὡπλισμένῳ.

ΜΕΝΕΛΑΟΣ

ἡ γλῶσσά σου τὸν θυμὸν ὡς δεινὸν τρέφει.

ΤΕΥΚΡΟΣ

ξὺν τῷ δικαίῳ γὰρ μέγ᾽ ἔξεστιν φρονεῖν.

ΜΕΝΕΛΑΟΣ

δίκαια γὰρ τόνδ᾽ εὐτυχεῖν κτείναντά με;

ΤΕΥΚΡΟΣ

κτείναντα; δεινόν γ᾽ εἶπας, εἰ καὶ ζῇς θανών.

ΜΕΝΕΛΑΟΣ

θεὸς γὰρ ἐκσῴζει με, τῷδε δ᾽ οἴχομαι.

ΤΕΥΚΡΟΣ

μή νυν ἀτίμα θεούς, θεοῖς σεσωμένος.

heralds, and the general! But I would never turn about on account of your noise, so long as you are the man you are.

CHORUS

Neither do I care for such language in time of troubles; hard words sting, however just they are.

MENELAUS

The archer seems to have no small pride.

TEUCER

Yes, for the art I practise is no mean one.

MENELAUS

Your boasts would be loud indeed, if you were to acquire a shield.

TEUCER

With no shield I could deal with you fully armed.

MENELAUS

What fierce anger your tongue supplies with sustenance!

TEUCER

Yes, one can feel pride when one has justice on one's side.

MENELAUS

Is it just that this man should be honoured when he was my murderer?

TEUCER

Your murderer? You have said a strange thing, if you have died but are alive.

MENELAUS

Yes, a god has kept me safe, but for Ajax I am dead.

TEUCER

Then do not refuse honour to the gods, seeing that the gods preserved you.

ΜΕΝΕΛΑΟΣ

ἐγὼ γὰρ ἂν ψέξαιμι δαιμόνων νόμους;

ΤΕΥΚΡΟΣ

εἰ τοὺς θανόντας οὐκ ἐᾷς θάπτειν παρών.

ΜΕΝΕΛΑΟΣ

τούς γ' αὐτὸς αὑτοῦ πολεμίους· οὐ γὰρ καλόν;

ΤΕΥΚΡΟΣ

ἦ σοὶ γὰρ Αἴας πολέμιος προὔστη ποτέ;

ΜΕΝΕΛΑΟΣ

μισοῦντ' ἐμίσει· καὶ σὺ τοῦτ' ἠπίστασο.

ΤΕΥΚΡΟΣ

κλέπτης γὰρ αὐτοῦ ψηφοποιὸς ηὑρέθης.

ΜΕΝΕΛΑΟΣ

ἐν τοῖς δικασταῖς, οὐκ ἐμοί, τόδ' ἐσφάλη.

ΤΕΥΚΡΟΣ

πόλλ' ἂν καλῶς λάθρᾳ σὺ κλέψειας κακά.

ΜΕΝΕΛΑΟΣ

τοῦτ' εἰς ἀνίαν τοὔπος ἔρχεταί τινι.

ΤΕΥΚΡΟΣ

οὐ μᾶλλον, ὡς ἔοικεν, ἢ λυπήσομεν.

ΜΕΝΕΛΑΟΣ

ἕν σοι φράσω· τόνδ' ἐστὶν οὐχὶ θαπτέον.

1132 notam interrogationis posuit Dobree
1137 καλῶς L: κακῶς cett.

MENELAUS

Why, would I find fault with the laws of the gods?

TEUCER

Yes, if you stand there and forbid the burial of the dead.

MENELAUS

Yes, that of my own enemies; is it not honourable?

TEUCER

Did Ajax ever stand against you as an enemy?

MENELAUS

We hated one another; and you knew this.

TEUCER

Yes, you were shown to have cheated in the voting.

MENELAUS

This set-back was the work of the judges, not my work.

TEUCER

You could speciously bring off many evil frauds without men knowing.

MENELAUS

This speech is tending towards pain for someone.

TEUCER

To no more pain, I think, for me than for you.

MENELAUS

I will say one word to you; this man must not be buried!

ΤΕΥΚΡΟΣ

ἀλλ᾿ ἀντακούσῃ τοῦθ᾿ ἕν, ὡς τεθάψεται.

ΜΕΝΕΛΑΟΣ

ἤδη ποτ᾿ εἶδον ἄνδρ᾿ ἐγὼ γλώσσῃ θρασὺν
ναύτας ἐφορμήσαντα χειμῶνος τὸ πλεῖν,
ᾧ φθέγμ᾿ ἂν οὐκ ἐνηῦρες, ἡνίκ᾿ ἐν κακῷ
χειμῶνος εἴχετ᾿, ἀλλ᾿ ὑφ᾿ εἵματος κρυφεὶς
πατεῖν παρεῖχε τῷ θέλοντι ναυτίλων.
οὕτω δὲ καὶ σὲ καὶ τὸ σὸν λάβρον στόμα
σμικροῦ νέφους τάχ᾿ ἄν τις ἐκπνεύσας μέγας
χειμὼν κατασβέσειε τὴν πολλὴν βοήν.

ΤΕΥΚΡΟΣ

ἐγὼ δέ γ᾿ ἄνδρ᾿ ὄπωπα μωρίας πλέων,
ὃς ἐν κακοῖς ὕβριζε τοῖσι τῶν πέλας.
κᾆτ᾿ αὐτὸν εἰσιδών τις ἐμφερὴς ἐμοὶ
ὀργήν θ᾿ ὁμοῖος εἶπε τοιοῦτον λόγον,
"ὤνθρωπε, μὴ δρᾶ τοὺς τεθνηκότας κακῶς·
εἰ γὰρ ποήσεις, ἴσθι πημανούμενος."
τοιαῦτ᾿ ἄνολβον ἄνδρ᾿ ἐνουθέτει παρών.
ὁρῶ δέ τοί νιν, κἄστιν, ὡς ἐμοὶ δοκεῖ,
οὐδείς ποτ᾿ ἄλλος ἢ σύ. μῶν ᾐνιξάμην;

ΜΕΝΕΛΑΟΣ

ἄπειμι· καὶ γὰρ αἰσχρόν, εἰ πύθοιτό τις
λόγοις κολάζειν ᾧ βιάζεσθαι πάρα.

ΤΕΥΚΡΟΣ

ἄφερπέ νυν. κἀμοὶ γὰρ αἴσχιστον κλύειν
ἀνδρὸς ματαίου φλαῦρ᾿ ἔπη μυθουμένου.

TEUCER

But you shall hear one word in reply, that he shall be buried!

MENELAUS

In the past I have seen a man of reckless speech urging sailors to sail during a storm. But one heard no word from him when he was in the grip of the storm's attack; he huddled up under his cloak and allowed any sailor who wished to trample on him. Just so shall a small cloud issue in a mighty tempest that shall blow upon you and your loud mouth and put a stop to all your shouting.

TEUCER

And I have seen a man full of stupidity, who harried others in their time of troubles. And then a man like me and of the same temper saw him, and spoke such words as these: "Fellow, do not persecute the dead; for if you do so, know that you shall suffer pain!" That was how he rebuked the miserable man directly; and I see that man, and he is, I think, none other than you. Do I speak in riddles?

MENELAUS

I shall depart; it would be disgraceful if anyone learned that I was chastising with words when I could use force.

TEUCER

Be off, then, for for me too it is utterly disgraceful to listen to a futile fellow speaking foolish words.

Exit MENELAUS.

1141 τοῦθ' ἕν Wecklein: τοῦτον codd. plerique
1144 ἐνηῦρες Hartung: ἂν ηὗρες codd.

ΧΟΡΟΣ

ἔσται μεγάλης ἔριδός τις ἀγών.
ἀλλ᾿ ὡς δύνασαι, Τεῦκρε, ταχύνας
σπεῦσον κοίλην κάπετόν τιν᾿ ἰδεῖν
τῷδ᾿, ἔνθα βροτοῖς τὸν ἀείμνηστον
τάφον εὐρώεντα καθέξει.

ΤΕΥΚΡΟΣ

καὶ μὴν ἐς αὐτὸν καιρὸν οἵδε πλησίοι
πάρεισιν ἀνδρὸς τοῦδε παῖς τε καὶ γυνή,
τάφον περιστελοῦντε δυστήνου νεκροῦ.
ὦ παῖ, πρόσελθε δεῦρο, καὶ σταθεὶς πέλας
ἱκέτης ἔφαψαι πατρός, ὅς σ᾿ ἐγείνατο.
θάκει δὲ προστρόπαιος ἐν χεροῖν ἔχων
κόμας ἐμὰς καὶ τῆσδε καὶ σαυτοῦ τρίτον,
ἱκτήριον θησαυρόν. εἰ δέ τις στρατοῦ
βίᾳ σ᾿ ἀποσπάσειε τοῦδε τοῦ νεκροῦ,
κακὸς κακῶς ἄθαπτος ἐκπέσοι χθονός,
γένους ἅπαντος ῥίζαν ἐξημημένος,
αὔτως ὅπωσπερ τόνδ᾿ ἐγὼ τέμνω πλόκον.
ἔχ᾿ αὐτόν, ὦ παῖ, καὶ φύλασσε, μηδέ σε
κινησάτω τις, ἀλλὰ προσπεσὼν ἔχου,
ὑμεῖς τε μὴ γυναῖκες ἀντ᾿ ἀνδρῶν πέλας
παρέστατ᾿, ἀλλ᾿ ἀρήγετ᾿, ἔστ᾿ ἐγὼ μόλω
τάφου μεληθεὶς τῷδε, κἂν μηδεὶς ἐᾷ.

ΧΟΡΟΣ

τίς ἄρα νέατος, ἐς πότε λή- στρ. α´
ξει πολυπλάγκτων ἐτέων ἀριθμός,

CHORUS

There will be a struggle arising from a great dispute! Come, as quickly as you can, Teucer, hasten to find a hollow trench for this man, where he shall occupy the dank tomb that shall ever be remembered by mortals.

Enter TECMESSA *and* EURYSACES.

TEUCER

Yes, at this very moment here are this man's son and wife, come to adorn the tomb of the hapless corpse. Boy, come here and, standing close by, clasp as a suppliant the father who begot you. Sit there in supplication, holding a lock of mine and one of hers and thirdly one of your own, a store of instruments of supplication! And if any of the army tries to drag you by force away from this corpse, may that man perish out of the earth without burial, evilly as befits an evil man, with the seed of all his house cut off, even as I now cut this hair! Hold him, boy, and guard him! Let no one move you, but throw yourself upon him and keep hold. And do you men not stand around like women, but render aid, until I return from taking care of this grave, even if everyone forbids it.

Exit TEUCER.

CHORUS

What will be the final number of the wandering years? When will their count end, the years that bring for me the

τὰν ἄπαυστον αἰὲν ἐμοὶ δορυσσοή-
των μόχθων ἄταν ἐπάγων
ἂν τὰν εὐρώδη Τροΐαν,
δύστανον ὄνειδος Ἑλλάνων;
ὄφελε πρότερον αἰθέρα δῦ- ἀντ. α′
ναι μέγαν ἢ τὸν πολύκοινον Ἅιδαν
κεῖνος ἀνήρ, ὃς στυγερῶν ἔδειξεν ὅ-
πλων Ἕλλασιν κοινὸν Ἄρη.
ὦ πόνοι πρόγονοι πόνων·
κεῖνος γὰρ ἔπερσεν ἀνθρώπους.
ἐκεῖνος οὐ στεφάνων οὔ- στρ. β′
τε βαθειᾶν κυλίκων νεῖ-
μεν ἐμοὶ τέρψιν ὁμιλεῖν,
οὔτε γλυκὺν αὐλῶν ὄτοβον δυσ-
μόρῳ, οὔτ᾽ ἐννυχίαν τέρψιν ἰαύειν·
ἐρώτων δ᾽ ἐρώτων ἀπέπαυσεν, ὤμοι.
κεῖμαι δ᾽ ἀμέριμνος οὕτως,
ἀεὶ πυκιναῖς δρόσοις
τεγγόμενος κόμας,
λυγρᾶς μνήματα Τροίας.
καὶ πρὶν μὲν ἐννυχίου δεί- ἀντ. β′
ματος ἦν μοι προβολὰ καὶ
βελέων θούριος Αἴας·
νῦν δ᾽ οὗτος ἀνεῖται στυγερῷ δαί-
μονι. τίς μοι, τίς ἔτ᾽ οὖν τέρψις ἐπέσται;
γενοίμαν ἵν᾽ ὑλᾶεν ἔπεστι πόντῳ
πρόβλημ᾽ ἁλίκλυστον, ἄκραν

ceaseless torment of the sufferings of battle, in the wide land of Troy, a mournful reproach for the Greeks?

That man should first have entered the mighty sky or Hades, common to all, who first showed to the Greeks how to league in war with hateful weapons! O sorrows progenitors of sorrows! for he was the ruin of mankind.

It was he that denied me the pleasure of garlands and of deep cups, and the delightful sound of pipes, to my sorrow, and the delight of sleep at night. And he cut me off from love, alas, from love! And I lie here uncared for, my hair ever drenched by the heavy dews, reminding me of miserable Troy.

And before my shield against nocturnal fear and arrows was mighty Ajax. But now he is made over to a hateful god. What joy, what joy yet remains for me? I wish I were where the wooded cape, beaten by the surf, projects

---

1190 ἂν τὰν Ahrens: ἀνὰ τὰν codd.: τάνδ᾽ ἂν Lobeck
1199 οὐ Hermann: οὔτε codd.
1202 δυσμόρῳ Blaydes: -μορος codd.
1211 αἰὲν νυχίου G. Wolff: <ἦν> νυχίου Günther
1218 πόντῳ Morstadt: πόντου codd.

ὑπὸ πλάκα Σουνίου,
τὰς ἱερὰς ὅπως
προσείποιμεν Ἀθάνας.

ΤΕΥΚΡΟΣ

καὶ μὴν ἰδὼν ἔσπευσα τὸν στρατηλάτην
Ἀγαμέμνον᾽ ἡμῖν δεῦρο τόνδ᾽ ὁρμώμενον·
δῆλος δέ μοὔστὶ σκαιὸν ἐκλύσων στόμα.

ΑΓΑΜΕΜΝΩΝ

σὲ δὴ τὰ δεινὰ ῥήματ᾽ ἀγγέλλουσί μοι
τλῆναι καθ᾽ ἡμῶν ὧδ᾽ ἀνοιμωκτεὶ χανεῖν.
σέ τοι, τὸν ἐκ τῆς αἰχμαλωτίδος λέγω·
ἦ που τραφεὶς ἂν μητρὸς εὐγενοῦς ἄπο
ὑψήλ᾽ ἐφώνεις κἀπ᾽ ἄκρων ὡδοιπόρεις,
ὅτ᾽ οὐδὲν ὢν τοῦ μηδὲν ἀντέστης ὕπερ,
κοὔτε στρατηγοὺς οὔτε ναυάρχους μολεῖν
ἡμᾶς Ἀχαιῶν οὔτε σοῦ διωμόσω,
ἀλλ᾽ αὐτὸς ἄρχων, ὡς σὺ φής, Αἴας ἔπλει.
ταῦτ᾽ οὐκ ἀκούειν μεγάλα πρὸς δούλων κακά;
ποίου κέκραγας ἀνδρὸς ὧδ᾽ ὑπέρφρονα,
ποῦ βάντος ἢ ποῦ στάντος οὗπερ οὐκ ἐγώ;
οὐκ ἆρ᾽ Ἀχαιοῖς ἄνδρες εἰσὶ πλὴν ὅδε;
πικροὺς ἔοιγμεν τῶν Ἀχιλλείων ὅπλων
ἀγῶνας Ἀργείοισι κηρῦξαι τότε,
εἰ πανταχοῦ φανούμεθ᾽ ἐκ Τεύκρου κακοί,
κοὐκ ἀρκέσει ποθ᾽ ὑμὶν οὐδ᾽ ἡσσημένοις
εἴκειν ἃ τοῖς πολλοῖσιν ἤρεσκεν κριταῖς,
ἀλλ᾽ αἰὲν ἡμᾶς ἢ κακοῖς βαλεῖτέ που
ἢ σὺν δόλῳ κεντήσεθ᾽ οἱ λελειμμένοι.

over the sea, beneath the high plateau of Sunium, so that I could salute sacred Athens!

Enter TEUCER

TEUCER

Now I have made haste, since I saw the general Agamemnon advancing this way towards us; and it is clear that he will open his mouth in jarring speech.

Enter AGAMEMNON.

AGAMEMNON

It is you who they report has had the insolence to utter these strong words against us, and with impunity! It is you, the son of the captive woman, that I address! You would have used high words, I think, and have walked on the tips of your toes if you had been the son of a noble mother, since you who are nothing have championed him who is also nothing, and have declared on oath that we did not come as commanders nor as leaders of the fleet over the Achaeans or over you, but that Ajax sailed—so you say—as his own chief. Is it not a great scandal that we hear this from slaves? What sort of man was he about whom you speak so arrogantly? Where did he go and where did he stand where I did not? Have the Achaeans, then, no men but him? We are likely to regret having announced a contest for the arms of Achilles if we are to be denounced as evil in every way by Teucer, and even when you are defeated you will not bow to the decision of the majority of judges, but will always shower us with abuse or stab at us from ambush, you that are left. If such

ἐκ τῶνδε μέντοι τῶν τρόπων οὐκ ἄν ποτε
κατάστασις γένοιτ' ἂν οὐδενὸς νόμου,
εἰ τοὺς δίκῃ νικῶντας ἐξωθήσομεν
καὶ τοὺς ὄπισθεν ἐς τὸ πρόσθεν ἄξομεν.
ἀλλ' εἰρκτέον τάδ' ἐστίν· οὐ γὰρ οἱ πλατεῖς
οὐδ' εὐρύνωτοι φῶτες ἀσφαλέστατοι,
ἀλλ' οἱ φρονοῦντες εὖ κρατοῦσι πανταχοῦ.
μέγας δὲ πλευρὰ βοῦς ὑπὸ σμικρᾶς ὅμως
μάστιγος ὀρθὸς εἰς ὁδὸν πορεύεται.
καὶ σοὶ προσέρπον τοῦτ' ἐγὼ τὸ φάρμακον
ὁρῶ τάχ', εἰ μὴ νοῦν κατακτήσῃ τινά·
ὃς τἀνδρὸς οὐκέτ' ὄντος, ἀλλ' ἤδη σκιᾶς,
θαρσῶν ὑβρίζεις κἀξελευθεροστομεῖς.
οὐ σωφρονήσεις; οὐ μαθὼν ὃς εἶ φύσιν
ἄλλον τιν' ἄξεις ἄνδρα δεῦρ' ἐλεύθερον,
ὅστις πρὸς ἡμᾶς ἀντὶ σοῦ λέξει τὰ σά;
σοῦ γὰρ λέγοντος οὐκέτ' ἂν μάθοιμ' ἐγώ·
τὴν βάρβαρον γὰρ γλῶσσαν οὐκ ἐπαΐω.

ΧΟΡΟΣ

εἴθ' ὑμὶν ἀμφοῖν νοῦς γένοιτο σωφρονεῖν·
τούτου γὰρ οὐδὲν σφῷν ἔχω λῷον φράσαι.

ΤΕΥΚΡΟΣ

φεῦ, τοῦ θανόντος ὡς ταχεῖά τις βροτοῖς
χάρις διαρρεῖ καὶ προδοῦσ' ἁλίσκεται,
εἰ σοῦ γ' ὅδ' ἀνὴρ οὐδ' ἐπὶ σμικρὸν λόγον,
Αἴας, ἔτ' ἴσχει μνῆστιν, οὗ σὺ πολλάκις
τὴν σὴν προτείνων προὔκαμες ψυχὴν δορί·
ἀλλ' οἴχεται δὴ πάντα ταῦτ' ἐρριμμένα.

behaviour is allowed, no law can be established, if we are to thrust aside those who have justly won and bring to the front those who were behind. No, we must put a stop to this! It is not stout and broad-shouldered men who are the most reliable, but it is men of good sense that everywhere prevail. A huge ox goes straight along the road, guided by a small goad. And I see this remedy in store for you, soon, if you do not acquire some sense; you who when the man is no more, but is already a ghost, confidently insult us with speech uncontrolled! Will you not get some sense? Will you not learn who you are and bring another man here who is a free man to speak for you instead of you yourself? I could not understand, were you the speaker, since I do not know the barbarian language.

CHORUS

I wish you could both have the wisdom to be sensible; I have nothing better than that to say to you.

TEUCER

Alas, how swiftly does gratitude to the dead flow away among men and how soon is it caught betraying them, if this man does not bear you in mind, Ajax, even to a small extent, this man whom you often protected, risking your own life! But all this is cast away and gone! You who just

---

1257 *τἀνδρὸς* Wecklein: *ἀνδρὸς* codd.
1268 *σμικρὸν λόγον* Reiske: *-ων -ῶν* Lrpa

ὦ πολλὰ λέξας ἄρτι κἀνόητ᾽ ἔπη,
οὐ μνημονεύεις οὐκέτ᾽ οὐδέν, ἡνίκα
ἑρκέων ποθ᾽ ὑμᾶς ἐντὸς ἐγκεκλῃμένους,
ἤδη τὸ μηδὲν ὄντας ἐν τροπῇ δορός,
ἐρρύσατ᾽ ἐλθὼν μοῦνος, ἀμφὶ μὲν νεῶν
ἄκροισιν ἤδη ναυτικοῖς θ᾽ ἑδωλίοις
πυρὸς φλέγοντος, ἐς δὲ ναυτικὰ σκάφη
πηδῶντος ἄρδην Ἕκτορος τάφρων ὕπερ;
τίς ταῦτ᾽ ἀπεῖρξεν; οὐχ ὅδ᾽ ἦν ὁ δρῶν τάδε,
ὃν οὐδαμοῦ φής, οὗ σὺ μή, βῆναι ποδί;
ἆρ᾽ ὑμὶν οὗτος ταῦτ᾽ ἔδρασεν ἔνδικα;
χὤτ᾽ αὖθις αὐτὸς Ἕκτορος μόνος μόνου,
λαχών τε κἀκέλευστος, ἦλθεν ἀντίος,
οὐ δραπέτην τὸν κλῆρον ἐς μέσον καθείς,
ὑγρᾶς ἀρούρας βῶλον, ἀλλ᾽ ὃς εὐλόφου
κυνῆς ἔμελλε πρῶτος ἅλμα κουφιεῖν;
ὅδ᾽ ἦν ὁ πράσσων ταῦτα, σὺν δ᾽ ἐγὼ παρών,
ὁ δοῦλος, οὑκ τῆς βαρβάρου μητρὸς γεγώς.
δύστηνε, ποῖ βλέπων ποτ᾽ αὐτὰ καὶ θροεῖς;
οὐκ οἶσθα σοῦ πατρὸς μὲν ὃς προὔφυ πατὴρ
τἀρχαῖον ὄντα Πέλοπα βάρβαρον Φρύγα;
Ἀτρέα δ᾽, ὃς αὖ σ᾽ ἔσπειρε, δυσσεβέστατον
προθέντ᾽ ἀδελφῷ δεῖπνον οἰκείων τέκνων;
αὐτὸς δὲ μητρὸς ἐξέφυς Κρήσσης, ἐφ᾽ ᾗ
λαβὼν ἐπακτὸν ἄνδρ᾽ ὁ φιτύσας πατὴρ
ἐφῆκεν ἐλλοῖς ἰχθύσιν διαφθοράν.
τοιοῦτος ὢν τοιῷδ᾽ ὀνειδίζεις σποράν;
ὃς ἐκ πατρὸς μέν εἰμι Τελαμῶνος γεγώς,

now spoke so many foolish words, have you no memory of the time when you were shut up inside your fence, already reduced to nothing by the turn taken by the battle, and this man came alone and saved you, when fire was blazing about the decks of the ships at their sterns, and Hector was leaping high over the moat onto the hulls of the ships? Who put a stop to this? was it not he who did this deed, he who you said went nowhere where you did not go? Was this action of his criminal? And again when he came against Hector, man to man, by lot and without orders, having thrown in a token that was no runaway, no lump of wet earth, but one that was bound to leap first out of the crested helmet?[a] It was he that did this, and I was there with him, the slave, the child of the barbarian mother. Wretch, where are you looking when you speak these words? Do you not know that the father of your father, Pelops, was by origin a barbarous Phrygian? And that Atreus, your parent, set before his brother a most impious meal, the flesh of his children? And you yourself are the son of a Cretan mother, whom your father, finding a lover with her, sent to be destroyed by dumb fishes. Does such a man as you reproach with his origin such a

[a] Each of the different contenders for the privilege of fighting Hector in the duel threw into a helmet a marked token, and the owner of the first token to come out when the helmet was shaken was the winner.

1274 ἐντὸς a (coni. Musgrave): οὗτος Lrpat
1281 οὗ σὺ μή, βῆναι J. Krauss: οὐδὲ συμβῆναι codd.
1292 τἀρχαῖον Ll.-J.: ἀρχαῖον codd.

ὅστις στρατοῦ τὰ πρῶτ᾽ ἀριστεύσας ἐμὴν
ἴσχει ξύνευνον μητέρ᾽, ἣ φύσει μὲν ἦν
βασίλεια, Λαομέδοντος· ἔκκριτον δέ νιν
δώρημ᾽ ἐκείνῳ ᾽δωκεν Ἀλκμήνης γόνος.
ἆρ᾽ ὧδ᾽ ἄριστος ἐξ ἀριστέοιν δυοῖν
βλαστὼν ἂν αἰσχύνοιμι τοὺς πρὸς αἵματος,
οὓς νῦν σὺ τοιοῖσδ᾽ ἐν πόνοισι κειμένους
ὠθεῖς ἀθάπτους, οὐδ᾽ ἐπαισχύνῃ λέγων;
εὖ νυν τόδ᾽ ἴσθι, τοῦτον εἰ βαλεῖτέ που,
βαλεῖτε χἠμᾶς τρεῖς ὁμοῦ συγκειμένους,
ἐπεὶ καλόν μοι τοῦδ᾽ ὑπερπονουμένῳ
θανεῖν προδήλως μᾶλλον ἢ τῆς σῆς ὑπὲρ
γυναικός, ἢ σοῦ τοῦ θ᾽ ὁμαίμονος λέγω;
πρὸς ταῦθ᾽ ὅρα μὴ τοὐμόν, ἀλλὰ καὶ τὸ σόν.
ὡς εἴ με πημανεῖς τι, βουλήσῃ ποτὲ
καὶ δειλὸς εἶναι μᾶλλον ἢ ᾽ν ἐμοὶ θρασύς.

ΧΟΡΟΣ

ἄναξ Ὀδυσσεῦ, καιρὸν ἴσθ᾽ ἐληλυθώς,
εἰ μὴ ξυνάψων, ἀλλὰ συλλύσων πάρει.

ΟΔΥΣΣΕΥΣ

τί δ᾽ ἔστιν, ἄνδρες; τηλόθεν γὰρ ᾐσθόμην
βοὴν Ἀτρειδῶν τῷδ᾽ ἐπ᾽ ἀλκίμῳ νεκρῷ.

ΑΓΑΜΕΜΝΩΝ

οὐ γὰρ κλυόντες ἐσμὲν αἰσχίστους λόγους,
ἄναξ Ὀδυσσεῦ, τοῦδ᾽ ὑπ᾽ ἀνδρὸς ἀρτίως;

1312 σοῦ τοῦ θ᾽ Hertel: τοῦ σοῦ θ᾽ codd.

one as I, whose father was Telamon, who as the army's greatest prize for valour won as bedfellow my mother, who was by birth a princess, daughter of Laomedon, and she was given as a special gift by Alcmene's son? Would I, thus born the noble son of two noble parents, shame my relation, whom, as he lies low in misery, you would expel unburied, and feel no shame for your words? Know it for certain, if you hurl him aside, you shall hurl aside also the three of us along with him, since I am proud to die before all fighting for him rather than for your wife, or shall I say for you and your brother? In face of that, think not of my position, but your own; since if you do me harm, you shall live to wish you had been cowardly rather than brave in dealing with me.

Enter ODYSSEUS.

CHORUS

Lord Odysseus, know that you have come at the right moment, if you have come not to make the tangle worse, but to untie it!

ODYSSEUS

What is it, sirs? From far off I heard loud cries of the sons of Atreus over this valiant corpse.

AGAMEMNON

Why, had we not heard shameful words from this man just now, my lord Odysseus?

ΟΔΥΣΣΕΥΣ

ποίους; ἐγὼ γὰρ ἀνδρὶ συγγνώμην ἔχω
κλύοντι φλαῦρα συμβαλεῖν ἔπη κακά.

ΑΓΑΜΕΜΝΩΝ

ἤκουσεν αἰσχρά· δρῶν γὰρ ἦν τοιαῦτ᾽ ἐμέ.

ΟΔΥΣΣΕΥΣ

τί γάρ σ᾽ ἔδρασεν, ὥστε καὶ βλάβην ἔχειν;

ΑΓΑΜΕΜΝΩΝ

οὔ φησ᾽ ἐάσειν τόνδε τὸν νεκρὸν ταφῆς
ἄμοιρον, ἀλλὰ πρὸς βίαν θάψειν ἐμοῦ.

ΟΔΥΣΣΕΥΣ

ἔξεστιν οὖν εἰπόντι τἀληθῆ φίλῳ
σοὶ μηδὲν ἧσσον ἢ πάρος ξυνηρετεῖν;

ΑΓΑΜΕΜΝΩΝ

εἴπ᾽· ἦ γὰρ εἴην οὐκ ἂν εὖ φρονῶν, ἐπεὶ
φίλον σ᾽ ἐγὼ μέγιστον Ἀργείων νέμω.

ΟΔΥΣΣΕΥΣ

ἄκουέ νυν. τὸν ἄνδρα τόνδε πρὸς θεῶν
μὴ τλῇς ἄθαπτον ὧδ᾽ ἀναλγήτως βαλεῖν·
μηδ᾽ ἡ βία σε μηδαμῶς νικησάτω
τοσόνδε μισεῖν ὥστε τὴν δίκην πατεῖν.
κἀμοὶ γὰρ ἦν ποθ᾽ οὗτος ἔχθιστος στρατοῦ,
ἐξ οὗ ᾽κράτησα τῶν Ἀχιλλείων ὅπλων,
ἀλλ᾽ αὐτὸν ἔμπας ὄντ᾽ ἐγὼ τοιόνδ᾽ ἐμοὶ
οὔ τἂν ἀτιμάσαιμ᾽ ἄν, ὥστε μὴ λέγειν
ἕν᾽ ἄνδρ᾽ ἰδεῖν ἄριστον Ἀργείων, ὅσοι
Τροίαν ἀφικόμεσθα, πλὴν Ἀχιλλέως.

ODYSSEUS

What words? I can feel with a man who hurls insults when he has heard hard words.

AGAMEMNON

He heard shameful words, because his acts towards me were shameful.

ODYSSEUS

What did he do to you so as to injure you?

AGAMEMNON

He says he will not leave this corpse unburied, but will bury it against my will.

ODYSSEUS

Then may a friend tell the truth to a friend and assist you no less than I have done till now?

AGAMEMNON

Speak! Indeed I should be foolish not to let you, since I regard you as my greatest friend among the Argives.

ODYSSEUS

Listen, then! I beg you not to venture to cast this man out ruthlessly, unburied. Violence must not so prevail on you that you trample justice under foot! For me too he was once my chief enemy in the army, ever since I became the owner of the arms of Achilles; but though he was such in regard to me, I would not so far fail to do him honour as to deny that he was the most valiant man among the

---

1336 *ἔχθιστος*] an *οὔχθιστος*?

1339 *οὔ τἂν ἀτιμάσαιμ' ἄν* Elmsley: *οὐκ ἂν ἀτιμάσαιμ' ἄν* lrp: *οὔκουν ἀτιμάσαιμ' ἄν* a

ὥστ' οὐκ ἂν ἐνδίκως γ' ἀτιμάζοιτό σοι·
οὐ γάρ τι τοῦτον, ἀλλὰ τοὺς θεῶν νόμους
φθείροις ἄν. ἄνδρα δ' οὐ δίκαιον, εἰ θάνοι,
βλάπτειν τὸν ἐσθλόν, οὐδ' ἐὰν μισῶν κυρῇς.

ΑΓΑΜΕΜΝΩΝ

σὺ ταῦτ', Ὀδυσσεῦ, τοῦδ' ὑπερμαχεῖς ἐμοί;

ΟΔΥΣΣΕΥΣ

ἔγωγ'· ἐμίσουν δ', ἡνίκ' ἦν μισεῖν καλόν.

ΑΓΑΜΕΜΝΩΝ

οὐ γὰρ θανόντι καὶ προσεμβῆναί σε χρή;

ΟΔΥΣΣΕΥΣ

μὴ χαῖρ', Ἀτρείδη, κέρδεσιν τοῖς μὴ καλοῖς.

ΑΓΑΜΕΜΝΩΝ

τόν τοι τύραννον εὐσεβεῖν οὐ ῥᾴδιον.

ΟΔΥΣΣΕΥΣ

ἀλλ' εὖ λέγουσι τοῖς φίλοις τιμὰς νέμειν.

ΑΓΑΜΕΜΝΩΝ

κλύειν τὸν ἐσθλὸν ἄνδρα χρὴ τῶν ἐν τέλει.

ΟΔΥΣΣΕΥΣ

παῦσαι· κρατεῖς τοι τῶν φίλων νικώμενος.

ΑΓΑΜΕΜΝΩΝ

μέμνησ' ὁποίῳ φωτὶ τὴν χάριν δίδως.

ΟΔΥΣΣΕΥΣ

ὅδ' ἐχθρὸς ἀνήρ, ἀλλὰ γενναῖός ποτ' ἦν.

1348 πρὸς ἐμβῆναι Blaydes

Argives, of all that came to Troy, except Achilles. And so you cannot dishonour him without injustice; for you would be destroying not him, but the laws of the gods. It is unjust to injure a noble man, if he is dead, even if it happens that you hate him.

AGAMEMNON

Odysseus, are you fighting for this man against me?

ODYSSEUS

Yes! I hated him when it was honourable to hate him.

AGAMEMNON

Now that he is dead, should you not trample on him?

ODYSSEUS

Son of Atreus, do not take pleasure in a superiority that is ignoble!

AGAMEMNON

It is not easy for a ruler to avoid impiety.

ODYSSEUS

But he should honour his friends when they give good advice.

AGAMEMNON

The noble man should obey those in authority.

ODYSSEUS

Enough! You win, when you give in to your friends.

AGAMEMNON

Remember what sort of man is the recipient of your kindness.

ODYSSEUS

This man was an enemy, but he was noble.

ΑΓΑΜΕΜΝΩΝ

τί ποτε ποήσεις; ἐχθρὸν ὧδ᾽ αἰδῇ νέκυν;

ΟΔΥΣΣΕΥΣ

νικᾷ γὰρ ἁρετή με τῆς ἔχθρας πλέον.

ΑΓΑΜΕΜΝΩΝ

τοιοίδε μέντοι φῶτες οὔμπληκτοι βροτῶν.

ΟΔΥΣΣΕΥΣ

ἦ κάρτα πολλοὶ νῦν φίλοι καὖθις πικροί.

ΑΓΑΜΕΜΝΩΝ

τοιούσδ᾽ ἐπαινεῖς δῆτα σὺ κτᾶσθαι φίλους;

ΟΔΥΣΣΕΥΣ

σκληρὰν ἐπαινεῖν οὐ φιλῶ ψυχὴν ἐγώ.

ΑΓΑΜΕΜΝΩΝ

ἡμᾶς σὺ δειλοὺς τῇδε θἠμέρᾳ φανεῖς.

ΟΔΥΣΣΕΥΣ

ἄνδρας μὲν οὖν Ἕλλησι πᾶσιν ἐνδίκους.

ΑΓΑΜΕΜΝΩΝ

ἄνωγας οὖν με τὸν νεκρὸν θάπτειν ἐᾶν;

ΟΔΥΣΣΕΥΣ

ἔγωγε· καὶ γὰρ αὐτὸς ἐνθάδ᾽ ἵξομαι.

ΑΓΑΜΕΜΝΩΝ

ἦ πάνθ᾽ ὁμοῖα· πᾶς ἀνὴρ αὑτῷ πονεῖ.

ΟΔΥΣΣΕΥΣ

τῷ γάρ με μᾶλλον εἰκὸς ἢ ᾽μαυτῷ πονεῖν;

AGAMEMNON

What is it you will do? Have you such respect for the corpse of an enemy?

ODYSSEUS

His excellence weighs more with me than his enmity.

AGAMEMNON

That is what inconsistent men are like.

ODYSSEUS

In truth many people are now friends and later enemies.

AGAMEMNON

Do you approve of making friends of such people?

ODYSSEUS

It is not my way to approve of a rigid mind.

AGAMEMNON

On this day you will make us seem cowards.

ODYSSEUS

No, men who are just in the sight of all the Greeks.

AGAMEMNON

Then are you telling me to allow this body to be buried?

ODYSSEUS

I am; why, I myself shall come to this same pass!

AGAMEMNON

It is always the same! Every man works for himself.

ODYSSEUS

For whom am I likely to work if not for myself?

1357 πλέον C: πολύ cett.
1358 οὔμπληκτοι Blaydes: ἔμπληκτοι codd.

ΑΓΑΜΕΜΝΩΝ

σὸν ἆρα τοὔργον, οὐκ ἐμὸν κεκλήσεται.

ΟΔΥΣΣΕΥΣ

ὧδ' ἢν ποήσῃς, πανταχῇ χρηστός γ' ἔσῃ.

ΑΓΑΜΕΜΝΩΝ

ἀλλ' εὖ γε μέντοι τοῦτ' ἐπίστασ', ὡς ἐγὼ
σοὶ μὲν νέμοιμ' ἂν τῆσδε καὶ μείζω χάριν,
οὗτος δὲ κἀκεῖ κἀνθάδ' ὢν ἔμοιγ' ὁμῶς
ἔχθιστος ἔσται. σοὶ δὲ δρᾶν ἔξεσθ' ἃ χρῇς.

ΧΟΡΟΣ

ὅστις σ', Ὀδυσσεῦ, μὴ λέγει γνώμῃ σοφὸν
φῦναι, τοιοῦτον ὄντα, μῶρός ἐστ' ἀνήρ.

ΟΔΥΣΣΕΥΣ

καὶ νῦν γε Τεύκρῳ τἀπὸ τοῦδ' ἀγγέλλομαι,
ὅσον τότ' ἐχθρὸς ἦ, τοσόνδ' εἶναι φίλος.
καὶ τὸν θανόντα τόνδε συνθάπτειν θέλω,
καὶ ξυμπονεῖν καὶ μηδὲν ἐλλείπειν ὅσων
χρὴ τοῖς ἀρίστοις ἀνδράσιν πονεῖν βροτούς.

ΤΕΥΚΡΟΣ

ἄριστ' Ὀδυσσεῦ, πάντ' ἔχω σ' ἐπαινέσαι
λόγοισι· καί μ' ἔψευσας ἐλπίδος πολύ.
τούτῳ γὰρ ὢν ἔχθιστος Ἀργείων ἀνὴρ
μόνος παρέστης χερσίν, οὐδ' ἔτλης παρὼν
θανόντι τῷδε ζῶν ἐφυβρίσαι μέγα,
ὡς ὁ στρατηγὸς οὑπιβρόντητος μολὼν
αὐτός τε χὼ ξύναιμος ἠθελησάτην

AGAMEMNON

Then it shall be called your action, not mine.

ODYSSEUS

If you perform this action, in any case you will do well.

AGAMEMNON

Indeed you can be sure of this, that to you I would accord a favour still greater than this one. But he both here and there alike shall be a deadly enemy to me. But you may do as you wish.

Exit AGAMEMNON.

CHORUS

Odysseus, whoever says that you are not wise in your judgment, when you are like this, is a fool!

ODYSSEUS

And now for the future I proclaim to Teucer that I am as much a friend as I was then an enemy; and I wish to join in burying the dead man, and to help and to leave undone none of the things that one should do for the noblest of mortals.

TEUCER

Noble Odysseus, in my speech I can approve you in every matter; and you have altogether belied my expectations. You were this man's greatest enemy among the Argives, but you alone stood by him actively, and refused to stand there and mock him when you were living and he dead, when the deluded general and his brother wished to do

1369 ὧδ' ἦν Broadhead (ὧδ' Polle): ὡς ἂν codd.
1373 χρῇς Dindorf: χρή codd. 1377 ᾗ Elmsley: ἦν codd.
1379 ὅσων Zc s.l., coni. Porson: ὅσον cett.

λωβητὸν αὐτὸν ἐκβαλεῖν ταφῆς ἄτερ.
τοιγάρ σφ᾿ Ὀλύμπου τοῦδ᾿ ὁ πρεσβεύων πατὴρ
μνήμων τ᾿ Ἐρινὺς καὶ τελεσφόρος Δίκη
κακοὺς κακῶς φθείρειαν, ὥσπερ ἤθελον
τὸν ἄνδρα λώβαις ἐκβαλεῖν ἀναξίως.
σὲ δ᾿, ὦ γεραιοῦ σπέρμα Λαέρτου πατρός,
τάφου μὲν ὀκνῶ τοῦδ᾿ ἐπιψαύειν ἐᾶν,
μὴ τῷ θανόντι τοῦτο δυσχερὲς ποῶ·
τὰ δ᾿ ἄλλα καὶ ξύμπρασσε, κεἴ τινα στρατοῦ
θέλεις κομίζειν, οὐδὲν ἄλγος ἕξομεν.
ἐγὼ δὲ τἄλλα πάντα πορσυνῶ· σὺ δὲ
ἀνὴρ καθ᾿ ἡμᾶς ἐσθλὸς ὢν ἐπίστασο.

ΟΔΥΣΣΕΥΣ

ἀλλ᾿ ἤθελον μέν· εἰ δὲ μή ᾿στί σοι φίλον
πράσσειν τάδ᾿ ἡμᾶς, εἶμ᾿ ἐπαινέσας τὸ σόν.

ΤΕΥΚΡΟΣ

ἅλις· ἤδη γὰρ πολὺς ἐκτέταται
χρόνος. ἀλλ᾿ οἱ μὲν κοίλην κάπετον
χερσὶ ταχύνετε, τοὶ δ᾿ ὑψίβατον
τρίποδ᾿ ἀμφίπυρον λουτρῶν ὁσίων
θέσθ᾿ ἐπίκαιρον·
μία δ᾿ ἐκ κλισίας ἀνδρῶν ἴλη
τὸν ὑπασπίδιον κόσμον φερέτω.
παῖ, σὺ δὲ πατρός γ᾿, ὅσον ἰσχύεις,
φιλότητι θιγὼν πλευρὰς σὺν ἐμοὶ
τάσδ᾿ ἐπικούφιζ᾿· ἔτι γὰρ θερμαὶ
σύριγγες ἄνω φυσῶσι μέλαν

him outrage and cast him out without a funeral. For that, may the father who is first on Olympus and the unforgetting Erinys and Justice who accomplishes her ends destroy them cruelly, as they are cruel, they who wished to cast this man out outrageously in unworthy fashion. But I am reluctant, seed of ancient Laertes, to allow you to set your hand to this grave, for fear of doing a thing displeasing to the dead. But for the rest do you help us, and if you like to bring any other man from the army, we shall not be aggrieved. I will see to all the rest; but do you know that in your dealings with us you have been noble!

ODYSSEUS

Well, I would have wished to; but if it is not your pleasure that I should do this, I will depart, respecting your position.

TEUCER

Enough! for already much time has elapsed. Let some speedily dig a deep trench, and others place high up a tripod over the fire to receive the holy water, as the occasion requires. And let one group of men bring from the hut the armour that he wore. Boy, do you, so far as your strength allows, lovingly lay your hand upon your father and with me lift his body; for still the hot channels are

1402–20 del. Dawe (1402–13 μένος del. Nauck)

μένος. ἀλλ' ἄγε πᾶς, φίλος ὅστις ἀνὴρ
φησὶ παρεῖναι, σούσθω, βάτω,
τῷδ' ἀνδρὶ πονῶν τῷ πάντ' ἀγαθῷ
†κοὐδενί πω λῴονι θνητῶν†
[Αἴαντος, ὅτ' ἦν, τότε φωνῶ.]

ΧΟΡΟΣ

ἦ πολλὰ βροτοῖς ἔστιν ἰδοῦσιν
γνῶναι· πρὶν ἰδεῖν δ' οὐδεὶς μάντις
τῶν μελλόντων ὅ τι πράξει.

1416 corruptum et forte interpolatum puto
1417 del. Hermann

spouting upwards the black blood. Come, let every man who claims to be here in friendship make haste, and set forth, labouring for this man, in all things excellent [and never yet did you serve a nobler among mortals . . . of Ajax, when he lived, I say].

CHORUS

Mortals can judge of many things when they have seen them; but before seeing it no man can prophesy what his fortune shall be in the future.

ELECTRA

ΤΑ ΤΟΥ ΔΡΑΜΑΤΟΣ ΠΡΟΣΩΠΑ

Παιδαγωγός
Ὀρέστης
Ἠλέκτρα
Χορὸς ἐπιχωρίων παρθένων
Χρυσόθεμις
Κλυταιμήστρα
Αἴγισθος

DRAMATIS PERSONAE

Old slave
Orestes
Electra
Chorus of Argive maidens
Chrysothemis
Clytemnestra
Aegisthus

MUTES

Pylades
Servant girl
Attendants

Scene: In front of the palace at Mycenae.
Time: Some twenty years after the Trojan War.

ΗΛΕΚΤΡΑ

ΠΑΙΔΑΓΩΓΟΣ

Ὦ τοῦ στρατηγήσαντος ἐν Τροίᾳ ποτὲ
Ἀγαμέμνονος παῖ, νῦν ἐκεῖν' ἔξεστί σοι
παρόντι λεύσσειν, ὧν πρόθυμος ἦσθ' ἀεί.
τὸ γὰρ παλαιὸν Ἄργος οὑπόθεις τόδε,
τῆς οἰστροπλῆγος ἄλσος Ἰνάχου κόρης·
αὕτη δ', Ὀρέστα, τοῦ λυκοκτόνου θεοῦ
ἀγορὰ Λύκειος· οὑξ ἀριστερᾶς δ' ὅδε
Ἥρας ὁ κλεινὸς ναός· οἷ δ' ἱκάνομεν,
φάσκειν Μυκήνας τὰς πολυχρύσους ὁρᾶν,
πολύφθορόν τε δῶμα Πελοπιδῶν τόδε,
ὅθεν σε πατρὸς ἐκ φονῶν ἐγώ ποτε
πρὸς σῆς ὁμαίμου καὶ κασιγνήτης λαβὼν
ἤνεγκα κἀξέσωσα κἀξεθρεψάμην
τοσόνδ' ἐς ἥβης, πατρὶ τιμωρὸν φόνου.
νῦν οὖν, Ὀρέστα καὶ σὺ φίλτατε ξένων
Πυλάδη, τί χρὴ δρᾶν ἐν τάχει βουλευτέον·
ὡς ἡμὶν ἤδη λαμπρὸν ἡλίου σέλας
ἑῷα κινεῖ φθέγματ' ὀρνίθων σαφῆ
μέλαινά τ' ἄστρων ἐκλέλοιπεν εὐφρόνη.
πρὶν οὖν τιν' ἀνδρῶν ἐξοδοιπορεῖν στέγης,
ξυνάπτετον λόγοισιν· ὡς ἐνταῦθ' †ἐμὲν
ἵν' οὐκέτ' ὀκνεῖν καιρός, ἀλλ' ἔργων ἀκμή.

ELECTRA

Enter ORESTES, PYLADES, *and the* OLD SLAVE. *They stand before the central door of the stage building, which represents the palace of Mycenae.*

OLD SLAVE

Son of Agamemnon who once led the army before Troy, now you can gaze with your own eyes on what you have always longed to see! This is the ancient Argos for which you used to long, the precinct of the daughter of Inachus whom the gadfly stung; and this, Orestes, is the Lycean marketplace of the wolf-killing god;[a] this to the left is the famous temple of Hera; and at the place where we have arrived, you may say that you see Mycenae, rich in gold, and the house of the sons of Pelops here, rich in disasters, from which I once carried you, after your father's murder, receiving you from your own sister, and kept you safe and raised you up to this stage of youthful vigour, to avenge your father's murder. So now, Orestes, and you, dearest of hosts, Pylades, you must speedily decide what you must do; for already we hear the morning voices of the birds whom the bright beam of the sun is arousing, and the black night of stars has departed. So before any man leaves the house you must take counsel, since in this place this is no occasion to hesitate, but it is time to act.

[a] Apollo.

---

1 del. Haslam (vid. *Sophoclea* p. 42)
11 φονῶν Dindorf: φόνων codd.
21 ἐνταῦθα μὲν Handley 22 ἵν'] fort. ἔστ' (ἦν Handley)

ΟΡΕΣΤΗΣ

ὦ φίλτατ᾽ ἀνδρῶν προσπόλων, ὥς μοι σαφῆ
σημεῖα φαίνεις ἐσθλὸς εἰς ἡμᾶς γεγώς.
ὥσπερ γὰρ ἵππος εὐγενής, κἂν ᾖ γέρων,
ἐν τοῖσι δεινοῖς θυμὸν οὐκ ἀπώλεσεν,
ἀλλ᾽ ὀρθὸν οὖς ἵστησιν, ὡσαύτως δὲ σὺ
ἡμᾶς τ᾽ ὀτρύνεις καὐτὸς ἐν πρώτοις ἕπῃ.
τοιγὰρ τὰ μὲν δόξαντα δηλώσω, σὺ δὲ
ὀξεῖαν ἀκοὴν τοῖς ἐμοῖς λόγοις διδούς,
εἰ μή τι καιροῦ τυγχάνω, μεθάρμοσον.
ἐγὼ γὰρ ἡνίχ᾽ ἱκόμην τὸ Πυθικὸν
μαντεῖον, ὡς μάθοιμ᾽ ὅτῳ τρόπῳ πατρὶ
δίκας ἀροίμην τῶν φονευσάντων πάρα,
χρῇ μοι τοιαῦθ᾽ ὁ Φοῖβος ὧν πεύσῃ τάχα·
ἄσκευον αὐτὸν ἀσπίδων τε καὶ στρατοῦ
δόλοισι κλέψαι χειρὸς ἐνδίκου σφαγάς.
ὅτ᾽ οὖν τοιόνδε χρησμὸν εἰσηκούσαμεν,
σὺ μὲν μολών, ὅταν σε καιρὸς εἰσάγῃ,
δόμων ἔσω τῶνδ᾽, ἴσθι πᾶν τὸ δρώμενον,
ὅπως ἂν εἰδὼς ἡμὶν ἀγγείλῃς σαφῆ.
οὐ γάρ σε μὴ γήρᾳ τε καὶ χρόνῳ μακρῷ
γνῶσ᾽, οὐδ᾽ ὑποπτεύσουσιν, ὧδ᾽ ἠνθισμένον.
λόγῳ δὲ χρῶ τοιῷδ᾽, ὅτι ξένος μὲν εἶ
Φωκέως παρ᾽ ἀνδρὸς Φανοτέως ἥκων· ὁ γὰρ
μέγιστος αὐτοῖς τυγχάνει δορυξένων.
ἄγγελλε δ᾽ ὅρκον προστιθεὶς ὁθούνεκα
τέθνηκ᾽ Ὀρέστης ἐξ ἀναγκαίας τύχης,
ἄθλοισι Πυθικοῖσιν ἐκ τροχηλάτων

ORESTES

Dearest of retainers, how clearly you show your loyalty to us! Just as a noble horse, even if he is old, does not lose his spirit in a time of danger, but pricks up his ear, just so do you urge us on and yourself are foremost in support. So I will explain my decisions, and do you lend a prompt ear to my words, and if I do not hit the mark, correct me! When I went to the Pythian oracle to learn how I might get vengeance for my father on his murderers, Phoebus gave me a prophecy which you shall soon hear; that alone, without the help of armed men or of an army, I should accomplish by cunning the slaughter done by a righteous hand. Then, since this is the nature of the oracle I heard, do you go into this house, when you have the chance to enter it, and find out everything that they are doing, so that you can report to us with certain knowledge. They will never know you, grizzled as you are with age and the passage of time, and they will not suspect you. Tell this story, that you are a foreigner come from Phanoteus the Phocian—for he is the greatest of their allies—and tell them, speaking on oath, that Orestes is dead by an accident, having fallen from his moving chariot in the Pythian

---

33 πατρὶ L^{ac}K: πατρὸς cett.
37 ἐνδίκου Lange: -ους codd.
45 Φωκέως Bentley: -εὺς codd.
47 ὅρκον Reiske: ὅρκῳ codd.

δίφρων κυλισθείς· ὧδ᾽ ὁ μῦθος ἑστάτω.
ἡμεῖς δὲ πατρὸς τύμβον, ὡς ἐφίετο,
λοιβαῖσι πρῶτον καὶ καρατόμοις χλιδαῖς
στέψαντες, εἶτ᾽ ἄψορρον ἥξομεν πάλιν,
τύπωμα χαλκόπλευρον ἠρμένοι χεροῖν,
ὃ καὶ σὺ θάμνοις οἶσθά που κεκρυμμένον,
ὅπως λόγῳ κλέπτοντες ἡδεῖαν φάτιν
φέρωμεν αὐτοῖς, τοὐμὸν ὡς ἔρρει δέμας
φλογιστὸν ἤδη καὶ κατηνθρακωμένον.
τί γάρ με λυπεῖ τοῦθ᾽, ὅταν λόγῳ θανὼν
ἔργοισι σωθῶ κἀξενέγκωμαι κλέος;
δοκῶ μέν, οὐδὲν ῥῆμα σὺν κέρδει κακόν.
ἤδη γὰρ εἶδον πολλάκις καὶ τοὺς σοφοὺς
λόγῳ μάτην θνῄσκοντας· εἶθ᾽, ὅταν δόμους
ἔλθωσιν αὖθις, ἐκτετίμηνται πλέον·
ὣς κἄμ᾽ ἐπαυχῶ τῆσδε τῆς φήμης ἄπο
δεδορκότ᾽ ἐχθροῖς ἄστρον ὣς λάμψειν ἔτι.
ἀλλ᾽, ὦ πατρῴα γῆ θεοί τ᾽ ἐγχώριοι,
δέξασθέ μ᾽ εὐτυχοῦντα ταῖσδε ταῖς ὁδοῖς,
σύ τ᾽, ὦ πατρῷον δῶμα· σοῦ γὰρ ἔρχομαι
δίκῃ καθαρτὴς πρὸς θεῶν ὡρμημένος·
καὶ μή μ᾽ ἄτιμον τῆσδ᾽ ἀποστείλητε γῆς,
ἀλλ᾽ ἀρχέπλουτον καὶ καταστάτην δόμων.
εἴρηκα μέν νυν ταῦτα· σοὶ δ᾽ ἤδη, γέρον,
τὸ σὸν μελέσθω βάντι φρουρῆσαι χρέος.
νὼ δ᾽ ἔξιμεν· καιρὸς γάρ, ὅσπερ ἀνδράσιν
μέγιστος ἔργου παντός ἐστ᾽ ἐπιστάτης.

games; let that be your tale! And we will first honour my father's tomb, as the god commanded, with libations and with a tribute of luxuriant hair; then we will return once more, carrying in our hands the bronze urn which as you know is hidden in the bushes, so that we can deceive them with our story and bring them happy news, that my body has already been burnt to ashes. How can this hurt me, if I am dead in fiction, but in fact am safe and can win glory? I think, no word that brings you gain is bad. Yes, often in the past I have known clever men dead in fiction but not dead; and then when they return home the honour they receive is all the greater. Just so I believe that as a result of this story, alive, I shall shine like a star upon my enemies. But do you, my native land, and you, gods of the place, receive me in good fortune on this mission, and you, house of my fathers! For I come in justice to cleanse you, sped on my way by the gods. And do not send me from the land dishonoured, but let me control my riches and set my house upon its feet! That is my speech; and do you now, old man, make it your business to go and attend to what you have to do. And we two will be off; it is the moment, and the moment is the chief determiner of every action for men.

ΗΛΕΚΤΡΑ

ἰώ μοί μοι δύστηνος.

ΠΑΙΔΑΓΩΓΟΣ

καὶ μὴν θυρῶν ἔδοξα προσπόλων τινὸς
ὑποστενούσης ἔνδον αἰσθέσθαι, τέκνον.

ΟΡΕΣΤΗΣ

ἆρ' ἐστὶν ἡ δύστηνος Ἠλέκτρα; θέλεις
μείνωμεν αὐτοῦ κἀπακούσωμεν γόων;

ΠΑΙΔΑΓΩΓΟΣ

ἥκιστα. μηδὲν πρόσθεν ἢ τὰ Λοξίου
πειρώμεθ' ἔρδειν κἀπὸ τῶνδ' ἀρχηγετεῖν,
πατρὸς χέοντες λουτρά· ταῦτα γὰρ φέρειν
νίκην τέ φημι καὶ κράτος τῶν δρωμένων.

ΗΛΕΚΤΡΑ

ὦ φάος ἁγνὸν
καὶ γῆς ἰσόμοιρ' ἀήρ, ὥς μοι
πολλὰς μὲν θρήνων ᾠδάς,
πολλὰς δ' ἀντήρεις ᾔσθου
στέρνων πλαγὰς αἱμασσομένων,
ὁπόταν δνοφερὰ νὺξ ὑπολειφθῇ·
τὰ δὲ παννυχίδων κήδη στυγεραὶ
ξυνίσασ' εὐναὶ μογερῶν οἴκων,
ὅσα τὸν δύστηνον ἐμὸν θρηνῶ
πατέρ', ὃν κατὰ μὲν βάρβαρον αἶαν
φοίνιος Ἄρης οὐκ ἐξένισεν,
μήτηρ δ' ἡμὴ χὼ κοινολεχὴς

ELECTRA

From inside the palace comes the voice of ELECTRA

Ah me, ah me, alas!

OLD SLAVE

Why, I thought I heard one of the slaves behind the door groaning, my son!

ORESTES

Is it the unfortunate Electra? Would you like us to stay here and listen to her laments?

OLD SLAVE

But no! Let us attempt nothing before obeying Loxias, and begin from that, pouring libations to your father; I say that that brings victory and success in what has to be done!

Exeunt by one of the side passages ORESTES, PYLADES, *and the* OLD SLAVE. *From the palace, enter* ELECTRA.

ELECTRA

O holy light and air that has an equal share of earth, how many dirges have you heard me sing, and how many blows have you heard me aim against my bleeding breast, when dusky night has been left behind! And my hateful bed in the miserable house knows of the sorrows of my sleepless nights, how often I lament for my unhappy father, whom the bloody war-god did not make his guest in a barbarian land, but my mother and her bedfellow,

---

81 κἀπακούσωμεν Nauck: κἀν- codd.

84–85 φέρειν . . . φημι Tournier: φέρει νίκην τ' ἐφ' ἡμῖν codd.

92 κήδη Fröhlich: ἤδη codd.

93 οἴκων pat: οἰκιῶν lrp: οἴκτων Blaydes (fort. iam Bentley)

Αἴγισθος ὅπως δρῦν ὑλοτόμοι
σχίζουσι κάρα φονίῳ πελέκει.
κοὐδεὶς τούτων οἶκτος ἀπ᾽ ἄλλης
ἢ ᾽μοῦ φέρεται, σοῦ, πάτερ, οὕτως
αἰκῶς οἰκτρῶς τε θανόντος.
ἀλλ᾽ οὐ μὲν δὴ
λήξω θρήνων στυγερῶν τε γόων,
ἔστ᾽ ἂν παμφεγγεῖς ἄστρων
ῥιπάς, λεύσσω δὲ τόδ᾽ ἦμαρ,
μὴ οὐ τεκνολέτειρ᾽ ὥς τις ἀηδὼν
ἐπὶ κωκυτῷ τῶνδε πατρῴων
πρὸ θυρῶν ἠχὼ πᾶσι προφωνεῖν.
ὦ δῶμ᾽ Ἀίδου καὶ Περσεφόνης,
ὦ χθόνι᾽ Ἑρμῆ καὶ πότνι᾽ Ἀρά,
σεμναί τε θεῶν παῖδες Ἐρινύες,
αἳ τοὺς ἀδίκως θνῄσκοντας ὁρᾶθ᾽,
αἳ τοὺς εὐνὰς ὑποκλεπτομένους,
ἔλθετ᾽, ἀρήξατε, τείσασθε πατρὸς
φόνον ἡμετέρου,
καί μοι τὸν ἐμὸν πέμψατ᾽ ἀδελφόν.
μούνη γὰρ ἄγειν οὐκέτι σωκῶ
λύπης ἀντίρροπον ἄχθος.

ΧΟΡΟΣ

ὦ παῖ παῖ δυστανοτάτας στρ. α´
Ἠλέκτρα ματρός, τίς ἀεὶ
τάκει σ᾽ ὧδ᾽ ἀκόρεστος οἰμωγὰ
τὸν πάλαι ἐκ δολερᾶς ἀθεώτατα

Aegisthus, split his head with a murderous axe, as woodmen split an oak. And from none but me does your due of lamentation come, father, though your death was so dreadful and so pitiful!

But I shall not cease from my dirges and miserable lamentations, so long as I look upon the sparkling of the bright stars, and upon this light of day, like the nightingale, slayer of her young, crying out loud and making loud proclamation to all before my father's doors. O house of Hades and Persephone, O Hermes of the underworld and powerful Curse, and Erinyes, revered children of the gods who look upon those wrongfully done to death, who look upon those who dishonour the marriage bed in secret, come, bring help, avenge the murder of our father, and send to me my brother! For I have no longer strength to bear alone the burden of grief that weighs me down.

The Chorus of Argive women enter the orchestra.

CHORUS

Electra, daughter of a wretched mother, what is this lament that wastes you away, never content to cease, over Agamemnon, long since brought down in unholy fashion

---

102 *αἰκῶς* Hermann e Σ: *ἀδίκως* codd.

113–14 *ὁρᾶθ', αἳ* Dobree: *ὁρᾶτε* codd.

123 *τάκει σ' ὧδ' ἀκόρεστος οἰμωγὰ* Kricala: *τάκεις . . . ἀκόρεστον οἰμωγὰν* codd.

124 *ἀθεώτατα* Porson: *ἀθεωτάτας* codd.

μματρὸς ἁλόντ᾿ ἀπάταις Ἀγαμέμνονα
κακᾷ τε χειρὶ πρόδοτον; ὡς ὁ τάδε πορὼν
ὄλοιτ᾿, εἴ μοι θέμις τάδ᾿ αὐδᾶν.

ΗΛΕΚΤΡΑ

ὦ γενέθλα γενναίων,
ἥκετ᾿ ἐμῶν καμάτων παραμύθιον·
οἶδά τε καὶ ξυνίημι τάδ᾿, οὔ τί με
φυγγάνει, οὐδ᾿ ἐθέλω προλιπεῖν τόδε,
μὴ οὐ τὸν ἐμὸν στενάχειν πατέρ᾿ ἄθλιον.
ἀλλ᾿ ὦ παντοίας φιλότητος ἀμειβόμεναι χάριν,
ἐᾶτέ μ᾿ ὧδ᾿ ἀλύειν,
αἰαῖ, ἱκνοῦμαι.

ΧΟΡΟΣ

ἀλλ᾿ οὔτοι τόν γ᾿ ἐξ Ἀίδα ἀντ. α´
παγκοίνου λίμνας πατέρ᾿ ἀν-
στάσεις οὔτε γόοισιν, οὐ λιταῖς·
ἀλλ᾿ ἀπὸ τῶν μετρίων ἐπ᾿ ἀμήχανον
ἄλγος ἀεὶ στενάχουσα διόλλυσαι,
ἐν οἷς ἀνάλυσίς ἐστιν οὐδεμία κακῶν.
τί μοι τῶν δυσφόρων ἐφίῃ;

ΗΛΕΚΤΡΑ

νήπιος ὃς τῶν οἰκτρῶς
οἰχομένων γονέων ἐπιλάθεται.
ἀλλ᾿ ἐμέ γ᾿ ἁ στονόεσσ᾿ ἄραρεν φρένας,
ἃ Ἴτυν αἰὲν Ἴτυν ὀλοφύρεται,
ὄρνις ἀτυζομένα, Διὸς ἄγγελος.

by a plot through your mother's cunning, and sent to his doom by her cruel hand? May the doer perish, if it is right for me to speak this word!

ELECTRA

O race of noble ones, you have come to comfort me in my sorrows; I know and understand, and it does not escape me, yet I am unwilling to give over and not to lament for my unhappy father. You who repay kindness in every sort of friendship, allow me thus to wander, alas, I beg you!

CHORUS

But you will never raise up your father from the lake of Hades, to which all must come, by weeping or by prayers! No, leaving moderation aside and plunging into grief irresistible you lament ever, to your ruin. In this there is no way of undoing evil; why are you set on misery?

ELECTRA

Foolish is he who forgets the piteous end of parents! Ever in my mind is the lamenting one, she[a] who mourns always for Itys, for Itys, she the bird distraught, the

[a] The nightingale, who had once been Procne, wife of Tereus.

---

129 post γενναίων add. πατέρων lrpa: τοκέων pt, del. Monk
139 λιταῖσ(ιν) codd.: ἄνταις Hermann: εὐχαῖς Erfurdt

ἰὼ παντλάμων Νιόβα, σὲ δ᾽ ἔγωγε νέμω θεόν,
ἅτ᾽ ἐν τάφῳ πετραίῳ,
αἰαῖ, δακρύεις.

ΧΟΡΟΣ

οὔτοι σοὶ μούνᾳ, στρ. β′
τέκνον, ἄχος ἐφάνη βροτῶν,
πρὸς ὅ τι σὺ τῶν ἔνδον εἶ περισσά,
οἷς ὁμόθεν εἶ καὶ γονᾷ ξύναιμος,
οἵα Χρυσόθεμις ζώει καὶ Ἰφιάνασσα,
κρυπτᾷ τ᾽ ἀχέων ἐν ἥβᾳ
ὄλβιος, ὃν ἁ κλεινὰ
γᾶ ποτε Μυκηναίων
δέξεται εὐπατρίδαν, Διὸς εὔφρονι
βήματι μολόντα τάνδε γᾶν Ὀρέσταν.

ΗΛΕΚΤΡΑ

ὅν γ᾽ ἐγὼ ἀκάματα προσμένουσ᾽ ἄτεκνος,
τάλαιν᾽ ἀνύμφευτος αἰὲν οἰχνῶ,
δάκρυσι μυδαλέα, τὸν ἀνήνυτον
οἶτον ἔχουσα κακῶν· ὁ δὲ λάθεται
ὧν τ᾽ ἔπαθ᾽ ὧν τ᾽ ἐδάη. τί γὰρ οὐκ ἐμοὶ
ἔρχεται ἀγγελίας ἀπατώμενον;
ἀεὶ μὲν γὰρ ποθεῖ,
ποθῶν δ᾽ οὐκ ἀξιοῖ φανῆναι.

ΧΟΡΟΣ

θάρσει μοι, θάρσει, ἀντ. β′
τέκνον. ἔτι μέγας οὐρανῷ

messenger of Zeus! Ah, Niobe who endured every sorrow, I regard you as a goddess, you who in your rocky tomb, alas, lament!

CHORUS

Not to you alone among mortals, my child, has sorrow been made manifest, a sorrow that you suffer beyond others in the house with whom you share your lineage and your blood, such as Chrysothemis and Iphianassa—and Orestes, he who is happy in his youth concealed from painful things, he whom the famous land of the Mycenaeans shall receive, glorious in his ancestry, when he comes to this land, brought by the kindly aid of Zeus.

ELECTRA

Yes, he whom I unwearyingly await, lost, without child or bridegroom, drenched in tears, with my never-ending fate of sorrows! But he forgets what he has suffered and what he has learned. Why, which of his messages does not end in disappointment? Always he feels the longing, but for all his longing he does not think fit to appear!

CHORUS

Have courage, my child, courage! Zeus is still great in

---

164 *ὅν γ᾽ ἐγὼ* Hermann: *ὃν ἔγωγ᾽* codd.

174 post *μέγας* add. *ἐν* codd., del. Livineius: *μέγας ἔτ᾽ ἐν* Hermann

Ζεύς, ὃς ἐφορᾷ πάντα καὶ κρατύνει·
ᾧ τὸν ὑπεραλγῆ χόλον νέμουσα
μήθ' οἷς ἐχθαίρεις ὑπεράχθεο μήτ' ἐπιλάθου·
χρόνος γὰρ εὐμαρὴς θεός.
οὔτε γὰρ ὁ τὰν Κρῖσαν
βούνομον ἔχων ἀκτὰν
παῖς Ἀγαμεμνονίδας ἀπερίτροπος
οὔθ' ὁ παρὰ τὸν Ἀχέροντα θεὸς ἀνάσσων.

ΗΛΕΚΤΡΑ

ἀλλ' ἐμὲ μὲν ὁ πολὺς ἀπολέλοιπεν ἤδη
βίοτος ἀνέλπιστον, οὐδ' ἔτ' ἀρκῶ·
ἅτις ἄνευ τεκέων κατατάκομαι,
ἇς φίλος οὔτις ἀνὴρ ὑπερίσταται,
ἀλλ' ἁπερεί τις ἔποικος ἀναξία
οἰκονομῶ θαλάμους πατρός, ὧδε μὲν
ἀεικεῖ σὺν στολᾷ,
κεναῖς δ' ἀμφίσταμαι τραπέζαις.

ΧΟΡΟΣ

οἰκτρὰ μὲν νόστοις αὐδά, στρ. γ´
οἰκτρὰ δ' ἐν κοίταις πατρῴαις,
ὅτε οἱ παγχάλκων ἀνταία
γενύων ὡρμάθη πλαγά.
δόλος ἦν ὁ φράσας, ἔρος ὁ κτείνας,
δεινὰν δεινῶς προφυτεύσαντες
μορφάν, εἴτ' οὖν θεὸς εἴτε βροτῶν
ἦν ὁ ταῦτα πράσσων.

heaven, he who surveys all things and rules them; make over to him your grievous anger; do not be angry in excess against your enemies, yet do not forget; time is a god that brings relief. He who occupies the pastures of Crisa on the coast, the son of Agamemnon, is not remiss, neither is the god who rules beside Acheron.

ELECTRA

But much of my life has already abandoned me without hope, and my strength is failing! Yes, I melt away without offspring, I who have no husband to protect me, but like a lowborn slave serve in the chambers of my father, in such mean attire as this, and stand at empty tables!

CHORUS

Piteous was the cry at his return, piteous as your father lay there, when the blow of the brazen axe came straight upon him! Cunning was the teacher, passion was the killer; horribly they brought into being a shape horrible, whether it was a god or a mortal who was the doer.

---

186 *ἀνέλπιστον* Dindorf: -*ος* codd.
195 *οἱ* Hermann: *σοι* codd.

ΗΛΕΚΤΡΑ

ὦ πασᾶν κείνα πλέον ἁμέρα
ἐλθοῦσ᾽ ἐχθίστα δή μοι·
ὦ νύξ, ὦ δείπνων ἀρρήτων
ἔκπαγλ᾽ ἄχθη·
τοῖς ἐμὸς ἴδε πατὴρ
θανάτους αἰκεῖς διδύμαιν χειροῖν,
αἳ τὸν ἐμὸν εἷλον βίον
πρόδοτον, αἵ μ᾽ ἀπώλεσαν·
οἷς θεὸς ὁ μέγας Ὀλύμπιος
ποίνιμα πάθεα παθεῖν πόροι,
μηδέ ποτ᾽ ἀγλαΐας ἀποναίατο
τοιάδ᾽ ἀνύσαντες ἔργα.

ΧΟΡΟΣ

φράζου μὴ πόρσω φωνεῖν. ἀντ. γ´
οὐ γνώμαν ἴσχεις ἐξ οἵων
τὰ παρόντ᾽; οἰκείας εἰς ἄτας
ἐμπίπτεις οὕτως αἰκῶς;
πολὺ γάρ τι κακῶν ὑπερεκτήσω,
σᾷ δυσθύμῳ τίκτουσ᾽ αἰεὶ
ψυχᾷ πολέμους· τάδε—τοῖς δυνατοῖς
οὐκ ἐριστά—τλᾶθι.

ΗΛΕΚΤΡΑ

ἐν δεινοῖς δείν᾽ ἠναγκάσθην·
ἔξοιδ᾽, οὐ λάθει μ᾽ ὀργά.
ἀλλ᾽ ἐν γὰρ δεινοῖς οὐ σχήσω
ταύτας ἄτας,

ELECTRA

O day that came most hateful of all days to me! O night, o pain appalling of the feast unspeakable, at which my father saw grim death dealt him by two hands, hands that betrayed and took away my life, hands that brought me death! May the great god of Olympus give them suffering in return, and may they never have joy of their splendour, they who did such a deed!

CHORUS

Take care, speak no more! Do you not understand from what beginnings the present came? Do you so grimly plunge into ruin of your own making? You have got yourself evil in excess by ever creating wars for your sorrowful soul! Put up with this! You cannot struggle against those in power!

ELECTRA

Dreadful actions were forced on me by dreadful things; I know it well, my passion does not escape me! But amid these dreadful things I shall not hold back from this ruinous action, so long as life maintains me! Who indeed

---

205 τοῖς Johnson: τοὺς codd. ἴδε Brunck: εἶδε codd.
219–20 vv. sic interpunxit Jackson
220 τλᾶθι Wakefield: πλάθειν codd.
221 ἐν δεινοῖς <δείν'> ἠναγκάσθην Kaibel: alii alia

ὄφρα με βίος ἔχῃ.
τίνι γάρ ποτ᾽ ἄν, ὦ φιλία γενέθλα,
πρόσφορον ἀκούσαιμ᾽ ἔπος,
τίνι φρονοῦντι καίρια;
ἄνετέ μ᾽ ἄνετε παράγοροι.
τάδε γὰρ ἄλυτα κεκλήσεται·
οὐδέ ποτ᾽ ἐκ καμάτων ἀποπαύσομαι
ἀνάριθμος ὧδε θρήνων.

ΧΟΡΟΣ

ἀλλ᾽ οὖν εὐνοίᾳ γ᾽ αὐδῶ, ἐπ.
μάτηρ ὡσεί τις πιστά,
μὴ τίκτειν σ᾽ ἄταν ἄταις.

ΗΛΕΚΤΡΑ

καὶ τί μέτρον κακότατος ἔφυ; φέρε,
πῶς ἐπὶ τοῖς φθιμένοις ἀμελεῖν καλόν;
ἐν τίνι τοῦτ᾽ ἔβλαστ᾽ ἀνθρώπων;
μήτ᾽ εἴην ἔντιμος τούτοις
μήτ᾽, εἴ τῳ πρόσκειμαι χρηστῷ,
ξυνναίοιμ᾽ εὔκηλος, γονέως
ἐκτίμους ἴσχουσα πτέρυγας
ὀξυτόνων γόων.
εἰ γὰρ ὁ μὲν θανὼν γᾶ τε καὶ οὐδὲν ὢν
κείσεται τάλας,
οἱ δὲ μὴ πάλιν
δώσουσ᾽ ἀντιφόνους δίκας,
ἔρροι τ᾽ ἂν αἰδὼς
ἁπάντων τ᾽ εὐσέβεια θνατῶν.

would think, dear sisters, that I could hear a word of comfort, who that thinks rightly? Leave me, leave me, you that would console me! For this shall be called insoluble, and I shall never have respite from my sorrows, with my numberless laments!

CHORUS

Well, I speak as a well-wisher, like a mother in whom you can have trust, telling you not to create misery by means of misery!

ELECTRA

And what limit is there to my torment? Come, how can it be honourable to have no thought for the dead? Who among men has such an instinct? May I never enjoy honour among such people, and never may I live contentedly with any good thing I may have, if I restrain the wings of loud lamentation, dishonouring my father. For if the dead man is to lie there as earth and nothingness, unhappy one, and they are not to pay the penalty, murdered in their turn, that would be the end of reverence and of the piety of all mortals!

---

241 γονέως Morstadt: γονέων codd.
249 τ' ἂν] τἂν Martin

ΧΟΡΟΣ

ἐγὼ μέν, ὦ παῖ, καὶ τὸ σὸν σπεύδουσ᾽ ἅμα
καὶ τοὐμὸν αὐτῆς ἦλθον· εἰ δὲ μὴ καλῶς
λέγω, σὺ νίκα· σοὶ γὰρ ἑψόμεσθ᾽ ἅμα.

ΗΛΕΚΤΡΑ

αἰσχύνομαι μέν, ὦ γυναῖκες, εἰ δοκῶ
πολλοῖσι θρήνοις δυσφορεῖν ὑμῖν ἄγαν.
ἀλλ᾽, ἡ βία γὰρ ταῦτ᾽ ἀναγκάζει με δρᾶν,
σύγγνωτε. πῶς γάρ, ἥτις εὐγενὴς γυνή,
πατρῷ᾽ ὁρῶσα πήματ᾽, οὐ δρῴη τάδ᾽ ἄν,
ἁγὼ κατ᾽ ἦμαρ καὶ κατ᾽ εὐφρόνην ἀεὶ
θάλλοντα μᾶλλον ἢ καταφθίνονθ᾽ ὁρῶ;
ᾗ πρῶτα μὲν τὰ μητρός, ἥ μ᾽ ἐγείνατο,
ἔχθιστα συμβέβηκεν· εἶτα δώμασιν
ἐν τοῖς ἐμαυτῆς τοῖς φονεῦσι τοῦ πατρὸς
ξύνειμι, κἀκ τῶνδ᾽ ἄρχομαι κἀκ τῶνδέ μοι
λαβεῖν θ᾽ ὁμοίως καὶ τὸ τητᾶσθαι πέλει.
ἔπειτα ποίας ἡμέρας δοκεῖς μ᾽ ἄγειν,
ὅταν θρόνοις Αἴγισθον ἐνθακοῦντ᾽ ἴδω
τοῖσιν πατρῴοις, εἰσίδω δ᾽ ἐσθήματα
φοροῦντ᾽ ἐκείνῳ ταὐτά, καὶ παρεστίους
σπένδοντα λοιβὰς ἔνθ᾽ ἐκεῖνον ὤλεσεν,
ἴδω δὲ τούτων τὴν τελευταίαν ὕβριν,
τὸν αὐτοέντην ἡμὶν ἐν κοίτῃ πατρὸς
ξὺν τῇ ταλαίνῃ μητρί, μητέρ᾽ εἰ χρεὼν
ταύτην προσαυδᾶν τῷδε συγκοιμωμένην.
ἡ δ᾽ ὧδε τλήμων ὥστε τῷ μιάστορι

CHORUS

I have come, daughter, in your interest and also in my own. But if what I say is wrong, have your own way, because we shall follow you.

ELECTRA

I am ashamed, women, if you think I grieve too much with my numerous laments; but since a hard compulsion forces me to do this, you must bear with me! Why, how could any woman nobly born not do this, looking at the sufferings of her father's house, sufferings which I see by day and night always growing worse and not declining? First, my relation with the mother who bore me is one of bitter enmity; next, I am living in my own home with my father's murderers; they are my rulers, and it rests with them whether I receive or go without. And then what kind of days do you think I pass when I see Aegisthus sitting on my father's throne, and when I see him wearing the same clothes he wore, and pouring libations by the same hearth at which he murdered him; and when I see their final outrage, the murderer in my father's bed with my miserable mother, if she can be called mother when she sleeps with him? But she is so abandoned that she lives with the polluter, having no fear of any Erinys; but

253 ἅμα] fort. ἄρα

272 αὐτοέντην Lγρ: αὐτοφόντην cett.

ξύνεστ', Ἐρινὺν οὔτιν' ἐκφοβουμένη·
ἀλλ' ὥσπερ ἐγγελῶσα τοῖς ποιουμένοις,
εὑροῦσ' ἐκείνην ἡμέραν, ἐν ᾗ τότε
πατέρα τὸν ἀμὸν ἐκ δόλου κατέκτανεν,
ταύτῃ χοροὺς ἵστησι καὶ μηλοσφαγεῖ
θεοῖσιν ἔμμην' ἱερὰ τοῖς σωτηρίοις.
ἐγὼ δ' ὁρῶσα δύσμορος κατὰ στέγας
κλαίω, τέτηκα, κἀπικωκύω πατρὸς
τὴν δυστάλαιναν δαῖτ' ἐπωνομασμένην
αὐτὴ πρὸς αὐτήν· οὐδὲ γὰρ κλαῦσαι πάρα
τοσόνδ' ὅσον μοι θυμὸς ἡδονὴν φέρει.
αὕτη γὰρ ἡ λόγοισι γενναία γυνὴ
φωνοῦσα τοιάδ' ἐξονειδίζει κακά,
"ὦ δύσθεον μίσημα, σοὶ μόνῃ πατὴρ
τέθνηκεν; ἄλλος δ' οὔτις ἐν πένθει βροτῶν;
κακῶς ὄλοιο, μηδέ σ' ἐκ γόων ποτὲ
τῶν νῦν ἀπαλλάξειαν οἱ κάτω θεοί."
τάδ' ἐξυβρίζει· πλὴν ὅταν κλύῃ τινὸς
ἥξοντ' Ὀρέστην· τηνικαῦτα δ' ἐμμανὴς
βοᾷ παραστᾶσ', "οὐ σύ μοι τῶνδ' αἰτία;
οὐ σὸν τόδ' ἐστὶ τοὔργον, ἥτις ἐκ χερῶν
κλέψασ' Ὀρέστην τῶν ἐμῶν ὑπεξέθου;
ἀλλ' ἴσθι τοι τείσουσά γ' ἀξίαν δίκην."
τοιαῦθ' ὑλακτεῖ, σὺν δ' ἐποτρύνει πέλας
ὁ κλεινὸς αὐτῇ ταὐτὰ νυμφίος παρών,
ὁ πάντ' ἄναλκις οὗτος, ἡ πᾶσα βλάβη,
ὁ σὺν γυναιξὶ τὰς μάχας ποιούμενος.
ἐγὼ δ' Ὀρέστην τῶνδε προσμένουσ' ἀεὶ

as though she is gloating over what she has done, she finds the day on which she treacherously killed my father and on it sets up dances and slaughters cattle, sacrificing monthly victims to the gods that have preserved her. But I, poor creature, in the house weep, and pine away, and lament alone and to myself the abominable feast that bears my father's name; for I am not permitted even to weep as much as my heart desires. Yes, this woman, who is said to be so noble, gives tongue and utters insults such as these: "Accursed, hateful creature, are you the only one that has lost a father? Does no other mortal mourn a loss? May you perish miserably, and may the gods below never release you from your lamentations!" These are her insults; only when she hears anyone say that Orestes will come, then she stands by me in a fury and shouts, "Are not you the cause of this? Is this not your work, you who stole Orestes out of my arms and smuggled him away? Well, know that you will pay the penalty you deserve!" She barks out words like these, and her noble husband stands by her to encourage her, this utter coward, this total plague, this man who fights his battles with women's aid. And as I wait forever for

278 εὑροῦσ'] τηροῦσ' Reiske
298 τείσουσά γ'] τείσουσ' ἔτ' Blaydes

παυστῆρ᾽ ἐφήξειν ἡ τάλαιν᾽ ἀπόλλυμαι.
μέλλων γὰρ ἀεὶ δρᾶν τι τὰς οὔσας τέ μου
καὶ τὰς ἀπούσας ἐλπίδας διέφθορεν.
ἐν οὖν τοιούτοις οὔτε σωφρονεῖν, φίλαι,
οὔτ᾽ εὐσεβεῖν πάρεστιν· ἀλλ᾽ ἐν τοῖς κακοῖς
πολλή ᾽στ᾽ ἀνάγκη κἀπιτηδεύειν κακά.

ΧΟΡΟΣ

φέρ᾽ εἰπέ, πότερον ὄντος Αἰγίσθου πέλας
λέγεις τάδ᾽ ἡμῖν, ἢ βεβῶτος ἐκ δόμων;

ΗΛΕΚΤΡΑ

ἦ κάρτα. μὴ δόκει μ᾽ ἄν, εἴπερ ἦν πέλας,
θυραῖον οἰχνεῖν· νῦν δ᾽ ἀγροῖσι τυγχάνει.

ΧΟΡΟΣ

ἦ δὴ ἂν ἐγὼ θαρσοῦσα μᾶλλον ἐς λόγους
τοὺς σοὺς ἱκοίμην, εἴπερ ὧδε ταῦτ᾽ ἔχει.

ΗΛΕΚΤΡΑ

ὡς νῦν ἀπόντος ἱστόρει· τί σοι φίλον;

ΧΟΡΟΣ

καὶ δή σ᾽ ἐρωτῶ, τοῦ κασιγνήτου τί φής,
ἥξοντος, ἢ μέλλοντος; εἰδέναι θέλω.

ΗΛΕΚΤΡΑ

φησίν γε· φάσκων δ᾽ οὐδὲν ὧν λέγει ποεῖ.

ΧΟΡΟΣ

φιλεῖ γὰρ ὀκνεῖν πρᾶγμ᾽ ἀνὴρ πράσσων μέγα.

312 ἦ] καὶ Meineke

Orestes to come and put a stop to this, I perish in my misery, for by always putting off his action he has destroyed the hopes I had and the hopes I had not! When things are so, my friends, there can be no good sense or piety, but since things are bad, then inevitably one's conduct must be bad also.

CHORUS

Tell me, is Aegisthus near while you are saying this, or is he away from home?

ELECTRA

Indeed he is away! Do not suppose that I would be wandering out of doors if he were near! But now he is in the country.

CHORUS

To be sure I would converse with you with more confidence, if indeed this is so.

ELECTRA

Know that he is now away and ask your question; what is your pleasure?

CHORUS

Well, I ask you, what do you say about your brother? Will he come, or will he put off coming? I would like to know.

ELECTRA

He says that he will come; but though he says so, he does none of the things he says he will do.

CHORUS

Yes, a man often hesitates when he is engaged in a great task.

ΗΛΕΚΤΡΑ

καὶ μὴν ἔγωγ᾽ ἔσωσ᾽ ἐκεῖνον οὐκ ὄκνῳ.

ΧΟΡΟΣ

θάρσει· πέφυκεν ἐσθλός, ὥστ᾽ ἀρκεῖν φίλοις.

ΗΛΕΚΤΡΑ

πέποιθ᾽, ἐπεί τἂν οὐ μακρὰν ἔζων ἐγώ.

ΧΟΡΟΣ

μὴ νῦν ἔτ᾽ εἴπῃς μηδέν· ὡς δόμων ὁρῶ
τὴν σὴν ὅμαιμον, ἐκ πατρὸς ταὐτοῦ φύσιν,
Χρυσόθεμιν, ἔκ τε μητρός, ἐντάφια χεροῖν
φέρουσαν, οἷα τοῖς κάτω νομίζεται.

ΧΡΥΣΟΘΕΜΙΣ

τίν᾽ αὖ σὺ τήνδε πρὸς θυρῶνος ἐξόδοις
ἐλθοῦσα φωνεῖς, ὦ κασιγνήτη, φάτιν,
κοὐδ᾽ ἐν χρόνῳ μακρῷ διδαχθῆναι θέλεις
θυμῷ ματαίῳ μὴ χαρίζεσθαι κενά;
καίτοι τοσοῦτόν γ᾽ οἶδα κἀμαυτήν, ὅτι
ἀλγῶ ᾽πὶ τοῖς παροῦσιν· ὥστ᾽ ἄν, εἰ σθένος
λάβοιμι, δηλώσαιμ᾽ ἂν οἷ᾽ αὐτοῖς φρονῶ.
νῦν δ᾽ ἐν κακοῖς μοι πλεῖν ὑφειμένῃ δοκεῖ,
καὶ μὴ δοκεῖν μὲν δρᾶν τι, πημαίνειν δὲ μή.
τοιαῦτα δ᾽ ἄλλα καὶ σὲ βούλομαι ποεῖν.
καίτοι τὸ μὲν δίκαιον οὐχ ᾗ ᾽γὼ λέγω,
ἀλλ᾽ ᾗ σὺ κρίνεις. εἰ δ᾽ ἐλευθέραν με δεῖ
ζῆν, τῶν κρατούντων ἐστὶ πάντ᾽ ἀκουστέα.

ELECTRA

Well, it was not by hesitation that I saved him!

CHORUS

Be assured, he is of noble nature, so he will help his friends.

ELECTRA

I believe it, since otherwise I would not have remained long alive.

CHORUS

Now say no more; for I see your sister, born of the same father and the same mother, Chrysothemis, carrying from the house offerings such as men make to those below the earth.

Enter CHRYSOTHEMIS.

CHRYSOTHEMIS

What are these things that you have come out to say by the door we leave the house by, my sister? And will you not learn, after so long, not to indulge in futile fashion your useless anger? Why, I know this much about myself, that the present situation grieves me; so that if I had the power I should show them what are my feelings towards them. But as things are I think that in time of trouble I must lower my sails, and not seem to perform some deed, but do them no harm; and I would like you to follow suit. I know, justice lies not in what I say, but in what you judge; but if I am to live in freedom, I must obey those in power in everything.

ΗΛΕΚΤΡΑ

δεινόν γέ σ' οὖσαν πατρὸς οὗ σὺ παῖς ἔφυς
κείνου λελῆσθαι, τῆς δὲ τικτούσης μέλειν.
ἅπαντα γάρ σοι τἀμὰ νουθετήματα
κείνης διδακτά, κοὐδὲν ἐκ σαυτῆς λέγεις.
ἐπεί γ' ἑλοῦ σὺ θἄτερ', ἢ φρονεῖν κακῶς,
ἢ τῶν φίλων φρονοῦσα μὴ μνήμην ἔχειν·
ἥτις λέγεις μὲν ἀρτίως, ὡς εἰ λάβοις
σθένος, τὸ τούτων μῖσος ἐκδείξειας ἄν·
ἐμοῦ δὲ πατρὶ πάντα τιμωρουμένης
οὔτε ξυνέρδεις τήν τε δρῶσαν ἐκτρέπεις.
οὐ ταῦτα πρὸς κακοῖσι δειλίαν ἔχει;
ἐπεὶ δίδαξον, ἢ μάθ' ἐξ ἐμοῦ, τί μοι
κέρδος γένοιτ' ἂν τῶνδε ληξάσῃ γόων.
οὐ ζῶ; κακῶς μέν, οἶδ', ἐπαρκούντως δ' ἐμοί.
λυπῶ δὲ τούτους, ὥστε τῷ τεθνηκότι
τιμὰς προσάπτειν, εἴ τις ἔστ' ἐκεῖ χάρις.
σὺ δ' ἡμὶν ἡ μισοῦσα μισεῖς μὲν λόγῳ,
ἔργῳ δὲ τοῖς φονεῦσι τοῦ πατρὸς ξύνει.
ἐγὼ μὲν οὖν οὐκ ἄν ποτ', οὐδ' εἴ μοι τὰ σὰ
μέλλοι τις οἴσειν δῶρ', ἐφ' οἷσι νῦν χλιδᾷς,
τούτοις ὑπεικάθοιμι· σοὶ δὲ πλουσία
τράπεζα κείσθω καὶ περιρρείτω βίος.
ἐμοὶ γὰρ ἔστω τοὐμὲ μὴ λυπεῖν μόνον
βόσκημα· τῆς σῆς δ' οὐκ ἐρῶ τιμῆς λαχεῖν.
οὐδ' ἂν σύ, σώφρων γ' οὖσα. νῦν δ' ἐξὸν πατρὸς
πάντων ἀρίστου παῖδα κεκλῆσθαι, καλοῦ

ELECTRA

It is terrible that you, the daughter of your father, forget him and respect your mother; for all your lecturing of me is learned from her, and none of what you say comes from yourself. Why, choose one or the other, either to be foolish or to be wise but forgetful of your own, you that said just now that if you had power you would show how much you hate them, but when I do all I can to honour my father, do not act with me and try to deter me from my action! Does this not add to your woes the reproach of being a coward? Why, explain to me, or learn from me, what I would gain if I left off these lamentations. Do I not live, miserably, but sufficiently for me? And I give pain to them, so that I do honour to the dead, if any pleasure can be felt where the dead are. But you who say you hate them hate them in words, but in your actions you keep company with your father's murderers. Well, I would never give in to them, not even if someone were to offer me your privileges, on which you now plume yourself; but you may have a rich diet and your life may comfortably flow on. For me it is food enough not to give pain to myself, and I have no desire to enjoy your honours. Neither would you, if you thought rightly; but as things are, when you could be called the daughter of the noblest of men, be called the child of your mother! In that way

345 ἐπεί γ᾽ ἑλοῦ σὺ Ll.-J.: ἔπειθ᾽ ἑλοῦ γε codd.
363 μὴ λυπεῖν μόνον] μὴ λυποῦν μόνον Erfurdt

τῆς μητρός. οὕτω γὰρ φανῇ πλείστοις κακή,
θανόντα πατέρα καὶ φίλους προδοῦσα σούς.

ΧΟΡΟΣ

μηδὲν πρὸς ὀργὴν πρὸς θεῶν· ὡς τοῖς λόγοις
ἔνεστιν ἀμφοῖν κέρδος, εἰ σὺ μὲν μάθοις
τοῖς τῆσδε χρῆσθαι, τοῖς δὲ σοῖς αὕτη πάλιν.

ΧΡΥΣΟΘΕΜΙΣ

ἐγὼ μέν, ὦ γυναῖκες, ἠθάς εἰμί πως
τῶν τῆσδε μύθων· οὐδ᾽ ἂν ἐμνήσθην ποτέ,
εἰ μὴ κακὸν μέγιστον εἰς αὐτὴν ἰὸν
ἤκουσ᾽, ὃ ταύτην τῶν μακρῶν σχήσει γόων.

ΗΛΕΚΤΡΑ

φέρ᾽ εἰπὲ δὴ τὸ δεινόν. εἰ γὰρ τῶνδέ μοι
μεῖζόν τι λέξεις, οὐκ ἂν ἀντείποιμ᾽ ἔτι.

ΧΡΥΣΟΘΕΜΙΣ

ἀλλ᾽ ἐξερῶ σοι πᾶν ὅσον κάτοιδ᾽ ἐγώ.
μέλλουσι γάρ σ᾽, εἰ τῶνδε μὴ λήξεις γόων,
ἐνταῦθα πέμψειν ἔνθα μή ποθ᾽ ἡλίου
φέγγος προσόψῃ, ζῶσα δ᾽ ἐν κατηρεφεῖ
στέγῃ χθονὸς τῆσδ᾽ ἐκτὸς ὑμνήσεις κακά.
πρὸς ταῦτα φράζου, καί με μή ποθ᾽ ὕστερον
παθοῦσα μέμψῃ. νῦν γὰρ ἐν καλῷ φρονεῖν.

ΗΛΕΚΤΡΑ

ἦ ταῦτα δή με καὶ βεβούλευνται ποεῖν;

ΧΡΥΣΟΘΕΜΙΣ

μάλισθ᾽· ὅταν περ οἴκαδ᾽ Αἴγισθος μόλῃ.

you will seem to most people a traitor, who have betrayed your dead father and those who are your own!

CHORUS

I beg you, say nothing in anger! There is profit in the words of both, if you would learn to make use of hers and she in turn of yours.

CHRYSOTHEMIS

For my part, women, I am accustomed somehow to her way of speaking; and I should not have spoken of these things, if it were not that I have heard of a great evil coming upon her, which will restrain her from her long lamentations.

ELECTRA

Come, tell me what is the terrible thing! If you are going to tell me of something worse than my present condition, I shall argue with you no more.

CHRYSOTHEMIS

Well, I will tell you all I know! If you do not leave off these lamentations, they plan to send you to where you shall no longer see the light of the sun, but while still alive in a dungeon, outside this country, you shall bewail your troubles. In the face of that take thought, and do not blame me later, after you have suffered; now you have the chance to show good sense!

ELECTRA

Is that what they have decided to do to me?

CHRYSOTHEMIS

Yes, whenever Aegisthus returns home.

---

382 ἐκτὸς] ἐντὸς Schenkl

ΗΛΕΚΤΡΑ

ἀλλ᾽ ἐξίκοιτο τοῦδέ γ᾽ οὕνεκ᾽ ἐν τάχει.

ΧΡΥΣΟΘΕΜΙΣ

τίν᾽, ὦ τάλαινα, τόνδ᾽ ἐπηράσω λόγον;

ΗΛΕΚΤΡΑ

ἐλθεῖν ἐκεῖνον, εἴ τι τῶνδε δρᾶν νοεῖ.

ΧΡΥΣΟΘΕΜΙΣ

ὅπως πάθῃς τί χρῆμα; ποῦ ποτ᾽ εἶ φρενῶν;

ΗΛΕΚΤΡΑ

ὅπως ἀφ᾽ ὑμῶν ὡς προσώτατ᾽ ἐκφύγω.

ΧΡΥΣΟΘΕΜΙΣ

βίου δὲ τοῦ παρόντος οὐ μνείαν ἔχεις;

ΗΛΕΚΤΡΑ

καλὸς γὰρ οὑμὸς βίοτος ὥστε θαυμάσαι.

ΧΡΥΣΟΘΕΜΙΣ

ἀλλ᾽ ἦν ἄν, εἰ σύ γ᾽ εὖ φρονεῖν ἠπίστασο.

ΗΛΕΚΤΡΑ

μή μ᾽ ἐκδίδασκε τοῖς φίλοις εἶναι κακήν.

ΧΡΥΣΟΘΕΜΙΣ

ἀλλ᾽ οὐ διδάσκω· τοῖς κρατοῦσι δ᾽ εἰκαθεῖν.

ELECTRA
So far as that goes, let him arrive quickly!

CHRYSOTHEMIS
Unhappy one, what is this imprecation that you have uttered against yourself?

ELECTRA
That he should come, if he is minded to do any of these things.

CHRYSOTHEMIS
So that what may happen to you? What kind of madness is this?

ELECTRA
So that I can escape as far away as possible from you all.

CHRYSOTHEMIS
But do you feel no concern for the kind of life you now enjoy?

ELECTRA
Yes, my life is wonderfully agreeable!

CHRYSOTHEMIS
Why, it would be, if you knew how to think sensibly!

ELECTRA
Do not try to teach me to be disloyal to my own!

CHRYSOTHEMIS
It is not that that I am trying to teach you, but to yield to those in power.

ΗΛΕΚΤΡΑ

σὺ ταῦτα θῶπευ᾽· οὐκ ἐμοὺς τρόπους λέγεις.

ΧΡΥΣΟΘΕΜΙΣ

καλόν γε μέντοι μὴ ᾽ξ ἀβουλίας πεσεῖν.

ΗΛΕΚΤΡΑ

πεσούμεθ᾽, εἰ χρή, πατρὶ τιμωρούμενοι.

ΧΡΥΣΟΘΕΜΙΣ

πατὴρ δὲ τούτων, οἶδα, συγγνώμην ἔχει.

ΗΛΕΚΤΡΑ

ταῦτ᾽ ἐστὶ τἄπη πρὸς κακῶν ἐπαινέσαι.

ΧΡΥΣΟΘΕΜΙΣ

σὺ δ᾽ οὐχὶ πείσῃ καὶ συναινέσεις ἐμοί;

ΗΛΕΚΤΡΑ

οὐ δῆτα. μή πω νοῦ τοσόνδ᾽ εἴην κενή.

ΧΡΥΣΟΘΕΜΙΣ

χωρήσομαί τἄρ᾽ οἷπερ ἐστάλην ὁδοῦ.

ΗΛΕΚΤΡΑ

ποῖ δ᾽ ἐμπορεύῃ; τῷ φέρεις τάδ᾽ ἔμπυρα;

ΧΡΥΣΟΘΕΜΙΣ

μήτηρ με πέμπει πατρὶ τυμβεῦσαι χοάς.

ELECTRA

That kind of subservience is for you! What you suggest is not my way!

CHRYSOTHEMIS

But honour requires that one should not come to grief through foolishness.

ELECTRA

I shall come to grief, if I must, defending the honour of my father.

CHRYSOTHEMIS

But our father, I know, excuses this.

ELECTRA

These are the kind of words that cowards approve of.

CHRYSOTHEMIS

But will you not comply and join with me in approving them?

ELECTRA

No! May I never be so empty-headed!

CHRYSOTHEMIS

Then I will depart on the mission I was sent on.

ELECTRA

Where are you going? For whom are you carrying these vessels?

CHRYSOTHEMIS

My mother is sending me to offer libations at my father's tomb.

ΗΛΕΚΤΡΑ

πῶς εἶπας; ἦ τῷ δυσμενεστάτῳ βροτῶν;

ΧΡΥΣΟΘΕΜΙΣ

ὃν ἔκταν᾽ αὐτή· τοῦτο γὰρ λέξαι θέλεις.

ΗΛΕΚΤΡΑ

ἐκ τοῦ φίλων πεισθεῖσα; τῷ τοῦτ᾽ ἤρεσεν;

ΧΡΥΣΟΘΕΜΙΣ

ἐκ δείματός του νυκτέρου, δοκεῖν ἐμοί.

ΗΛΕΚΤΡΑ

ὦ θεοὶ πατρῷοι, συγγένεσθέ γ᾽ ἀλλὰ νῦν.

ΧΡΥΣΟΘΕΜΙΣ

ἔχεις τι θάρσος τοῦδε τοῦ τάρβους πέρι;

ΗΛΕΚΤΡΑ

εἴ μοι λέγοις τὴν ὄψιν, εἴποιμ᾽ ἂν τότε.

ΧΡΥΣΟΘΕΜΙΣ

ἀλλ᾽ οὐ κάτοιδα πλὴν ἐπὶ σμικρὸν φράσαι.

ΗΛΕΚΤΡΑ

λέγ᾽ ἀλλὰ τοῦτο. πολλά τοι σμικροὶ λόγοι
ἔσφηλαν ἤδη καὶ κατώρθωσαν βροτούς.

ΧΡΥΣΟΘΕΜΙΣ

λόγος τις αὐτήν ἐστιν εἰσιδεῖν πατρὸς
τοῦ σοῦ τε κἀμοῦ δευτέραν ὁμιλίαν
ἐλθόντος ἐς φῶς· εἶτα τόνδ᾽ ἐφέστιον
πῆξαι λαβόντα σκῆπτρον οὑφόρει ποτὲ
αὐτός, τανῦν δ᾽ Αἴγισθος· ἔκ τε τοῦδ᾽ ἄνω

ELECTRA

What did you say? Libations to her worst enemy among mankind?

CHRYSOTHEMIS

To the man she killed; that is what you mean.

ELECTRA

Which of her friends persuaded her? Who approved this?

CHRYSOTHEMIS

I think it was some midnight terror.

ELECTRA

Gods of my fathers, come to my help now at last!

CHRYSOTHEMIS

Does this fear of hers give you some kind of confidence?

ELECTRA

If you could tell me her dream, then I could say.

CHRYSOTHEMIS

But I know and can tell you only a little.

ELECTRA

Well, tell me that! Telling about little things has often in the past brought disaster or success to mortals.

CHRYSOTHEMIS

They say that she was once more in company with your father and mine, who had come to the world of light; and then he took the staff which he used to carry, and which Aegisthus carries now, and planted it beside the hearth;

βλαστεῖν βρύοντα θαλλόν, ᾧ κατάσκιον
πᾶσαν γενέσθαι τὴν Μυκηναίων χθόνα.
τοιαῦτά του παρόντος, ἡνίχ' Ἡλίῳ
δείκνυσι τοὔναρ, ἔκλυον ἐξηγουμένου.
πλείω δὲ τούτων οὐ κάτοιδα, πλὴν ὅτι
πέμπει μ' ἐκείνη τοῦδε τοῦ φόβου χάριν.
[πρός νυν θεῶν σε λίσσομαι τῶν ἐγγενῶν
ἐμοὶ πιθέσθαι μηδ' ἀβουλίᾳ πεσεῖν·
εἰ γάρ μ' ἀπώσῃ, σὺν κακῷ μέτει πάλιν.]

ΗΛΕΚΤΡΑ

ἀλλ', ὦ φίλη, τούτων μὲν ὧν ἔχεις χεροῖν
τύμβῳ προσάψῃς μηδέν· οὐ γάρ σοι θέμις
οὐδ' ὅσιον ἐχθρᾶς ἀπὸ γυναικὸς ἱστάναι
κτερίσματ' οὐδὲ λουτρὰ προσφέρειν πατρί·
ἀλλ' ἢ πνοαῖσιν ἢ βαθυσκαφεῖ κόνει
κρύψον νιν, ἔνθα μή ποτ' εἰς εὐνὴν πατρὸς
τούτων πρόσεισι μηδέν· ἀλλ' ὅταν θάνῃ,
κειμήλι' αὐτῇ ταῦτα σῳζέσθω κάτω.
ἀρχὴν δ' ἄν, εἰ μὴ τλημονεστάτη γυνὴ
πασῶν ἔβλαστε, τάσδε δυσμενεῖς χοὰς
οὐκ ἄν ποθ' ὅν γ' ἔκτεινε τῷδ' ἐπέστεφε.
σκέψαι γὰρ εἴ σοι προσφιλῶς αὐτῇ δοκεῖ
γέρα τάδ' οὑν τάφοισι δέξεσθαι νέκυς
ὑφ' ἧς θανὼν ἄτιμος ὥστε δυσμενὴς
ἐμασχαλίσθη κἀπὶ λουτροῖσιν κάρᾳ
κηλῖδας ἐξέμαξεν. ἆρα μὴ δοκεῖς
λυτήρι' αὐτῇ ταῦτα τοῦ φόνου φέρειν;

and from it grew up a fruitful bough, which overshadowed all the land of the Mycenaeans. That is the story I heard from someone who was present when she told her dream to the Sun. But I know no more than this, except that it is because of this fear that she is sending me. [So I implore you by the gods of the family to do as I say, and not to come to grief through folly; for if you repulse me, you will regret it and will come to me again.]

ELECTRA

My dear, do not place on the tomb any of the things you are carrying! It is not right in the eyes of gods or men that you should place burial offerings or bring libations from a hateful woman to our father. Throw them to the winds, or hide them deep in the dust, where none of them will approach my father's place of rest; but let them be preserved down below as possessions for her when she comes to die! Had she not been the most shameless of all women, she would never have placed these hateful libations on the tomb of him whom she murdered. Yes, see if you think the dead man in the tomb will receive these honours in a manner favourable to her, to her who killed him without honour, like an enemy, mutilated his corpse and by way of ablution wiped off the bloodstains on his head! Can you believe that these offerings will absolve

---

428–30 del. Morstadt

443 δέξεσθαι Heath: -ασθαι codd.

οὐκ ἔστιν. ἀλλὰ ταῦτα μὲν μέθες· σὺ δὲ
τεμοῦσα κρατὸς βοστρύχων ἄκρας φόβας
κἀμοῦ ταλαίνης, σμικρὰ μὲν τάδ', ἀλλ' ὅμως
ἅχω, δὸς αὐτῷ, τήνδε λιπαρῆ τρίχα
καὶ ζῶμα τοὐμὸν οὐ χλιδαῖς ἠσκημένον.
αἰτοῦ δὲ προσπίτνουσα γῆθεν εὐμενῆ
ἡμῖν ἀρωγὸν αὐτὸν εἰς ἐχθροὺς μολεῖν,
καὶ παῖδ' Ὀρέστην ἐξ ὑπερτέρας χερὸς
ἐχθροῖσιν αὐτοῦ ζῶντ' ἐπεμβῆναι ποδί,
ὅπως τὸ λοιπὸν αὐτὸν ἀφνεωτέραις
χερσὶ στέφωμεν ἢ τανῦν δωρούμεθα.
οἶμαι μὲν οὖν, οἶμαί τι κἀκείνῳ μέλειν
πέμψαι τάδ' αὐτῇ δυσπρόσοπτ' ὀνείρατα·
ὅμως δ', ἀδελφή, σοί θ' ὑπούργησον τάδε
ἐμοί τ' ἀρωγά, τῷ τε φιλτάτῳ βροτῶν
πάντων, ἐν Ἅιδου κειμένῳ κοινῷ πατρί.

ΧΟΡΟΣ

πρὸς εὐσέβειαν ἡ κόρη λέγει· σὺ δέ,
εἰ σωφρονήσεις, ὦ φίλη, δράσεις τάδε.

ΧΡΥΣΟΘΕΜΙΣ

δράσω· τὸ γὰρ δίκαιον οὐκ ἔχει λόγον
δυοῖν ἐρίζειν, ἀλλ' ἐπισπεύδει τὸ δρᾶν.
πειρωμένῃ δὲ τῶνδε τῶν ἔργων ἐμοὶ
σιγὴ παρ' ὑμῶν πρὸς θεῶν ἔστω, φίλαι·
ὡς εἰ τάδ' ἡ τεκοῦσα πεύσεται, πικρὰν
δοκῶ με πεῖραν τήνδε τολμήσειν ἔτι.

her of the murder? It cannot be! Abandon these, and cut locks from your hair and from that of this unhappy person—a small gift, but all that I possess—and give them to him, this hair denoting supplication and my girdle, decorated with no ornaments. Kneel and pray him to come in kindness from below the earth to help us against our enemies, and pray that his son Orestes may get the upper hand and may trample, alive and well, upon his enemies, so that in the future we may honour him with hands richer than those with which we now bring him gifts! I believe, yes, I believe that it is he who was concerned to send these ugly dreams to her. But none the less, my sister, perform this service in aid of both yourself and me, and of the dearest of all mortals, the father of us both who lies in Hades.

CHORUS

The girl's words are pious; and if you are wise, my dear, you will perform this action.

CHRYSOTHEMIS

I will; for when an act is right, reason demands that two voices should not contend, but hastens on the deed. But when I attempt the task, dear friends, do you, I beg you, keep silent, for if my mother hears of this, I think I shall have reason to regret my daring venture.

Exit CHRYSOTHEMIS; ELECTRA *remains on stage during the singing of the First Stasimon.*

---

459 μέλειν Nauck et Blaydes: μέλον codd.
466 τί γάρ; δίκαιον. Günther
467 ἐπισπεύδει Stobaeus: -ειν codd.

ΧΟΡΟΣ

εἰ μὴ 'γὼ παράφρων μάντις ἔφυν καὶ στρ.
γνώμας λειπομένα σοφᾶς,
εἶσιν ἁ πρόμαντις
Δίκα, δίκαια φερομένα χεροῖν κράτη·
μέτεισιν, ὦ τέκνον, οὐ μακροῦ χρόνου.
ὕπεστί μοι θάρσος
ἁδυπνόων κλυοῦσαν
ἀρτίως ὀνειράτων.
οὐ γάρ ποτ' ἀμναστεῖ γ' ὁ φύ-
σας σ' Ἑλλάνων ἄναξ,
οὐδ' ἁ παλαιὰ χαλκόπλη-
κτος ἀμφήκης γένυς,
ἅ νιν κατέπεφνεν αἰσχίσταις ἐν αἰκείαις.
ἥξει καὶ πολύπους καὶ πολύχειρ ἁ ἀντ.
δεινοῖς κρυπτομένα λόχοις
χαλκόπους Ἐρινύς.
ἄλεκτρ' ἄνυμφα γὰρ ἐπέβα μιαιφόνων
γάμων ἁμιλλήμαθ' οἷσιν οὐ θέμις.
πρὸ τῶνδέ τοι θάρσος
μήποτε μήποθ' ἡμῖν
ἀψεγὲς πελᾶν τέρας
τοῖς δρῶσι καὶ συνδρῶσιν. ἤ-
τοι μαντεῖαι βροτῶν
οὐκ εἰσὶν ἐν δεινοῖς ὀνεί-
ροις οὐδ' ἐν θεσφάτοις,
εἰ μὴ τόδε φάσμα νυκτὸς εὖ κατασχήσει.
ὦ Πέλοπος ἁ πρόσθεν ἐπ.

CHORUS

If I am not a mistaken prophet, lacking in wise judgment, Justice that has predicted the outcome shall come, carrying off just triumph with her strength; she shall come after them, my child, in no short space of time. Confidence is in my mind, now that I have heard the dream that breathes sweetly on us. For the lord of the Greeks who begot you will never be unmindful, and neither will the ancient brazen axe with double edge that slew him in a shameful outrage.

She shall come, with many feet and many hands, she who lurks in dire ambush, the brazen-clawed Erinys! For the drive to a polluting marriage, that brought an accursed bed, an accursed bridal, came upon those for whom it was forbidden. Therefore I have confidence that the portent will never come in a manner welcome to the doers and the partners in the deed. Indeed there is no prophecy for mortals in fearsome dreams or oracles, if this apparition in the night is not to find due fulfillment.

O ride of Pelops long ago,[a] bringer of many sorrows,

[a] Pelops, the founder of the dynasty, won his bride Hippodameia by defeating her father, Oenomaus, in a chariot race; thirteen previous suitors had been defeated by Oenomaus and put to death. Pelops won by bribing Oenomaus' charioteer, Myrtilus, to loosen the lynchpins of his master's chariot; when Myrtilus claimed his reward, Pelops killed him.

---

492 ἐπέβα] -αν R, coni. Blaydes
495 θάρσος Wunder: μ' ἔχει θάρσος rP: μ' ἔχει cett.
496 μήποτέ σφιν Günther

πολύπονος ἱππεία,
ὡς ἔμολες αἰανὴς
τᾷδε γᾷ.
εὖτε γὰρ ὁ ποντισθεὶς
Μυρτίλος ἐκοιμάθη,
παγχρύσων δίφρων
δυστάνοις αἰκείαις
πρόρριζος ἐκριφθείς,
οὔ τί πω
ἔλιπεν ἐκ τοῦδ᾽ οἴκου
πολύπονος αἰκεία.

ΚΛΥΤΑΙΜΗΣΤΡΑ

ἀνειμένη μέν, ὡς ἔοικας, αὖ στρέφῃ.
οὐ γὰρ πάρεστ᾽ Αἴγισθος, ὅς σ᾽ ἐπεῖχ᾽ ἀεὶ
μή τοι θυραίαν γ᾽ οὖσαν αἰσχύνειν φίλους·
νῦν δ᾽ ὡς ἄπεστ᾽ ἐκεῖνος, οὐδὲν ἐντρέπῃ
ἐμοῦ γε· καίτοι πολλὰ πρὸς πολλούς με δὴ
ἐξεῖπας ὡς θρασεῖα καὶ πέρα δίκης
ἄρχω, καθυβρίζουσα καὶ σὲ καὶ τὰ σά.
ἐγὼ δ᾽ ὕβριν μὲν οὐκ ἔχω, κακῶς δέ σε
λέγω κακῶς κλύουσα πρὸς σέθεν θαμά.
πατὴρ γάρ, οὐδὲν ἄλλο, σοὶ πρόσχημ᾽ ἀεί,
ὡς ἐξ ἐμοῦ τέθνηκεν. ἐξ ἐμοῦ· καλῶς
ἔξοιδα· τῶνδ᾽ ἄρνησις οὐκ ἔνεστί μοι.
ἡ γὰρ Δίκη νιν εἷλεν, οὐκ ἐγὼ μόνη,
ᾗ χρῆν σ᾽ ἀρήγειν, εἰ φρονοῦσ᾽ ἐτύγχανες.
ἐπεὶ πατὴρ οὗτος σός, ὃν θρηνεῖς ἀεί,

how dire was your effect upon this land! For since Myrtilus fell asleep, plunged into the sea, hurled headlong from the golden chariot with cruel torment, never yet has the torment of many troubles departed from this house.

Enter CLYTEMNESTRA.

CLYTEMNESTRA

You are ranging about once more, it seems, at large; because Aegisthus is not here, he who always used to prevent you from shaming your family at least outside the house. But now that he is away, you show no respect for me; and you have declared often and to many people that I am insolent and rule unjustly, doing violence to you and what is yours. I do no violence, but I abuse you because you often abuse me. Your father, and nothing else, is always your pretext, because I killed him. I know it well; I cannot deny it. Yes, Justice was his killer, not I alone, and you would take her side, if you happened to have sense. Why, that father of yours, whom you are always lament-

τὴν σὴν ὅμαιμον μοῦνος Ἑλλήνων ἔτλη
θῦσαι θεοῖσιν, οὐκ ἴσον καμὼν ἐμοὶ
λύπης, ὅτ᾽ ἔσπειρ᾽, ὥσπερ ἡ τίκτουσ᾽ ἐγώ.
εἶέν· δίδαξον δή με <τοῦτο>· τοῦ χάριν
ἔθυσεν αὐτήν; πότερον Ἀργείων ἐρεῖς;
ἀλλ᾽ οὐ μετῆν αὐτοῖσι τήν γ᾽ ἐμὴν κτανεῖν.
ἀλλ᾽ ἀντ᾽ ἀδελφοῦ δῆτα Μενέλεω κτανὼν
τἄμ᾽ οὐκ ἔμελλε τῶνδέ μοι δώσειν δίκην;
πότερον ἐκείνῳ παῖδες οὐκ ἦσαν διπλοῖ,
οὓς τῆσδε μᾶλλον εἰκὸς ἦν θνῄσκειν, πατρὸς
καὶ μητρὸς ὄντας, ἧς ὁ πλοῦς ὅδ᾽ ἦν χάριν;
ἢ τῶν ἐμῶν Ἅιδης τιν᾽ ἵμερον τέκνων
ἢ τῶν ἐκείνης ἔσχε δαίσασθαι πλέον;
ἢ τῷ πανώλει πατρὶ τῶν μὲν ἐξ ἐμοῦ
παίδων πόθος παρεῖτο, Μενέλεω δ᾽ ἐνῆν;
οὐ ταῦτ᾽ ἀβούλου καὶ κακοῦ γνώμην πατρός;
δοκῶ μέν, εἰ καὶ σῆς δίχα γνώμης λέγω.
φαίη δ᾽ ἂν ἡ θανοῦσά γ᾽, εἰ φωνὴν λάβοι.
ἐγὼ μὲν οὖν οὐκ εἰμὶ τοῖς πεπραγμένοις
δύσθυμος· εἰ δὲ σοὶ δοκῶ φρονεῖν κακῶς,
γνώμην δικαίαν σχοῦσα τοὺς πέλας ψέγε.

ΗΛΕΚΤΡΑ

ἐρεῖς μὲν οὐχὶ νῦν γέ μ᾽ ὡς ἄρξασά τι
λυπηρὸν εἶτα σοῦ τάδ᾽ ἐξήκουσ᾽ ὕπο·
ἀλλ᾽ ἢν ἐφῇς μοι, τοῦ τεθνηκότος θ᾽ ὕπερ
λέξαιμ᾽ ἂν ὀρθῶς τῆς κασιγνήτης θ᾽ ὁμοῦ.

ing, alone among the Greeks brought himself to sacrifice your sister to the gods,[a] though he felt less pain when he begot her than I did when I bore her. So, explain this! For whose sake did he sacrifice her? Will you say for that of the Argives? But they had no right to kill her, who was mine. But if he killed her who was mine for his brother Menelaus, was he not to pay the penalty to me? Had not Menelaus two children, who ought to have died in preference to her, since it was for the sake of their father and mother that the voyage took place? Had Hades a desire to feast on my children rather on hers? Or did your accursed father feel sorrow for the children of Menelaus, but none for mine? Is that not like a father who was foolish and lacked judgment? I think so, even if I differ from your judgment. She who died would say so, if she could acquire a voice. I for my part feel no regret at what was done; and if I seem to you to think wrongly, do you acquire a just judgment before finding fault with others!

ELECTRA

This time you shall not say that I was first to say something painful and then heard these things from you! But if you will allow me, I wish to speak on behalf of the dead man and of my sister also.

[a] Iphigeneia, sacrificed by Agamemnon because this was the only way of enabling the Greek fleet to leave Aulis for Troy.

---

534 <τοῦτο>· τοῦ χάριν Schmalfeld: τοῦ χάριν τίνος lra: τοῦ χάριν τίνων L in linea, pt

ΚΛΥΤΑΙΜΗΣΤΡΑ

καὶ μὴν ἐφίημ᾽· εἰ δέ μ᾽ ὧδ᾽ ἀεὶ λόγους
ἐξῆρχες, οὐκ ἂν ἦσθα λυπηρὰ κλύειν.

ΗΛΕΚΤΡΑ

καὶ δὴ λέγω σοι. πατέρα φὴς κτεῖναι. τίς ἂν
τούτου λόγος γένοιτ᾽ ἂν αἰσχίων ἔτι,
εἴτ᾽ οὖν δικαίως εἴτε μή; λέξω δέ σοι,
ὡς οὐ δίκῃ γ᾽ ἔκτεινας, ἀλλά σ᾽ ἔσπασεν
πειθὼ κακοῦ πρὸς ἀνδρός, ᾧ τανῦν ξύνει.
ἐροῦ δὲ τὴν κυναγὸν Ἄρτεμιν τίνος
ποινὰς τὰ πολλὰ πνεύματ᾽ ἔσχ᾽ ἐν Αὐλίδι·
ἢ ᾽γὼ φράσω· κείνης γὰρ οὐ θέμις μαθεῖν.
πατήρ ποθ᾽ οὑμός, ὡς ἐγὼ κλύω, θεᾶς
παίζων κατ᾽ ἄλσος ἐξεκίνησεν ποδοῖν
στικτὸν κεράστην ἔλαφον, οὗ κατὰ σφαγὰς
ἐκκομπάσας ἔπος τι τυγχάνει βαλών.
κἀκ τοῦδε μηνίσασα Λητῴα κόρη
κατεῖχ᾽ Ἀχαιούς, ἕως πατὴρ ἀντίσταθμον
τοῦ θηρὸς ἐκθύσειε τὴν αὑτοῦ κόρην.
ὧδ᾽ ἦν τὰ κείνης θύματ᾽· οὐ γὰρ ἦν λύσις
ἄλλη στρατῷ πρὸς οἶκον οὐδ᾽ εἰς Ἴλιον.
ἀνθ᾽ ὧν βιασθεὶς πολλά τ᾽ ἀντιβὰς μόλις
ἔθυσεν αὐτήν, οὐχὶ Μενέλεω χάριν.
εἰ δ᾽ οὖν, ἐρῶ γὰρ καὶ τὸ σόν, κεῖνον θέλων
ἐπωφελῆσαι ταῦτ᾽ ἔδρα, τούτου θανεῖν
χρῆν αὐτὸν οὕνεκ᾽ ἐκ σέθεν; ποίῳ νόμῳ;
ὅρα τιθεῖσα τόνδε τὸν νόμον βροτοῖς
μὴ πῆμα σαυτῇ καὶ μετάγνοιαν τίθῃς.

CLYTEMNESTRA

Well, I allow you! If you had always begun your speeches in such a manner, you would not have been painful to listen to.

ELECTRA

Then I will speak! You say that you killed my father. What words could carry more disgrace than that, whether your act was just or not? And I will tell you that you did not kill him justly, but were impelled by persuasion coming from an evil man, with whom you are now living. Ask the huntress Artemis what action she requited when she stilled the many winds in Aulis! Or I will tell you, since we are forbidden to learn from her. My father, as I have been told, was sporting in the sacred grove of the goddess and by his footfall started up a dappled, horned stag, and when he killed it chanced to let fall a boastful word. In her anger at this Leto's daughter detained the Achaeans, until in requital for the beast my father sacrificed his own daughter. That was how she came to be sacrificed; for there was no other means of releasing the army to go home or to go to Troy. It was for this that he sacrificed her, against his will and after much resistance, not for the sake of Menelaus. But even if he had done so to help him, for I will state your version also, was that a reason for him to die at your hands? According to what law? Take care that in laying down this law for mortals you are not laying down pain and repentance for yourself! For if we

---

560 λέξω] δείξω Morstadt
571 ἕως Fröhlich: ὡς codd.
575 τ' ἀντιβὰς Walter: κἀντιβὰς codd.

εἰ γὰρ κτενοῦμεν ἄλλον ἀντ' ἄλλου, σύ τοι
πρώτη θάνοις ἄν, εἰ δίκης γε τυγχάνοις.
ἀλλ' εἰσόρα μὴ σκῆψιν οὐκ οὖσαν τίθης.
εἰ γὰρ θέλεις, δίδαξον ἀνθ' ὅτου τανῦν
αἴσχιστα πάντων ἔργα δρῶσα τυγχάνεις,
ἥτις ξυνεύδεις τῷ παλαμναίῳ, μεθ' οὗ
πατέρα τὸν ἀμὸν πρόσθεν ἐξαπώλεσας,
καὶ παιδοποιεῖς, τοὺς δὲ πρόσθεν εὐσεβεῖς
κἀξ εὐσεβῶν βλαστόντας ἐκβαλοῦσ' ἔχεις.
πῶς ταῦτ' ἐπαινέσαιμ' ἄν; ἢ καὶ ταῦτ' ἐρεῖς
ὡς τῆς θυγατρὸς ἀντίποινα λαμβάνεις;
αἰσχρῶς δ', ἐάν περ καὶ λέγῃς. οὐ γὰρ καλὸν
ἐχθροῖς γαμεῖσθαι τῆς θυγατρὸς οὕνεκα.
ἀλλ' οὐ γὰρ οὐδὲ νουθετεῖν ἔξεστί σε,
ἣ πᾶσαν ἵης γλῶσσαν ὡς τὴν μητέρα
κακοστομοῦμεν. καί σ' ἔγωγε δεσπότιν
ἢ μητέρ' οὐκ ἔλασσον εἰς ἡμᾶς νέμω,
ἣ ζῶ βίον μοχθηρόν, ἔκ τε σοῦ κακοῖς
πολλοῖς ἀεὶ ξυνοῦσα τοῦ τε συννόμου.
ὁ δ' ἄλλος ἔξω, χεῖρα σὴν μόλις φυγών,
τλήμων Ὀρέστης δυστυχῆ τρίβει βίον·
ὃν πολλὰ δή μέ σοι τρέφειν μιάστορα
ἐπῃτιάσω· καὶ τόδ', εἴπερ ἔσθενον,
ἔδρων ἄν, εὖ τοῦτ' ἴσθι. τοῦδέ γ' οὕνεκα
κήρυσσέ μ' εἰς ἅπαντας, εἴτε χρῇς κακὴν
εἴτε στόμαργον εἴτ' ἀναιδείας πλέαν.

591 καὶ ταῦτ' Dobree: καὶ τοῦτ' codd.
606 χρῇς Wunder: χρὴ codd.

are to take a life for a life, you should die first, if you were to get what you deserve. But take care you are not putting forward an excuse that has no substance! For come, pray explain why you are doing the most shameful thing of all, you who are sleeping with the guilty one, with whom in time past you killed my father, and getting children by him, while you have cast out your earlier children who are god-fearing and born of a god-fearing father! How could I approve of this? Or will you say that this too is taken in payment for your daughter? If you do say it, it will be a shameful thing to say; for it is not honourable to mate with enemies for your daughter's sake! But no, one cannot even counsel you, who with every manner of expression declare that I abuse my mother; and I think you more a tyrant than a mother towards us, I who live a miserable life, living always with many torments that come from you and from your mate. And the other wears away an unhappy life, far away, he who barely escaped your violence, the unfortunate Orestes. Often you have accused me of bringing him up to punish you; and I would have done so, know it, had I had the power. So far as that goes, proclaim me to all, whether you like to call me bad or loud-mouthed or full of

εἰ γὰρ πέφυκα τῶνδε τῶν ἔργων ἴδρις,
σχεδόν τι τὴν σὴν οὐ καταισχύνω φύσιν.

ΧΟΡΟΣ

[one line missing]
ὁρῶ μένος πνέουσαν· εἰ δὲ σὺν δίκῃ
ξύνεστι, τοῦδε φροντίδ' οὐκέτ' εἰσορῶ.

ΚΛΥΤΑΙΜΗΣΤΡΑ

ποίας δ' ἐμοὶ δεῖ πρός γε τήνδε φροντίδος,
ἥτις τοιαῦτα τὴν τεκοῦσαν ὕβρισεν,
καὶ ταῦτα τηλικοῦτος; ἆρά σοι δοκεῖ
χωρεῖν ἂν ἐς πᾶν ἔργον αἰσχύνης ἄτερ;

ΗΛΕΚΤΡΑ

εὖ νυν ἐπίστω τῶνδέ μ' αἰσχύνην ἔχειν,
κεἰ μὴ δοκῶ σοι· μανθάνω δ' ὁθούνεκα
ἔξωρα πράσσω κοὐκ ἐμοὶ προσεικότα.
ἀλλ' ἡ γὰρ ἐκ σοῦ δυσμένεια καὶ τὰ σὰ
ἔργ' ἐξαναγκάζει με ταῦτα δρᾶν βίᾳ·
αἰσχροῖς γὰρ αἰσχρὰ πράγματ' ἐκδιδάσκεται.

ΚΛΥΤΑΙΜΗΣΤΡΑ

ὦ θρέμμ' ἀναιδές, ἦ σ' ἐγὼ καὶ τἄμ' ἔπη
καὶ τἄργα τἀμὰ πόλλ' ἄγαν λέγειν ποεῖ.

ΗΛΕΚΤΡΑ

σύ τοι λέγεις νιν, οὐκ ἐγώ. σὺ γὰρ ποεῖς
τοὔργον· τὰ δ' ἔργα τοὺς λόγους εὑρίσκεται.

609 post hunc versum lacunam statuit Ll.-J. (ex. gr. <καὶ μήν σ', ἄνασσα, τῶν λόγων τῶν τῆσδ' ὕπο>)

shamelessness; for if I am expert in such behaviour, I think I am no unworthy child of yours!

CHORUS

<Why, now, lady, at her words> I see you breathing forth anger; but I do not see you considering whether she has justice with her.

CLYTEMNESTRA

And what sort of consideration do I need to have for her, who has insulted her mother in such a fashion, and that at such an age? Do you not think she would go as far as any action, without shame?

ELECTRA

You may know that I feel shame at this, even if you do not think so, and I am aware that my actions are wrong for my age and unlike my nature. But it is the hostility that comes from you and your actions that force me to act thus against my will; for shocking behaviour is taught by shocking things.

CLYTEMNESTRA

Shameless creature, in truth I and my words and my actions make you say all too much!

ELECTRA

It is you that say these things, not I; for you do the deed, and it is deeds that find the words.

ΚΛΥΤΑΙΜΗΣΤΡΑ

ἀλλ᾿ οὐ μὰ τὴν δέσποιναν Ἄρτεμιν θράσους
τοῦδ᾿ οὐκ ἀλύξεις, εὖτ᾿ ἂν Αἴγισθος μόλῃ.

ΗΛΕΚΤΡΑ

ὁρᾷς; πρὸς ὀργὴν ἐκφέρῃ, μεθεῖσά με
λέγειν ἃ χρῄζοιμ᾿, οὐδ᾿ ἐπίστασαι κλύειν.

ΚΛΥΤΑΙΜΗΣΤΡΑ

οὔκουν ἐάσεις οὐδ᾿ ὑπ᾿ εὐφήμου βοῆς
θῦσαί μ᾿, ἐπειδὴ σοί γ᾿ ἐφῆκα πᾶν λέγειν;

ΗΛΕΚΤΡΑ

ἐῶ, κελεύω, θῦε, μηδ᾿ ἐπαιτιῶ
τοὐμὸν στόμ᾿· ὡς οὐκ ἂν πέρα λέξαιμ᾿ ἔτι.

ΚΛΥΤΑΙΜΗΣΤΡΑ

ἔπαιρε δὴ σὺ θύμαθ᾿ ἡ παροῦσά μοι
πάγκαρπ᾿, ἄνακτι τῷδ᾿ ὅπως λυτηρίους
εὐχὰς ἀνάσχω δειμάτων, ἃ νῦν ἔχω.
κλύοις ἂν ἤδη, Φοῖβε προστατήριε,
κεκρυμμένην μου βάξιν. οὐ γὰρ ἐν φίλοις
ὁ μῦθος, οὐδὲ πᾶν ἀναπτύξαι πρέπει
πρὸς φῶς παρούσης τῆσδε πλησίας ἐμοί,
μὴ σὺν φθόνῳ τε καὶ πολυγλώσσῳ βοῇ
σπείρῃ ματαίαν βάξιν εἰς πᾶσαν πόλιν.
ἀλλ᾿ ὧδ᾿ ἄκουε· τῇδε γὰρ κἀγὼ φράσω.
ἃ γὰρ προσεῖδον νυκτὶ τῇδε φάσματα
δισσῶν ὀνείρων, ταῦτά μοι, Λύκει᾿ ἄναξ,
εἰ μὲν πέφηνεν ἐσθλά, δὸς τελεσφόρα,

CLYTEMNESTRA

Why, by the lady Artemis, you shall not escape the consequences of this insolence when Aegisthus comes!

ELECTRA

Do you see? You are carried away into anger, when you had set me free to say what I wished, and you do not know how to listen.

CLYTEMNESTRA

Will you not even allow me to sacrifice without ill-omened utterance, now that I have permitted you to say all you wished?

ELECTRA

I do allow you, I beg you, sacrifice, and do not blame my speech; for I will say no more.

CLYTEMNESTRA

(*addressing an attendant carrying a tray of offerings, and later the statue of Apollo Agyieus that stands on the stage*) Raise up the offering of many fruits, you who are with me, so that I may lift up to the lord here prayers for release from the fears I now suffer. Listen, Phoebus our protector, to my secret words; for I do not speak among friends, nor is it proper for me to unfold all to the light while she stands near me, in case in her hatred and with her shouting of much verbiage she should spread vain rumours through the whole city. No, listen in this fashion, for this is how I shall speak!

Grant, Lycian lord, that if the visions in two dreams that I saw last night are favourable, they may be accom-

---

628 μεθεῖσα] παρεῖσα H, probat Dawe | με Ll.-J.: μοι codd.

εἰ δ' ἐχθρά, τοῖς ἐχθροῖσιν ἔμπαλιν μέθες·
καὶ μή με πλούτου τοῦ παρόντος εἴ τινες
δόλοισι βουλεύουσιν ἐκβαλεῖν, ἐφῇς,
ἀλλ' ὧδέ μ' αἰεὶ ζῶσαν ἀβλαβεῖ βίῳ
δόμους Ἀτρειδῶν σκῆπτρά τ' ἀμφέπειν τάδε,
φίλοισί τε ξυνοῦσαν οἷς ξύνειμι νῦν,
εὐημεροῦσαν καὶ τέκνοις ὅσων ἐμοὶ
δύσνοια μὴ πρόσεστιν ἢ λύπη πικρά.
ταῦτ', ὦ Λύκει' Ἄπολλον, ἵλεως κλυὼν
δὸς πᾶσιν ἡμῖν ὥσπερ ἐξαιτούμεθα.
τὰ δ' ἄλλα πάντα καὶ σιωπώσης ἐμοῦ
ἐπαξιῶ σε δαίμον' ὄντ' ἐξειδέναι·
τοὺς ἐκ Διὸς γὰρ εἰκός ἐστι πάνθ' ὁρᾶν.

ΠΑΙΔΑΓΩΓΟΣ

ξέναι γυναῖκες, πῶς ἂν εἰδείην σαφῶς
εἰ τοῦ τυράννου δώματ' Αἰγίσθου τάδε;

ΧΟΡΟΣ

τάδ' ἐστίν, ὦ ξέν'· αὐτὸς ᾔκασας καλῶς.

ΠΑΙΔΑΓΩΓΟΣ

ἦ καὶ δάμαρτα τήνδ' ἐπεικάζων κυρῶ
κείνου; πρέπει γὰρ ὡς τύραννος εἰσορᾶν.

ΧΟΡΟΣ

μάλιστα πάντων· ἥδε σοι κείνη πάρα.

ΠΑΙΔΑΓΩΓΟΣ

ὦ χαῖρ', ἄνασσα. σοὶ φέρων ἥκω λόγους
ἡδεῖς φίλου παρ' ἀνδρὸς Αἰγίσθῳ θ' ὁμοῦ.

plished, but if they are inimical, send them back upon my enemies! And if some persons are plotting to rob me of the wealth I now enjoy, do not allow it, but grant that I may always live a life unharmed, ruling the house of the Atreidae and this kingdom, living with the friends with whom I now live, enjoying prosperity, and with those of my children from whom no enmity or bitter pain attaches to me. Hear this, Lycian Apollo, with kindness and grant to all of us that which we are praying for! The rest I think that you, who are a god, know well, even if I say nothing; for the children of Zeus can surely see all things.

Enter OLD SLAVE.

OLD SLAVE

Ladies of Mycenae, how can I know for certain if this is the house of the king Aegisthus?

CHORUS

This is it, stranger; your own guess is correct.

OLD SLAVE

Should I be right in guessing this lady is his wife? She has the aspect of a queen.

CHORUS

Yes, indeed! Here she is!

OLD SLAVE

Hail, royal lady! I bring to you and to Aegisthus good news from a friend.

---

653 τέκνοις Xr s.l., coni. Benedict: τέκνων cett.

ΚΛΥΤΑΙΜΗΣΤΡΑ

ἐδεξάμην τὸ ῥηθέν· εἰδέναι δέ σου
πρώτιστα χρῄζω τίς σ᾽ ἀπέστειλεν βροτῶν.

ΠΑΙΔΑΓΩΓΟΣ

Φανοτεὺς ὁ Φωκεύς, πρᾶγμα πορσύνων μέγα.

ΚΛΥΤΑΙΜΗΣΤΡΑ

τὸ ποῖον, ὦ ξέν᾽; εἰπέ. παρὰ φίλου γὰρ ὢν
ἀνδρός, σάφ᾽ οἶδα, προσφιλεῖς λέξεις λόγους.

ΠΑΙΔΑΓΩΓΟΣ

τέθνηκ᾽ Ὀρέστης· ἐν βραχεῖ ξυνθεὶς λέγω.

ΗΛΕΚΤΡΑ

οἲ ᾽γὼ τάλαιν᾽, ὄλωλα τῇδ᾽ ἐν ἡμέρᾳ.

ΚΛΥΤΑΙΜΗΣΤΡΑ

τί φής, τί φής, ὦ ξεῖνε; μὴ ταύτης κλύε.

ΠΑΙΔΑΓΩΓΟΣ

θανόντ᾽ Ὀρέστην νῦν τε καὶ πάλαι λέγω.

ΗΛΕΚΤΡΑ

ἀπωλόμην δύστηνος, οὐδέν εἰμ᾽ ἔτι.

ΚΛΥΤΑΙΜΗΣΤΡΑ

σὺ μὲν τὰ σαυτῆς πρᾶσσ᾽, ἐμοὶ δὲ σύ, ξένε,
τἀληθὲς εἰπέ, τῷ τρόπῳ διόλλυται;

ΠΑΙΔΑΓΩΓΟΣ

κἀπεμπόμην πρὸς ταῦτα καὶ τὸ πᾶν φράσω.
κεῖνος γὰρ ἐλθὼν ἐς τὸ κλεινὸν Ἑλλάδος
πρόσχημ᾽ ἀγῶνος Δελφικῶν ἄθλων χάριν,

CLYTEMNESTRA

I accept the omen! But first I want to know from you who among mortals sent you.

OLD SLAVE

Phanoteus the Phocian, furthering an important matter.

CLYTEMNESTRA

What is that, stranger? Tell me, for you come, I know, from a friend, and the words you utter will be friendly words.

OLD SLAVE

Orestes is dead! There you have it in a word!

ELECTRA

Ah me, misery! I am lost this day!

CLYTEMNESTRA

What are you saying? What, stranger? Do not listen to her!

OLD SLAVE

I said then and I say now that Orestes is dead.

ELECTRA

Misery, I am ruined, I am no more!

CLYTEMNESTRA

Do you mind your own business; but do you, stranger, tell me the truth! How did he die?

OLD SLAVE

I was sent for this purpose and I will tell you all! He came to the pride of Greece, the contest, for the sake of Delphic

ὅτ᾽ ᾔσθετ᾽ ἀνδρὸς ὀρθίων γηρυμάτων
δρόμον προκηρύξαντος, οὗ πρώτη κρίσις,
εἰσῆλθε λαμπρός, πᾶσι τοῖς ἐκεῖ σέβας·
δρόμου δ᾽ ἰσώσας τῇ φύσει τὰ τέρματα
νίκης ἔχων ἐξῆλθε πάντιμον γέρας.
χὤπως μὲν ἐν παύροισι πολλά σοι λέγω,
οὐκ οἶδα τοιοῦδ᾽ ἀνδρὸς ἔργα καὶ κράτη·
ἓν δ᾽ ἴσθ᾽· ὅσων γὰρ εἰσεκήρυξαν βραβῆς,
[†δρόμων διαύλων πένταθλ᾽ ἃ νομίζεται, †]
τούτων ἐνεγκὼν πάντα τἀπινίκια
ὠλβίζετ᾽, Ἀργεῖος μὲν ἀνακαλούμενος,
ὄνομα δ᾽ Ὀρέστης, τοῦ τὸ κλεινὸν Ἑλλάδος
Ἀγαμέμνονος στράτευμ᾽ ἀγείραντός ποτε.
καὶ ταῦτα μὲν τοιαῦθ᾽· ὅταν δέ τις θεῶν
βλάπτῃ, δύναιτ᾽ ἂν οὐδ᾽ ἂν ἰσχύων φυγεῖν.
κεῖνος γὰρ ἄλλης ἡμέρας, ὅθ᾽ ἱππικῶν
ἦν ἡλίου τέλλοντος ὠκύπους ἀγών,
εἰσῆλθε πολλῶν ἁρματηλατῶν μέτα.
εἷς ἦν Ἀχαιός, εἷς ἀπὸ Σπάρτης, δύο
Λίβυες ζυγωτῶν ἁρμάτων ἐπιστάται·
κἀκεῖνος ἐν τούτοισι Θεσσαλὰς ἔχων
ἵππους, ὁ πέμπτος· ἕκτος ἐξ Αἰτωλίας
ξανθαῖσι πώλοις· ἕβδομος Μάγνης ἀνήρ·
ὁ δ᾽ ὄγδοος λεύκιππος, Αἰνιὰν γένος·
ἔνατος Ἀθηνῶν τῶν θεοδμήτων ἄπο·
Βοιωτὸς ἄλλος, δέκατον ἐκπληρῶν ὄχον.
στάντες δ᾽ ὅθ᾽ αὐτοὺς οἱ τεταγμένοι βραβῆς
κλήροις ἔπηλαν καὶ κατέστησαν δίφρους,

prizes, and when he heard the loud pronouncement of the man who proclaimed the race, which is decided first, he entered the course a brilliant figure, admired by all. He made the result of the race correspond with his appearance, and emerged holding the greatly honoured prize of victory. To tell much in few words, I do not know of the deeds and triumphs of any other such man; but one thing you may know, that he carried off all the prizes in every contest that the judges proclaimed [, the races on the double track that are the custom], and men called him fortunate. He was proclaimed as an Argive, by name Orestes, son of Agamemnon who once gathered the famous armament of Greece. So far, things stood thus; but when one of the gods does mischief, not even a mighty man can escape.

For on another day, when at sunrise there was the speedy contest of the chariot horses, he entered the lists with many charioteers. One was an Achaean, one from Sparta, two were Libyans, masters of yoked cars, another among them had Thessalian mares, the fifth; the sixth came from Aetolia, with chestnut colts; the seventh was Magnesian; the eighth had white horses, an Aenian; the ninth came from Athens, built by gods; another was Boeotian, filling the tenth chariot. They took their stand where the appointed judges had sorted them with lots

683 γηρυμάτων Herwerden: κηρυγμάτων codd.
688 παύροισι πολλὰ Bergk: πολλοῖσι παῦρα codd.
691 del. Porson
709 ὅθ' αὐτοὺς pa: ὅτ' αὐτοὺς Lrp: ὅθι σφιν Wecklein
710 κλήροις] -ους p, coni. Wunder

χαλκῆς ὑπαὶ σάλπιγγος ᾖξαν· οἱ δ' ἅμα
ἵπποις ὁμοκλήσαντες ἡνίας χεροῖν
ἔσεισαν· ἐν δὲ πᾶς ἐμεστώθη δρόμος
κτύπου κροτητῶν ἁρμάτων· κόνις δ' ἄνω
φορεῖθ'· ὁμοῦ δὲ πάντες ἀναμεμειγμένοι
φείδοντο κέντρων οὐδέν, ὡς ὑπερβάλοι
χνόας τις αὐτῶν καὶ φρυάγμαθ' ἱππικά.
ὁμοῦ γὰρ ἀμφὶ νῶτα καὶ τροχῶν βάσεις
ἤφριζον, εἰσέβαλλον ἱππικαὶ πνοαί.
 κεῖνος δ' ὑπ' αὐτὴν ἐσχάτην στήλην ἔχων
ἔχριμπτ' ἀεὶ σύριγγα, δεξιὸν δ' ἀνεὶς
σειραῖον ἵππον εἶργε τὸν προσκείμενον.
καὶ πρὶν μὲν ὀρθοὶ πάντες ἕστασαν δίφροις·
ἔπειτα δ' Αἰνιᾶνος ἀνδρὸς ἄστομοι
πῶλοι βίᾳ φέρουσιν, ἐκ δ' ὑποστροφῆς
τελοῦντες ἕκτον ἕβδομόν τ' ἤδη δρόμον
μέτωπα συμπαίουσι Βαρκαίοις ὄχοις·
κἀντεῦθεν ἄλλος ἄλλον ἐξ ἑνὸς κακοῦ
ἔθραυε κἀνέπιπτε, πᾶν δ' ἐπίμπλατο
ναυαγίων Κρισαῖον ἱππικῶν πέδον.
γνοὺς δ' οὑξ Ἀθηνῶν δεινὸς ἡνιοστρόφος
ἔξω παρασπᾷ κἀνοκωχεύει παρεὶς
κλύδων' ἔφιππον ἐν μέσῳ κυκώμενον.
 ἤλαυνε δ' ἔσχατος μέν, ὑστέρας ἔχων
πώλους, Ὀρέστης, τῷ τέλει πίστιν φέρων·
ὅπως δ' ὁρᾷ μόνον νιν ἐλλελειμμένον,
ὀξὺν δι' ὤτων κέλαδον ἐνσείσας θοαῖς
πώλοις διώκει, κἀξισώσαντε ζυγὰ

and placed their chariots, and at the sound of the brazen trumpet darted off. Shouting to their horses, the drivers gripped the reins and shook them loose; the whole course resounded with the clash of rattling chariots; the dust rose up; and all close together, they did not spare the use of their goads, each hoping to pass the wheels and the snorting horses of the others; for about their backs and their wheels below alike the breath of the horses touched them with its foam.

And Orestes, keeping his horses near the pillar at the end, each time grazed the post, and giving his right-hand trace-horse room he tried to block off his pursuer. At first all had stood upright in their chariots; but then the hard-mouthed colts of the Aenian, carrying him on in his despite, on the turn as they finished the sixth and began the seventh round dashed their foreheads against the chariot from Barce. One driver crashed into and smashed another in a single disaster, and then the whole plain of Crisa was filled with the wreckage of chariots. Seeing this, the cunning charioteer from Athens pulled his horses away and paused, avoiding the surge of chariots all confused in the middle of the course.

Orestes was driving last, keeping his horses in the rear, confident in the result; and when he saw that the Athenian alone was left, he sent a sharp command through the

---

718–22 hos versus post 740 traiecit Dawe (720–22 iam Piccolomini)

723 δίφροις Kp: -οι Lrpa

736 ὅπως δ' r, fort. L: ὁ δ' ὡς cett.

ἠλαυνέτην, τότ᾽ ἄλλος, ἄλλοθ᾽ ἅτερος
κάρα προβάλλων ἱππικῶν ὀχημάτων.
καὶ τοὺς μὲν ἄλλους πάντας ἀσφαλὴς δρόμους
ὠρθοῦθ᾽ ὁ τλήμων ὀρθὸς ἐξ ὀρθῶν δίφρων·
ἔπειτα λύων ἡνίαν ἀριστερὰν
κάμπτοντος ἵππου λανθάνει στήλην ἄκραν
παίσας· ἔθραυσε δ᾽ ἄξονος μέσας χνόας,
κἀξ ἀντύγων ὤλισθε· σὺν δ᾽ ἑλίσσεται
τμητοῖς ἱμᾶσι· τοῦ δὲ πίπτοντος πέδῳ
πῶλοι διεσπάρησαν ἐς μέσον δρόμον.
στρατὸς δ᾽ ὅπως ὁρᾷ νιν ἐκπεπτωκότα
δίφρων, ἀνωτότυξε τὸν νεανίαν,
οἷ᾽ ἔργα δράσας οἷα λαγχάνει κακά,
φορούμενος πρὸς οὖδας, ἄλλοτ᾽ οὐρανῷ
σκέλη προφαίνων, ἔστε νιν διφρηλάται,
μόλις κατασχεθόντες ἱππικὸν δρόμον,
ἔλυσαν αἱματηρόν, ὥστε μηδένα
γνῶναι φίλων ἰδόντ᾽ ἂν ἄθλιον δέμας.
καί νιν πυρᾷ κέαντες εὐθὺς ἐν βραχεῖ
χαλκῷ μέγιστον σῶμα δειλαίας σποδοῦ
φέρουσιν ἄνδρες Φωκέων τεταγμένοι,
ὅπως πατρῴας τύμβον ἐκλάχῃ χθονός.
τοιαῦτά σοι ταῦτ᾽ ἐστίν, ὡς μὲν ἐν λόγοις
ἀλγεινά, τοῖς δ᾽ ἰδοῦσιν, οἵπερ εἴδομεν,
μέγιστα πάντων ὧν ὄπωπ᾽ ἐγὼ κακῶν.

741 ἀσφαλὴς Reiske: -εῖς codd.
750 ἀνωτότυξε Herwerden: ἀνωλόλυξε codd.

ears of his swift horses and went after him. They brought their chariots level and drove on, with the head now of one, now of the other projecting from the chariots. Throughout all the other rounds the man and his chariot remained upright; then as the horse turned he relaxed his left-hand rein, and unawares he struck the end of the pillar. He broke the axle box, slid over the rail, and was caught in the reins, and as he fell upon the ground the horses plunged wildly into the middle of the course.

And when the crowd saw his fall from the chariot, they cried out with pity for the young man, seeing what misfortunes followed upon such deeds, as at one moment he was borne earthwards, at another with legs skywards, until the charioteers with difficulty checked the horses' career and released him, all bloody, so that none of his friends that saw him could have recognised his wretched shape. Men appointed from among the Phocians burned him on a pyre, and at once carried in a small urn of bronze his mighty form, now miserable dust, so that he should be accorded burial in the land of his fathers. Such was this event, terrible to relate, and for those that saw it, as we did, the worst disaster of all that I have beheld.

257–60 del. Günther

758 *μέγιστον σῶμα* Lrpat: *-ου -ατος* N et s.l. p, quo recepto *δειλὴν σποδόν* Wecklein *δειλαίας σποδοῦ*] *-αν -όν* s.l. p

ΧΟΡΟΣ

φεῦ φεῦ· τὸ πᾶν δὴ δεσπόταισι τοῖς πάλαι
πρόρριζον, ὡς ἔοικεν, ἔφθαρται γένος.

ΚΛΥΤΑΙΜΗΣΤΡΑ

ὦ Ζεῦ, τί ταῦτα, πότερον εὐτυχῆ λέγω,
ἢ δεινὰ μέν, κέρδη δέ; λυπηρῶς δ᾽ ἔχει,
εἰ τοῖς ἐμαυτῆς τὸν βίον σῴζω κακοῖς.

ΠΑΙΔΑΓΩΓΟΣ

τί δ᾽ ὧδ᾽ ἀθυμεῖς, ὦ γύναι, τῷ νῦν λόγῳ;

ΚΛΥΤΑΙΜΗΣΤΡΑ

δεινὸν τὸ τίκτειν ἐστίν· οὐδὲ γὰρ κακῶς
πάσχοντι μῖσος ὧν τέκῃ προσγίγνεται.

ΠΑΙΔΑΓΩΓΟΣ

μάτην ἄρ᾽ ἡμεῖς, ὡς ἔοικεν, ἥκομεν.

ΚΛΥΤΑΙΜΗΣΤΡΑ

οὔτοι μάτην γε. πῶς γὰρ ἂν μάτην λέγοις;
εἴ μοι θανόντος πίστ᾽ ἔχων τεκμήρια
προσῆλθες, ὅστις τῆς ἐμῆς ψυχῆς γεγώς,
μαστῶν ἀποστὰς καὶ τροφῆς ἐμῆς, φυγὰς
ἀπεξενοῦτο· καί μ᾽, ἐπεὶ τῆσδε χθονὸς
ἐξῆλθεν, οὐκέτ᾽ εἶδεν· ἐγκαλῶν δέ μοι
φόνους πατρῴους δείν᾽ ἐπηπείλει τελεῖν·
ὥστ᾽ οὔτε νυκτὸς ὕπνον οὔτ᾽ ἐξ ἡμέρας
ἐμὲ στεγάζειν ἡδύν, ἀλλ᾽ ὁ προστατῶν
χρόνος διῆγέ μ᾽ αἰὲν ὡς θανουμένην.
νῦν δ᾽—ἡμέρᾳ γὰρ τῇδ᾽ ἀπηλλάγην φόβου

CHORUS

Alas, alas! The whole family of our ancient masters, it seems, is destroyed root and branch.

CLYTEMNESTRA

O Zeus! What of this? Am I to call it fortunate, or terrible, but beneficial? It is painful, if I preserve my life by means of my own calamities.

OLD SLAVE

Why are you thus despondent, lady, at the news?

CLYTEMNESTRA

Giving birth is a strange thing; even when they treat one badly, one does not hate one's children.

OLD SLAVE

It seems then, that my coming was in vain.

CLYTEMNESTRA

Never in vain! How can you say "in vain" if you have come bringing sure proof of the death of one who, though sprung from my life, turned away from the nurture of my breast, and became a foreigner in exile. After he left this land he never saw me, but he reproached me with his father's murder and swore to do terrible things, so that neither by night nor day would sweet sleep cover me, but from one moment to another I lived like one about to die. But now—for on this day I have been freed from the fear

---

783 ἀπηλλάγην KrN: -αγμαι lpa

πρὸς τῆσδ᾽ ἐκείνου θ᾽· ἥδε γὰρ μείζων βλάβη
ξύνοικος ἦν μοι, τοὐμὸν ἐκπίνουσ᾽ ἀεὶ
ψυχῆς ἄκρατον αἷμα—νῦν δ᾽ ἕκηλά που
τῶν τῆσδ᾽ ἀπειλῶν οὕνεχ᾽ ἡμερεύσομεν.

ΗΛΕΚΤΡΑ

οἴμοι τάλαινα· νῦν γὰρ οἰμῶξαι πάρα,
Ὀρέστα, τὴν σὴν ξυμφοράν, ὅθ᾽ ὧδ᾽ ἔχων
πρὸς τῆσδ᾽ ὑβρίζῃ μητρός. ἆρ᾽ ἔχω καλῶς;

ΚΛΥΤΑΙΜΗΣΤΡΑ

οὔτοι σύ· κεῖνος δ᾽ ὡς ἔχει καλῶς ἔχει.

ΗΛΕΚΤΡΑ

ἄκουε, Νέμεσι τοῦ θανόντος ἀρτίως.

ΚΛΥΤΑΙΜΗΣΤΡΑ

ἤκουσεν ὧν δεῖ κἀπεκύρωσεν καλῶς.

ΗΛΕΚΤΡΑ

ὕβριζε· νῦν γὰρ εὐτυχοῦσα τυγχάνεις.

ΚΛΥΤΑΙΜΗΣΤΡΑ

οὔκουν Ὀρέστης καὶ σὺ παύσετον τάδε;

ΗΛΕΚΤΡΑ

πεπαύμεθ᾽ ἡμεῖς, οὐχ ὅπως σὲ παύσομεν.

ΚΛΥΤΑΙΜΗΣΤΡΑ

πολλῶν ἂν ἥκοις, ὦ ξέν᾽, ἄξιος φίλος,
εἰ τήνδ᾽ ἔπαυσας τῆς πολυγλώσσου βοῆς.

inspired by this woman here and him—yes, she was a worse mischief, living with me and all the time sucking my very life-blood—now we shall spend our days, I think, securely, for any threats of hers.

ELECTRA

Ah, miserable me! Now I can lament your disaster, Orestes, when in this plight you are insulted by this mother of yours! Am I not well off?

CLYTEMNESTRA

Not so; but as he is he is well off.

ELECTRA

Hear this, Nemesis,[a] of the one who lately died!

CLYTEMNESTRA

Nemesis has heard what she needed to hear and has decided well.

ELECTRA

Insult me! Now is your moment of good fortune.

CLYTEMNESTRA

Then will not Orestes and you put a stop to this?

ELECTRA

We have been stopped, far from our stopping you!

CLYTEMNESTRA

You would be a friend deserving much, stranger, if you had put a stop to her loud verbiage.

[a] Nemesis is a power that sees that each man receives his due.

---

790 ἔχω F. W. Schmidt: ἔχει codd.
791 οὔτοι σὺ] οὐ σοί γε Reiske
797 φίλος G: φιλεῖν l: τυχεῖν cett.

ΠΑΙΔΑΓΩΓΟΣ

οὔκουν ἀποστείχοιμ᾽ ἄν, εἰ τάδ᾽ εὖ κυρεῖ;

ΚΛΥΤΑΙΜΗΣΤΡΑ

ἥκιστ᾽· ἐπείπερ οὔτ᾽ ἐμοῦ κατάξι᾽ ἂν
πράξειας οὔτε τοῦ πορεύσαντος ξένου.
ἀλλ᾽ εἴσιθ᾽ εἴσω· τήνδε δ᾽ ἔκτοθεν βοᾶν
ἔα τά θ᾽ αὑτῆς καὶ τὰ τῶν φίλων κακά.

ΗΛΕΚΤΡΑ

ἆρ᾽ ὑμὶν ὡς ἀλγοῦσα κὠδυνωμένη
δεινῶς δακρῦσαι κἀπικωκῦσαι δοκεῖ
τὸν υἱὸν ἡ δύστηνος ὧδ᾽ ὀλωλότα;
ἀλλ᾽ ἐγγελῶσα φροῦδος. ὦ τάλαιν᾽ ἐγώ·
Ὀρέστα φίλταθ᾽, ὥς μ᾽ ἀπώλεσας θανών.
ἀποσπάσας γὰρ τῆς ἐμῆς οἴχῃ φρενὸς
αἵ μοι μόναι παρῆσαν ἐλπίδων ἔτι,
σὲ πατρὸς ἥξειν ζῶντα τιμωρόν ποτε
κἀμοῦ ταλαίνης. νῦν δὲ ποῖ με χρὴ μολεῖν;
μόνη γάρ εἰμι, σοῦ τ᾽ ἀπεστερημένη
καὶ πατρός. ἤδη δεῖ με δουλεύειν πάλιν
ἐν τοῖσιν ἐχθίστοισιν ἀνθρώπων ἐμοί,
φονεῦσι πατρός. ἆρά μοι καλῶς ἔχει;
ἀλλ᾽ οὔ τι μὴν ἔγωγε τοῦ λοιποῦ χρόνου
ἔσομαι ξύνοικος, ἀλλὰ τῇδε πρὸς πύλῃ
παρεῖσ᾽ ἐμαυτὴν ἄφιλος αὑανῶ βίον.
πρὸς ταῦτα καινέτω τις, εἰ βαρύνεται,
τῶν ἔνδον ὄντων· ὡς χάρις μέν, ἢν κτάνῃ,
λύπη δ᾽, ἐὰν ζῶ· τοῦ βίου δ᾽ οὐδεὶς πόθος.

OLD SLAVE

Then may I depart, if all is well?

CLYTEMNESTRA

Never! That would be treatment unworthy of me and of the friend who sent you! Come in, and leave her outside to scream out her sorrows and those of her friends!

CLYTEMNESTRA and the OLD SLAVE go into the palace.

ELECTRA

Do you think the wretched woman weeps for and laments her dead son as though she feels grief and pain? No, she is gone, gloating. Misery me! Dearest Orestes, how you have killed me by your death! You have carried away with you, out of my mind, the only hopes I still possessed, that you would one day come to avenge our father and my wretched self. But now where can I go? I am alone, deprived of you and of my father. Now once more must I be a slave among the mortals I hate most, my father's murderers. Are things well with me? But in the future I shall not live with them, but by this gate I shall let myself go and without a friend waste away my life. In face of that let any of those inside kill me, if he resents me; to die will be a pleasure, to survive will be a pain, and I have no desire for life.

---

818 *ἔσομαι ξύνοικος* Dawes: *ξύνοικος ἔσ(σ)ομ'* codd.: *ξύνοικος εἴσειμ'* Hermann

ΧΟΡΟΣ

ποῦ ποτε κεραυνοὶ Διός, ἢ ποῦ — στρ. α´
φαέθων Ἅλιος, εἰ ταῦτ᾽ ἐφορῶντες
κρύπτουσιν ἕκηλοι;

ΗΛΕΚΤΡΑ

ἒ ἕ, αἰαῖ.

ΧΟΡΟΣ

ὦ παῖ, τί δακρύεις;

ΗΛΕΚΤΡΑ

φεῦ.

ΧΟΡΟΣ

μηδὲν μέγ᾽ ἀύσῃς.

ΗΛΕΚΤΡΑ

ἀπολεῖς.

ΧΟΡΟΣ

πῶς;

ΗΛΕΚΤΡΑ

εἰ τῶν φανερῶς οἰχομένων
εἰς Ἀίδαν ἐλπίδ᾽ ὑποίσεις, κατ᾽ ἐμοῦ τακομένας
μᾶλλον ἐπεμβάσῃ.

ΧΟΡΟΣ

οἶδα γὰρ ἄνακτ᾽ Ἀμφιάρεων χρυ- — ἀντ. α´
σοδέτοις ἕρκεσι κρυφθέντα γυναικῶν
καὶ νῦν ὑπὸ γαίας—

824 lacunam post ἐφορῶντες statuit Musgrave (vid. 838); an <μάκαρες> supplendum?

CHORUS

Where are the thunderbolts of Zeus, and where is the blazing Sun, if they look on this and peacefully conceal it?

ELECTRA

Woe, woe, ah me!

CHORUS

Daughter, why do you weep?

ELECTRA

Alas!

CHORUS

Utter no loud cry!

ELECTRA

You will kill me!

CHORUS

How so?

ELECTRA

If you suggest a hope resting on those who we can see have gone to Hades, you will trample yet harder on me as I melt away.

CHORUS

Why, I know that the lord Amphiaraus was brought low by the golden necklaces of women,[a] and now below the earth . . .

[a] Amphiaraus died betrayed by his wife Eriphyle, who had been bribed with a golden necklace; their son Alcmaeon later avenged his father by killing his mother.

---

838 *γυναικῶν* Brunck: *γυναικῶν ἀπάταις* Lrpa

ΗΛΕΚΤΡΑ

ἒ ἔ, ἰώ.

ΧΟΡΟΣ

πάμψυχος ἀνάσσει.

ΗΛΕΚΤΡΑ

φεῦ.

ΧΟΡΟΣ

φεῦ δῆτ'· ὀλοὰ γ' ἆρ'—

ΗΛΕΚΤΡΑ

ἐδάμη.

ΧΟΡΟΣ

ναί.

ΗΛΕΚΤΡΑ

οἶδ' οἶδ'· ἐφάνη γὰρ μελέτωρ
ἀμφὶ τὸν ἐν πένθει· ἐμοὶ δ' οὔτις ἔτ' ἔσθ'· ὃς γὰρ ἔτ' ἦν
φροῦδος ἀναρπασθείς.

ΧΟΡΟΣ

δειλαία δειλαίων κυρεῖς. στρ. β´

ΗΛΕΚΤΡΑ

κἀγὼ τοῦδ' ἴστωρ, ὑπερίστωρ,
πανσύρτῳ παμμήνῳ πολλῶν
δεινῶν στυγνῶν τ' αἰῶνι.

ELECTRA

Woe, woe, ah me!

CHORUS

He is a king, with full power of mind.[a]

ELECTRA

Alas!

CHORUS

Alas indeed! The killer at least . . .

ELECTRA

. . . was done to death.

CHORUS

Yes!

ELECTRA

I know, I know! For there appeared a champion for the mourning one; but for me there is none, for he whom I had is gone, snatched away.

CHORUS

Wretched are you, and wretched is your fate!

ELECTRA

I too know this, and know it all too well, I whose life is a torrent of things terrible and hateful that does not abate in any month.

[a] Like another great prophet, Tiresias (*Od.* 10.495), Amphiaraus retained his full mental powers, unlike the other dead.

---

844 γ' ἆρ' Ll.-J.: γὰρ codd.

852 αἰῶνι Hermann: ἀχέων Krpa (et L ex ἀχ..ων correctum): ἄχθει olim Hermann, τε post δεινῶν addito

ΧΟΡΟΣ

εἴδομεν ἃ θροεῖς.

ΗΛΕΚΤΡΑ

μή μέ νυν μηκέτι
παραγάγῃς, ἵν' οὐ—

ΧΟΡΟΣ

τί φής;

ΗΛΕΚΤΡΑ

πάρεισιν ἐλπίδων ἔτι κοινοτόκων
εὐπατριδᾶν ἀρωγαί.

ΧΟΡΟΣ

πᾶσιν θνατοῖς ἔφυ μόρος. ἀντ. β'

ΗΛΕΚΤΡΑ

ἦ καὶ χαλάργοις ἐν ἁμίλλαις
οὕτως, ὡς κείνῳ δυστάνῳ,
τμητοῖς ὁλκοῖς ἐγκῦρσαι;

ΧΟΡΟΣ

ἄσκοπος ἁ λώβα.

ΗΛΕΚΤΡΑ

πῶς γὰρ οὔκ; εἰ ξένος
ἄτερ ἐμᾶν χερῶν—

ΧΟΡΟΣ

παπαῖ.

ELECTRA

CHORUS

We have seen the things you speak of.

ELECTRA

Bring me no longer to where there are not . . .

CHORUS

What are you saying?

ELECTRA

. . . still present the supports that come from hopes for noble ones of the same stock.

CHORUS

For all mortals there is an end.

ELECTRA

But an end amid the hooves of racing horses, such as came to that unhappy one, entangled in the reins?

CHORUS

Unconscionable is the horror!

ELECTRA

Surely it is so; if in a foreign land, without my touch . . .

CHORUS

Alas!

ΗΛΕΚΤΡΑ

κέκευθεν, οὔτε του τάφου ἀντιάσας
οὔτε γόων παρ' ἡμῶν.

ΧΡΥΣΟΘΕΜΙΣ

ὑφ' ἡδονῆς τοι, φιλτάτη, διώκομαι
τὸ κόσμιον μεθεῖσα σὺν τάχει μολεῖν.
φέρω γὰρ ἡδονάς τε κἀνάπαυλαν ὧν
πάροιθεν εἶχες καὶ κατέστενες κακῶν.

ΗΛΕΚΤΡΑ

πόθεν δ' ἂν εὕροις τῶν ἐμῶν σὺ πημάτων
ἄρηξιν, οἷς ἴασις οὐκ ἔνεστ' ἔτι;

ΧΡΥΣΟΘΕΜΙΣ

πάρεστ' Ὀρέστης ἡμίν, ἴσθι τοῦτ' ἐμοῦ
κλύουσ', ἐναργῶς, ὥσπερ εἰσορᾷς ἐμέ.

ΗΛΕΚΤΡΑ

ἀλλ' ἦ μέμηνας, ὦ τάλαινα, κἀπὶ τοῖς
σαυτῆς κακοῖσι κἀπὶ τοῖς ἐμοῖς γελᾷς;

ΧΡΥΣΟΘΕΜΙΣ

μὰ τὴν πατρῴαν ἑστίαν, ἀλλ' οὐχ ὕβρει
λέγω τάδ', ἀλλ' ἐκεῖνον ὡς παρόντα νῷν.

ΗΛΕΚΤΡΑ

οἴμοι τάλαινα· καὶ τίνος βροτῶν λόγον
τόνδ' εἰσακούσασ' ὧδε πιστεύεις ἄγαν;

ΧΡΥΣΟΘΕΜΙΣ

ἐγὼ μὲν ἐξ ἐμοῦ τε κοὐκ ἄλλου σαφῆ
σημεῖ' ἰδοῦσα τῷδε πιστεύω λόγῳ.

ELECTRA

He is buried, having had no funeral or lament from us.

Enter CHRYSOTHEMIS.

CHRYSOTHEMIS

Delight, dearest one, spurs me to come fast, letting go care for dignity! For I bring happiness and relief from your previous troubles, over which you have lamented.

ELECTRA

And where could you find help for my sorrows, for which it is impossible to see a remedy?

CHRYSOTHEMIS

We have Orestes here—know this from me—unmistakably, just as you see me!

ELECTRA

Are you mad, poor creature, and are you mocking my troubles and your own?

CHRYSOTHEMIS

No, by the hearth of our father, I do not speak in mockery, but I tell you that we have him here!

ELECTRA

Ah me! and from whom among mortals have you heard this story to which you give excessive credence?

CHRYSOTHEMIS

I believe this story because I have seen sure signs with my own eyes, and have not heard it from another.

---

876 ἴασις L s.l., pZr Suda: ἴασιν cett. | οὐκ] οὐκέτ' p | ἔνεστ'] ἔστιν p | ἔτι L s.l., p: ἰδεῖν cett.

ΗΛΕΚΤΡΑ

τίν', ὦ τάλαιν', ἰδοῦσα πίστιν; ἐς τί μοι
βλέψασα θάλπῃ τῷδ' ἀνηφαίστῳ πυρί;

ΧΡΥΣΟΘΕΜΙΣ

πρός νυν θεῶν ἄκουσον, ὡς μαθοῦσά μου
τὸ λοιπὸν ἢ φρονοῦσαν ἢ μώραν λέγῃς.

ΗΛΕΚΤΡΑ

σὺ δ' οὖν λέγ', εἴ σοι τῷ λόγῳ τις ἡδονή.

ΧΡΥΣΟΘΕΜΙΣ

καὶ δὴ λέγω σοι πᾶν ὅσον κατειδόμην.
ἐπεὶ γὰρ ἦλθον πατρὸς ἀρχαῖον τάφον,
ὁρῶ κολώνης ἐξ ἄκρας νεορρύτους
πηγὰς γάλακτος καὶ περιστεφῆ κύκλῳ
πάντων ὅσ' ἔστιν ἀνθέων θήκην πατρός.
ἰδοῦσα δ' ἔσχον θαῦμα, καὶ περισκοπῶ
μή πού τις ἡμῖν ἐγγὺς ἐγχρίμπτει βροτῶν.
ὡς δ' ἐν γαλήνῃ πάντ' ἐδερκόμην τόπον,
τύμβου προσεῖρπον ἆσσον· ἐσχάτης δ' ὁρῶ
πυρᾶς νεώρη βόστρυχον τετμημένον.
κεὐθὺς τάλαιν' ὡς εἶδον, ἐμπαίει τί μοι
ψυχῇ σύνηθες ὄμμα, φιλτάτου βροτῶν
πάντων Ὀρέστου τοῦθ' ὁρᾶν τεκμήριον·
καὶ χερσὶ βαστάσασα δυσφημῶ μὲν οὔ,
χαρᾷ δὲ πίμπλημ' εὐθὺς ὄμμα δακρύων.
καὶ νῦν θ' ὁμοίως καὶ τότ' ἐξεπίσταμαι
μή του τόδ' ἀγλάισμα πλὴν κείνου μολεῖν.
τῷ γὰρ προσήκει πλήν γ' ἐμοῦ καὶ σοῦ τόδε;

ELECTRA

What have you seen that proves it? What do you look to, that you are warm with this fire not of Hephaestus?

CHRYSOTHEMIS

Listen, I beg you, so that you can learn it from me and then pronounce me sensible or foolish!

ELECTRA

Well, speak, if speaking gives you any pleasure!

CHRYSOTHEMIS

Then I will tell you all I saw. When I approached our father's ancient tomb, I saw on top of the mound freshly flowing streams of milk, and my father's urn crowned with a ring of every kind of flower. Seeing, I wondered, and looked about in case any person was nearby. But when I had calmly looked about the whole place, I drew near to the tomb; and on the edge of the pyre, I saw a newly cut lock of hair. And the moment that I saw it, ah! a familiar source of light struck me; I beheld a token of him among mortals whom I love the most, Orestes! I took it in my hands, and uttered no ill-omened word, but at once my eyes filled with tears of joy. And I know now, just as I knew then, that this ornament came from none but him. For to whom does this pertain but to you and to me? and

---

888 ἀνηφαίστῳ Bergk: ἀνηκέστῳ codd.
900–1 ἐσχάτης . . . πυρᾶς] -ῃ . . . -ᾷ Schaefer

κἀγὼ μὲν οὐκ ἔδρασα, τοῦτ᾽ ἐπίσταμαι,
οὐδ᾽ αὖ σύ· πῶς γάρ; ᾗ γε μηδὲ πρὸς θεοὺς
ἔξεστ᾽ ἀκλαύτῳ τῆσδ᾽ ἀποστῆναι στέγης.
ἀλλ᾽ οὐδὲ μὲν δὴ μητρὸς οὔθ᾽ ὁ νοῦς φιλεῖ
τοιαῦτα πράσσειν οὔτε δρῶσ᾽ ἐλάνθαν᾽ ἄν·
ἀλλ᾽ ἔστ᾽ Ὀρέστου ταῦτα τἀπιτύμβια.
ἀλλ᾽, ὦ φίλη, θάρσυνε. τοῖς αὐτοῖσί τοι
οὐχ αὑτὸς αἰεὶ δαιμόνων παραστατεῖ.
νῷν δ᾽ ἦν ὁ πρόσθε στυγνός· ἡ δὲ νῦν ἴσως
πολλῶν ὑπάρξει κῦρος ἡμέρα καλῶν.

ΗΛΕΚΤΡΑ

φεῦ, τῆς ἀνοίας ὥς σ᾽ ἐποικτίρω πάλαι.

ΧΡΥΣΟΘΕΜΙΣ

τί δ᾽ ἔστιν; οὐ πρὸς ἡδονὴν λέγω τάδε;

ΗΛΕΚΤΡΑ

οὐκ οἶσθ᾽ ὅποι γῆς οὐδ᾽ ὅποι γνώμης φέρῃ.

ΧΡΥΣΟΘΕΜΙΣ

πῶς δ᾽ οὐκ ἐγὼ κάτοιδ᾽ ἅ γ᾽ εἶδον ἐμφανῶς;

ΗΛΕΚΤΡΑ

τέθνηκεν, ὦ τάλαινα· τἀκ κείνου δέ σοι
σωτήρι᾽ ἔρρει· μηδὲν ἐς κεῖνόν γ᾽ ὅρα.

ΧΡΥΣΟΘΕΜΙΣ

οἴμοι τάλαινα· τοῦ τάδ᾽ ἤκουσας βροτῶν;

I did not do it, that I know, neither did you; how could you, who cannot leave this house even to go to the gods without ruing it? As for our mother, it is not her way to do such things, nor could she have done it without our knowing. No, these offerings at the tomb come from Orestes. Come, my dear, take courage! The same fortune does not always attend the same person, and our fortune in the past was hateful; but perhaps this day shall confirm our possession of much good.

ELECTRA

Alas, how I have been pitying you for your folly all this while!

CHRYSOTHEMIS

What is it? Do my words not please you?

ELECTRA

You do not know where your feet or your thoughts are carrying you!

CHRYSOTHEMIS

But how can I not know what I saw with my own eyes?

ELECTRA

He is dead, poor creature! Your chance of salvation by him is lost; do not look to him!

CHRYSOTHEMIS

Ah me! From whom among mortals did you hear this?

---

914 *ἐλάνθαν' ἂν* Heath: *ἐλάνθανεν* codd.

915 *τἀπιτύμβια* Dindorf: *τἀπιτίμια* codd.

918 *ὅ* Ll.-J.: *τὰ* codd.

924 *τὰκ κείνου* Canter: *τἀκείνου* codd.

ΗΛΕΚΤΡΑ

τοῦ πλησίον παρόντος, ἡνίκ᾽ ὤλλυτο.

ΧΡΥΣΟΘΕΜΙΣ

καὶ ποῦ 'στιν οὗτος; θαῦμά τοί μ᾽ ὑπέρχεται.

ΗΛΕΚΤΡΑ

κατ᾽ οἶκον, ἡδὺς οὐδὲ μητρὶ δυσχερής.

ΧΡΥΣΟΘΕΜΙΣ

οἴμοι τάλαινα· τοῦ γὰρ ἀνθρώπων ποτ᾽ ἦν
τὰ πολλὰ πατρὸς πρὸς τάφον κτερίσματα;

ΗΛΕΚΤΡΑ

οἶμαι μάλιστ᾽ ἔγωγε τοῦ τεθνηκότος
μνημεῖ᾽ Ὀρέστου ταῦτα προσθεῖναί τινα.

ΧΡΥΣΟΘΕΜΙΣ

ὢ δυστυχής· ἐγὼ δὲ σὺν χαρᾷ λόγους
τοιούσδ᾽ ἔχουσ᾽ ἔσπευδον, οὐκ εἰδυῖ᾽ ἄρα
ἵν᾽ ἦμεν ἄτης· ἀλλὰ νῦν, ὅθ᾽ ἱκόμην,
τά τ᾽ ὄντα πρόσθεν ἄλλα θ᾽ εὑρίσκω κακά.

ΗΛΕΚΤΡΑ

οὕτως ἔχει σοι ταῦτ᾽· ἐὰν δ᾽ ἐμοὶ πίθῃ,
τῆς νῦν παρούσης πημονῆς λύσεις βάρος.

ΧΡΥΣΟΘΕΜΙΣ

ἦ τοὺς θανόντας ἐξαναστήσω ποτέ;

ΗΛΕΚΤΡΑ

†οὐκ ἔσθ᾽ ὅ γ᾽† εἶπον· οὐ γὰρ ὧδ᾽ ἄφρων ἔφυν.

941 ἔσθ᾽ ὅ γ᾽ L s.l., Rpa: ἔσθ᾽ ὅδ᾽ LG: τοῦτό γ᾽ Blaydes

ELECTRA

From the man who was close at hand when he perished.

CHRYSOTHEMIS

And where is he? Wonder is creeping over me.

ELECTRA

In the house, to my mother's pleasure, not to her distaste.

CHRYSOTHEMIS

Ah me! Then from what man did the many offerings to my father's tomb come?

ELECTRA

I think someone put them there as memorials of the dead Orestes.

CHRYSOTHEMIS

Ah, misery me! and I was hurrying with such news in my delight, not knowing, as it proved, in what a plight we were! But now that I am here I find our old troubles and others also.

ELECTRA

That is how things stand; but if you will obey me, you will lighten the weight of our present pain.

CHRYSOTHEMIS

Shall I ever make the dead rise again?

ELECTRA

That is not what I said! I am not such a fool!

ΧΡΥΣΟΘΕΜΙΣ

τί γὰρ κελεύεις ὧν ἐγὼ φερέγγυος;

ΗΛΕΚΤΡΑ

τλῆναί σε δρῶσαν ἂν ἐγὼ παραινέσω.

ΧΡΥΣΟΘΕΜΙΣ

ἀλλ᾽ εἴ τις ὠφέλειά γ᾽, οὐκ ἀπώσομαι.

ΗΛΕΚΤΡΑ

ὅρα, πόνου τοι χωρὶς οὐδὲν εὐτυχεῖ.

ΧΡΥΣΟΘΕΜΙΣ

ὁρῶ. ξυνοίσω πᾶν ὅσονπερ ἂν σθένω.

ΗΛΕΚΤΡΑ

ἄκουε δή νυν ᾗ βεβούλευμαι τελεῖν.
παρουσίαν μὲν οἶσθα καὶ σύ που φίλων
ὡς οὔτις ἡμῖν ἐστιν, ἀλλ᾽ Ἅιδης λαβὼν
ἀπεστέρηκε καὶ μόνα λελείμμεθον.
ἐγὼ δ᾽ ἕως μὲν τὸν κασίγνητον βίῳ
θάλλοντ᾽ ἔτ᾽ εἰσήκουον, εἶχον ἐλπίδας
φόνου ποτ᾽ αὐτὸν πράκτορ᾽ ἵξεσθαι πατρός·
νῦν δ᾽ ἡνίκ᾽ οὐκέτ᾽ ἔστιν, ἐς σὲ δὴ βλέπω,
ὅπως τὸν αὐτόχειρα πατρῴου φόνου
ξὺν τῇδ᾽ ἀδελφῇ μὴ κατοκνήσεις κτανεῖν
Αἴγισθον· οὐδὲν γάρ σε δεῖ κρύπτειν μ᾽ ἔτι.
ποῖ γὰρ μενεῖς ῥάθυμος, ἐς τίν᾽ ἐλπίδων
βλέψασ᾽ ἔτ᾽ ὀρθήν; ᾗ πάρεστι μὲν στένειν
πλούτου πατρῴου κτῆσιν ἐστερημένῃ,
πάρεστι δ᾽ ἀλγεῖν ἐς τοσόνδε τοῦ χρόνου

CHRYSOTHEMIS

Then what is it you command that lies within my power?

ELECTRA

That you bring yourself to do what I advise.

CHRYSOTHEMIS

Why, if it will bring any help, I shall not reject it.

ELECTRA

Remember, there is no success without hard work.

CHRYSOTHEMIS

I know; I will help as far as my strength allows.

ELECTRA

Then hear what I have determined to accomplish! You know, I think, that we have no friends here, but that Hades has taken them from us and we are left alone. So long as I still heard that my brother was alive and well, I had hopes that he would one day come to avenge his father's murder. But now that he is no more, I look to you, not to be afraid to kill with me your sister the author of our father's murder, Aegisthus; I must conceal nothing from you any more! Why, how long will you wait, doing nothing? To what hope that still stands upright can you look? You can lament at being cheated of the possession of your father's wealth, and you can grieve at growing

952 θάλλοντ' ἔτ' Reiske: θάλλοντά τ' codd.

ἄλεκτρα γηράσκουσαν ἀνυμέναιά τε.
καὶ τῶνδε μέντοι μηκέτ᾽ ἐλπίσῃς ὅπως
τεύξῃ ποτ᾽· οὐ γὰρ ὧδ᾽ ἄβουλός ἐστ᾽ ἀνὴρ
Αἴγισθος ὥστε σόν ποτ᾽ ἢ κἀμὸν γένος
βλαστεῖν ἐᾶσαι, πημονὴν αὑτῷ σαφῆ.
ἀλλ᾽ ἢν ἐπίσπῃ τοῖς ἐμοῖς βουλεύμασιν,
πρῶτον μὲν εὐσέβειαν ἐκ πατρὸς κάτω
θανόντος οἴσῃ τοῦ κασιγνήτου θ᾽ ἅμα·
ἔπειτα δ᾽, ὥσπερ ἐξέφυς, ἐλευθέρα
καλῇ τὸ λοιπὸν καὶ γάμων ἐπαξίων
τεύξῃ· φιλεῖ γὰρ πρὸς τὰ χρηστὰ πᾶς ὁρᾶν.
λόγων γε μὴν εὔκλειαν οὐχ ὁρᾷς ὅσην
σαυτῇ τε κἀμοὶ προσβαλεῖς πεισθεῖσ᾽ ἐμοί;
τίς γάρ ποτ᾽ ἀστῶν ἢ ξένων ἡμᾶς ἰδὼν
τοιοῖσδ᾽ ἐπαίνοις οὐχὶ δεξιώσεται,
"ἴδεσθε τώδε τὼ κασιγνήτω, φίλοι,
ὣ τὸν πατρῷον οἶκον ἐξεσωσάτην,
ὣ τοῖσιν ἐχθροῖς εὖ βεβηκόσιν ποτὲ
ψυχῆς ἀφειδήσαντε προὐστήτην φόνου.
τούτω φιλεῖν χρή, τώδε χρὴ πάντας σέβειν·
τώδ᾽ ἔν θ᾽ ἑορταῖς ἔν τε πανδήμῳ πόλει
τιμᾶν ἅπαντας οὕνεκ᾽ ἀνδρείας χρεών."
τοιαῦτά τοι νὼ πᾶς τις ἐξερεῖ βροτῶν,
ζώσαιν θανούσαιν θ᾽ ὥστε μὴ ᾽κλιπεῖν κλέος.
ἀλλ᾽, ὦ φίλη, πείσθητι, συμπόνει πατρί,
σύγκαμν᾽ ἀδελφῷ, παῦσον ἐκ κακῶν ἐμέ,
παῦσον δὲ σαυτήν, τοῦτο γιγνώσκουσ᾽, ὅτι
ζῆν αἰσχρὸν αἰσχρῶς τοῖς καλῶς πεφυκόσιν.

older to this point in time without a wedding and without a marriage. And think no longer that you will ever get these things; Aegisthus is not so stupid a man as to allow your children or mine to come into being, bringing obvious trouble for himself. But if you fall in with my counsels, first you will earn credit for piety from our dead father below, and also from our brother; and further, for the future you will be called free, that which you are by nature, and you will obtain a worthy marriage; for what is excellent draws the eyes of all. Then as to fame on the lips of men, do you not see how much you will add to you and me if you obey me? Which of the citizens or strangers when he sees us will not greet us with praise? "Look on these sisters, friends, who preserved their father's house, who when their enemies were firmly based took no thought of their lives, but stood forth to avenge murder! All should love them, all should reverence them; all should honour them at feasts and among the assembled citizens for their courage!" Such things will be said of us by all men, so that in life and death our fame will never die. Come, my dear, comply, work with your father, labour with your brother, save me from my sorrows, and save yourself, recognising that a shameful life is shameful for those nobly born!

ΧΟΡΟΣ

ἐν τοῖς τοιούτοις ἐστὶν ἡ προμηθία
καὶ τῷ λέγοντι καὶ κλύοντι σύμμαχος.

ΧΡΥΣΟΘΕΜΙΣ

καὶ πρίν γε φωνεῖν, ὦ γυναῖκες, εἰ φρενῶν
ἐτύγχαν' αὕτη μὴ κακῶν, ἐσῴζετ' ἂν
τὴν εὐλάβειαν, ὥσπερ οὐχὶ σῴζεται.
ποῖ γάρ ποτε βλέψασα τοιοῦτον θράσος
αὐτή θ' ὁπλίζῃ κἄμ' ὑπηρετεῖν καλεῖς;
οὐκ εἰσορᾷς; γυνὴ μὲν οὐδ' ἀνὴρ ἔφυς,
σθένεις δ' ἔλασσον τῶν ἐναντίων χερί.
δαίμων δὲ τοῖς μὲν εὐτυχὴς καθ' ἡμέραν,
ἡμῖν δ' ἀπορρεῖ κἀπὶ μηδὲν ἔρχεται.
τίς οὖν τοιοῦτον ἄνδρα βουλεύων ἑλεῖν
ἄλυπος ἄτης ἐξαπαλλαχθήσεται;
ὅρα κακῶς πράσσοντε μὴ μείζω κακὰ
κτησώμεθ', εἴ τις τούσδ' ἀκούσεται λόγους.
λύει γὰρ ἡμᾶς οὐδὲν οὐδ' ἐπωφελεῖ
βάξιν καλὴν λαβόντε δυσκλεῶς θανεῖν.
[οὐ γὰρ θανεῖν ἔχθιστον, ἀλλ' ὅταν θανεῖν
χρῄζων τις εἶτα μηδὲ τοῦτ' ἔχῃ λαβεῖν.]
ἀλλ' ἀντιάζω, πρὶν πανωλέθρους τὸ πᾶν
ἡμᾶς τ' ὀλέσθαι κἀξερημοῦσθαι γένος,
κατάσχες ὀργήν. καὶ τὰ μὲν λελεγμένα
ἄρρητ' ἐγώ σοι κἀτελῆ φυλάξομαι,
αὐτὴ δὲ νοῦν σχὲς ἀλλὰ τῷ χρόνῳ ποτέ,
σθένουσα μηδὲν τοῖς κρατοῦσιν εἰκαθεῖν.

CHORUS

In such matters as these forethought is an ally both for him who speaks and him who listens.

CHRYSOTHEMIS

Before giving tongue, women, she would have preserved caution, if she had good sense, but she does not preserve it! Why, with what aim in view do you arm yourself with such rashness and call on me to second you? Do you not see? You are a woman, not a man, and your strength is less than that of your adversaries. Their fortune prospers day by day, and ours ebbs away and comes to nothing. Who, then, shall plan to kill such a man and emerge unscathed by disaster? Take care that in our ill fortune we do not get for ourselves yet more trouble, if anybody hears these words! We get no help and no profit if we acquire fair fame, but an ignoble death. [It is not death that is the most hateful thing, but to wish for death and have not even that in one's power.] I beseech you, before we perish altogether and wipe out our family, restrain your passion! I will guard your words unspoken and unrealised, and do you in the end at least acquire the sense to yield to those in power when you have no strength!

---

995 *βλέψασα* Π 6: *ἐμβλέψασα* lrpat

1007–8 del. Nauck

1010 *κἐξερημοῦσθαι* Blaydes: *ἐξερημῶσαι* codd.

ΧΟΡΟΣ

πείθου. προνοίας οὐδὲν ἀνθρώποις ἔφυ
κέρδος λαβεῖν ἄμεινον οὐδὲ νοῦ σοφοῦ.

ΗΛΕΚΤΡΑ

ἀπροσδόκητον οὐδὲν εἴρηκας· καλῶς δ'
ᾔδη σ' ἀπορρίψουσαν ἁπηγγελλόμην.
ἀλλ' αὐτόχειρί μοι μόνῃ τε δραστέον
τοὔργον τόδ'· οὐ γὰρ δὴ κενόν γ' ἀφήσομεν.

ΧΡΥΣΟΘΕΜΙΣ

φεῦ·
εἴθ' ὤφελες τοιάδε τὴν γνώμην πατρὸς
θνῄσκοντος εἶναι· πᾶν γὰρ ἂν κατειργάσω.

ΗΛΕΚΤΡΑ

ἀλλ' ἦ φύσιν γε, τὸν δὲ νοῦν ἥσσων τότε.

ΧΡΥΣΟΘΕΜΙΣ

ἄσκει τοιαύτη νοῦν δι' αἰῶνος μένειν.

ΗΛΕΚΤΡΑ

ὡς οὐχὶ συνδράσουσα νουθετεῖς τάδε.

ΧΡΥΣΟΘΕΜΙΣ

εἰκὸς γὰρ ἐγχειροῦντα καὶ πράσσειν κακῶς.

ΗΛΕΚΤΡΑ

ζηλῶ σε τοῦ νοῦ, τῆς δὲ δειλίας στυγῶ.

ΧΡΥΣΟΘΕΜΙΣ

ἀνέξομαι κλύουσα χὤταν εὖ λέγῃς.

1022 πᾶν Dawes: πάντα codd. γὰρ ἂν L[ac]KpXs: γὰρ rpa
1023 ἦ Elmsley: ἦν codd.

CHORUS

Comply! There is nothing more profitable for human beings than foresight and wise thinking.

ELECTRA

You have said nothing that surprises me; I knew well that you would reject what I proposed. Well, I must do this deed single-handed and alone! For I will not leave it unattempted.

CHRYSOTHEMIS

Ah! I wish you had shown such resolution when our father perished; you would have carried all before you!

ELECTRA

By nature I was the same, but then I had less understanding.

CHRYSOTHEMIS

Practise so as to keep such understanding throughout life!

ELECTRA

Your lecturing me thus means that you will not act with me!

CHRYSOTHEMIS

No, for it is likely that the attempt would fail!

ELECTRA

I envy your good sense, but I hate you for your cowardice.

CHRYSOTHEMIS

I will put up with hearing this as well as when you praise me!

ΗΛΕΚΤΡΑ

ἀλλ᾽ οὔ ποτ᾽ ἐξ ἐμοῦ γε μὴ πάθῃς τόδε.

ΧΡΥΣΟΘΕΜΙΣ

μακρὸς τὸ κρῖναι ταῦτα χὠ λοιπὸς χρόνος.

ΗΛΕΚΤΡΑ

ἄπελθε· σοὶ γὰρ ὠφέλησις οὐκ ἔνι.

ΧΡΥΣΟΘΕΜΙΣ

ἔνεστιν· ἀλλὰ σοὶ μάθησις οὐ πάρα.

ΗΛΕΚΤΡΑ

ἐλθοῦσα μητρὶ ταῦτα πάντ᾽ ἔξειπε σῇ.

ΧΡΥΣΟΘΕΜΙΣ

οὐδ᾽ αὖ τοσοῦτον ἔχθος ἐχθαίρω σ᾽ ἐγώ.

ΗΛΕΚΤΡΑ

ἀλλ᾽ οὖν ἐπίστω γ᾽ οἷ μ᾽ ἀτιμίας ἄγεις.

ΧΡΥΣΟΘΕΜΙΣ

ἀτιμίας μὲν οὔ, προμηθίας δὲ σοῦ.

ΗΛΕΚΤΡΑ

τῷ σῷ δικαίῳ δῆτ᾽ ἐπισπέσθαι με δεῖ;

ΧΡΥΣΟΘΕΜΙΣ

ὅταν γὰρ εὖ φρονῇς, τόθ᾽ ἡγήσῃ σὺ νῷν.

ΗΛΕΚΤΡΑ

ἦ δεινὸν εὖ λέγουσαν ἐξαμαρτάνειν.

ΧΡΥΣΟΘΕΜΙΣ

εἴρηκας ὀρθῶς ᾧ σὺ πρόσκεισαι κακῷ.

ELECTRA
But you will never suffer that from me!

CHRYSOTHEMIS
There will be a long time in the future to decide that!

ELECTRA
Go! There is no help in you!

CHRYSOTHEMIS
There is; but there is no readiness to learn in you.

ELECTRA
Go and tell all this to your mother!

CHRYSOTHEMIS
No, I do not hate you so much as that!

ELECTRA
Well, know to what point of dishonour you are bringing me!

CHRYSOTHEMIS
Not of dishonour, but of care for you!

ELECTRA
Must I comply with your notion of what is right?

CHRYSOTHEMIS
Yes, when you are sensible, then you shall be our leader.

ELECTRA
It is sad when one who speaks so well goes wrong!

CHRYSOTHEMIS
You have perfectly described your own trouble!

ΗΛΕΚΤΡΑ

τί δ'; οὐ δοκῶ σοι ταῦτα σὺν δίκῃ λέγειν;

ΧΡΥΣΟΘΕΜΙΣ

ἀλλ' ἔστιν ἔνθα χἠ δίκη βλάβην φέρει.

ΗΛΕΚΤΡΑ

τούτοις ἐγὼ ζῆν τοῖς νόμοις οὐ βούλομαι.

ΧΡΥΣΟΘΕΜΙΣ

ἀλλ' εἰ ποήσεις ταῦτ', ἐπαινέσεις ἐμέ.

ΗΛΕΚΤΡΑ

καὶ μὴν ποήσω γ' οὐδὲν ἐκπλαγεῖσά σε.

ΧΡΥΣΟΘΕΜΙΣ

καὶ τοῦτ' ἀληθές, οὐδὲ βουλεύσῃ πάλιν;

ΗΛΕΚΤΡΑ

βουλῆς γὰρ οὐδέν ἐστιν ἔχθιον κακῆς.

ΧΡΥΣΟΘΕΜΙΣ

φρονεῖν ἔοικας οὐδὲν ὧν ἐγὼ λέγω.

ΗΛΕΚΤΡΑ

πάλαι δέδοκται ταῦτα κοὐ νεωστί μοι.

[ΧΡΥΣΟΘΕΜΙΣ

ἄπειμι τοίνυν· οὔτε γὰρ σὺ τἄμ' ἔπη
τολμᾷς ἐπαινεῖν οὔτ' ἐγὼ τοὺς σοὺς τρόπους.

ΗΛΕΚΤΡΑ

ἀλλ' εἴσιθ'. οὔ σοι μὴ μεθέψομαί ποτε,
οὐδ' ἢν σφόδρ' ἱμείρουσα τυγχάνῃς· ἐπεὶ
πολλῆς ἀνοίας καὶ τὸ θηρᾶσθαι κενά.]

ELECTRA
What? Do you not think that what I say is right?

CHRYSOTHEMIS
But there are times when being right does one harm.

ELECTRA
I do not wish to live by rules like that.

CHRYSOTHEMIS
Well, if you do do this, you will end by approving my words.

ELECTRA
Well, I shall do it, in no way scared by you!

CHRYSOTHEMIS
Is that really so, and will you not think again?

ELECTRA
Yes, because there is nothing worse than wrong thinking.

CHRYSOTHEMIS
You seem to understand none of what I say.

ELECTRA
I decided all this long ago, not lately.

[CHRYSOTHEMIS
Then I shall go; for you will not approve my words and I shall not approve your ways.

ELECTRA
Why, go indoors! I shall never follow you, however much you may desire it; it is great folly to engage in a vain chase.]

1050–54 interpolatos esse censeo: 1052–57 del. Morstadt: 1050–51 Sophoclis Phaedrae tribuit Stobaeus 3.2.29

ΧΡΥΣΟΘΕΜΙΣ

ἀλλ᾽ εἰ σεαυτῇ τυγχάνεις δοκοῦσά τι
φρονεῖν, φρόνει τοιαῦθ᾽· ὅταν γὰρ ἐν κακοῖς
ἤδη βεβήκῃς, τἄμ᾽ ἐπαινέσεις ἔπη.

ΧΟΡΟΣ

τί τοὺς ἄνωθεν φρονιμωτάτους οἰωνοὺς — στρ. α΄
ἐσορώμενοι τροφᾶς κη-
δομένους ἀφ᾽ ὧν τε βλάστω-
σιν ἀφ᾽ ὧν τ᾽ ὄνησιν εὕρω-
σι, τάδ᾽ οὐκ ἐπ᾽ ἴσας τελοῦμεν;
ἀλλ᾽ οὐ τὰν Διὸς ἀστραπὰν
καὶ τὰν οὐρανίαν Θέμιν
δαρὸν οὐκ ἀπόνητοι.
ὦ χθονία βροτοῖσι φάμα,
κατά μοι βόασον οἰκτρὰν
ὄπα τοῖς ἔνερθ᾽ Ἀτρείδαις,
ἀχόρευτα φέρουσ᾽ ὀνείδη.
ὅτι σφὶν ἤδη τὰ μὲν ἐκ δόμων νοσεῖται, — ἀντ. α΄
τὰ δὲ πρὸς τέκνων διπλῆ φύ-
λοπις οὐκέτ᾽ ἐξισοῦται
φιλοτασίῳ διαίτᾳ.
πρόδοτος δὲ μόνα σαλεύει
ἁ παῖς, οἶτον ἀεὶ πατρὸς
δειλαία στενάχουσ᾽ ὅπως
ἁ πάνδυρτος ἀηδών,
οὔτε τι τοῦ θανεῖν προμηθὴς
τό τε μὴ βλέπειν ἑτοίμα,

CHRYSOTHEMIS

Well, if you think you are showing some sense, think like that! For when you are already in trouble, you will approve my words.

Exit CHRYSOTHEMIS.

CHORUS

Why, when we see birds above that are so wise taking care to sustain those that give them life and pleasure, do we not render the same services? But by Zeus' lightning and divine justice in the sky, trouble shall soon follow! O voice that for mortals travels below the earth, cry out a sad message to the Atreidae below, carrying a joyless message of dishonour!

Tell them that their house suffers from a plague, and that the strife between their children is no longer levelled out in loving life together! But the daughter is betrayed and alone tosses on the sea, ever lamenting her father's fate in sorrow, like the ever-grieving nightingale, reckless of death and ready to renounce the light, if she can bring

1070 *σφὶν* Schaefer: *σφίσιν* Lrpa | *νοσεῖται* Paris. gr. 2794: *νοσεῖ* codd. plerique

1075 *ἁ παῖς, οἶτον* Heath: *Ἠλέκτρα τὸν* codd.

διδύμαν ἑλοῦσ᾽ Ἐρινύν.
τίς ἂν εὔπατρις ὧδε βλάστοι;
οὐδεὶς τῶν ἀγαθῶν <ἂν> στρ. β′
ζῶν κακῶς εὔκλειαν αἰσχῦναι θέλοι
νώνυμος, ὦ παῖ παῖ·
ὡς καὶ σὺ πάγκλαυτον αἰ-
ῶνα κλεινὸν εἵλου,
ἄκος καλὸν καθοπλίσα-
σα δύο φέρειν <ἐν> ἑνὶ λόγῳ,
σοφά τ᾽ ἀρίστα τε παῖς κεκλῆσθαι.
ζῴης μοι καθύπερθεν ἀντ. β′
χειρὶ καὶ πλούτῳ τεῶν ἐχθρῶν ὅσον
νῦν ὑπόχειρ ναίεις·
ἐπεί σ᾽ ἐφηύρηκα μοί-
ρᾳ μὲν οὐκ ἐν ἐσθλᾷ
βεβῶσαν, ἃ δὲ μέγιστ᾽ ἔβλα-
στε νόμιμα, τῶνδε φερομέναν
ἄριστα τᾷ Ζηνὸς εὐσεβείᾳ.

ΟΡΕΣΤΗΣ

ἆρ᾽, ὦ γυναῖκες, ὀρθά τ᾽ εἰσηκούσαμεν
ὀρθῶς θ᾽ ὁδοιποροῦμεν ἔνθα χρῄζομεν;

ΧΟΡΟΣ

τί δ᾽ ἐξερευνᾷς καὶ τί βουληθεὶς πάρει;

ΟΡΕΣΤΗΣ

Αἴγισθον ἔνθ᾽ ᾤκηκεν ἱστορῶ πάλαι.

down the twin Erinyes. Who could be so loyal to her father?

No one who is noble consents to sully his fame by a miserable life without glory, my child, my child! Thus have you chosen a glorious life bathed in tears, giving a weapon to a noble remedy, so that you win on one score twofold praise, being called a daughter wise and noble.

May you live as much above your enemies in strength and wealth as now you are below them! For I have found you enjoying no happy fate, and yet winning the highest prize in the observance of the greatest laws, by your piety towards Zeus.

Enter ORESTES *and* PYLADES, *with two attendants,* ORESTES *carrying an urn.*

ORESTES

Ladies, have we heard right instructions, and are we on the right way to where we wish to go?

CHORUS

What are you looking for? and what is the purpose that brings you here?

ORESTES

For a while I have been asking where Aegisthus lives.

1082 ‹ἂν› Schneidewin: ‹γὰρ› Hermann

1083 θέλοι Schneidewin: θέλει codd.

1086 κλεινὸν Sirks: κοινὸν codd.

1087 ἄκος Ll.-J.: τὸ μὴ codd.

1091 χειρὶ V et Eustath.: χερὶ cett. | τεῶν Hermann: τῶν codd.

1092 ὑπόχειρ Musgrave: ὑπὸ χεῖρα codd.

1097 Ζηνὸς Lγρt: Διὸς cett.

ΧΟΡΟΣ

ἀλλ᾽ εὖ θ᾽ ἱκάνεις χὠ φράσας ἀζήμιος.

ΟΡΕΣΤΗΣ

τίς οὖν ἂν ὑμῶν τοῖς ἔσω φράσειεν ἂν
ἡμῶν ποθεινὴν κοινόπουν παρουσίαν;

ΧΟΡΟΣ

ἥδ᾽, εἰ τὸν ἄγχιστόν γε κηρύσσειν χρεών.

ΟΡΕΣΤΗΣ

ἴθ᾽, ὦ γύναι, δήλωσον εἰσελθοῦσ᾽ ὅτι
Φωκῆς ματεύουσ᾽ ἄνδρες Αἴγισθόν τινες.

ΗΛΕΚΤΡΑ

οἴμοι τάλαιν᾽, οὐ δή ποθ᾽ ἧς ἠκούσαμεν
φήμης φέροντες ἐμφανῆ τεκμήρια;

ΟΡΕΣΤΗΣ

οὐκ οἶδα τὴν σὴν κληδόν᾽· ἀλλά μοι γέρων
ἐφεῖτ᾽ Ὀρέστου Στροφίος ἀγγεῖλαι πέρι.

ΗΛΕΚΤΡΑ

τί δ᾽ ἔστιν, ὦ ξέν᾽; ὥς μ᾽ ὑπέρχεται φόβος.

ΟΡΕΣΤΗΣ

φέροντες αὐτοῦ σμικρὰ λείψαν᾽ ἐν βραχεῖ
τεύχει θανόντος, ὡς ὁρᾷς, κομίζομεν.

ΗΛΕΚΤΡΑ

οἲ ᾽γὼ τάλαινα, τοῦτ᾽ ἐκεῖν᾽, ἤδη σαφές·
πρόχειρον ἄχθος, ὡς ἔοικε, δέρκομαι.

CHORUS

You have come the right way, and whoever directed you cannot be faulted.

ORESTES

Then which among you could report to those inside the presence of us both, a presence long desired?

CHORUS

This lady, if the nearest ought to announce it.

ORESTES

Go in, lady, and tell them that some Phocians are looking for Aegisthus.

ELECTRA

Ah me, surely you are not bringing manifest proof of the story which we heard?

ORESTES

I do not know about your story; but the aged Strophius told me to bring the news about Orestes.

ELECTRA

What is it, stranger? How fear steals over me!

ORESTES

He is dead, and we are carrying in a small urn the little that remains of him to bring it here.

ELECTRA

Ah me, that is it, it is now clear! It seems I see the burden ready to hand.

ΟΡΕΣΤΗΣ

εἴπερ τι κλαίεις τῶν Ὀρεστείων κακῶν,
τόδ᾽ ἄγγος ἴσθι σῶμα τοὐκείνου στέγον.

ΗΛΕΚΤΡΑ

ὦ ξεῖνε, δός νυν πρὸς θεῶν, εἴπερ τόδε
κέκευθεν αὐτὸν τεῦχος, ἐς χεῖρας λαβεῖν,
ὅπως ἐμαυτὴν καὶ γένος τὸ πᾶν ὁμοῦ
ξὺν τῇδε κλαύσω κἀποδύρωμαι σποδῷ.

ΟΡΕΣΤΗΣ

δόθ᾽, ἥτις ἐστί, προσφέροντες· οὐ γὰρ ὡς
ἐν δυσμενείᾳ γ᾽ οὖσ᾽ ἐπαιτεῖται τόδε,
ἀλλ᾽ ἢ φίλων τις, ἢ πρὸς αἵματος φύσιν.

ΗΛΕΚΤΡΑ

ὦ φιλτάτου μνημεῖον ἀνθρώπων ἐμοὶ
ψυχῆς Ὀρέστου λοιπόν, ὥς σ᾽ ἀπ᾽ ἐλπίδων
οὐχ ὧνπερ ἐξέπεμπον εἰσεδεξάμην.
νῦν μὲν γὰρ οὐδὲν ὄντα βαστάζω χεροῖν,
δόμων δέ σ᾽, ὦ παῖ, λαμπρὸν ἐξέπεμψ᾽ ἐγώ.
ὡς ὤφελον πάροιθεν ἐκλιπεῖν βίον,
πρὶν ἐς ξένην σε γαῖαν ἐκπέμψαι χεροῖν
κλέψασα ταῖνδε κἀνασώσασθαι φόνου,
ὅπως θανὼν ἔκεισο τῇ τόθ᾽ ἡμέρᾳ,
τύμβου πατρῴου κοινὸν εἰληχὼς μέρος.
νῦν δ᾽ ἐκτὸς οἴκων κἀπὶ γῆς ἄλλης φυγὰς
κακῶς ἀπώλου, σῆς κασιγνήτης δίχα·
κοὔτ᾽ ἐν φίλαισι χερσὶν ἡ τάλαιν᾽ ἐγὼ
λουτροῖς σ᾽ ἐκόσμησ᾽ οὔτε παμφλέκτου πυρὸς

ORESTES

If you have any tears for the woes of Orestes, know that this vessel contains his body.

ELECTRA

Stranger, I beg you, give it to me to hold, if this casket really contains him, so that I may weep and lament for myself and my whole family together with these ashes!

ORESTES

Take it and give it to her, whoever she is! She is not making this request in enmity, but she is clearly one of his friends or a relation.

ELECTRA

O remaining memorial of the life of the dearest of men to me, Orestes, how far from the hopes with which I sent you off do I receive you back! Now you are nothing, and I hold you in my hands; but you were glorious, brother, when I sent you from the house. How I wish that I had departed from life before I stole you with these hands, saving you from murder, and sent you to a foreign land, so that you could have died and lain here on that day, getting a share in your father's tomb! But now you have died miserably, far from home, an exile in another land, without your sister. And I, unhappy one, did not wash you with loving hands or take up the sad burden, as is proper, from

---

1125 τίς <ἐστιν> Fröhlich, deleto φύσιν

ἀνειλόμην, ὡς εἰκός, ἄθλιον βάρος,
ἀλλ᾽ ἐν ξένησι χερσὶ κηδευθεὶς τάλας
σμικρὸς προσήκεις ὄγκος ἐν σμικρῷ κύτει.
οἴμοι τάλαινα τῆς ἐμῆς πάλαι τροφῆς
ἀνωφελήτου, τὴν ἐγὼ θάμ᾽ ἀμφὶ σοὶ
πόνῳ γλυκεῖ παρέσχον. οὔτε γάρ ποτε
μητρὸς σύ γ᾽ ἦσθα μᾶλλον ἢ κἀμοῦ φίλος,
οὔθ᾽ οἱ κατ᾽ οἶκον ἦσαν ἀλλ᾽ ἐγὼ τροφός,
ἐγὼ δ᾽ ἀδελφὴ σοὶ προσηυδώμην ἀεί.
νῦν δ᾽ ἐκλέλοιπε πάντ᾽ ἐν ἡμέρᾳ μιᾷ
θανόντι σὺν σοί. πάντα γὰρ συναρπάσας,
θύελλ᾽ ὅπως, βέβηκας. οἴχεται πατήρ·
τέθνηκ᾽ ἐγὼ σοί· φροῦδος αὐτὸς εἶ θανών·
γελῶσι δ᾽ ἐχθροί· μαίνεται δ᾽ ὑφ᾽ ἡδονῆς
μήτηρ ἀμήτωρ, ἧς ἐμοὶ σὺ πολλάκις
φήμας λάθρᾳ προὔπεμπες ὡς φανούμενος
τιμωρὸς αὐτός. ἀλλὰ ταῦθ᾽ ὁ δυστυχὴς
δαίμων ὁ σός τε κἀμὸς ἐξαφείλετο,
ὅς σ᾽ ὧδέ μοι προὔπεμψεν ἀντὶ φιλτάτης
μορφῆς σποδόν τε καὶ σκιὰν ἀνωφελῆ.
οἴμοι μοι.
ὦ δέμας οἰκτρόν. φεῦ φεῦ.
ὦ δεινοτάτας, οἴμοι μοι,
πεμφθεὶς κελεύθους, φίλταθ᾽, ὥς μ᾽ ἀπώλεσας·
ἀπώλεσας δῆτ᾽, ὦ κασίγνητον κάρα.
τοιγὰρ σὺ δέξαι μ᾽ ἐς τὸ σὸν τόδε στέγος,
τὴν μηδὲν ἐς τὸ μηδέν, ὡς σὺν σοὶ κάτω
ναίω τὸ λοιπόν. καὶ γὰρ ἡνίκ᾽ ἦσθ᾽ ἄνω,

the blazing fire, but you were given burial, miserable one, by foreign hands, and come as a little substance in a little urn. Alas for my care for you long ago, gone for nothing, the care I often rendered, delighting in my labour! You were never your mother's more than you were mine, and the women in the house were not your nurses, but always you called me nurse and called me sister! And now all this has vanished in one day, with your death; like a whirlwind, you have gone, carrying off everything! My father is gone; you have killed me; you yourself are dead and gone. Our enemies are laughing; and our evil mother is mad with delight, she whom you often said, in secret messages, that you yourself would come and punish. But your unhappy fate and mine has taken this away, sending me instead of your dearest form ashes and a useless shadow. Alas! Pitiable corpse, alack! You who have travelled on a terrible path, dearest one, how you have destroyed me! Yes, you have destroyed me, my brother! Therefore do you receive me into this mansion of yours, receive me who am nothing into nothingness, so that in future I may

---

1149 πάντ' Greg. Cypr. (coni. Blaydes): ταῦτ' codd.

ξὺν σοὶ μετεῖχον τῶν ἴσων· καὶ νῦν ποθῶ
τοῦ σοῦ θανοῦσα μὴ ἀπολείπεσθαι τάφου.
τοὺς γὰρ θανόντας οὐχ ὁρῶ λυπουμένους.

ΧΟΡΟΣ

θνητοῦ πέφυκας πατρός, Ἠλέκτρα, φρόνει·
θνητὸς δ' Ὀρέστης· ὥστε μὴ λίαν στένε·
πᾶσιν γὰρ ἡμῖν τοῦτ' ὀφείλεται παθεῖν.

ΟΡΕΣΤΗΣ

φεῦ φεῦ, τί λέξω; ποῖ λόγων ἀμηχανῶν
ἔλθω; κρατεῖν γὰρ οὐκέτι γλώσσης σθένω.

ΗΛΕΚΤΡΑ

τί δ' ἔσχες ἄλγος; πρὸς τί τοῦτ' εἰπὼν κυρεῖς;

ΟΡΕΣΤΗΣ

ἦ σὸν τὸ κλεινὸν εἶδος Ἠλέκτρας τόδε;

ΗΛΕΚΤΡΑ

τόδ' ἔστ' ἐκεῖνο, καὶ μάλ' ἀθλίως ἔχον.

ΟΡΕΣΤΗΣ

οἴμοι ταλαίνης ἆρα τῆσδε συμφορᾶς.

ΗΛΕΚΤΡΑ

οὐ δή ποτ', ὦ ξέν', ἀμφ' ἐμοὶ στένεις τάδε;

ΟΡΕΣΤΗΣ

ὦ σῶμ' ἀτίμως κἀθέως ἐφθαρμένον.

ΗΛΕΚΤΡΑ

οὔτοι ποτ' ἄλλην ἢ 'μὲ δυσφημεῖς, ξένε.

1170 del. Zippmann
1173 = Aristophanis fr. 468, 2 K.-A. (e Polyido)

live with you below. Yes, for when you were above, I shared your fate, and now I desire to die and not to be excluded from your tomb; for I see that the dead suffer no pain.

CHORUS

You are the child of a mortal father, Electra, remember, and Orestes was mortal; so do not lament too much! This is a debt which all of us must pay.

ORESTES

Ah, ah, what can I say? Where can I go, since words fail me? I can no longer control my tongue!

ELECTRA

What is your trouble? Why do you say that?

ORESTES

Is it the illustrious person of Electra that is here?

ELECTRA

This is it, and in a sorry state.

ORESTES

Alas, then, for this miserable disaster!

ELECTRA

Surely it is not over me that you are lamenting, stranger!

ORESTES

O body dishonoured and godlessly ruined!

ELECTRA

It is none other than I that your ill-omened words describe, stranger!

ΟΡΕΣΤΗΣ

φεῦ τῆς ἀνύμφου δυσμόρου τε σῆς τροφῆς.

ΗΛΕΚΤΡΑ

τί δή ποτ', ὦ ξέν', ὧδ' ἐπισκοπῶν στένεις;

ΟΡΕΣΤΗΣ

ὅσ' οὐκ ἄρ' ᾔδη τῶν ἐμῶν ἐγὼ κακῶν.

ΗΛΕΚΤΡΑ

ἐν τῷ διέγνως τοῦτο τῶν εἰρημένων;

ΟΡΕΣΤΗΣ

ὁρῶν σε πολλοῖς ἐμπρέπουσαν ἄλγεσιν.

ΗΛΕΚΤΡΑ

καὶ μὴν ὁρᾷς γε παῦρα τῶν ἐμῶν κακῶν.

ΟΡΕΣΤΗΣ

καὶ πῶς γένοιτ' ἂν τῶνδ' ἔτ' ἐχθίω βλέπειν;

ΗΛΕΚΤΡΑ

ὁθούνεκ' εἰμὶ τοῖς φονεῦσι σύντροφος.

ΟΡΕΣΤΗΣ

τοῖς τοῦ; πόθεν τοῦτ' ἐξεσήμηνας κακόν;

ΗΛΕΚΤΡΑ

τοῖς πατρός. εἶτα τοῖσδε δουλεύω βίᾳ.

ΟΡΕΣΤΗΣ

τίς γάρ σ' ἀνάγκῃ τῇδε προστρίβει βροτῶν;

1185 ὅσ' Plüss: ὡς codd.
1193 προστρίβει Wilson: προτρέπει codd.

ELECTRA

ORESTES

Alas for your unmarried, miserable way of life!

ELECTRA

Why do you look at me like this, stranger, and lament?

ORESTES

So how few of my own sorrows I knew!

ELECTRA

What has been said to show you that?

ORESTES

My seeing that you are marked by many sorrows.

ELECTRA

Why, you can see only a few of my miseries!

ORESTES

And how could anything be more hateful to behold than this?

ELECTRA

Because I live with the murderers!

ORESTES

Whose murderers? From where comes the evil that you hint at?

ELECTRA

My father's; and then they have enslaved me by force.

ORESTES

Who is it that afflicts you with this constraint?

ΗΛΕΚΤΡΑ

μήτηρ καλεῖται· μητρὶ δ' οὐδὲν ἐξισοῖ.

ΟΡΕΣΤΗΣ

τί δρῶσα; πότερα χερσίν, ἢ λύμῃ βίου;

ΗΛΕΚΤΡΑ

καὶ χερσὶ καὶ λύμαισι καὶ πᾶσιν κακοῖς.

ΟΡΕΣΤΗΣ

οὐδ' οὑπαρήξων οὐδ' ὁ κωλύσων πάρα;

ΗΛΕΚΤΡΑ

οὐ δῆθ'· ὃς ἦν γάρ μοι σὺ προὔθηκας σποδόν.

ΟΡΕΣΤΗΣ

ὦ δύσποτμ', ὡς ὁρῶν σ' ἐποικτίρω πάλαι.

ΗΛΕΚΤΡΑ

μόνος βροτῶν νυν ἴσθ' ἐποικτίρας ποτέ.

ΟΡΕΣΤΗΣ

μόνος γὰρ ἥκω τοῖσι σοῖς ἀλγῶν κακοῖς.

ΗΛΕΚΤΡΑ

οὐ δή ποθ' ἡμῖν ξυγγενὴς ἥκεις ποθέν;

ΟΡΕΣΤΗΣ

ἐγὼ φράσαιμ' ἄν, εἰ τὸ τῶνδ' εὔνουν πάρα.

ΗΛΕΚΤΡΑ

ἀλλ' ἐστὶν εὔνουν, ὥστε πρὸς πιστὰς ἐρεῖς.

ΟΡΕΣΤΗΣ

μέθες τόδ' ἄγγος νυν, ὅπως τὸ πᾶν μάθῃς.

ELECTRA
She is called my mother, but she does nothing like a mother.

ORESTES
What does she do? Does she show violence, or does she lead you a hard life?

ELECTRA
She uses violence, and hardship, and every kind of torment.

ORESTES
And is there no one to help you or to prevent it?

ELECTRA
No! You have shown me the ashes of the one I had!

ORESTES
Unhappy one, I have long looked on you with pity!

ELECTRA
Then know that you are the only person who has pitied me.

ORESTES
Yes, I am the only one who has come and felt pain at your troubles.

ELECTRA
Surely you are not a kinsman from somewhere?

ORESTES
I would tell you, if we can trust these women's loyalty.

ELECTRA
They are loyal, so you can trust them when you speak.

ORESTES
Then let go that vessel, so that you can learn all!

ΗΛΕΚΤΡΑ

μὴ δῆτα πρὸς θεῶν τοῦτό μ᾽ ἐργάσῃ, ξένε.

ΟΡΕΣΤΗΣ

πιθοῦ λέγοντι κοὐχ ἁμαρτήσῃ ποτέ.

ΗΛΕΚΤΡΑ

μὴ πρὸς γενείου μὴ ᾽ξέλῃ τὰ φίλτατα.

ΟΡΕΣΤΗΣ

οὔ φημ᾽ ἐάσειν.

ΗΛΕΚΤΡΑ

ὢ τάλαιν᾽ ἐγὼ σέθεν,
Ὀρέστα, τῆς σῆς εἰ στερήσομαι ταφῆς.

ΟΡΕΣΤΗΣ

εὔφημα φώνει· πρὸς δίκης γὰρ οὐ στένεις.

ΗΛΕΚΤΡΑ

πῶς τὸν θανόντ᾽ ἀδελφὸν οὐ δίκῃ στένω;

ΟΡΕΣΤΗΣ

οὔ σοι προσήκει τήνδε προσφωνεῖν φάτιν.

ΗΛΕΚΤΡΑ

οὕτως ἄτιμός εἰμι τοῦ τεθνηκότος;

ΟΡΕΣΤΗΣ

ἄτιμος οὐδενὸς σύ· τοῦτο δ᾽ οὐχὶ σόν.

ΗΛΕΚΤΡΑ

εἴπερ γ᾽ Ὀρέστου σῶμα βαστάζω τόδε.

ΟΡΕΣΤΗΣ

ἀλλ᾽ οὐκ Ὀρέστου, πλὴν λόγῳ γ᾽ ἠσκημένον.

ELECTRA

Do not do that to me, I beg you, stranger!

ORESTES

Do as I say, and you will never go wrong!

ELECTRA

By your beard, do not take from me what I love most!

ORESTES

I say I will not let you keep it!

ELECTRA

I am unhappy, Orestes, if I am cheated of the power to give you burial!

ORESTES

Say nothing that is ill-omened! You have no reason to lament!

ELECTRA

How can I have no reason to lament my dead brother?

ORESTES

It is not right for you to call him that!

ELECTRA

Am I so refused honour with regard to the dead man?

ORESTES

You are refused no honour; but this does not belong to you!

ELECTRA

It does, if it is the body of Orestes that I hold here.

ORESTES

It is not Orestes, except in pretence!

ΗΛΕΚΤΡΑ

ποῦ δ' ἔστ' ἐκείνου τοῦ ταλαιπώρου τάφος;

ΟΡΕΣΤΗΣ

οὐκ ἔστι· τοῦ γὰρ ζῶντος οὐκ ἔστιν τάφος.

ΗΛΕΚΤΡΑ

πῶς εἶπας, ὦ παῖ;

ΟΡΕΣΤΗΣ

ψεῦδος οὐδὲν ὧν λέγω.

ΗΛΕΚΤΡΑ

ἦ ζῇ γὰρ ἁνήρ;

ΟΡΕΣΤΗΣ

εἴπερ ἔμψυχός γ' ἐγώ.

ΗΛΕΚΤΡΑ

ἦ γὰρ σὺ κεῖνος;

ΟΡΕΣΤΗΣ

τήνδε προσβλέψασά μου
σφραγῖδα πατρὸς ἔκμαθ' εἰ σαφῆ λέγω.

ΗΛΕΚΤΡΑ

ὦ φίλτατον φῶς.

ΟΡΕΣΤΗΣ

φίλτατον, συμμαρτυρῶ.

ΗΛΕΚΤΡΑ

ὦ φθέγμ', ἀφίκου;

ELECTRA
But where is the tomb of that unhappy one?

ORESTES
There is none; a living man does not have a tomb!

ELECTRA
What did you say, young man?

ORESTES
All that I say is true!

ELECTRA
Then is the man alive?

ORESTES
If I am living!

ELECTRA
Then are you he?

ORESTES
Look at this seal that was my father's, and learn whether I speak the truth!

ELECTRA
O dearest light!

ORESTES
Dearest, I too can witness!

ELECTRA
Voice, have you come?

ΟΡΕΣΤΗΣ

μηκέτ᾽ ἄλλοθεν πύθῃ.

ΗΛΕΚΤΡΑ

ἔχω σε χερσίν;

ΟΡΕΣΤΗΣ

ὡς τὰ λοίπ᾽ ἔχοις ἀεί.

ΗΛΕΚΤΡΑ

ὦ φίλταται γυναῖκες, ὦ πολίτιδες,
ὁρᾶτ᾽ Ὀρέστην τόνδε, μηχαναῖσι μὲν
θανόντα, νῦν δὲ μηχαναῖς σεσωμένον.

ΧΟΡΟΣ

ὁρῶμεν, ὦ παῖ, κἀπὶ συμφοραῖσί μοι
γεγηθὸς ἕρπει δάκρυον ὀμμάτων ἄπο.

ΗΛΕΚΤΡΑ

ἰὼ γοναί, στρ.
γοναὶ σωμάτων ἐμοὶ φιλτάτων,
ἐμόλετ᾽ ἀρτίως,
ἐφηύρετ᾽, ἤλθετ᾽, εἴδεθ᾽ οὓς ἐχρῄζετε.

ΟΡΕΣΤΗΣ

πάρεσμεν· ἀλλὰ σῖγ᾽ ἔχουσα πρόσμενε.

ΗΛΕΚΤΡΑ

τί δ᾽ ἔστιν;

ΟΡΕΣΤΗΣ

σιγᾶν ἄμεινον, μή τις ἔνδοθεν κλύῃ.

ELECTRA

ORESTES

Ask it of no other!

ELECTRA

Do I hold you in my arms?

ORESTES

So may you always hold me!

ELECTRA

Dearest women, fellow townswomen, you see here Orestes, dead by a stratagem, and now by a stratagem preserved!

CHORUS

We see him, daughter, and a tear of rejoicing at your fortune comes from our eyes!

ELECTRA

Dearest of bodies ever engendered, now you have come; you have found, you have arrived, you have seen those whom you desired!

ORESTES

I am here; but keep silent, and wait!

ELECTRA

What is the matter?

ORESTES

It is best to keep silent, in case anyone inside should hear.

ΗΛΕΚΤΡΑ

ἀλλ᾽ οὐ τὰν θεὰν τὰν ἀεὶ ἀδμήταν,
τόδε μὲν οὔποτ᾽ ἀξιώσω τρέσαι,
περισσὸν ἄχθος ἔνδον
γυναικῶν ὃ ναίει.

ΟΡΕΣΤΗΣ

ὅρα γε μὲν δὴ κἀν γυναιξὶν ὡς Ἄρης
ἔνεστιν· εὖ δ᾽ ἔξοισθα πειραθεῖσά που.

ΗΛΕΚΤΡΑ

ὀττοτοῖ ὀττοτοῖ,
ἀνέφελον ἐνέβαλες οὔποτε καταλύσιμον,
οὐδέ ποτε λησόμενον ἁμέτερον
οἷον ἔφυ κακόν.

ΟΡΕΣΤΗΣ

ἔξοιδα καὶ ταῦτ᾽· ἀλλ᾽ ὅταν παρουσία
φράζῃ, τότ᾽ ἔργων τῶνδε μεμνῆσθαι χρεών.

ΗΛΕΚΤΡΑ

ὁ πᾶς ἐμοί, ἀντ.
ὁ πᾶς ἂν πρέποι παρὼν ἐννέπειν
τάδε δίκᾳ χρόνος.
μόλις γὰρ ἔσχον νῦν ἐλεύθερον στόμα.

ΟΡΕΣΤΗΣ

ξύμφημι κἀγώ· τοιγαροῦν σῴζου τόδε.

ΗΛΕΚΤΡΑ

τί δρῶσα;

ELECTRA

By Artemis, her who is ever virgin, this I shall never deign to be afraid of, the women that stay inside, vainly burdening the earth!

ORESTES

But remember that women too have martial valour; and you know it well, I think, from experience.

ELECTRA

Alas, alas! You have brought to mind the nature of our sorrow, never to be veiled, never to be undone, never to forget!

ORESTES

I know that also! But when their presence prompts us, that will be the moment to recall these deeds.

ELECTRA

The whole, the whole of time could aptly by its presence justly prompt these words! Now only with difficulty have I had my lips set free!

ORESTES

I too say so! Therefore guard that freedom!

ELECTRA

By what action?

1239 ἀλλ᾽ οὐ (vel ἀλλ᾽ οὐ μὰ) codd.: οὐ Seidler : μὰ Hartung | Ἄρτεμιν] θεὰν Steinhart | ἀεὶ Arndt: αἰὲν codd.

1242 ὃ ναίει Viketos: ὃν αἰεί codd.

1246 ἐνέβαλες ΣL: ἐπ- codd.: ὑπ- Vat. gr. 40

ΟΡΕΣΤΗΣ

οὗ μή 'στι καιρὸς μὴ μακρὰν βούλου λέγειν.

ΗΛΕΚΤΡΑ

τίς ἀνταξίαν σοῦ γε πεφηνότος
μεταβάλοιτ' ἂν ὧδε σιγὰν λόγων;
ἐπεί σε νῦν ἀφράστως
ἀέλπτως τ' ἐσεῖδον.

ΟΡΕΣΤΗΣ

τότ' εἶδες, ὅτε θεοί μ' ἐπώτρυναν μολεῖν
<×–∪–×–∪–×–∪–>

ΗΛΕΚΤΡΑ

ἔφρασας ὑπερτέραν
τᾶς πάρος ἔτι χάριτος, εἴ σε θεὸς ἐπόρισεν
ἁμέτερα πρὸς μέλαθρα· δαιμόνιον
αὐτὸ τίθημ' ἐγώ.

ΟΡΕΣΤΗΣ

τὰ μέν σ' ὀκνῶ χαίρουσαν εἰργαθεῖν, τὰ δὲ
δέδοικα λίαν ἡδονῇ νικωμένην.

ΗΛΕΚΤΡΑ

ἰὼ χρόνῳ ἐπ.
μακρῷ φιλτάταν ὁδὸν ἐπαξιώ-
σας ὧδέ μοι φανῆναι,
μή τί με, πολύστονον ὧδ' ἰδὼν—

ΟΡΕΣΤΗΣ

τί μὴ ποήσω;

ORESTES

Do not wish to speak at length when it is not the moment!

ELECTRA

Who could exchange speech for a silence worthy of your appearance, since now I have looked upon you, a thing beyond thought and beyond hope?

ORESTES

You looked on me when the gods had spurred me on to come ‹................ ....›

ELECTRA

You have spoken of a grace even beyond the former grace, if a god brought you to our house; I think it the action of a god.

ORESTES

I am unwilling to restrain your joy, but I am afraid of your excessive surrender to delight.

ELECTRA

Hail, you who after long years deigned to make a journey dear to me and to appear! Seeing me thus, stricken by my sorrows, do not . . .

ORESTES

Do not do what?

1260 ἀνταξίαν Ll.-J. post Arndt: οὖν ἀξίαν LrpZr: οὖν ἂν ἀξίαν pa σοῦ γε Seidler: γε σοῦ codd.

1264 ἐπώτρυναν Reiske: ὤτρυναν codd.

1266 ἐπόρισαν Fröhlich: ἐπῶρσεν codd. plerique

1275 πολύπονον J, coni. Hermann

ΗΛΕΚΤΡΑ

μή μ' ἀποστερήσῃς
τῶν σῶν προσώπων ἡδονὰν μεθέσθαι.

ΟΡΕΣΤΗΣ

ἦ κάρτα κἂν ἄλλοισι θυμοίμην ἰδών.

ΗΛΕΚΤΡΑ

ξυναινεῖς;

ΟΡΕΣΤΗΣ

τί μὴν οὔ;

ΗΛΕΚΤΡΑ

ὦ φίλ', ἔκλυον
ἃν ἐγὼ οὐδ' ἂν ἤλπισ' αὐδάν.
<ἀλλ' ὅμως ἐπ>έσχον ὀργὰν ἄναυδον
οὐδὲ σὺν βοᾷ κλύουσ' ἁ τάλαινα.
νῦν δ' ἔχω σε· προὐφάνης δὲ
φιλτάταν ἔχων πρόσοψιν,
ἇς ἐγὼ οὐδ' ἂν ἐν κακοῖς λαθοίμαν.

ΟΡΕΣΤΗΣ

τὰ μὲν περισσεύοντα τῶν λόγων ἄφες,
καὶ μήτε μήτηρ ὡς κακὴ δίδασκέ με
μήθ' ὡς πατρῴαν κτῆσιν Αἴγισθος δόμων
ἀντλεῖ, τὰ δ' ἐκχεῖ, τὰ δὲ διασπείρει μάτην·
χρόνου γὰρ ἄν σοι καιρὸν ἐξείργοι λόγος.
ἃ δ' ἁρμόσει μοι τῷ παρόντι νῦν χρόνῳ
σήμαιν', ὅπου φανέντες ἢ κεκρυμμένοι
γελῶντας ἐχθροὺς παύσομεν τῇ νῦν ὁδῷ.

ELECTRA

Do not cheat me by making me forgo the comfort of your face!

ORESTES

Indeed I would be angry if I saw this in another!

ELECTRA

Do you consent?

ORESTES

Of course I do!

ELECTRA

Dear one, I heard a voice I never would have thought to hear; but none the less I held back my passion in silence, nor did I cry out as I listened. But now I have you; you have appeared, with your dear aspect, which I can never forget even in times of trouble.

ORESTES

Let go all superfluous words, and do not explain to me that our mother is evil, nor that Aegisthus is dissipating the wealth of our father's house by waste and aimless spending; for the recital would deprive you of the moment for action. But tell me what will suit the present time, where we must appear or where we must hide to put a stop to our enemies' laughter by our present expedi-

---

1280 μὴν Seidler: μὴ codd.
1281 φίλ' p, coni. Wunder: φίλαι cett.
1283 ex. gr. suppl. Ll.-J.
1292 ἐξείργοι] ἐξαιροῖ Hartung: ἐξαίρῃ Suda

τούτῳ δ᾽ ὅπως μήτηρ σε μὴ ᾽πιγνώσεται
φαιδρῷ προσώπῳ νῷν ἐπελθόντοιν δόμους·
ἀλλ᾽ ὡς ἐπ᾽ ἄτῃ τῇ μάτην λελεγμένῃ
στέναζ᾽· ὅταν γὰρ εὐτυχήσωμεν, τότε
χαίρειν παρέσται καὶ γελᾶν ἐλευθέρως.

ΗΛΕΚΤΡΑ

ἀλλ᾽, ὦ κασίγνηθ᾽, ὧδ᾽ ὅπως καὶ σοὶ φίλον
καὶ τοὐμὸν ἔσται, τάσδ᾽ ἐπεὶ τὰς ἡδονὰς
πρὸς σοῦ λαβοῦσα κοὐκ ἐμὰς ἐκτησάμην.
κοὐδ᾽ ἄν σε λυπήσασα δεξαίμην βραχὺ
αὐτὴ μέγ᾽ εὑρεῖν κέρδος· οὐ γὰρ ἂν καλῶς
ὑπηρετοίην τῷ παρόντι δαίμονι.
ἀλλ᾽ οἶσθα μὲν τἀνθένδε, πῶς γὰρ οὔ; κλυὼν
ὁθούνεκ᾽ Αἴγισθος μὲν οὐ κατὰ στέγας,
μήτηρ δ᾽ ἐν οἴκοις· ἣν σὺ μὴ δείσῃς ποθ᾽ ὡς
γέλωτι τοὐμὸν φαιδρὸν ὄψεται κάρα.
μῖσός τε γὰρ παλαιὸν ἐντέτηκέ μοι,
κἀπεί σ᾽ ἐσεῖδον, οὔ ποτ᾽ ἐκλήξω χαρᾷ
δακρυρροοῦσα. πῶς γὰρ ἂν λήξαιμ᾽ ἐγώ,
ἥτις μιᾷ σε τῇδ᾽ ὁδῷ θανόντα τε
καὶ ζῶντ᾽ ἐσεῖδον; εἴργασαι δέ μ᾽ ἄσκοπα·
ὥστ᾽, εἰ πατήρ μοι ζῶν ἵκοιτο, μηκέτ᾽ ἂν
τέρας νομίζειν αὐτό, πιστεύειν δ᾽ ὁρᾶν.
ὅτ᾽ οὖν τοιαύτην ἡμὶν ἐξήκεις ὁδόν,
ἄρχ᾽ αὐτὸς ὥς σοι θυμός. ὡς ἐγὼ μόνη
οὐκ ἂν δυοῖν ἥμαρτον· ἢ γὰρ ἂν καλῶς
ἔσωσ᾽ ἐμαυτήν, ἢ καλῶς ἀπωλόμην.

tion. And see to it that our mother does not learn your state from that joyous countenance when we go into the house, but lament as though the disaster falsely told of were the truth! When we are triumphant, then we shall be able to rejoice and laugh in freedom.

ELECTRA

Brother, your pleasure shall be mine also, since I got my delight from you and it is not my own; and I would not accept great gain for myself at the price of small pain to you; for that would be poor service to the god prevailing at this moment. Well, you know how things lie here, of course; you have heard that Aegisthus is not in the house, but that my mother is at home. Do not be afraid that she will ever see my face radiant with smiles; for long since hatred for her has seeped into me, and now that I have seen you, I shall never cease to weep for joy. How could I cease to do so, when on this one occasion I have seen you dead and living? Your effect on me has been amazing, so that if my father were to return alive, I should not now think it a miracle, but should believe I saw him. So since you have come to us in such a fashion, direct me yourself according to your will. For if I had been alone, I should have had one of two things; either I should have saved myself with honour, or I should have perished with honour.

1296 τούτῳ Ll.-J.: οὕτω(ς) codd.
1302 τάσδ᾽ ἐπεὶ Brunck: τῇδ᾽· ἐπεὶ codd.
1312 χαρᾷ Schaefer: χαρᾶς codd.

ΟΡΕΣΤΗΣ

σιγᾶν ἐπῄνεσ'· ὡς ἐπ' ἐξόδῳ κλύω
τῶν ἔνδοθεν χωροῦντος.

ΗΛΕΚΤΡΑ

εἴσιτ', ὦ ξένοι,
ἄλλως τε καὶ φέροντες οἷ' ἂν οὔτε τις
δόμων ἀπώσαιτ' οὔτ' ἂν ἡσθείη λαβών.

ΠΑΙΔΑΓΩΓΟΣ

ὦ πλεῖστα μῶροι καὶ φρενῶν τητώμενοι,
πότερα παρ' οὐδὲν τοῦ βίου κήδεσθ' ἔτι,
ἢ νοῦς ἔνεστιν οὔτις ὑμὶν ἐγγενής,
ὅτ' οὐ παρ' αὐτοῖς ἀλλ' ἐν αὐτοῖσιν κακοῖς
τοῖσιν μεγίστοις ὄντες οὐ γιγνώσκετε;
ἀλλ' εἰ σταθμοῖσι τοῖσδε μὴ 'κύρουν ἐγὼ
πάλαι φυλάσσων, ἦν ἂν ἡμὶν ἐν δόμοις
τὰ δρώμεν' ὑμῶν πρόσθεν ἢ τὰ σώματα·
νῦν δ' εὐλάβειαν τῶνδε προὐθέμην ἐγώ.
καὶ νῦν ἀπαλλαχθέντε τῶν μακρῶν λόγων
καὶ τῆς ἀπλήστου τῆσδε σὺν χαρᾷ βοῆς
εἴσω παρέλθεθ', ὡς τὸ μὲν μέλλειν κακὸν
ἐν τοῖς τοιούτοις ἔστ', ἀπηλλάχθαι δ' ἀκμή.

ΟΡΕΣΤΗΣ

πῶς οὖν ἔχει τἀντεῦθεν εἰσιόντι μοι;

ΠΑΙΔΑΓΩΓΟΣ

καλῶς· ὑπάρχει γάρ με μὴ γνῶναί τινα.

ORESTES

I counsel silence; for I hear at the door one of the people within is coming.

ELECTRA

Go inside, strangers, especially since you are carrying what no one would refuse to admit but what no one would be glad to have.

Enter OLD SLAVE.

OLD SLAVE

You utter fools, you senseless people, do you take no heed any longer for your lives, or have you no inborn sense, that you fail to see that you are not merely close to but are in the midst of the greatest dangers? Why, had I not been watching by these doorposts long since, your doings would have been in the house sooner than your persons! But as it is I have taken care in this matter. And now get clear of your long speeches and of the cries of joy of which you are never weary, and come, since on such occasions delay is dangerous, and it is the moment to make an end of it!

ORESTES

How then shall I find things when I go in?

OLD SLAVE

Good; we have this advantage, that no one knows me.

1322–23 (usque ad χωροῦντος) Hermann, 1322–25 Dawe choro tribuunt, uterque Σ verbis fretus

1332 ἡμὶν Blaydes: ἡμῖν p: ὑμὶν fere cett.

1340 με Doederlein: σε codd.

ΟΡΕΣΤΗΣ

ἤγγειλας, ὡς ἔοικεν, ὡς τεθνηκότα.

ΠΑΙΔΑΓΩΓΟΣ

εἷς τῶν ἐν Ἅιδου μάνθαν᾽ ἐνθάδ᾽ ὢν ἀνήρ.

ΟΡΕΣΤΗΣ

χαίρουσιν οὖν τούτοισιν; ἢ τίνες λόγοι;

ΠΑΙΔΑΓΩΓΟΣ

τελουμένων εἴποιμ᾽ ἄν· ὡς δὲ νῦν ἔχει
καλῶς τὰ κείνων πάντα, καὶ τὰ μὴ καλῶς.

ΗΛΕΚΤΡΑ

τίς οὗτός ἐστ᾽, ἀδελφέ; πρὸς θεῶν φράσον.

ΟΡΕΣΤΗΣ

οὐχὶ ξυνίης;

ΗΛΕΚΤΡΑ

οὐδέ γ᾽ ᾐσθόμην σφέ πω.

ΟΡΕΣΤΗΣ

οὐκ οἶσθ᾽ ὅτῳ μ᾽ ἔδωκας ἐς χεῖράς ποτε;

ΗΛΕΚΤΡΑ

ποίῳ; τί φωνεῖς;

ΟΡΕΣΤΗΣ

οὗ τὸ Φωκέων πέδον
ὑπεξεπέμφθην σῇ προμηθίᾳ χεροῖν.

ΗΛΕΚΤΡΑ

ἦ κεῖνος οὗτος ὅν ποτ᾽ ἐκ πολλῶν ἐγὼ
μόνον προσηῦρον πιστὸν ἐν πατρὸς φόνῳ;

ORESTES

You have reported, it seems, that I am dead.

OLD SLAVE

Know that here you are one of those in Hades.

ORESTES

Then are they pleased at that, or what are they saying?

OLD SLAVE

I will tell you when the thing is being finished; as things are, all is well with them, even what is not well.

ELECTRA

Who is this, brother? Tell me, I beg you.

ORESTES

Do you not see?

ELECTRA

I have never even seen him!

ORESTES

Do you not know the man into whose hands you once put me?

ELECTRA

What man? What are you saying?

ORESTES

The man by whose guidance I was conveyed through your foresight to the Phocian plain.

ELECTRA

Is this the one out of many whom I found loyal once when my father was murdered?

1341 ἔοικέ μ' Fröhlich: ἔοικεν codd.
1347 ᾐσθόμην σφέ πω Wilson: ἐς θυμὸν φέρω codd.

ΟΡΕΣΤΗΣ

ὅδ᾽ ἐστί. μή μ᾽ ἔλεγχε πλείοσιν λόγοις.

ΗΛΕΚΤΡΑ

ὦ φίλτατον φῶς· ὦ μόνος σωτὴρ δόμων
Ἀγαμέμνονος, πῶς ἦλθες; ἦ σὺ κεῖνος εἶ,
ὃς τόνδε κἄμ᾽ ἔσωσας ἐκ πολλῶν πόνων;
ὦ φίλταται μὲν χεῖρες, ἥδιστον δ᾽ ἔχων
ποδῶν ὑπηρέτημα, πῶς οὕτω πάλαι
ξυνών μ᾽ ἔληθες οὐδ᾽ ἔσαινες, ἀλλά με
λόγοις ἀπώλλυς, ἔργ᾽ ἔχων ἥδιστ᾽ ἐμοί;
χαῖρ᾽, ὦ πάτερ· πατέρα γὰρ εἰσορᾶν δοκῶ·
χαῖρ᾽· ἴσθι δ᾽ ὡς μάλιστά σ᾽ ἀνθρώπων ἐγὼ
ἤχθηρα κἀφίλησ᾽ ἐν ἡμέρᾳ μιᾷ.

ΠΑΙΔΑΓΩΓΟΣ

ἀρκεῖν δοκεῖ μοι· τοὺς γὰρ ἐν μέσῳ λόγους—
πολλαὶ κυκλοῦνται νύκτες ἡμέραι τ᾽ ἴσαι,
αἳ ταῦτά σοι δείξουσιν, Ἠλέκτρα, σαφῆ.
σφῷν δ᾽ ἐννέπω ᾽γὼ τοῖν παρεστώτοιν ὅτι
νῦν καιρὸς ἔρδειν· νῦν Κλυταιμήστρα μόνη·
νῦν οὔτις ἀνδρῶν ἔνδον· εἰ δ᾽ ἐφέξετον,
φροντίζεθ᾽ ὡς τούτοις τε καὶ σοφωτέροις
ἄλλοισι τούτων πλείοσιν μαχούμενοι.

1359 ἔσαινες Ll.-J.: ἔφαινες codd.
1367 ᾽γὼ Hermann: γε codd.
1368 Κλυταιμήστρα L: -μνήστρα cett.
1370–71 τούτοις . . . τούτων] ἄλλοισι καὶ σοφωτέροις τούτων παλαισταῖς ex. gr. Nauck

ELECTRA

ORESTES

This is he! Spare no more words to question me!

ELECTRA

O dearest day, O only preserver of the house of Agamemnon, how have you come? Are you he who saved him and me from many troubles? O dearest hands, O most delightful feet, how could you be so long with me without my knowing or my recognising you? But you were killing me with what you said, though what you did brought me delight. Hail, father—for I think I see a father—hail, and know that I have hated you and loved you in one day as I have no other mortal!

OLD SLAVE

I think that is enough; as for the story of the time between, many nights and many days are rolling on that shall reveal this to you, Electra, in truth. But I say to you who stand here that now is the time to act; now Clytemnestra is alone; now none of the men is inside; but if you hold back, consider that you will have to fight with these and with others more numerous and better skilled.

ΟΡΕΣΤΗΣ

οὐκ ἂν μακρῶν ἔθ᾽ ἡμὶν οὐδὲν ἂν λόγων,
Πυλάδη, τόδ᾽ εἴη τοὔργον, ἀλλ᾽ ὅσον τάχος
χωρεῖν ἔσω, πατρῷα προσκύσανθ᾽ ἕδη
θεῶν, ὅσοιπερ πρόπυλα ναίουσιν τάδε.

ΗΛΕΚΤΡΑ

ἄναξ Ἄπολλον, ἵλεως αὐτοῖν κλύε,
ἐμοῦ τε πρὸς τούτοισιν, ἥ σε πολλὰ δὴ
ἀφ᾽ ὧν ἔχοιμι λιπαρεῖ προὔστην χερί.
νῦν δ᾽, ὦ Λύκει᾽ Ἄπολλον, ἐξ οἵων ἔχω
αἰτῶ, προπίτνω, λίσσομαι, γενοῦ πρόφρων
ἡμῖν ἀρωγὸς τῶνδε τῶν βουλευμάτων
καὶ δεῖξον ἀνθρώποισι τἀπιτίμια
τῆς δυσσεβείας οἷα δωροῦνται θεοί.

ΧΟΡΟΣ

ἴδεθ᾽ ὅπου προνέμεται στρ.
τὸ δυσέριστον αἷμα φυσῶν Ἄρης.
βεβᾶσιν ἄρτι δωμάτων ὑπόστεγοι
μετάδρομοι κακῶν πανουργημάτων
ἄφυκτοι κύνες,
ὥστ᾽ οὐ μακρὰν ἔτ᾽ ἀμμενεῖ
τοὐμὸν φρενῶν ὄνειρον αἰωρούμενον.
παράγεται γὰρ ἐνέρων ἀντ.
δολιόπους ἀρωγὸς εἴσω στέγας,
ἀρχαιόπλουτα πατρὸς εἰς ἑδώλια,
νεακόνητον αἷμα χειροῖν ἔχων·
ὁ Μαίας δὲ παῖς

ORESTES

Pylades, our work requires no further long speeches, but we must go inside at once, when we have saluted the seats of my fathers' gods, all that live in this porch.

ORESTES, PYLADES and the OLD SLAVE enter the palace. ELECTRA now addresses the statue of Apollo.

ELECTRA

Lord Apollo, hear them favorably, and hear me also, me who have often stood before you in supplication, making an offering from what I had. But now, Lycian Apollo, with the things I have, I ask, I fall before you, I implore, be an active helper in this plan and show mortals with what wages the gods reward impiety!

ELECTRA follows the others into the palace.

CHORUS

See where Ares advances, breathing blood born of strife! Already they have gone beneath the house's roof, the hounds, not to be fled from, that pursue evil crimes, so that the vision of my mind shall not long wait in suspense!

For the crafty champion of the dead is entering the house, to the seat of his father with its ancient wealth, bearing a weapon newly sharpened for a deed of blood!

1380 προπίτνω A: προπιτνῶ vel προσπιτνῶ codd. plerique: προπίπτω Jebb

Ἑρμῆς σφ᾽ ἄγει δόλον σκότῳ
κρύψας πρὸς αὐτὸ τέρμα κοὐκέτ᾽ ἀμμένει.

ΗΛΕΚΤΡΑ

ὦ φίλταται γυναῖκες, ἄνδρες αὐτίκα στρ.
τελοῦσι τοὔργον· ἀλλὰ σῖγα πρόσμενε.

ΧΟΡΟΣ

πῶς δή; τί νῦν πράσσουσιν;

ΗΛΕΚΤΡΑ

ἡ μὲν ἐς τάφον
λέβητα κοσμεῖ, τὼ δ᾽ ἐφέστατον πέλας.

ΧΟΡΟΣ

σὺ δ᾽ ἐκτὸς ᾖξας πρὸς τί;

ΗΛΕΚΤΡΑ

φρουρήσουσ᾽ ὅπως
Αἴγισθος <ἡμᾶς> μὴ λάθῃ μολὼν ἔσω.

ΚΛΥΤΑΙΜΗΣΤΡΑ

αἰαῖ. ἰὼ στέγαι
φίλων ἐρῆμοι, τῶν δ᾽ ἀπολλύντων πλέαι.

ΗΛΕΚΤΡΑ

βοᾷ τις ἔνδον. οὐκ ἀκούετ᾽, ὦ φίλαι;

ΧΟΡΟΣ

ἤκουσ᾽ ἀνήκουστα δύσ-
τανος, ὥστε φρῖξαι.

ΚΛΥΤΑΙΜΗΣΤΡΑ

οἴμοι τάλαιν᾽. Αἴγισθε, ποῦ ποτ᾽ ὢν κυρεῖς;

And Maia's son, Hermes, hides the plot in darkness and brings him to the very end, nor does he delay!

ELECTRA comes out of the palace.

ELECTRA

Dearest women, the men will speedily finish the work! But wait in silence!

CHORUS

How now? What are they about?

ELECTRA

She is preparing the urn for burial, and those two are standing by her.

CHORUS

But why have you darted out?

ELECTRA

I must watch in case we should fail to see Aegisthus coming in.

From the palace comes the

voice of CLYTEMNESTRA

Alas! Ah, the house is empty of friends, but full of killers!

ELECTRA

Someone inside is crying out! Do you not hear, my friends?

CHORUS

I heard a cry dreadful to hear, that made me shudder!

voice of CLYTEMNESTRA

Ah me! Aegisthus, where are you?

1403 <ἡμᾶς> suppl. Reiske (interpretatio est in J): pro Αἴγισθος reponit Jackson ὁ θεοῖσιν ἐχθρὸς

ΗΛΕΚΤΡΑ

ἰδοὺ μάλ᾿ αὖ θροεῖ τις.

ΚΛΥΤΑΙΜΗΣΤΡΑ

ὦ τέκνον τέκνον,
οἴκτιρε τὴν τεκοῦσαν.

ΗΛΕΚΤΡΑ

ἀλλ᾿ οὐκ ἐκ σέθεν
ᾠκτίρεθ᾿ οὗτος οὐδ᾿ ὁ γεννήσας πατήρ.

ΧΟΡΟΣ

ὦ πόλις, ὦ γενεὰ τάλαινα, νῦν σοι
μοῖρα καθημερία φθίνει φθίνει.

ΚΛΥΤΑΙΜΗΣΤΡΑ

ὤμοι πέπληγμαι.

ΗΛΕΚΤΡΑ

παῖσον, εἰ σθένεις, διπλῆν.

ΚΛΥΤΑΙΜΗΣΤΡΑ

ὤμοι μάλ᾿ αὖθις.

ΗΛΕΚΤΡΑ

εἰ γὰρ Αἰγίσθῳ γ᾿ ὁμοῦ.

ΧΟΡΟΣ

τελοῦσ᾿ ἀραί· ζῶσιν οἱ
γᾶς ὑπαὶ κείμενοι.
παλίρρυτον γὰρ αἷμ᾿ ὑπεξαιροῦσι τῶν κτανόντων
οἱ πάλαι θανόντες.

ELECTRA

There, again someone is crying out!

voice of CLYTEMNESTRA

My child, my child, have pity on your mother!

ELECTRA

But you had no pity on him, nor on the father who begot him!

CHORUS

O city, O unhappy race, now the fate that was yours from day to day is dying, dying!

voice of CLYTEMNESTRA

Ah, I am struck!

ELECTRA

Strike twice as hard, if you have the strength!

voice of CLYTEMNESTRA

Ah, again!

ELECTRA

I wish it were Aegisthus too!

CHORUS

The curses are at work! Those who lie beneath the ground are living, for the blood of the killers flows in turn, drained by those who perished long ago!

1413 σοι Hermann: σε codd.
1416 γ' Hermann: θ' LRpat
1418 ὑπαὶ κείμενοι Brunck: ὑποκείμενοι codd.
1420 παλίρρυτον Bothe: πολύρρυτον codd.

καὶ μὴν πάρεισιν οἵδε· φοινία δὲ χεὶρ ἀντ.
στάζει θυηλῆς Ἄρεος, οὐδ᾽ ἔχω ψέγειν.

ΗΛΕΚΤΡΑ

Ὀρέστα, πῶς κυρεῖ τάδ᾽;

ΟΡΕΣΤΗΣ

ἐν δόμοισι μὲν
καλῶς, Ἀπόλλων εἰ καλῶς ἐθέσπισεν.

ΗΛΕΚΤΡΑ

τέθνηκεν ἡ τάλαινα;

ΟΡΕΣΤΗΣ

μηκέτ᾽ ἐκφοβοῦ
μητρῷον ὥς σε λῆμ᾽ ἀτιμάσει ποτέ.

ΗΛΕΚΤΡΑ

⟨–∪∪–∪×
×–∪–×–∪–×–∪–

ΟΡΕΣΤΗΣ

×–∪–×–∪–×–∪–⟩

ΧΟΡΟΣ

παύσασθε, λεύσσω γὰρ Αἴ-
γισθον ἐκ προδήλου.

ΟΡΕΣΤΗΣ

⟨×–∪–×–∪–×–∪–⟩

ΗΛΕΚΤΡΑ

ὦ παῖδες, οὐκ ἄψορρον;

Look, they are here! And a bloody hand drips with a sacrifice to Ares, nor can I find fault with it!

Enter ORESTES *and* PYLADES.

ELECTRA

Orestes, how is it with you?

ORESTES

In the house all is well, if Apollo prophesied well.

ELECTRA

Is the wretched woman dead?

ORESTES

Never fear that your mother's arrogance will again dishonour you!

[*Two lines of* ELECTRA'S *and one of* ORESTES' *are missing.*]

CHORUS

Cease! for I see Aegisthus in the distance!

[*A line of* ORESTES' *is missing.*]

ELECTRA

Boys, get back!

1422–23 coryphaeo tribuit Hermann, Electrae fere codd.

1424 κυρεῖ] κυρεῖτε Reisig, Elmsley | τάδ'; ἐν Kolster: τὰν codd.: δέ; τὰν Hermann

1426 τέθνηκεν ἡ τάλαινα; Electrae tribuit Erfurdt, Oresti codd.

1427 post hunc versum lacunam statuit Erfurdt, post 1429 Seidler

1430 ποῦ Hermann, qui in vv. 1430–32 personarum vices distinxit

ΟΡΕΣΤΗΣ

εἰσορᾶτε ποῦ

τὸν ἄνδρ᾿;

ΗΛΕΚΤΡΑ

ἐφ᾿ ἡμῖν οὗτος ἐκ προαστίου
χωρεῖ γεγηθὼς <–∪–×–∪–>.

ΧΟΡΟΣ

βᾶτε κατ᾿ ἀντιθύρων ὅσον τάχιστα,
νῦν, τὰ πρὶν εὖ θέμενοι, τάδ᾿ ὡς πάλιν—

ΟΡΕΣΤΗΣ

θάρσει· τελοῦμεν.

ΗΛΕΚΤΡΑ

ᾗ νοεῖς ἔπειγε νῦν.

ΟΡΕΣΤΗΣ

καὶ δὴ βέβηκα.

ΗΛΕΚΤΡΑ

τἀνθάδ᾿ ἂν μέλοιτ᾿ ἐμοί.

ΧΟΡΟΣ

δι᾿ ὠτὸς ἂν παῦρά γ᾿ ὡς
ἠπίως ἐννέπειν
πρὸς ἄνδρα τόνδε συμφέροι, λαθραῖον ὡς ὀρούσῃ
πρὸς δίκας ἀγῶνα.

1435 ᾗ. . . . .νῦν Electrae tribuit Erfurdt, Oresti codd.
1437–41 choro tribuit t, Electrae codd.

ORESTES
Where do you see the man?

ELECTRA
With a smile on his face he is coming towards us from the outskirts of the city . . .

CHORUS
Go through the inner door as fast as you can, so that you can now, having settled the earlier business, settle this also!

ORESTES
Be confident, we shall accomplish it!

ELECTRA
Hurry then to where you mean to go!

ORESTES
See, I am on my way!

ELECTRA
Leave matters here to me!

Exeunt ORESTES *and* PYLADES.

CHORUS
It would be well to utter in his ear a few gentle words, so that he may rush into the hidden ordeal Justice has ready for him.

Enter AEGISTHUS.

ΑΙΓΙΣΘΟΣ

τίς οἶδεν ὑμῶν ποῦ ποθ' οἱ Φωκῆς ξένοι,
οὕς φασ' Ὀρέστην ἡμὶν ἀγγεῖλαι βίον
λελοιπόθ' ἱππικοῖσιν ἐν ναυαγίοις;
σέ τοι, σὲ κρίνω, ναὶ σέ, τὴν ἐν τῷ πάρος
χρόνῳ θρασεῖαν· ὡς μάλιστα σοὶ μέλειν
οἶμαι, μάλιστα δ' ἂν κατειδυῖαν φράσαι.

ΗΛΕΚΤΡΑ

ἔξοιδα· πῶς γὰρ οὐχί; συμφορᾶς γὰρ ἂν
ἔξωθεν εἴην τῶν ἐμῶν γε φιλτάτων.

ΑΙΓΙΣΘΟΣ

ποῦ δῆτ' ἂν εἶεν οἱ ξένοι; δίδασκέ με.

ΗΛΕΚΤΡΑ

ἔνδον· φίλης γὰρ προξένου κατήνυσαν.

ΑΙΓΙΣΘΟΣ

ἦ καὶ θανόντ' ἤγγειλαν ὡς ἐτητύμως;

ΗΛΕΚΤΡΑ

οὔκ, ἀλλὰ κἀπέδειξαν, οὐ λόγῳ μόνον.

ΑΙΓΙΣΘΟΣ

πάρεστ' ἄρ' ἡμῖν ὥστε κἀμφανῆ μαθεῖν;

ΗΛΕΚΤΡΑ

πάρεστι δῆτα καὶ μάλ' ἄζηλος θέα.

ΑΙΓΙΣΘΟΣ

ἦ πολλὰ χαίρειν μ' εἶπας οὐκ εἰωθότως.

1445 ναὶ Reiske: καὶ codd.

AEGISTHUS

Which of you knows where are the Phocian strangers who they say have announced that Orestes has lost his life in the wreck of a chariot? You, it is you I ask, so insolent in former times, for I think you have it most at heart, and can tell me best from knowledge!

ELECTRA

I know it well, of course, for else I would be far from the calamity of those I love most.

AEGISTHUS

Then where are the strangers? Tell me!

ELECTRA

Inside; they have found a kindly hostess.

AEGISTHUS

Did they in truth announce that he was dead?

ELECTRA

No, they even proved it, not by word only.

AEGISTHUS

So can we even see with our own eyes?

ELECTRA

We can, and it is a most unenviable sight.

AEGISTHUS

Your words have given me much pleasure, not a usual thing.

ΗΛΕΚΤΡΑ

χαίροις ἄν, εἴ σοι χαρτὰ τυγχάνει τάδε.

ΑΙΓΙΣΘΟΣ

οἴγειν πύλας ἄνωγα κἀναδεικνύναι
πᾶσιν Μυκηναίοισιν Ἀργείοις θ' ὁρᾶν,
ὡς εἴ τις αὐτῶν ἐλπίσιν κεναῖς πάρος
ἐξῄρετ' ἀνδρὸς τοῦδε, νῦν ὁρῶν νεκρὸν
στόμια δέχηται τἀμά, μηδὲ πρὸς βίαν
ἐμοῦ κολαστοῦ προστυχὼν φύσῃ φρένας.

ΗΛΕΚΤΡΑ

καὶ δὴ τελεῖται τἀπ' ἐμοῦ· τῷ γὰρ χρόνῳ
νοῦν ἔσχον, ὥστε συμφέρειν τοῖς κρείσσοσιν.

ΑΙΓΙΣΘΟΣ

ὦ Ζεῦ, δέδορκα φάσμ' ἄνευ φθόνου μὲν οὐ
πεπτωκός· εἰ δ' ἔπεστι νέμεσις οὐ λέγω.
χαλᾶτε πᾶν κάλυμμ' ἀπ' ὀφθαλμῶν, ὅπως
τὸ συγγενές τοι κἀπ' ἐμοῦ θρήνων τύχῃ.

ΟΡΕΣΤΗΣ

αὐτὸς σὺ βάσταζ'. οὐκ ἐμὸν τόδ', ἀλλὰ σόν,
τὸ ταῦθ' ὁρᾶν τε καὶ προσηγορεῖν φίλως.

ΑΙΓΙΣΘΟΣ

ἀλλ' εὖ παραινεῖς, κἀπιπείσομαι· σὺ δέ,
εἴ που κατ' οἶκον ἡ Κλυταιμήστρα, κάλει.

1458 v. sic restituit Wilamowitz (*οἴγειν* iam Wecklein): *σιγᾶν ἄνωγα κἀναδεικνύναι πύλας* fere codd.

ELECTRA

You may feel pleasure, if this truly pleases you.

AEGISTHUS

I tell you to open the doors and to reveal the sight to all the Mycenaeans and the Argives, so that if anyone was previously buoyed up by vain hopes centered on this man, he may now see him a corpse and accept my bridle, and not need violent chastisement from me to teach him sense.

ELECTRA

See, what is required from me is being accomplished! In time I have learned sense, so as to be in accord with those more powerful.

The doors of the palace are opened, and a covered bier is visible inside, with ORESTES *and* PYLADES *standing beside it.*

AEGISTHUS

O Zeus, I see a vision that has fallen not without the envy of the gods; if righteous anger too attends it, I do not say! Remove every covering from the eyes, so that I too can lament for my relation!

ORESTES

Handle it yourself! It is not mine, but yours to look on this and to speak loving words!

AEGISTHUS

Your advice is good, and I shall take it; but do you call Clytemnestra, if she is in the house!

1473 ἥ t: μοι Lpa: om. GR | Κλυταιμήστρα Lpc: -μνήστρα fere cett., fort. ex. gr. ἔστιν ἡ δάμαρ

ΟΡΕΣΤΗΣ

αὕτη πέλας σοῦ· μηκέτ' ἄλλοσε σκόπει.

ΑΙΓΙΣΘΟΣ

οἴμοι, τί λεύσσω;

ΟΡΕΣΤΗΣ

τίνα φοβῇ; τίν' ἀγνοεῖς;

ΑΙΓΙΣΘΟΣ

τίνων ποτ' ἀνδρῶν ἐν μέσοις ἀρκυστάτοις
πέπτωχ' ὁ τλήμων;

ΟΡΕΣΤΗΣ

οὐ γὰρ αἰσθάνῃ πάλαι
ζῶν τοῖς θανοῦσιν οὕνεκ' ἀνταυδᾷς ἴσα;

ΑΙΓΙΣΘΟΣ

οἴμοι, ξυνῆκα τοὔπος· οὐ γὰρ ἔσθ' ὅπως
ὅδ' οὐκ Ὀρέστης ἔσθ' ὁ προσφωνῶν ἐμέ.

ΟΡΕΣΤΗΣ

καὶ μάντις ὢν ἄριστος ἐσφάλλου πάλαι;

ΑΙΓΙΣΘΟΣ

ὄλωλα δὴ δείλαιος. ἀλλά μοι πάρες
κἂν σμικρὸν εἰπεῖν.

ΗΛΕΚΤΡΑ

μὴ πέρα λέγειν ἔα,
πρὸς θεῶν, ἀδελφέ, μηδὲ μηκύνειν λόγους.
[τί γὰρ βροτῶν ἂν σὺν κακοῖς μεμειγμένων
θνῄσκειν ὁ μέλλων τοῦ χρόνου κέρδος φέροι;]
ἀλλ' ὡς τάχιστα κτεῖνε καὶ κτανὼν πρόθες

ORESTES

She is here near you; cease to look elsewhere!

AEGISTHUS lifts the covering.

AEGISTHUS

Ah, what do I see?

ORESTES

Whom are you afraid of? Whom do you not recognize?

AEGISTHUS

Who are the men into whose trap I have fallen, unluckily?

ORESTES

Do you not see that for some time you, still living, have been bandying words with the dead?

AEGISTHUS

Alas, I understand your words! It must be that this is Orestes who is speaking to me!

ORESTES

Are you so good at guessing, and have you been deceived so long?

AEGISTHUS

Disaster, I am lost! But let me speak one brief word!

ELECTRA

Let him say no more, I beg you, brother; allow no long speech! [For when mortals are involved in ruin, what does the man whose death is delayed gain by the time?] No, kill him at once and then set him before those who

---

1485–86 om. L[ac] (sed praebet L), del. Dindorf

ταφεῦσιν ὧν τόνδ' εἰκός ἐστι τυγχάνειν,
ἄποπτον ἡμῶν. ὡς ἐμοὶ τόδ' ἂν κακῶν
μόνον γένοιτο τῶν πάλαι λυτήριον.

ΟΡΕΣΤΗΣ

χωροῖς ἂν εἴσω σὺν τάχει· λόγων γὰρ οὐ
νῦν ἐστιν ἁγών, ἀλλὰ σῆς ψυχῆς πέρι.

ΑΙΓΙΣΘΟΣ

τί δ' ἐς δόμους ἄγεις με; πῶς, τόδ' εἰ καλὸν
τοὔργον, σκότου δεῖ, κοὐ πρόχειρος εἶ κτανεῖν;

ΟΡΕΣΤΗΣ

μὴ τάσσε· χώρει δ' ἔνθαπερ κατέκτανες
πατέρα τὸν ἁμόν, ὡς ἂν ἐν ταὐτῷ θάνῃς.

ΑΙΓΙΣΘΟΣ

ἦ πᾶσ' ἀνάγκη τήνδε τὴν στέγην ἰδεῖν
τά τ' ὄντα καὶ μέλλοντα Πελοπιδῶν κακά;

ΟΡΕΣΤΗΣ

τὰ γοῦν σ'· ἐγώ σοι μάντις εἰμὶ τῶνδ' ἄκρος.

ΑΙΓΙΣΘΟΣ

ἀλλ' οὐ πατρῴαν τὴν τέχνην ἐκόμπασας.

ΟΡΕΣΤΗΣ

πόλλ' ἀντιφωνεῖς, ἡ δ' ὁδὸς βραδύνεται.
ἀλλ' ἕρφ'.

ΑΙΓΙΣΘΟΣ

ὑφηγοῦ.

ΟΡΕΣΤΗΣ

σοὶ βαδιστέον πάρος.

should properly give him burial, out of our sight, since for me this would be the only release from ancient woes!

ORESTES

Go inside at once! It is not talk, but your life, that is the issue.

AEGISTHUS

Why do you force me into the house? If this act is honourable, why must it be in darkness, and why are you not ready to kill me?

ORESTES

Give me no orders! Go to where you killed my father, so that you may die in the same place!

AEGISTHUS

Is it needful that this house should witness the present and the future woes of the Pelopids?

ORESTES

It shall witness yours, at least; I am a good prophet in this matter.

AEGISTHUS

Why, your father lacked the skill you boast of!

ORESTES

You utter long replies, and the going is delayed! Go!

AEGISTHUS

Lead the way!

ORESTES

You must go first!

1497 πάντ' West

ΑΙΓΙΣΘΟΣ

ἦ μὴ φύγω σε;

ΟΡΕΣΤΗΣ

μὴ μὲν οὖν καθ' ἡδονὴν
θάνῃς· φυλάξαι δεῖ με τοῦτό σοι πικρόν.
χρῆν δ' εὐθὺς εἶναι τήνδε τοῖς πᾶσιν δίκην,
ὅστις πέρα πράσσειν γε τῶν νόμων θέλοι,
κτείνειν· τὸ γὰρ πανοῦργον οὐκ ἂν ἦν πολύ.

ΧΟΡΟΣ

ὦ σπέρμ' Ἀτρέως, ὡς πολλὰ παθὸν
δι' ἐλευθερίας μόλις ἐξῆλθες
τῇ νῦν ὁρμῇ τελεωθέν.

1505–7 del. Dindorf
1508–10 del. Ritter

AEGISTHUS

In case I should escape?

ORESTES

No, in case you should die where you please; I have to see that this tastes bitter for you. This punishment should come at once to all who would act outside the laws—death. Then crime would not abound!

Exit AEGISTHUS, *followed by* ORESTES *and* PYLADES.

CHORUS

Seed of Atreus, after many sufferings you have at last emerged in freedom, made complete by this day's enterprise!

OEDIPUS TYRANNUS

ΤΑ ΤΟΥ ΔΡΑΜΑΤΟΣ ΠΡΟΣΩΠΑ

Οἰδίπους
Ἱερεύς
Κρέων
Χορὸς γερόντων Θηβαίων
Τειρεσίας
Ἰοκάστη
Ἄγγελος
Θεράπων Λαΐου
Ἐξάγγελος

DRAMATIS PERSONAE

Oedipus
Priest
Creon
Chorus of Theban elders
Tiresias
Iocaste
Messenger
Shepherd
Second messenger

MUTES

Children
Daughters of Oedipus

Scene: In front of the palace at Thebes.
Time: Some two generations before the Trojan War.

ΟΙΔΙΠΟΥΣ ΤΥΡΑΝΝΟΣ

ΟΙΔΙΠΟΥΣ

Ὦ τέκνα, Κάδμου τοῦ πάλαι νέα τροφή,
τίνας ποθ᾽ ἕδρας τάσδε μοι θοάζετε
ἱκτηρίοις κλάδοισιν ἐξεστεμμένοι;
πόλις δ᾽ ὁμοῦ μὲν θυμιαμάτων γέμει,
ὁμοῦ δὲ παιάνων τε καὶ στεναγμάτων·
ἁγὼ δικαιῶν μὴ παρ᾽ ἀγγέλων, τέκνα,
ἄλλων ἀκούειν αὐτὸς ὧδ᾽ ἐλήλυθα,
ὁ πᾶσι κλεινὸς Οἰδίπους καλούμενος.
ἀλλ᾽, ὦ γεραιέ, φράζ᾽, ἐπεὶ πρέπων ἔφυς
πρὸ τῶνδε φωνεῖν, τίνι τρόπῳ καθέστατε,
δείσαντες ἢ στέρξαντες; ὡς θέλοντος ἂν
ἐμοῦ προσαρκεῖν πᾶν· δυσάλγητος γὰρ ἂν
εἴην τοιάνδε μὴ οὐ κατοικτίρων ἕδραν.

ΙΕΡΕΥΣ

ἀλλ᾽, ὦ κρατύνων Οἰδίπους χώρας ἐμῆς,
ὁρᾷς μὲν ἡμᾶς ἡλίκοι προσήμεθα
βωμοῖσι τοῖς σοῖς, οἱ μὲν οὐδέπω μακρὰν
πτέσθαι σθένοντες, οἱ δὲ σὺν γήρᾳ βαρεῖς·
ἱερεὺς ἐγὼ μὲν Ζηνός, οἵδε τ᾽ ᾐθέων
λεκτοί· τὸ δ᾽ ἄλλο φῦλον ἐξεστεμμένον

8 fort. om. Π 7: del. Wunder   11 στέργοντες Dawe

OEDIPUS TYRANNUS

A crowd consisting of the priest of Zeus and a number of children is sitting as suppliants before the altars in front of the palace of Oedipus; Oedipus comes out of the palace and addresses them.

OEDIPUS

Children, latest to be reared from the stock of Cadmus, why do you sit like this before me, with boughs of supplication wreathed with chaplets? and why is the city filled at the same time with incense, and with the sound of paeans and lamentations? Thinking it wrong to hear this from the report of others, my children, I have come myself, I who am called Oedipus, renowned to all.

Come, aged man, tell me, since it is fitting you should speak for these, what is your state, one of fear or one of longing? Know that I am willing to render every kind of aid; I would be hard of heart if I felt no pity at such a supplication.

PRIEST

Why, Oedipus, ruler of my land, you see the ages of us who are seated at your altars, some not yet able to fly far, others weighed down with age. I am the priest of Zeus, and these are chosen from the unmarried young; the

---

18 ἱερεύς Bentley: -εῖς codd.

ἀγοραῖσι θακεῖ, πρός τε Παλλάδος διπλοῖς
ναοῖς, ἐπ᾽ Ἰσμηνοῦ τε μαντείᾳ σποδῷ.
πόλις γάρ, ὥσπερ καὐτὸς εἰσορᾷς, ἄγαν
ἤδη σαλεύει κἀνακουφίσαι κάρα
βυθῶν ἔτ᾽ οὐχ οἵα τε φοινίου σάλου,
φθίνουσα μὲν κάλυξιν ἐγκάρποις χθονός,
φθίνουσα δ᾽ ἀγέλαις βουνόμοις, τόκοισί τε
ἀγόνοις γυναικῶν· ἐν δ᾽ ὁ πυρφόρος θεὸς
σκήψας ἐλαύνει, λοιμὸς ἔχθιστος, πόλιν,
ὑφ᾽ οὗ κενοῦται δῶμα Καδμεῖον· μέλας δ᾽
Ἅιδης στεναγμοῖς καὶ γόοις πλουτίζεται.
θεοῖσι μέν νυν οὐκ ἰσούμενόν σ᾽ ἐγὼ
οὐδ᾽ οἵδε παῖδες ἑζόμεσθ᾽ ἐφέστιοι,
ἀνδρῶν δὲ πρῶτον ἔν τε συμφοραῖς βίου
κρίνοντες ἔν τε δαιμόνων συναλλαγαῖς·
ὅς γ᾽ ἐξέλυσας ἄστυ Καδμεῖον μολὼν
σκληρᾶς ἀοιδοῦ δασμὸν ὃν παρείχομεν,
καὶ ταῦθ᾽ ὑφ᾽ ἡμῶν οὐδὲν ἐξειδὼς πλέον
οὐδ᾽ ἐκδιδαχθείς, ἀλλὰ προσθήκῃ θεοῦ
λέγῃ νομίζῃ θ᾽ ἡμὶν ὀρθῶσαι βίον.
νῦν δ᾽, ὦ κράτιστον πᾶσιν Οἰδίπου κάρα,
ἱκετεύομέν σε πάντες οἵδε πρόστροποι
ἀλκήν τιν᾽ εὑρεῖν ἡμίν, εἴτε του θεῶν
φήμην ἀκούσας εἴτ᾽ ἀπ᾽ ἀνδρὸς οἶσθά που·
ὡς τοῖσιν ἐμπείροισι καὶ τὰς ξυμφορὰς
ζώσας ὁρῶ μάλιστα τῶν βουλευμάτων.
ἴθ᾽, ὦ βροτῶν ἄριστ᾽, ἀνόρθωσον πόλιν·
ἴθ᾽, εὐλαβήθηθ᾽· ὡς σὲ νῦν μὲν ἥδε γῆ

other crowd that carries chaplets is seated in the marketplace, near the two temples of Pallas and the prophetic ashes of Ismenus. For the city, as you see yourself, is grievously tossed by storms, and still cannot lift its head from beneath the depths of the killing angry sea. A blight is on the buds that enclose the fruit, a blight is on the flocks of grazing cattle and on the women giving birth, killing their offspring; the fire-bearing god, hateful Pestilence, has swooped upon the city and harries it, emptying the house of Cadmus, and black Hades is a plutocrat in groans and weeping.[a]

It is not because we rank you with the gods that I and these children are seated at your hearth, but because we judge you to be the first of men, both in the incidents of life and in dealing with the higher powers. For it was you who came to the city of Cadmus and released us from the tribute we were paying, the tribute of the cruel singer;[b] and that with no special knowledge or instruction from us; no, it is by the extra strength given by a god that you are said and believed to have set right our life.

But now, Oedipus, mightiest man in the sight of all, all we suppliants implore you to find some protection for us, whether your knowledge comes from hearing a message from a god or from a man, perhaps; for I see that the setting together of counsels is most effective for those who have experience. Come, best of living men, raise up the city! Come, take care! For now this land calls you its

[a] 'Pluto,' one of the names of Hades, is derived from the word for 'wealth'; hence this grim pun. [b] The Sphinx.

---

21 ἐφ' Ἰσμηνοῦ Dawe dubitanter
31 ἰσούμενον] -ος Stanley

σωτῆρα κλῄζει τῆς πάρος προθυμίας,
ἀρχῆς δὲ τῆς σῆς μηδαμῶς μεμνῄμεθα
στάντες τ᾽ ἐς ὀρθὸν καὶ πεσόντες ὕστερον,
ἀλλ᾽ ἀσφαλείᾳ τήνδ᾽ ἀνόρθωσον πόλιν.
ὄρνιθι γὰρ καὶ τὴν τότ᾽ αἰσίῳ τύχην
παρέσχες ἡμῖν, καὶ τανῦν ἴσος γενοῦ.
ὡς εἴπερ ἄρξεις τῆσδε γῆς, ὥσπερ κρατεῖς,
ξὺν ἀνδράσιν κάλλιον ἢ κενῆς κρατεῖν·
ὡς οὐδέν ἐστιν οὔτε πύργος οὔτε ναῦς
ἐρῆμος ἀνδρῶν μὴ ξυνοικούντων ἔσω.

ΟΙΔΙΠΟΥΣ

ὦ παῖδες οἰκτροί, γνωτὰ κοὐκ ἄγνωτά μοι
προσήλθεθ᾽ ἱμείροντες, εὖ γὰρ οἶδ᾽ ὅτι
νοσεῖτε πάντες· καὶ νοσοῦντες, ὡς ἐγὼ
οὐκ ἔστιν ὑμῶν ὅστις ἐξ ἴσου νοσεῖ.
τὸ μὲν γὰρ ὑμῶν ἄλγος εἰς ἕν᾽ ἔρχεται
μόνον καθ᾽ αὑτόν, κοὐδέν᾽ ἄλλον, ἡ δ᾽ ἐμὴ
ψυχὴ πόλιν τε κἀμὲ καὶ σ᾽ ὁμοῦ στένει.
ὥστ᾽ οὐχ ὕπνῳ γ᾽ εὕδοντά μ᾽ ἐξεγείρετε,
ἀλλ᾽ ἴστε πολλὰ μέν με δακρύσαντα δή,
πολλὰς δ᾽ ὁδοὺς ἐλθόντα φροντίδος πλάνοις.
ἣν δ᾽ εὖ σκοπῶν ηὕρισκον ἴασιν μόνην,
ταύτην ἔπραξα· παῖδα γὰρ Μενοικέως
Κρέοντ᾽, ἐμαυτοῦ γαμβρόν, ἐς τὰ Πυθικὰ
ἔπεμψα Φοίβου δώμαθ᾽, ὡς πύθοιθ᾽ ὅ τι
δρῶν ἢ τί φωνῶν τήνδ᾽ ἐρυσαίμην πόλιν.
καί μ᾽ ἦμαρ ἤδη ξυμμετρούμενον χρόνῳ

preserver on account of the energy you showed before; and let it not be our memory of your reign that we were stood up straight at first only to fall later; no, raise up the city so that it does not fall! The good fortune you gave us before came with a favourable omen; be the same now! For if you are to continue ruling, as you govern now, better rule a land that has men than one that is empty, since a wall or a ship is nothing without men who live inside it.

OEDIPUS

Children, I pity you! I know, I am not ignorant of the desires with which you have come; yes, I know that you are all sick, and, sick as you are, none of you is as sick as I. Your pain comes upon each by himself and upon no other; but my soul mourns equally for the city and for myself and for you. And so you are not waking me from sleep, but know that I have shed many a tear, and have travelled many roads in the wanderings of reflection. The one remedy which, by careful thought, I have found I have applied; I have sent Creon, son of Menoeceus, my wife's brother, to the Pythian halls of Phoebus, so that he may learn by what deed or word I may protect this city. Already, when I compute the passage of the days, I am

---

49 *μεμνήμεθα* Herwerden, Nauck: -*ήμεθα* p: -*ώμεθα* Lra
54–57 del. van Deventer, 56–57 Reeve
65 *ἐνδόντα* Badham post Reiske

λυπεῖ τί πράσσει· τοῦ γὰρ εἰκότος πέρα
ἄπεστι, πλείω τοῦ καθήκοντος χρόνου.
ὅταν δ' ἵκηται, τηνικαῦτ' ἐγὼ κακὸς
μὴ δρῶν ἂν εἴην πάνθ' ὅσ' ἂν δηλοῖ θεός.

ΙΕΡΕΥΣ

ἀλλ' ἐς καλὸν σύ τ' εἶπας, οἵδε τ' ἀρτίως
Κρέοντα προσστείχοντα σημαίνουσί μοι.

ΟΙΔΙΠΟΥΣ

ὦναξ Ἄπολλον, εἰ γὰρ ἐν τύχῃ γέ τῳ
σωτῆρι βαίη λαμπρὸς ὥσπερ ὄμμα τι.

ΙΕΡΕΥΣ

ἀλλ' εἰκάσαι μέν, ἡδύς· οὐ γὰρ ἂν κάρα
πολυστεφὴς ὧδ' εἷρπε παγκάρπου δάφνης.

ΟΙΔΙΠΟΥΣ

τάχ' εἰσόμεσθα· ξύμμετρος γὰρ ὡς κλύειν.
ἄναξ, ἐμὸν κήδευμα, παῖ Μενοικέως,
τίν' ἡμὶν ἥκεις τοῦ θεοῦ φήμην φέρων;

ΚΡΕΩΝ

ἐσθλήν· λέγω γὰρ καὶ τὰ δύσφορ', εἰ τύχοι
κατ' ὀρθὸν ἐξιόντα, πάντ' ἂν εὐτυχεῖν.

ΟΙΔΙΠΟΥΣ

ἔστιν δὲ ποῖον τοὔπος; οὔτε γὰρ θρασὺς
οὔτ' οὖν προδείσας εἰμὶ τῷ γε νῦν λόγῳ.

79 προσστείχοντα R, coni. Erfurdt: προστ- cett.
81 λαμπρὸς] φαιδρὸς Nauck ὄμμα τι Wex: ὄμματι codd.

troubled, wondering how he fares; for he has been away longer than is natural, beyond the proper time. But when he comes, then I shall be a wretch if I fail to take any action that the god may indicate.

PRIEST

Why, you speak opportunely! These men are just signalling to me that Creon is approaching.

OEDIPUS

Lord Apollo, may he come radiant with preserving fortune, like a bright eye!

PRIEST

At a guess, he brings comfort; for else he would not be coming with a head crowned with luxuriant bay leaves.

OEDIPUS

We shall soon know, for he is close enough to hear. Lord, kinsman, son of Menoeceus, what word of the god have you come to bring us?

Enter CREON.

CREON

One that is good; I say that even troubles hard to bear, if they chance to turn out well, can bring good fortune.

OEDIPUS

But what is the message? What you are now saying makes me neither confident nor apprehensive.

ΚΡΕΩΝ

εἰ τῶνδε χρῄζεις πλησιαζόντων κλύειν,
ἑτοῖμος εἰπεῖν, εἴτε καὶ στείχειν ἔσω.

ΟΙΔΙΠΟΥΣ

ἐς πάντας αὔδα. τῶνδε γὰρ πλέον φέρω
τὸ πένθος ἢ καὶ τῆς ἐμῆς ψυχῆς πέρι.

ΚΡΕΩΝ

λέγοιμ᾽ ἂν οἷ᾽ ἤκουσα τοῦ θεοῦ πάρα.
ἄνωγεν ἡμᾶς Φοῖβος ἐμφανῶς, ἄναξ,
μίασμα χώρας, ὡς τεθραμμένον χθονὶ
ἐν τῇδ᾽, ἐλαύνειν μηδ᾽ ἀνήκεστον τρέφειν.

ΟΙΔΙΠΟΥΣ

ποίῳ καθαρμῷ; τίς ὁ τρόπος τῆς ξυμφορᾶς;

ΚΡΕΩΝ

ἀνδρηλατοῦντας, ἢ φόνῳ φόνον πάλιν
λύοντας, ὡς τόδ᾽ αἷμα χειμάζον πόλιν.

ΟΙΔΙΠΟΥΣ

ποίου γὰρ ἀνδρὸς τήνδε μηνύει τύχην;

ΚΡΕΩΝ

ἦν ἡμίν, ὦναξ, Λάιός ποθ᾽ ἡγεμὼν
γῆς τῆσδε, πρὶν σὲ τήνδ᾽ ἀπευθύνειν πόλιν.

ΟΙΔΙΠΟΥΣ

ἔξοιδ᾽ ἀκούων· οὐ γὰρ εἰσεῖδόν γέ πω.

ΚΡΕΩΝ

τούτου θανόντος νῦν ἐπιστέλλει σαφῶς
τοὺς αὐτοέντας χειρὶ τιμωρεῖν τινας.

CREON

If you wish to hear in these people's presence, I am ready to speak, or else to go inside.

OEDIPUS

Speak out to all! I lament more for these people than for my own life.

CREON

I will tell you what I heard from the god. The lord Phoebus orders us plainly to drive out from the land a pollution, one that has been nourished in this country, and not to nourish it till it cannot be cured.

OEDIPUS

With what means of purifying? what is the nature of the trouble?

CREON

By banishment, or by repaying killing with killing, since it is this bloodshed that has brought the storm upon the city.

OEDIPUS

And who is the man whose fate he is revealing?

CREON

King, Laius was once lord of this land, before you guided it.

OEDIPUS

I know from hearsay, for I never saw him.

CREON

He was killed, and the god now tells us plainly to punish his killers, whoever they may be.

---

107 τινας fere codd.: τινα Apc, Suda

ΟΙΔΙΠΟΥΣ

οἱ δ' εἰσὶ ποῦ γῆς; ποῦ τόδ' εὑρεθήσεται
ἴχνος παλαιᾶς δυστέκμαρτον αἰτίας;

ΚΡΕΩΝ

ἐν τῇδ' ἔφασκε γῇ. τὸ δὲ ζητούμενον
ἁλωτόν, ἐκφεύγει δὲ τἀμελούμενον.

ΟΙΔΙΠΟΥΣ

πότερα δ' ἐν οἴκοις, ἢ 'ν ἀγροῖς ὁ Λάιος
ἢ γῆς ἐπ' ἄλλης τῷδε συμπίπτει φόνῳ;

ΚΡΕΩΝ

θεωρός, ὡς ἔφασκεν, ἐκδημῶν πάλιν
πρὸς οἶκον οὐκέθ' ἵκεθ', ὡς ἀπεστάλη.

ΟΙΔΙΠΟΥΣ

οὐδ' ἄγγελός τις οὐδὲ συμπράκτωρ ὁδοῦ
κατεῖδ', ὅτου τις ἐκμαθὼν ἐχρήσατ' ἄν;

ΚΡΕΩΝ

θνῄσκουσι γάρ, πλὴν εἷς τις, ὃς φόβῳ φυγὼν
ὧν εἶδε πλὴν ἓν οὐδὲν εἶχ' εἰδὼς φράσαι.

ΟΙΔΙΠΟΥΣ

τὸ ποῖον; ἓν γὰρ πόλλ' ἂν ἐξεύροις μαθών,
ἀρχὴν βραχεῖαν εἰ λάβοις προθυμίας.

OEDIPUS

Where in the world are they? Where shall the track of an ancient guilt, hard to make out, be found?

CREON

He said, in this country. What one looks for can be caught, but what one neglects escapes.

OEDIPUS

Was it in the house, or in the fields, or in another country that Laius met this bloody end?

CREON

He left to go to Delphi, as he said, and never returned home from his journey.

OEDIPUS

Was the deed seen by no reporter, or companion of his journey, whose information one might have used?

CREON

No, they were all killed, except one, who ran away in terror and could tell nothing of what he saw for certain, except one thing.

OEDIPUS

One discovery might lead to many, when a little energy has given a start.

---

111 *ἐκφεύγει*] *-ειν* Valckenaer

114 *ἔφασκεν*] *-ον* Kousis

120 *ἐξεύροις μαθών* Ll.-J.: *ἐξεύροι μαθεῖν* codd. |]*υροι μαθ*[Π 7

121 *εἰ λάβοις προθυμίας* Ll.-J.: *λάβοιμεν ἐλπίδος* codd.:]..*μ*.[ita praebet Π 7 ut potius *υμ*∪– quam *οιμ*×–∪– habuisse videatur: *λάβοι τις ἐλπίδος* Herwerden

ΚΡΕΩΝ

λῃστὰς ἔφασκε συντυχόντας οὐ μιᾷ
ῥώμῃ κτανεῖν νιν, ἀλλὰ σὺν πλήθει χερῶν.

ΟΙΔΙΠΟΥΣ

πῶς οὖν ὁ λῃστής, εἴ τι μὴ ξὺν ἀργύρῳ
ἐπράσσετ᾿ ἐνθένδ᾿, ἐς τόδ᾿ ἂν τόλμης ἔβη;

ΚΡΕΩΝ

δοκοῦντα ταῦτ᾿ ἦν· Λαΐου δ᾿ ὀλωλότος
οὐδεὶς ἀρωγὸς ἐν κακοῖς ἐγίγνετο.

ΟΙΔΙΠΟΥΣ

κακὸν δὲ ποῖον ἐμποδὼν τυραννίδος
οὕτω πεσούσης εἶργε τοῦτ᾿ ἐξειδέναι;

ΚΡΕΩΝ

ἡ ποικιλῳδὸς Σφὶγξ τὸ πρὸς ποσὶ σκοπεῖν
μεθέντας ἡμᾶς τἀφανῆ προσήγετο.

ΟΙΔΙΠΟΥΣ

ἀλλ᾿ ἐξ ὑπαρχῆς αὖθις αὔτ᾿ ἐγὼ φανῶ.
ἐπαξίως γὰρ Φοῖβος, ἀξίως δὲ σὺ
πρὸ τοῦ θανόντος τήνδ᾿ ἔθεσθ᾿ ἐπιστροφήν·
ὥστ᾿ ἐνδίκως ὄψεσθε κἀμὲ σύμμαχον,
γῇ τῇδε τιμωροῦντα τῷ θεῷ θ᾿ ἅμα.
ὑπὲρ γὰρ οὐχὶ τῶν ἀπωτέρω φίλων
ἀλλ᾿ αὐτὸς αὑτοῦ τοῦτ᾿ ἀποσκεδῶ μύσος.
ὅστις γὰρ ἦν ἐκεῖνον ὁ κτανὼν τάχ᾿ ἂν
κἄμ᾿ ἂν τοιαύτῃ χειρὶ τιμωρεῖν θέλοι.
κείνῳ προσαρκῶν οὖν ἐμαυτὸν ὠφελῶ.

CREON

He said that robbers encountered them and killed him; he died not through one man's strength, but by the hands of many.

OEDIPUS

But how could the robber have reached this pitch of daring, unless there had been some payment of money from here?

CREON

That is what people thought; but after Laius' death no one came to help us in our trouble.

OEDIPUS

But when the throne had met with this disaster, what trouble prevented you from knowing all?

CREON

The Sphinx with her riddling song forced us to let go what was obscure and attend to what lay before our feet.

OEDIPUS

Well, I shall begin again and light up the obscurity. Phoebus is right, and you are right, to show this concern on behalf of the dead man, so that you shall see me also justly fighting for him, and defending the cause of this country and of the god. For it will not be on behalf of a distant friend, but for my own sake, that I shall drive away this pollution; whoever killed him may well wish to turn the same violence against me, so that in defending him I am helping myself.

ἀλλ᾽ ὡς τάχιστα, παῖδες, ὑμεῖς μὲν βάθρων
ἵστασθε, τούσδ᾽ ἄραντες ἱκτῆρας κλάδους,
ἄλλος δὲ Κάδμου λαὸν ὧδ᾽ ἀθροιζέτω,
ὡς πᾶν ἐμοῦ δράσοντος. ἢ γὰρ εὐτυχεῖς
σὺν τῷ θεῷ φανούμεθ᾽, ἢ πεπτωκότες.

ΙΕΡΕΥΣ

ὦ παῖδες, ἱστώμεσθα· τῶνδε γὰρ χάριν
καὶ δεῦρ᾽ ἔβημεν ὧν ὅδ᾽ ἐξαγγέλλεται.
Φοῖβος δ᾽ ὁ πέμψας τάσδε μαντείας ἅμα
σωτήρ θ᾽ ἵκοιτο καὶ νόσου παυστήριος.

ΧΟΡΟΣ

ὦ Διὸς ἁδυεπὲς φάτι, τίς ποτε τᾶς
πολυχρύσου στρ. α′
Πυθῶνος ἀγλαὰς ἔβας
Θήβας; ἐκτέταμαι φοβερὰν φρένα δείματι
πάλλων,
ἰήιε Δάλιε Παιάν,
ἀμφὶ σοὶ ἁζόμενος· τί μοι ἢ νέον
ἢ περιτελλομέναις ὥραις πάλιν ἐξανύσεις χρέος;
εἰπέ μοι, ὦ χρυσέας τέκνον Ἐλπίδος, ἄμβροτε
Φάμα.
πρῶτα σὲ κεκλόμενος, θύγατερ Διός, ἄμβροτ᾽
Ἀθάνα, ἀντ. α′
γαιάοχόν τ᾽ ἀδελφεὰν
Ἄρτεμιν, ἃ κυκλόεντ᾽ ἀγορᾶς θρόνον εὐκλέα
θάσσει,
καὶ Φοῖβον ἑκαβόλον, ἰώ,

Come, children, swiftly rise from the steps, taking away these boughs of supplication; and let another assemble here all the people of Cadmus, knowing that I shall take every measure. Either we shall succeed, with the god's help, or we shall perish.

PRIEST

Children, let us stand up; for his announcement is the thing for which we came; and may Phoebus, who sent these prophecies, come to preserve us and to put a stop to the plague!

The priest and the children leave; OEDIPUS *and* CREON *also leave. The Chorus of elderly Theban men enters the orchestra, and sings the opening ode, the parodos.*

CHORUS

Sweet-speaking message of Zeus,[a] what are you that have come from Pytho rich in gold to glorious Thebes? I am prostrated, my mind is shaken by terror, Delian healer invoked with cries, in awe of you, wondering what thing you will accomplish, perhaps new, perhaps coming again with the revolving seasons. Tell me, child of golden Hope, immortal oracle!

On you first I call, daughter of Zeus, immortal Athena, and I implore your sister who protects the land, Artemis, seated on her round throne, far-famed, in the market-

[a] Apollo derived his prophetic power from Zeus.

163 ἰὼ Heath: ἰὼ ἰὼ fere codd.: αἰτῶ Blaydes

τρισσοὶ ἀλεξίμοροι προφάνητέ μοι·
εἴ ποτε καὶ προτέρας ἄτας ὑπερορνυμένας πόλει
ἠνύσατ᾽ ἐκτοπίαν φλόγα πήματος, ἔλθετε καὶ νῦν.
ὦ πόποι, ἀνάριθμα γὰρ φέρω *στρ. β´*
πήματα· νοσεῖ δέ μοι πρόπας
στόλος, οὐδ᾽ ἔνι φροντίδος ἔγχος
ᾧ τις ἀλέξεται· οὔτε γὰρ ἔκγονα
κλυτᾶς χθονὸς αὔξεται οὔτε τόκοισιν
ἰηίων καμάτων ἀνέχουσι γυναῖκες.
ἄλλον δ᾽ ἂν ἄλλᾳ προσίδοις ἅπερ εὔπτερον ὄρνιν
κρεῖσσον ἀμαιμακέτου πυρὸς ὄρμενον
ἀκτὰν πρὸς ἑσπέρου θεοῦ·
ὧν πόλις ἀνάριθμος ὄλλυται· *ἀντ. β´*
νηλέα δὲ γένεθλα πρὸς πέδῳ
θαναταφόρα κεῖται ἀνοίκτως·
ἐν δ᾽ ἄλοχοι πολιαί τ᾽ ἔπι ματέρες
ἀκτὰν πάρα βώμιον ἄλλοθεν ἄλλαι
λυγρῶν πόνων ἱκτῆρες ἐπιστενάχουσιν.
παιὼν δὲ λάμπει στονόεσσά τε γῆρυς ὅμαυλος·
τῶν ὕπερ, ὦ χρυσέα θύγατερ Διός,
εὐῶπα πέμψον ἀλκάν.
Ἀρεά τε τὸν μαλερόν, ὃς *στρ. γ´*
νῦν ἄχαλκος ἀσπίδων
φλέγει με περιβόητος ἀν<ηψ> τιάζων,
παλίσσυτον δράμημα νωτίσαι πάτρας,
ἔπουρον εἴτ᾽ ἐς μέγαν
θάλαμον Ἀμφιτρίτας
εἴτ᾽ ἐς τὸν ἀπόξενον ὅρμων

place, and Phoebus the far-darter; appear to me, all three, to ward off doom! If in time past when destruction loomed over the city you drove the flames of ruin far away, come now also!

Ah, countless are the troubles that I bear! Sickness lies on all our company, and thought can find no weapon to repel it. The fruits of the glorious earth do not increase, and no births come to let women surmount the pains in which they cry out. You can see one here and one there, swifter than destroying fire, speed like a winged bird to the shore of the god whose home is in the West.

Countless are their deaths, and the city is perishing; unpitied her children lie on the ground, carried off by death, with none to lament; and by the row of altars wives and white-haired mothers on this side and on that groan as suppliants on account of their sad troubles. Loud rings out the hymn to the Healer and the sound of lamentation with it! For these things, golden daughter of Zeus, send the bright face of protection!

And may savage Ares, who now without the bronze of shields is scorching me as he attacks with shouts, turn his back and hasten from our land, carried back either to the great chamber of Amphitrite or to the Thracian billow

---

165 *ὑπερορνυμένας* Musgrave: *ὕπερ ὀρ-* codd.
175 *ἄλλᾳ* Dobree: *ἄλλῳ* codd.
186 *παιὼν* Π 8, L[ac]K: *παιὰν* cett.
188 *τῶν*] *τω*]*ν* Π 8: *ὧν* codd.
194 *ἔπουρον* LRpt: *ἄπ-* G[γρ]pa

Θρῄκιον κλύδωνα·
τελεῖν γάρ, εἴ τι νὺξ ἀφῇ,
τοῦτ᾽ ἐπ᾽ ἦμαρ ἔρχεται·
τόν, ὦ τᾶν πυρφόρων
ἀστραπᾶν κράτη νέμων,
ὦ Ζεῦ πάτερ, ὑπὸ σῷ φθίσον κεραυνῷ.
Λύκει᾽ ἄναξ, τά τε σὰ χρυ- ἀντ. γ´
σοστρόφων ἀπ᾽ ἀγκυλᾶν
βέλεα θέλοιμ᾽ ἂν ἀδάματ᾽ ἐνδατεῖσθαι
ἀρωγὰ προσταθέντα, τάς τε πυρφόρους
Ἀρτέμιδος αἴγλας, ξὺν αἷς
Λύκι᾽ ὄρεα διᾴσσει·
τὸν χρυσομίτραν τε κικλήσκω,
τᾶσδ᾽ ἐπώνυμον γᾶς,
οἰνῶπα Βάκχον, εὔιον
Μαινάδων ὁμόστολον,
πελασθῆναι φλέγοντ᾽
ἀγλαῶπι <–∪–>
πεύκᾳ ᾽πὶ τὸν ἀπότιμον ἐν θεοῖς θεόν.

ΟΙΔΙΠΟΥΣ

αἰτεῖς· ἃ δ᾽ αἰτεῖς, τἄμ᾽ ἐὰν θέλῃς ἔπη
κλύων δέχεσθαι τῇ νόσῳ θ᾽ ὑπηρετεῖν,
ἀλκὴν λάβοις ἂν κἀνακούφισιν κακῶν·
ἁγὼ ξένος μὲν τοῦ λόγου τοῦδ᾽ ἐξερῶ,
ξένος δὲ τοῦ πραχθέντος· οὐ γὰρ ἂν μακρὰν
ἴχνευον αὐτό, μὴ οὐκ ἔχων τι σύμβολον·
νῦν δ᾽, ὕστερος γὰρ ἀστὸς εἰς ἀστοὺς τελῶ,

bare of harbours! For if Night leaves anything undone, day follows to accomplish it. Him, father Zeus, you who wield the power of the lightning flashes, destroy with your thunderbolt!

Lord of Lycia,[a] I would gladly celebrate the invincible shafts coming from your golden bowstring as you stand by me bringing aid, and the fiery torches of Artemis, with which she darts through the Lycian mountains. And I call on him of the golden cap, him that gives his name to this land, ruddy-faced Bacchus, to whom they cry Euhoe, companion of the Maenads, to draw near with brightly blazing torch of pinewood against the god who lacks honour among the gods.

OEDIPUS has entered

OEDIPUS

You make a demand of me; and as to your demand, if you are willing to hear and to receive my words and to apply treatment to the sickness, you may get protection and relief from your troubles. I shall speak these words as a stranger to the story and a stranger to the deed; no, I could not get far on the track, unless I had some link with you. But as things are, since I have become a citizen with

[a] Apollo.

---

198 *τελεῖν* Hermann: *τέλει* codd.: *τελεῖ* Kayser, qui post *γάρ* interpunxit

200 *τόν, ὦ τᾶν* Hermann: *τόν, ὦ* Π 7, Lpat: *τᾶν, ὦ* r

214 ex. gr. suppl. <*σύμμαχον*> G. Wolff, <*νυκτέρῳ*> J.H.H. Schmidt

221 *αὐτὸ* lGγρp: *αὐτός* rpat post hunc v. lacunam statuit Groeneboom; ex. gr. <*πόλεως ἐπισπᾶν θανασίμους φόνου δίκας*> supplere possis

ὑμῖν προφωνῶ πᾶσι Καδμείοις τάδε·
ὅστις ποθ᾽ ὑμῶν Λάιον τὸν Λαβδάκου
κάτοιδεν ἀνδρὸς ἐκ τίνος διώλετο,
τοῦτον κελεύω πάντα σημαίνειν ἐμοί·
κεἰ μὲν φοβεῖται, τοὐπίκλημ᾽ ὑπεξελὼν
[one line missing]
αὐτὸς κατ᾽ αὑτοῦ·—πείσεται γὰρ ἄλλο μὲν
ἀστεργὲς οὐδέν, γῆς δ᾽ ἄπεισιν ἀβλαβής—
εἰ δ᾽ αὖ τις ἄλλον οἶδεν ἢ ᾽ξ ἄλλης χθονὸς
τὸν αὐτόχειρα, μὴ σιωπάτω· τὸ γὰρ
κέρδος τελῶ ᾽γὼ χἠ χάρις προσκείσεται.
εἰ δ᾽ αὖ σιωπήσεσθε, καί τις ἢ φίλου
δείσας ἀπώσει τοὔπος ἢ χαὐτοῦ τόδε,
ἃκ τῶνδε δράσω, ταῦτα χρὴ κλυεῖν ἐμοῦ.
τὸν ἄνδρ᾽ ἀπαυδῶ τοῦτον, ὅστις ἐστί, γῆς
τῆσδ᾽, ἧς ἐγὼ κράτη τε καὶ θρόνους νέμω,
μήτ᾽ ἐσδέχεσθαι μήτε προσφωνεῖν τινά,
μήτ᾽ ἐν θεῶν εὐχαῖσι μήτε θύμασιν
κοινὸν ποεῖσθαι, μήτε χέρνιβος νέμειν·
ὠθεῖν δ᾽ ἀπ᾽ οἴκων πάντας, ὡς μιάσματος
τοῦδ᾽ ἡμὶν ὄντος, ὡς τὸ Πυθικὸν θεοῦ
μαντεῖον ἐξέφηνεν ἀρτίως ἐμοί.
ἐγὼ μὲν οὖν τοιόσδε τῷ τε δαίμονι
τῷ τ᾽ ἀνδρὶ τῷ θανόντι σύμμαχος πέλω.
[κατεύχομαι δὲ τὸν δεδρακότ᾽, εἴτε τις
εἷς ὢν λέληθεν εἴτε πλειόνων μέτα,
κακὸν κακῶς νιν ἄμορον ἐκτρῖψαι βίον.
ἐπεύχομαι δ᾽, οἴκοισιν εἰ ξυνέστιος

the rest, though late, I utter to all Cadmeans this proclamation! Whoever among you knows at whose hands Laius, son of Labdacus, perished, him I command to tell me all! If he is afraid that if he removes the guilt <from the city, he will bring judgment of death> upon himself, well and good, he shall suffer nothing else unwelcome, but shall leave the land unharmed. But if someone knows another of you, or a foreigner, to be the killer, let him not be silent; for I can dispense rewards, and gratitude also shall be his. But if you remain silent, and someone, fearing for a friend or for himself, rejects this order—what I shall do then you must hear from me! I forbid all belonging to this land, over which I rule and sit upon the throne, to receive him or to speak to him, or to let him share in prayers and sacrifices to the gods, or to touch holy water; but all must drive him from their homes, since we are polluted, as the Pythian oracle of the god has just now revealed to me. This is how I shall fight side by side with the god and with the man who died.

[And I pray that the doer of the deed, whether a single man has gone undetected or he has acted with others, may wear away a miserable life in misery, miserable as he is. And I pray further that if he is by the hearth in my own

---

227 post hunc versum ex. gr. suppl. Ll.-J. *<πόλεως ἐπισπᾶν θανασίμους φόνου δίκας>* (cf. *Sophoclea*, 85)
229 *ἀβλαβής* pat: *ἀσφαλής* lrp
230 *ἤ 'ξ* Vauvilliers: *ἐξ* codd.
240 *χέρνιβος* LN: *χέρνιβας* cett.
246–51 del. Wecklein: post 272 traiecit amicus Dobraei

ἐν τοῖς ἐμοῖς γένοιτ' ἐμοῦ ξυνειδότος,
παθεῖν ἅπερ τοῖσδ' ἀρτίως ἠρασάμην.]
ὑμῖν δὲ ταῦτα πάντ' ἐπισκήπτω τελεῖν,
ὑπέρ τ' ἐμαυτοῦ, τοῦ θεοῦ τε, τῆσδέ τε
γῆς ὧδ' ἀκάρπως κἀθέως ἐφθαρμένης.
οὐδ' εἰ γὰρ ἦν τὸ πρᾶγμα μὴ θεήλατον,
ἀκάθαρτον ὑμᾶς εἰκὸς ἦν οὕτως ἐᾶν,
ἀνδρός γ' ἀρίστου βασιλέως τ' ὀλωλότος,
ἀλλ' ἐξερευνᾶν· νῦν δ' ἐπεὶ κυρῶ τ' ἐγὼ
ἔχων μὲν ἀρχάς, ἃς ἐκεῖνος εἶχε πρίν,
ἔχων δὲ λέκτρα καὶ γυναῖχ' ὁμόσπορον,
κοινῶν τε παίδων κοίν' ἄν, εἰ κείνῳ γένος
μὴ 'δυστύχησεν, ἦν ἂν ἐκπεφυκότα—
νῦν δ' ἐς τὸ κείνου κρᾶτ' ἐνήλαθ' ἡ τύχη·
ἀνθ' ὧν ἐγὼ τάδ', ὡσπερεὶ τοὐμοῦ πατρός,
ὑπερμαχοῦμαι κἀπὶ πάντ' ἀφίξομαι
ζητῶν τὸν αὐτόχειρα τοῦ φόνου λαβεῖν
τῷ Λαβδακείῳ παιδὶ Πολυδώρου τε καὶ
τοῦ πρόσθε Κάδμου τοῦ πάλαι τ' Ἀγήνορος.
καὶ ταῦτα τοῖς μὴ δρῶσιν εὔχομαι θεοὺς
μήτ' ἄροτον αὐτοῖς γῆς ἀνιέναι τινὰ
μήτ' οὖν γυναικῶν παῖδας, ἀλλὰ τῷ πότμῳ
τῷ νῦν φθερεῖσθαι κἄτι τοῦδ' ἐχθίονι.
ὑμῖν δὲ τοῖς ἄλλοισι Καδμείοις, ὅσοις
τάδ' ἔστ' ἀρέσκονθ', ἥ τε σύμμαχος Δίκη
χοἰ πάντες εὖ ξυνεῖεν εἰσαεὶ θεοί.

house with my own knowledge, I may suffer the fate with which I have just cursed others.]

And I charge you to bring all this about for my sake, for the sake of the god, and for the sake of this land, thus blasted with barrenness by the angry gods. For even had the matter not been forced upon you by the gods, it was not proper to leave the guilt thus unpurified, when a great man and a king had perished. No, you should have searched it out. But now, since I chance to hold the power which once he held, and to have a marriage and a wife in common with him, and since had he not been unfortunate in respect of issue our children would have had one mother—but as things are he has been struck down by fortune; on account of this I shall fight for him as though he had been my father, and shall go to every length in searching for the author of the murder done upon the son of Labdacus, sprung from Polydorus and from Cadmus before him and from Agenor long ago.

And for those who take no action I pray that the gods may not send up crops from the earth nor allow their women to bear children, but that they may perish by the fate that now afflicts them or by one yet worse. But beside you other Cadmeans, all who approve these words, may Justice fight and may all the gods ever graciously remain.

---

270 γῆς Vauvilliers: γῆν codd.

ΧΟΡΟΣ

ὥσπερ μ' ἀραῖον ἔλαβες, ὧδ', ἄναξ, ἐρῶ.
οὔτ' ἔκτανον γὰρ οὔτε τὸν κτανόντ' ἔχω
δεῖξαι. τὸ δὲ ζήτημα τοῦ πέμψαντος ἦν
Φοίβου τόδ' εἰπεῖν, ὅστις εἴργασταί ποτε.

ΟΙΔΙΠΟΥΣ

δίκαι' ἔλεξας· ἀλλ' ἀναγκάσαι θεοὺς
ἂν μὴ θέλωσιν οὐδ' <ἂν> εἷς δύναιτ' ἀνήρ.

ΧΟΡΟΣ

τὰ δεύτερ' ἐκ τῶνδ' ἂν λέγοιμ' ἁμοὶ δοκεῖ.

ΟΙΔΙΠΟΥΣ

εἰ καὶ τρίτ' ἐστί, μὴ παρῇς τὸ μὴ οὐ φράσαι.

ΧΟΡΟΣ

ἄνακτ' ἄνακτι ταὔθ' ὁρῶντ' ἐπίσταμαι
μάλιστα Φοίβῳ Τειρεσίαν, παρ' οὗ τις ἂν
σκοπῶν τάδ', ὦναξ, ἐκμάθοι σαφέστατα.

ΟΙΔΙΠΟΥΣ

ἀλλ' οὐκ ἐν ἀργοῖς οὐδὲ τοῦτ' ἐπράξαμεν.
ἔπεμψα γὰρ Κρέοντος εἰπόντος διπλοῦς
πομπούς· πάλαι δὲ μὴ παρὼν θαυμάζεται.

ΧΟΡΟΣ

καὶ μὴν τά γ' ἄλλα κωφὰ καὶ παλαί' ἔπη.

ΟΙΔΙΠΟΥΣ

τὰ ποῖα ταῦτα; πάντα γὰρ σκοπῶ λόγον.

ΧΟΡΟΣ

θανεῖν ἐλέχθη πρός τινων ὁδοιπόρων.

CHORUS

As you have put me upon oath, so, my lord, shall I speak. I did not kill him, neither can I point to the killer. But the enquiry was the task of Phoebus who has sent the message, so that he should tell us who it is that did the deed.

OEDIPUS

You are right; but to compel the gods when they are unwilling is a thing no man can do.

CHORUS

May I say what seems to me the next best thing?

OEDIPUS

If there is even a third best, do not omit to tell it me.

CHORUS

I know that he whose sight is closest to that of the lord Phoebus is the lord Tiresias; if one made enquiry of him, my lord, one might best learn the truth.

OEDIPUS

Why, I have not been idle in that matter either! For at Creon's bidding I sent two men to bring him; and I have long been wondering why he is not here.

CHORUS

All the rest, to be sure, is vague and ancient rumour.

OEDIPUS

What is that rumour? I am examining the whole question.

CHORUS

He was said to have been killed by people on the road.

---

281 suppl. Burton

287 *ἐπράξαμεν* Shilleto: *ἐπραξάμην* codd.

ΟΙΔΙΠΟΥΣ

ἤκουσα κἀγώ· τὸν δὲ δρῶντ᾽ οὐδεὶς ὁρᾷ.

ΧΟΡΟΣ

ἀλλ᾽ εἴ τι μὲν δὴ δείματός γ᾽ ἔχει μέρος
τὰς σὰς ἀκούων οὐ μενεῖ τοιάσδ᾽ ἀράς.

ΟΙΔΙΠΟΥΣ

ᾧ μή ᾽στι δρῶντι τάρβος, οὐδ᾽ ἔπος φοβεῖ.

ΧΟΡΟΣ

ἀλλ᾽ οὑξελέγξων νιν πάρεστιν· οἵδε γὰρ
τὸν θεῖον ἤδη μάντιν ὧδ᾽ ἄγουσιν, ᾧ
τἀληθὲς ἐμπέφυκεν ἀνθρώπων μόνῳ.

ΟΙΔΙΠΟΥΣ

ὦ πάντα νωμῶν Τειρεσία, διδακτά τε
ἄρρητά τ᾽ οὐράνιά τε καὶ χθονοστιβῆ,
πόλιν μέν, εἰ καὶ μὴ βλέπεις, φρονεῖς δ᾽ ὅμως
οἵᾳ νόσῳ σύνεστιν· ἧς σὲ προστάτην
σωτῆρά τ᾽, ὦναξ, μοῦνον ἐξευρίσκομεν.
Φοῖβος γάρ, εἰ καὶ μὴ κλύεις τῶν ἀγγέλων,
πέμψασιν ἡμῖν ἀντέπεμψεν, ἔκλυσιν
μόνην ἂν ἐλθεῖν τοῦδε τοῦ νοσήματος,
εἰ τοὺς κτανόντας Λάιον μαθόντες εὖ
κτείναιμεν, ἢ γῆς φυγάδας ἐκπεμψαίμεθα.
σὺ δ᾽ οὖν φθονήσας μήτ᾽ ἀπ᾽ οἰωνῶν φάτιν
μήτ᾽ εἴ τιν᾽ ἄλλην μαντικῆς ἔχεις ὁδόν,

293 δρῶντ᾽ anon. (1779): ἰδόντ᾽ codd.
297 νιν πάρεστιν Heimsoeth: αὐτὸν ἔστιν codd.

OEDIPUS

I also have heard that; but the doer remains invisible.

CHORUS

But if he has any particle of fear within him, he will not wait long, now that he has heard such curses pronounced by you.

OEDIPUS

He who is not afraid to do the deed is not frightened by a word.

CHORUS

But here is he who shall convict him; yes, already they are bringing in the godlike prophet, in whom alone among mankind truth is implanted.

Enter TIRESIAS, *led by the boy who is his guide.*

OEDIPUS

Tiresias, you who dispose all things, those that can be explained and those unspeakable, things in heaven and things that move on earth, even though you cannot see you know the nature of the sickness that besets the city; and you are the only champion and protector, lord, whom we can find. In case you have not heard the messengers, Phoebus when we sent to him sent back the message that release from this plague would come only if we learned for certain who were the killers of Laius and killed them, or sent them out of the country into exile. Well, do not grudge the use of a message from the birds or of any other road of prophecy that you possess, and save yourself and

ῥῦσαι σεαυτὸν καὶ πόλιν, ῥῦσαι δ' ἐμέ,
ῥῦσαι δὲ πᾶν μίασμα τοῦ τεθνηκότος.
ἐν σοὶ γὰρ ἐσμέν· ἄνδρα δ' ὠφελεῖν ἀφ' ὧν
ἔχοι τε καὶ δύναιτο κάλλιστος πόνων.

ΤΕΙΡΕΣΙΑΣ

φεῦ φεῦ, φρονεῖν ὡς δεινὸν ἔνθα μὴ τέλη
λύῃ φρονοῦντι. ταῦτα γὰρ καλῶς ἐγὼ
εἰδὼς διώλεσ'· οὐ γὰρ ἂν δεῦρ' ἱκόμην.

ΟΙΔΙΠΟΥΣ

τί δ' ἔστιν; ὡς ἄθυμος εἰσελήλυθας.

ΤΕΙΡΕΣΙΑΣ

ἄφες μ' ἐς οἴκους· ῥᾷστα γὰρ τὸ σόν τε σὺ
κἀγὼ διοίσω τοὐμόν, ἢν ἐμοὶ πίθῃ.

ΟΙΔΙΠΟΥΣ

οὔτ' ἔννομ' εἶπας οὔτε προσφιλῆ πόλει
τῇδ', ἥ σ' ἔθρεψε, τήνδ' ἀποστερῶν φάτιν.

ΤΕΙΡΕΣΙΑΣ

ὁρῶ γὰρ οὐδὲ σοὶ τὸ σὸν φώνημ' ἰὸν
πρὸς καιρόν· ὡς οὖν μηδ' ἐγὼ ταὐτὸν πάθω—

ΟΙΔΙΠΟΥΣ

μὴ πρὸς θεῶν φρονῶν γ' ἀποστραφῇς, ἐπεὶ
πάντες σε προσκυνοῦμεν οἵδ' ἱκτήριοι.

ΤΕΙΡΕΣΙΑΣ

πάντες γὰρ οὐ φρονεῖτ'. ἐγὼ δ' οὐ μή ποτε
τἄμ', ὡς ἂν εἴπω μὴ τὰ σ', ἐκφήνω κακά.

the city, and save me, and save us from all the pollution coming from the dead man. We are in your hands; and for a man to use his qualities and his powers to help is the noblest of labours.

TIRESIAS

Alas, alas, how dreadful it is to know when the knowledge does not benefit the knower! I knew this well, but I suppressed it; else I would not have come here.

OEDIPUS

What is the matter? How despondent you are, now that you have come!

TIRESIAS

Let me go home! You will find it easier to bear your fate and I mine, if you do as I say.

OEDIPUS

What you say is neither lawful nor friendly to this city, which reared you, since you are withholding this message.

TIRESIAS

It is because I see that your speech also does not hit the mark; therefore, so as not to have the same happen to me. . . .

OEDIPUS

If you know, I beg you, do not turn away from us, since we all implore you in supplication.

TIRESIAS

Yes, for all of you are ignorant; I shall never reveal my sorrows, not to mention yours.

---

325 sentententiam interrumpi vidit Wunder

ΟΙΔΙΠΟΥΣ

τί φής; ξυνειδὼς οὐ φράσεις, ἀλλ᾽ ἐννοεῖς
ἡμᾶς προδοῦναι καὶ καταφθεῖραι πόλιν;

ΤΕΙΡΕΣΙΑΣ

ἐγὼ οὔτ᾽ ἐμαυτὸν οὔτε σ᾽ ἀλγυνῶ. τί ταῦτ᾽
ἄλλως ἐλέγχεις; οὐ γὰρ ἂν πύθοιό μου.

ΟΙΔΙΠΟΥΣ

οὐκ, ὦ κακῶν κάκιστε, καὶ γὰρ ἂν πέτρου
φύσιν σύ γ᾽ ὀργάνειας, ἐξερεῖς ποτέ,
ἀλλ᾽ ὧδ᾽ ἄτεγκτος κἀτελεύτητος φανῇ;

ΤΕΙΡΕΣΙΑΣ

ὀργὴν ἐμέμψω τὴν ἐμήν, τὴν σὴν δ᾽ ὁμοῦ
ναίουσαν οὐ κατεῖδες, ἀλλ᾽ ἐμὲ ψέγεις.

ΟΙΔΙΠΟΥΣ

τίς γὰρ τοιαῦτ᾽ ἂν οὐκ ἂν ὀργίζοιτ᾽ ἔπη
κλύων, ἃ νῦν σὺ τήνδ᾽ ἀτιμάζεις πόλιν;

ΤΕΙΡΕΣΙΑΣ

ἥξει γὰρ αὐτά, κἂν ἐγὼ σιγῇ στέγω.

ΟΙΔΙΠΟΥΣ

οὔκουν ἅ γ᾽ ἥξει καὶ σὲ χρὴ λέγειν ἐμοί;

ΤΕΙΡΕΣΙΑΣ

οὐκ ἂν πέρα φράσαιμι. πρὸς τάδ᾽, εἰ θέλεις,
θυμοῦ δι᾽ ὀργῆς ἥτις ἀγριωτάτη.

OEDIPUS

What are you saying? You know, but you will not tell us, but are minded to betray us and to destroy the city?

TIRESIAS

I shall give pain neither to you nor to myself. Why do you question me in vain? You cannot learn from me.

OEDIPUS

Most villainous of villains—you would drive even a rock to fury! Will you never speak out, but be seen as inflexible and inconclusive?

TIRESIAS

You find fault with my temper, but you have not seen your own that lives with you, and you blame me.

OEDIPUS

Why, who would not be angry, hearing such words as those with which you now show disrespect for the city?

TIRESIAS

Yes, things will come of themselves, even if I veil it in silence.

OEDIPUS

Is not what will come just what you ought to tell me?

TIRESIAS

I will explain no further; in the face of that, pray rage with the most ferocious anger!

ΟΙΔΙΠΟΥΣ

καὶ μὴν παρήσω γ᾽ οὐδέν, ὡς ὀργῆς ἔχω,
ἅπερ ξυνίημ᾽. ἴσθι γὰρ δοκῶν ἐμοὶ
καὶ ξυμφυτεῦσαι τοὔργον, εἰργάσθαι θ᾽, ὅσον
μὴ χερσὶ καίνων· εἰ δ᾽ ἐτύγχανες βλέπων,
καὶ τοὔργον ἂν σοῦ τοῦτ᾽ ἔφην εἶναι μόνου.

ΤΕΙΡΕΣΙΑΣ

ἄληθες ἐννέπω σὲ τῷ κηρύγματι
ᾧπερ προεῖπας ἐμμένειν, κἀφ᾽ ἡμέρας
τῆς νῦν προσαυδᾶν μήτε τούσδε μήτ᾽ ἐμέ,
ὡς ὄντι γῆς τῆσδ᾽ ἀνοσίῳ μιάστορι.

ΟΙΔΙΠΟΥΣ

οὕτως ἀναιδῶς ἐξεκίνησας τόδε
τὸ ῥῆμα; καὶ ποῦ τοῦτο φεύξεσθαι δοκεῖς;

ΤΕΙΡΕΣΙΑΣ

πέφευγα· τἀληθὲς γὰρ ἰσχῦον τρέφω.

ΟΙΔΙΠΟΥΣ

πρὸς τοῦ διδαχθείς; οὐ γὰρ ἔκ γε τῆς τέχνης.

ΤΕΙΡΕΣΙΑΣ

πρὸς σοῦ· σὺ γάρ μ᾽ ἄκοντα προὐτρέψω λέγειν.

ΟΙΔΙΠΟΥΣ

ποῖον λόγον; λέγ᾽ αὖθις, ὡς μᾶλλον μάθω.

ΤΕΙΡΕΣΙΑΣ

οὐχὶ ξυνῆκας πρόσθεν; ἦ ᾽κπειρᾷ †λέγειν†;

351 προεῖπας Brunck: προσ- codd. 360 ἦ Ll.-J.: ἢ codd. λέγειν] λόγων L s.l.: λόγοις Günther

OEDIPUS

Well, I am so angry that I will leave unsaid nothing of what I understand! Know that I think that you shared in the planning of the deed and in its doing, except that you did not kill him with your own hands; and if you did not happen to be blind, I should have said that the deed was yours alone!

TIRESIAS

So? I call on you to abide by the proclamation you made earlier, and from this day on address neither these men nor me, since you are the unholy polluter of this land!

OEDIPUS

Have you so shamelessly started up this story? How do you think you will escape its consequences?

TIRESIAS

I have escaped; the truth I nurture has strength.

OEDIPUS

From whom have you learned it? Not, I think, from your prophetic art.

TIRESIAS

From you; it was you who forced me to speak against my will.

OEDIPUS

To say what? Tell me again, so that I can understand it better!

TIRESIAS

Did you not understand before? Are you trying to test me?

ΟΙΔΙΠΟΥΣ

οὐχ ὥστε γ᾽ εἰπεῖν γνωστόν· ἀλλ᾽ αὖθις φράσον.

ΤΕΙΡΕΣΙΑΣ

φονέα σέ φημι τἀνδρὸς οὗ ζητεῖς κυρεῖν.

ΟΙΔΙΠΟΥΣ

ἀλλ᾽ οὔ τι χαίρων δίς γε πημονὰς ἐρεῖς.

ΤΕΙΡΕΣΙΑΣ

εἴπω τι δῆτα κἄλλ᾽, ἵν᾽ ὀργίζῃ πλέον;

ΟΙΔΙΠΟΥΣ

ὅσον γε χρῄζεις· ὡς μάτην εἰρήσεται.

ΤΕΙΡΕΣΙΑΣ

λεληθέναι σέ φημι σὺν τοῖς φιλτάτοις
αἴσχισθ᾽ ὁμιλοῦντ᾽, οὐδ᾽ ὁρᾶν ἵν᾽ εἶ κακοῦ.

ΟΙΔΙΠΟΥΣ

ἦ καὶ γεγηθὼς ταῦτ᾽ ἀεὶ λέξειν δοκεῖς;

ΤΕΙΡΕΣΙΑΣ

εἴπερ τί γ᾽ ἐστὶ τῆς ἀληθείας σθένος.

ΟΙΔΙΠΟΥΣ

ἀλλ᾽ ἔστι, πλὴν σοί· σοὶ δὲ τοῦτ᾽ οὐκ ἔστ᾽, ἐπεὶ
τυφλὸς τά τ᾽ ὦτα τόν τε νοῦν τά τ᾽ ὄμματ᾽ εἶ.

ΤΕΙΡΕΣΙΑΣ

σὺ δ᾽ ἄθλιός γε ταῦτ᾽ ὀνειδίζων, ἃ σοὶ
οὐδεὶς ὃς οὐχὶ τῶνδ᾽ ὀνειδιεῖ τάχα.

OEDIPUS

Not so that I can say I know it; come, say it again!

TIRESIAS

I say that you are the murderer of the man whose murderer you are searching for!

OEDIPUS

You shall not get away with speaking disaster twice!

TIRESIAS

Shall I tell you another thing, to make you even angrier?

OEDIPUS

Tell me as much as you please, since your words will be wasted!

TIRESIAS

I say that you are living unawares in a shameful relationship with those closest to you, and cannot see the plight in which you are.

OEDIPUS

Do you believe that you will continue to repeat such things and go scot-free?

TIRESIAS

Yes, if the truth has any strength.

OEDIPUS

It has, except for you; you are without it, since you are blind in your ears, in your mind, and in your eyes.

TIRESIAS

It is sad that you utter these reproaches, which all men shall soon utter against you.

ΟΙΔΙΠΟΥΣ

μιᾶς τρέφῃ πρὸς νυκτός, ὥστε μήτ᾽ ἐμὲ
μήτ᾽ ἄλλον, ὅστις φῶς ὁρᾷ, βλάψαι ποτ᾽ ἄν.

ΤΕΙΡΕΣΙΑΣ

οὐ γάρ σε μοῖρα πρός γ᾽ ἐμοῦ πεσεῖν, ἐπεὶ
ἱκανὸς Ἀπόλλων, ᾧ τάδ᾽ ἐκπρᾶξαι μέλει.

ΟΙΔΙΠΟΥΣ

Κρέοντος, ἢ τοῦ ταῦτα τἀξευρήματα;

ΤΕΙΡΕΣΙΑΣ

Κρέων δέ σοι πῆμ᾽ οὐδέν, ἀλλ᾽ αὐτὸς σὺ σοί.

ΟΙΔΙΠΟΥΣ

ὦ πλοῦτε καὶ τυραννὶ καὶ τέχνη τέχνης
ὑπερφέρουσα τῷ πολυζήλῳ βίῳ,
ὅσος παρ᾽ ὑμῖν ὁ φθόνος φυλάσσεται,
εἰ τῆσδέ γ᾽ ἀρχῆς οὕνεχ᾽, ἣν ἐμοὶ πόλις
δωρητόν, οὐκ αἰτητόν, εἰσεχείρισεν,
ταύτης Κρέων ὁ πιστός, οὑξ ἀρχῆς φίλος,
λάθρᾳ μ᾽ ὑπελθὼν ἐκβαλεῖν ἱμείρεται,
ὑφεὶς μάγον τοιόνδε μηχανορράφον,
δόλιον ἀγύρτην, ὅστις ἐν τοῖς κέρδεσιν
μόνον δέδορκε, τὴν τέχνην δ᾽ ἔφυ τυφλός.
ἐπεὶ φέρ᾽ εἰπέ, ποῦ σὺ μάντις εἶ σαφής;
πῶς οὐχ, ὅθ᾽ ἡ ῥαψῳδὸς ἐνθάδ᾽ ἦν κύων,
ηὔδας τι τοῖσδ᾽ ἀστοῖσιν ἐκλυτήριον;
καίτοι τό γ᾽ αἴνιγμ᾽ οὐχὶ τοὐπιόντος ἦν
ἀνδρὸς διειπεῖν, ἀλλὰ μαντείας ἔδει·

OEDIPUS

You are sustained by darkness only, so that you could never harm me or any other man that sees the light.

TIRESIAS

No, it is not at my hand that you are destined to fall, since Apollo, who has it in mind to bring this about, will be sufficient.

OEDIPUS

Is it Creon, or who, that has made these discoveries?

TIRESIAS

Creon is not your trouble, but rather you yourself.

OEDIPUS

O riches and kingship and skill surpassing skill in a life much-envied, how great is the hatred that you store up, if it is for the sake of this royal power, which the city placed in my hands as a gift, though I had not asked it, that Creon the trusty, my friend from the first, has crept up to me and longs to throw me out, setting upon me this wizard hatcher of plots, this crafty beggar, who has sight only when it comes to profit, but in his art is blind!

Why, come, tell me, how can you be a true prophet? Why when the versifying hound[a] was here did not you speak some word that could release the citizens? Indeed, her riddle was not one for the first comer to explain! It

[a] The Sphinx, called a hound because she was the servant of the god who sent her.

376 σε . . . γ' ἐμοῦ Brunck: με . . . γε σοῦ Π 9 et codd.
378 του Π 9ac: σοῦ Π 9pc et codd.
379 δὲ] γε Brunck

ἣν οὔτ᾽ ἀπ᾽ οἰωνῶν σὺ προὐφάνης ἔχων
οὔτ᾽ ἐκ θεῶν του γνωτόν· ἀλλ᾽ ἐγὼ μολών,
ὁ μηδὲν εἰδὼς Οἰδίπους, ἔπαυσά νιν,
γνώμῃ κυρήσας οὐδ᾽ ἀπ᾽ οἰωνῶν μαθών·
ὃν δὴ σὺ πειρᾷς ἐκβαλεῖν, δοκῶν θρόνοις
παραστατήσειν τοῖς Κρεοντείοις πέλας.
κλαίων δοκεῖς μοι καὶ σὺ χὠ συνθεὶς τάδε
ἀγηλατήσειν· εἰ δὲ μὴ 'δόκεις γέρων
εἶναι, παθὼν ἔγνως ἂν οἷά περ φρονεῖς.

ΧΟΡΟΣ

ἡμῖν μὲν εἰκάζουσι καὶ τὰ τοῦδ᾽ ἔπη
ὀργῇ λελέχθαι καὶ τὰ σ᾽, Οἰδίπου, δοκεῖ.
δεῖ δ᾽ οὐ τοιούτων, ἀλλ᾽ ὅπως τὰ τοῦ θεοῦ
μαντεῖ᾽ ἄριστα λύσομεν, τόδε σκοπεῖν.

ΤΕΙΡΕΣΙΑΣ

εἰ καὶ τυραννεῖς, ἐξισωτέον τὸ γοῦν
ἴσ᾽ ἀντιλέξαι· τοῦδε γὰρ κἀγὼ κρατῶ.
οὐ γάρ τι σοὶ ζῶ δοῦλος, ἀλλὰ Λοξίᾳ·
ὥστ᾽ οὐ Κρέοντος προστάτου γεγράψομαι.
λέγω δ᾽, ἐπειδὴ καὶ τυφλόν μ᾽ ὠνείδισας·
σὺ καὶ δέδορκας κοὐ βλέπεις ἵν᾽ εἶ κακοῦ,
οὐδ᾽ ἔνθα ναίεις, οὐδ᾽ ὅτων οἰκεῖς μέτα—
ἆρ᾽ οἶσθ᾽ ἀφ᾽ ὧν εἶ; καὶ λέληθας ἐχθρὸς ὢν
τοῖς σοῖσιν αὐτοῦ νέρθε κἀπὶ γῆς ἄνω,
καί σ᾽ ἀμφιπλὴξ μητρός τε κἀπὸ τοῦ πατρὸς
ἐλᾷ ποτ᾽ ἐκ γῆς τῆσδε δεινόπους ἀρά,
βλέποντα νῦν μὲν ὄρθ᾽, ἔπειτα δὲ σκότον.
βοῆς δὲ τῆς σῆς ποῖος οὐκ ἐσθαλικών,

required prophetic skill, and you were exposed as having no knowledge from the birds or from the gods. No, it was I that came, Oedipus who knew nothing, and put a stop to her; I hit the mark by native wit, not by what I learned from birds. And it is I that you are trying to throw out, thinking that you will stand close to the throne of Creon. Both you and he who hatched this plan will regret, I think, your attempt to drive out the curse; and if you did not seem to be old, you would learn by suffering how dangerous are your thoughts.

CHORUS

As we reckon, both this man's words and your own, Oedipus, seem to have been spoken in anger. We need nothing like that, but we should consider how best we can accomplish the prophecy of the god.

TIRESIAS

Even though you are king, we may be equal so far as to answer word for word; for there I too have power, since I live not as your slave, but that of Loxias, so that I shall not be written down as Creon's partisan. And I say, since you have reproached me with my blindness, that you have sight, but cannot see what trouble you are in, nor where you are living, nor with whom you share your home. Do you know from what stock you come? First, you are unaware of being an enemy to your own beneath and above the earth, and, next, the two-pronged curse that comes from your mother and your father with deadly step shall one day drive you from this land; now you have sight, then shall you look on darkness. What Helicon, what

417 *κἀπὸ τοῦ* Π 7pc: *καὶ τοῦ σοῦ* codd.
420 *ἐσθαλικών* Blaydes, Herwerden: *ἔσται λιμήν* codd.

ποῖος Κιθαιρὼν οὐχὶ σύμφωνος τάχα,
ὅταν καταίσθῃ τὸν ὑμέναιον, ὃν δόμοις
ἄνορμον εἰσέπλευσας, εὐπλοίας τυχών;
ἄλλων δὲ πλῆθος οὐκ ἐπαισθάνῃ κακῶν,
ἅ γ' ἐξαϊστώσει σε σὺν τοῖς σοῖς τέκνοις.
πρὸς ταῦτα καὶ Κρέοντα καὶ τοὐμὸν στόμα
προπηλάκιζε. σοῦ γὰρ οὐκ ἔστιν βροτῶν
κάκιον ὅστις ἐκτριβήσεταί ποτε.

ΟΙΔΙΠΟΥΣ

ἦ ταῦτα δῆτ' ἀνεκτὰ πρὸς τούτου κλυεῖν;
οὐκ εἰς ὄλεθρον; οὐχὶ θᾶσσον αὖ πάλιν
ἄψορρος οἴκων τῶνδ' ἀποστραφεὶς ἄπει;

ΤΕΙΡΕΣΙΑΣ

οὐδ' ἱκόμην ἔγωγ' ἄν, εἰ σὺ μὴ 'κάλεις.

ΟΙΔΙΠΟΥΣ

οὐ γάρ τί σ' ᾔδη μῶρα φωνήσοντ', ἐπεὶ
σχολῇ σ' ἂν οἴκους τοὺς ἐμοὺς ἐστειλάμην.

ΤΕΙΡΕΣΙΑΣ

ἡμεῖς τοιοίδ' ἔφυμεν, ὡς μὲν σοὶ δοκεῖ,
μῶροι, γονεῦσι δ', οἵ σ' ἔφυσαν, ἔμφρονες.

ΟΙΔΙΠΟΥΣ

ποίοισι; μεῖνον. τίς δέ μ' ἐκφύει βροτῶν;

ΤΕΙΡΕΣΙΑΣ

ἥδ' ἡμέρα φύσει σε καὶ διαφθερεῖ.

425 ἅ γ' ἐξαϊστώσει σε σὺν Bergk: ἅ σ' ἐξισώσει σοί τε καὶ codd.

Cithaeron shall not soon echo your laments when you become aware of the marriage into whose dangerous harbour you sailed in your house, sped by a favouring wind? And there are other troubles you do not perceive, which shall annihilate you together with your children. In face of that cover with abuse Creon and this mouth of mine! For there is none among mortals that shall be more cruelly rooted out than you.

OEDIPUS

Is it bearable that I should hear these words from this man? Go to destruction! Turn at once your back and hasten home away from this house!

TIRESIAS

I would never have come, had you not sent for me.

OEDIPUS

No, I did not know that your words would be foolish; else I would hardly have summoned you to my house.

TIRESIAS

That is what I am; foolish, as you think, but the parents who gave you birth found me wise.

OEDIPUS

What parents? Wait! Who among mortals gave me birth?

TIRESIAS

This day shall be your parent and your destroyer.

---

430 *αὖ* Π 9 in linea, coni. G. Wolff: *οὐ* codd. et Π 7
433 *ᾔδη* Π 7 in margine: *ᾔδειν* codd.
434 *σχολῇ σ'* fere codd.: *σχολῇ γ'* H, v.l. in Π 9 | *ἐμούς* <*σ'*> Porson
435 *μὲν σοὶ*] *σοὶ μὲν* Schaefer

ΟΙΔΙΠΟΥΣ

ὡς πάντ' ἄγαν αἰνικτὰ κἀσαφῆ λέγεις.

ΤΕΙΡΕΣΙΑΣ

οὔκουν σὺ ταῦτ' ἄριστος εὑρίσκειν ἔφυς;

ΟΙΔΙΠΟΥΣ

τοιαῦτ' ὀνείδιζ' οἷς ἔμ' εὑρήσεις μέγαν.

ΤΕΙΡΕΣΙΑΣ

αὕτη γε μέντοι σ' ἡ τύχη διώλεσεν.

ΟΙΔΙΠΟΥΣ

ἀλλ' εἰ πόλιν τήνδ' ἐξέσωσ', οὔ μοι μέλει.

ΤΕΙΡΕΣΙΑΣ

ἄπειμι τοίνυν· καὶ σύ, παῖ, κόμιζέ με.

ΟΙΔΙΠΟΥΣ

κομιζέτω δῆθ'· ὡς παρὼν σύ γ' ἐμποδὼν
ὀχλεῖς, συθείς τ' ἂν οὐκ ἂν ἀλγύναις πλέον.

ΤΕΙΡΕΣΙΑΣ

εἰπὼν ἄπειμ' ὧν οὕνεκ' ἦλθον, οὐ τὸ σὸν
δείσας πρόσωπον· οὐ γὰρ ἔσθ' ὅπου μ' ὀλεῖς.
λέγω δέ σοι· τὸν ἄνδρα τοῦτον, ὃν πάλαι
ζητεῖς ἀπειλῶν κἀνακηρύσσων φόνον
τὸν Λαΐειον, οὗτός ἐστιν ἐνθάδε,
ξένος λόγῳ μέτοικος· εἶτα δ' ἐγγενὴς
φανήσεται Θηβαῖος, οὐδ' ἡσθήσεται
τῇ ξυμφορᾷ· τυφλὸς γὰρ ἐκ δεδορκότος
καὶ πτωχὸς ἀντὶ πλουσίου ξένην ἔπι
σκήπτρῳ προδεικνὺς γαῖαν ἐμπορεύσεται.

OEDIPUS

How riddling and obscure in excess are all your words!

TIRESIAS

Do you not excel in answering such riddles?

OEDIPUS

Yes, taunt me in matters in which you shall find me great!

TIRESIAS

But it is that very happening that has been your ruin.

OEDIPUS

Well, if I preserved this city, I do not care!

TIRESIAS

Then I shall go; boy, take me away!

OEDIPUS

Yes, let him take you! While you are here, you are an obstruction and a nuisance, and when you have left you will cause us no more grief.

TIRESIAS

I shall go, now that I have spoken of the things that brought me here, with no fear of your angry countenance; for it cannot be that you destroy me. And I say this to you: the man you have long been looking for, with threats and proclamations about the murder of Laius, that man is here! He is thought to be a stranger who has migrated here, but later he shall be revealed to be a native Theban, and the finding will bring him no pleasure; for he shall travel over strange land blind instead of seeing, poor

---

442 τύχῃ] τέχνῃ Bentley

φανήσεται δὲ παισὶ τοῖς αὑτοῦ ξυνὼν
ἀδελφὸς αὑτὸς καὶ πατήρ, κἀξ ἧς ἔφυ
γυναικὸς υἱὸς καὶ πόσις, καὶ τοῦ πατρὸς
ὁμόσπορός τε καὶ φονεύς. καὶ ταῦτ᾽ ἰὼν
εἴσω λογίζου· κἂν λάβῃς ἐψευσμένον,
φάσκειν ἔμ᾽ ἤδη μαντικῇ μηδὲν φρονεῖν.

ΧΟΡΟΣ

τίς ὅντιν᾽ ἁ θεσπιέπει- στρ. α΄
α Δελφὶς ᾗδε πέτρα
ἄρρητ᾽ ἀρρήτων τελέσαν-
τα φοινίαισι χερσίν;
ὥρα νιν ἀελλάδων
ἵππων σθεναρώτερον
φυγᾷ πόδα νωμᾶν.
ἔνοπλος γὰρ ἐπ᾽ αὐτὸν ἐπενθρῴσκει
πυρὶ καὶ στεροπαῖς ὁ Διὸς γενέτας,
δειναὶ δ᾽ ἅμ᾽ ἕπονται
Κῆρες ἀναπλάκητοι.
ἔλαμψε γὰρ τοῦ νιφόεν- ἀντ. α΄
τος ἀρτίως φανεῖσα
φήμα Παρνασοῦ τὸν ἄδη-
λον ἄνδρα πάντ᾽ ἰχνεύειν.
φοιτᾷ γὰρ ὑπ᾽ ἀγρίαν
ὕλαν ἀνά τ᾽ ἄντρα καὶ
πετραῖος ὁ ταῦρος,
μέλεος μελέῳ ποδὶ χηρεύων,

instead of rich, feeling his way with his stick. And he shall be revealed as being to his children whom he lives with both a brother and a father, and to his mother both a son and a husband, and to his father a sharer in his wife and a killer. Go inside and think this over, and if you find me to be mistaken, you may say at once that I have no wisdom in my prophecies!

Exit TIRESIAS; *and* OEDIPUS *leaves the stage and goes into the palace.*

CHORUS

Who is he that the oracular rock of Delphi sung as having done a deed worse than unspeakable with bloody hands? It is time for him to ply his foot in flight with strength mightier than that of the horses of the winds. For armed with fire and lightning there leaps upon him the son of Zeus, and after him come dread spirits of death that never miss their mark.

For lately flashed out the word from snowcapped Parnassus that all were to follow the track of the mysterious man. Yes, he travels through the wild jungle and through caves and over rocks, like a bull, limping sadly with sore-wounded foot, trying to leave far behind the prophecies

---

464 ᾗδε J. E. Powell: εἶδε K: εἶπε cett.

478 πετραῖος ὁ fort. Lac, sed non iam legitur: πετραῖος ὡς KRV: πέτραις ὡς Gp: πέτρας ὡς pat

τὰ μεσόμφαλα γᾶς ἀπονοσφίζων
μαντεῖα· τὰ δ᾽ ἀεὶ
ζῶντα περιποτᾶται.
δεινά με νῦν, δεινὰ ταράσσει στρ. β′
σοφὸς οἰωνοθέτας,
οὔτε δοκοῦντ᾽ οὔτ᾽ ἀποφάσκονθ᾽,
ὅ τι λέξω δ᾽ ἀπορῶ.
πέτομαι δ᾽ ἐλπίσιν οὔτ᾽ ἐν-
θάδ᾽ ὁρῶν οὔτ᾽ ὀπίσω.
τί γὰρ ἢ Λαβδακίδαις
ἢ τῷ Πολύβου νεῖ-
κος ἔκειτ᾽ οὔτε πάροιθέν
ποτ᾽ ἔγωγ᾽ οὔτε τανῦν πως
ἔμαθον, πρὸς ὅτου δὴ
βασάνῳ <–∪∪–>
ἐπὶ τὰν ἐπίδαμον
φάτιν εἶμ᾽ Οἰδιπόδα Λαβδακίδαις
ἐπίκουρος ἀδήλων θανάτων.
ἀλλ᾽ ὁ μὲν οὖν Ζεὺς ὅ τ᾽ Ἀπόλλων ἀντ. β′
ξυνετοὶ καὶ τὰ βροτῶν
εἰδότες· ἀνδρῶν δ᾽ ὅτι μάντις
πλέον ἢ ᾽γὼ φέρεται,
κρίσις οὐκ ἔστιν ἀληθής·
σοφίᾳ δ᾽ ἂν σοφίαν
παραμείψειεν ἀνήρ.
ἀλλ᾽ οὔποτ᾽ ἔγωγ᾽ ἄν,
πρὶν ἴδοιμ᾽ ὀρθὸν ἔπος, μεμ-
φομένων ἂν καταφαίην.

coming from earth's centre; but they hover about him, ever alive.

Grievous, grievous is the trouble caused me by the wise interpreter of omens; I neither believe it nor deny it, but I cannot tell what to say, and fly on the wings of hope, seeing neither the present nor the future. For what quarrel had the Labdacids or the son of Polybus neither before nor now have I learned, that I should put the matter to the test and go against the public fame of Oedipus to aid the Labdacids in the matter of mysterious deaths.

Well, Zeus and Apollo are wise and know the affairs of mortals; but when it comes to men, one cannot tell for sure that a prophet carries more weight than I; a man may surpass one kind of wisdom by means of another. But never, till I see the saying made unmistakable, shall I assent to those that find fault with him; for in sight of all

---

483 *με νῦν* Bergk: *μὲν οὖν* codd.

492 *πως* Ll.-J.: *πω* codd.

494 lacunam post *βασάνῳ* statuit Ritter, post *ἔμαθον* Campbell, post *ὅτου* Brunck, post *δὴ* Hermann: <*χρησάμενος*> suppl. Brunck, <*πίστιν ἔχων*> G. Wolff

φανερὰ γὰρ ἐπ᾽ αὐτῷ
πτερόεσσ᾽ ἦλθε κόρα
ποτέ, καὶ σοφὸς ὤφθη
βασάνῳ θ᾽ ἡδύπολις· τῷ ἀπ᾽ ἐμᾶς
φρενὸς οὔποτ᾽ ὀφλήσει κακίαν.

ΚΡΕΩΝ

ἄνδρες πολῖται, δείν᾽ ἔπη πεπυσμένος
κατηγορεῖν μου τὸν τύραννον Οἰδίπουν
πάρειμ᾽ ἀτλητῶν. εἰ γὰρ ἐν ταῖς ξυμφοραῖς
ταῖς νῦν δοκεῖ τι πρός γ᾽ ἐμοῦ πεπονθέναι
λόγοισιν εἴτ᾽ ἔργοισιν ἐς βλάβην φέρον,
οὔτοι βίου μοι τοῦ μακραίωνος πόθος,
φέροντι τήνδε βάξιν. οὐ γὰρ εἰς ἁπλοῦν
ἡ ζημία μοι τοῦ λόγου τούτου φέρει,
ἀλλ᾽ ἐς μέγιστον, εἰ κακὸς μὲν ἐν πόλει,
κακὸς δὲ πρὸς σοῦ καὶ φίλων κεκλήσομαι.

ΧΟΡΟΣ

ἀλλ᾽ ἦλθε μὲν δὴ τοῦτο τοὔνειδος, τάχ᾽ ἂν δ᾽
ὀργῇ βιασθὲν μᾶλλον ἢ γνώμῃ φρενῶν.

ΚΡΕΩΝ

τοὔπος δ᾽ ἐφάνθη ταῖς ἐμαῖς γνώμαις ὅτι
πεισθεὶς ὁ μάντις τοὺς λόγους ψευδεῖς λέγοι;

ΧΟΡΟΣ

ηὐδᾶτο μὲν τάδ᾽, οἶδα δ᾽ οὐ γνώμῃ τινί.

the winged maiden came against him once, and he was seen to be wise and approved as dear to the city; thus shall he never be convicted of crime by my judgment.

Enter CREON.

CREON

Men of the city, I am here in indignation, having heard that King Oedipus is accusing me with terrible words. If in the present crisis he thinks he has suffered at my hands anything tending to harm, whether by words or deeds, I have no desire for long life when I hear such things said. No, the damage done by such a saying tends to no simple matter, but to one of great moment, if I am to be called a traitor to the city and a traitor in your eyes and in those of my friends.

CHORUS

Well, this charge was uttered, but perhaps it was forced out by anger rather than by considered thought.

CREON

But was it openly said that the prophet was persuaded by my counsels to speak lies?

CHORUS

This was said, but I know that it was unconsidered.

---

509 *ποτε*] *τότε* Blaydes
510 *τὼς* Ll.-J.: *τῷ* Krap: *των* Π 7 | *ἀπ'*] *πρὸς* Elmsley
516 *δοκεῖ τι* Blaydes: *νομίζει* codd.
523 *δ'* Π 7, coni. M. Schmidt: om. codd.
525 *τοὔπος* Π 7, Kr, coni. Heimsoeth: *τοῦ πρὸς* Lp: *πρὸς τοῦ* a
527 *τινί* Ll.-J. (cf. 524): *τίνι* codd.

ΚΡΕΩΝ

ἐξ ὀμμάτων δ' ὀρθῶν τε κἀπ' ὀρθῆς φρενὸς
κατηγορεῖτο τοὐπίκλημα τοῦτό μου;

ΧΟΡΟΣ

οὐκ οἶδ'· ἃ γὰρ δρῶσ' οἱ κρατοῦντες οὐχ ὁρῶ.
[αὐτὸς δ' ὅδ' ἤδη δωμάτων ἔξω περᾷ.]

ΟΙΔΙΠΟΥΣ

οὗτος σύ, πῶς δεῦρ' ἦλθες; ἦ τοσόνδ' ἔχεις
τόλμης πρόσωπον ὥστε τὰς ἐμὰς στέγας
ἵκου, φονεὺς ὢν τοῦδε τἀνδρὸς ἐμφανῶς
λῃστής τ' ἐναργὴς τῆς ἐμῆς τυραννίδος;
φέρ' εἰπὲ πρὸς θεῶν, δειλίαν ἢ μωρίαν
ἰδών τιν' ἔν μοι ταῦτ' ἐβουλεύσω ποεῖν;
ἢ τοὔργον ὡς οὐ γνωριοῖμί σου τόδε
δόλῳ προσέρπον κοὐκ ἀλεξοίμην μαθών;
ἆρ' οὐχὶ μῶρόν ἐστι τοὐγχείρημά σου,
ἄνευ τε πλούτου καὶ φίλων τυραννίδα
θηρᾶν, ὃ πλήθει χρήμασίν θ' ἁλίσκεται;

ΚΡΕΩΝ

οἶσθ' ὡς πόησον; ἀντὶ τῶν εἰρημένων
ἴσ' ἀντάκουσον, κᾆτα κρῖν' αὐτὸς μαθών.

ΟΙΔΙΠΟΥΣ

λέγειν σὺ δεινός, μανθάνειν δ' ἐγὼ κακὸς
σοῦ· δυσμενῆ γὰρ καὶ βαρύν σ' ηὕρηκ' ἐμοί.

528 κἀπ' Π 7: κἀξ codd.
531 om. Π 7, del. H. J. Rose
537 ἔν μοι Reisig: ἐν ἐμοὶ codd.

CREON

But was it with a steady look and from a steady mind that this accusation was pronounced against me?

CHORUS

I do not know; for I cannot judge the doings of my rulers. [But here he comes himself, out of the house.]

Enter, suddenly, OEDIPUS.

OEDIPUS

You there, how have you dared come here? Have you such a shameless face that you have come to my house, though you are clearly the would-be murderer of its master and are seen to be the would-be robber of my kingdom? Come, tell me, I beg you, was it because you saw in me some cowardice or folly that you decided to act thus? Or did you think I would not recognise the act as yours, as it came stealthily against me, and would not learn of it and defend myself? Is not your attempt foolish, without wealth and without friends to try to steal a kingdom, a thing that is captured with massed supporters and with money?

CREON

Do you know what you should do? Listen fairly in turn to my words that reply to yours, and then judge when you have heard them!

OEDIPUS

You are a clever speaker, but I am a poor listener to you, for I have found you to be a bitter enemy to me.

---

541 πλούτου anon. (1803): πλήθους codd.
545 an βραδύς? (cf. 548)

ΚΡΕΩΝ

τοῦτ᾽ αὐτὸ νῦν μου πρῶτ᾽ ἄκουσον ὡς ἐρῶ.

ΟΙΔΙΠΟΥΣ

τοῦτ᾽ αὐτὸ μή μοι φράζ᾽, ὅπως οὐκ εἶ κακός.

ΚΡΕΩΝ

εἴ τοι νομίζεις κτῆμα τὴν αὐθαδίαν
εἶναί τι τοῦ νοῦ χωρίς, οὐκ ὀρθῶς φρονεῖς.

ΟΙΔΙΠΟΥΣ

εἴ τοι νομίζεις ἄνδρα συγγενῆ κακῶς
δρῶν οὐχ ὑφέξειν τὴν δίκην, οὐκ εὖ φρονεῖς.

ΚΡΕΩΝ

ξύμφημί σοι ταῦτ᾽ ἔνδικ᾽ εἰρῆσθαι· τὸ δὲ
πάθημ᾽ ὁποῖον φὴς παθεῖν δίδασκέ με.

ΟΙΔΙΠΟΥΣ

ἔπειθες, ἢ οὐκ ἔπειθες, ὡς χρείη μ᾽ ἐπὶ
τὸν σεμνόμαντιν ἄνδρα πέμψασθαί τινα;

ΚΡΕΩΝ

καὶ νῦν ἔθ᾽ αὐτός εἰμι τῷ βουλεύματι.

ΟΙΔΙΠΟΥΣ

πόσον τιν᾽ ἤδη δῆθ᾽ ὁ Λάιος χρόνον—

ΚΡΕΩΝ

δέδρακε ποῖον ἔργον; οὐ γὰρ ἐννοῶ.

ΟΙΔΙΠΟΥΣ

ἄφαντος ἔρρει θανασίμῳ χειρώματι;

ΚΡΕΩΝ

μακροὶ παλαιοί τ᾽ ἂν μετρηθεῖεν χρόνοι.

CREON

First of all, listen to this!

OEDIPUS

First of all, do not tell me that you are not a traitor!

CREON

If you believe that obstinacy without sense is worth possessing, you are not thinking wisely.

OEDIPUS

If you believe that you can harm a kinsman and not pay the penalty, you are unwise.

CREON

I agree that what you say is just; but tell me what it is you say I did to you!

OEDIPUS

Did you or did you not persuade me that I ought to send someone for the much-revered prophet?

CREON

Yes, I still stand by the advice I gave you.

OEDIPUS

How long is it now since Laius . . .

CREON

Did what? I do not understand.

OEDIPUS

Vanished from sight by a deadly stroke?

CREON

The count of years would run far back.

ΟΙΔΙΠΟΥΣ

τότ᾿ οὖν ὁ μάντις οὗτος ἦν ἐν τῇ τέχνῃ;

ΚΡΕΩΝ

σοφός γ᾿ ὁμοίως κἀξ ἴσου τιμώμενος.

ΟΙΔΙΠΟΥΣ

ἐμνήσατ᾿ οὖν ἐμοῦ τι τῷ τότ᾿ ἐν χρόνῳ;

ΚΡΕΩΝ

οὔκουν ἐμοῦ γ᾿ ἑστῶτος οὐδαμοῦ πέλας.

ΟΙΔΙΠΟΥΣ

ἀλλ᾿ οὐκ ἔρευναν τοῦ κανόντος ἔσχετε;

ΚΡΕΩΝ

παρέσχομεν, πῶς δ᾿ οὐχί; κοὐκ ἠκούσαμεν.

ΟΙΔΙΠΟΥΣ

πῶς οὖν τόθ᾿ οὗτος ὁ σοφὸς οὐκ ηὔδα τάδε;

ΚΡΕΩΝ

οὐκ οἶδ᾿· ἐφ᾿ οἷς γὰρ μὴ φρονῶ σιγᾶν φιλῶ.

ΟΙΔΙΠΟΥΣ

τοσόνδε γ᾿ οἶσθα καὶ λέγοις ἂν εὖ φρονῶν—

ΚΡΕΩΝ

ποῖον τόδ᾿; εἰ γὰρ οἶδά γ᾿, οὐκ ἀρνήσομαι.

ΟΙΔΙΠΟΥΣ

ὁθούνεκ᾿, εἰ μὴ σοὶ ξυνῆλθε, τὰς ἐμὰς
οὐκ ἄν ποτ᾿ εἶπε Λαΐου διαφθοράς.

566 κανόντος Herwerden: θανόντος codd.

OEDIPUS

Did the prophet in those days practise his craft?

CREON

He was just as wise and enjoyed equal honour.

OEDIPUS

Did he make any mention of me at that time?

CREON

Not while I was standing anywhere nearby.

OEDIPUS

But did you make no search for the killer?

CREON

We did, of course, but we heard nothing.

OEDIPUS

How came it, then, that this wise man did not tell you this?

CREON

I do not know; when I do not understand I like to say nothing.

OEDIPUS

But you know this much, and you would tell me if you were honest—

CREON

What thing? If I know, I shall not refuse.

OEDIPUS

That if he had not been in concert with you he would never have spoken of my killing Laius.

ΚΡΕΩΝ

εἰ μὲν λέγει τάδ', αὐτὸς οἶσθ'· ἐγὼ δέ σου
μαθεῖν δικαιῶ ταὔθ' ἅπερ κἀμοῦ σὺ νῦν.

ΟΙΔΙΠΟΥΣ

ἐκμάνθαν'· οὐ γὰρ δὴ φονεὺς ἁλώσομαι.

ΚΡΕΩΝ

τί δῆτ'; ἀδελφὴν τὴν ἐμὴν γήμας ἔχεις;

ΟΙΔΙΠΟΥΣ

ἄρνησις οὐκ ἔνεστιν ὧν ἀνιστορεῖς.

ΚΡΕΩΝ

ἄρχεις δ' ἐκείνῃ ταὐτὰ γῆς ἴσον νέμων;

ΟΙΔΙΠΟΥΣ

ἃν ᾖ θέλουσα πάντ' ἐμοῦ κομίζεται.

ΚΡΕΩΝ

οὔκουν ἰσοῦμαι σφῷν ἐγὼ δυοῖν τρίτος;

ΟΙΔΙΠΟΥΣ

ἐνταῦθα γὰρ δὴ καὶ κακὸς φαίνῃ φίλος.

ΚΡΕΩΝ

οὔκ, εἰ διδοίης γ' ὡς ἐγὼ σαυτῷ λόγον.
σκέψαι δὲ τοῦτο πρῶτον, εἴ τιν' ἂν δοκεῖς
ἄρχειν ἑλέσθαι ξὺν φόβοισι μᾶλλον ἢ
ἄτρεστον εὕδοντ', εἰ τά γ' αὔθ' ἕξει κράτη.
ἐγὼ μὲν οὖν οὔτ' αὐτὸς ἱμείρων ἔφυν
τύραννος εἶναι μᾶλλον ἢ τύραννα δρᾶν,

CREON

If he said that, you must know; but I claim the right to learn from you as much as you have just claimed to learn from me.

OEDIPUS

You shall learn all you wish; I shall not be proved to be the murderer.

CREON

Well, are you married to my sister?

OEDIPUS

It is impossible to answer no to your question.

CREON

And do you rule the land, allowing her an equal share in power?

OEDIPUS

Everything she wishes she obtains from me.

CREON

And am I not a third, equal to each of you?

OEDIPUS

That is where you are shown to be a traitorous friend.

CREON

Not if you reflect upon the matter as I do. Consider first this, whether you think anyone would choose to rule in terror rather than to rule while sleeping unafraid, if the power he has will be the same. Well, I am not the man to wish to be a king rather than to have royal power, nor is

---

576 *φονεύς* <γ'> Blaydes
586 *εἰ τά γ' αὔθ'*] *εἴ γε ταὔθ'* Broadhead

οὔτ᾽ ἄλλος ὅστις σωφρονεῖν ἐπίσταται.
νῦν μὲν γὰρ ἐκ σοῦ πάντ᾽ ἄνευ φόβου φέρω,
εἰ δ᾽ αὐτὸς ἦρχον, πολλὰ κἂν ἄκων ἔδρων.
πῶς δῆτ᾽ ἐμοὶ τυραννὶς ἡδίων ἔχειν
ἀρχῆς ἀλύπου καὶ δυναστείας ἔφυ;
οὔπω τοσοῦτον ἠπατημένος κυρῶ
ὥστ᾽ ἄλλα χρῄζειν ἢ τὰ σὺν κέρδει καλά.
νῦν πᾶσι χαίρω, νῦν με πᾶς ἀσπάζεται,
νῦν οἱ σέθεν χρῄζοντες ἐκκαλοῦσί με·
τὸ γὰρ τυχεῖν αὐτοῖσι πᾶν ἐνταῦθ᾽ ἔνι.
πῶς δῆτ᾽ ἐγὼ κεῖν᾽ ἂν λάβοιμ᾽ ἀφεὶς τάδε;
[οὐκ ἂν γένοιτο νοῦς κακὸς καλῶς φρονῶν.]
ἀλλ᾽ οὔτ᾽ ἐραστὴς τῆσδε τῆς γνώμης ἔφυν
οὔτ᾽ ἂν μετ᾽ ἄλλου δρῶντος ἂν τλαίην ποτέ.
καὶ τῶνδ᾽ ἔλεγχον τοῦτο μὲν Πυθώδ᾽ ἰὼν
πεύθου τὰ χρησθέντ᾽, εἰ σαφῶς ἤγγειλά σοι·
τοῦτ᾽ ἄλλ᾽, ἐάν με τῷ τερασκόπῳ λάβῃς
κοινῇ τι βουλεύσαντα, μή μ᾽ ἁπλῇ κτάνῃς
ψήφῳ, διπλῇ δέ, τῇ τ᾽ ἐμῇ καὶ σῇ, λαβών,
γνώμῃ δ᾽ ἀδήλῳ μή με χωρὶς αἰτιῶ.
οὐ γὰρ δίκαιον οὔτε τοὺς κακοὺς μάτην
χρηστοὺς νομίζειν οὔτε τοὺς χρηστοὺς κακούς.
[φίλον γὰρ ἐσθλὸν ἐκβαλεῖν ἴσον λέγω
καὶ τὸν παρ᾽ αὑτῷ βίοτον, ὃν πλεῖστον φιλεῖ.]
ἀλλ᾽ ἐν χρόνῳ γνώσῃ τάδ᾽ ἀσφαλῶς, ἐπεὶ
χρόνος δίκαιον ἄνδρα δείκνυσιν μόνος,
κακὸν δὲ κἂν ἐν ἡμέρᾳ γνοίης μιᾷ.

any man who knows how to think sensibly. As things are, I obtain everything from you without fear, and if I were the king, I would have to do many things against my will. How, indeed, is it pleasanter for me to be a king than to hold power and influence without grief? I am not so deluded as to wish for anything beyond what is honourable as well as profitable. Now everyone salutes me, everyone greets me; now those who want something from you take me aside, since they can get all they wish for if they do. How could I let this go to get that other place? [A mind that thinks sensibly cannot become evil]. Well, I have no love for this attitude, nor could I bring myself to act with another who did such a thing.

To put me to the test, go to Pytho and ask about the oracle, whether I reported it truly; and next, if you find me to have plotted with the soothsayer, doom me to death not with one vote, but with two, yours and my own, but do not accuse me by your own guess, upon a mere surmise. Both are unjust, wrongly to think bad men good and wrongly to think good men bad. [I think that for a man to cast off a true friend is equal to casting out his own way of life, which he most loves]. But in course of time you will learn this with certainty, since time alone reveals the just man, but the traitor you can learn to know in a single day.

---

600 del. G. Wolff

611–12 del. Ll.-J. (611–15 iam van Deventer)

ΧΟΡΟΣ

καλῶς ἔλεξεν εὐλαβουμένῳ πεσεῖν,
ἄναξ· φρονεῖν γὰρ οἱ ταχεῖς οὐκ ἀσφαλεῖς.

ΟΙΔΙΠΟΥΣ

ὅταν ταχύς τις οὑπιβουλεύων λάθρᾳ
χωρῇ, ταχὺν δεῖ κἀμὲ βουλεύειν πάλιν.
εἰ δ' ἡσυχάζων προσμενῶ, τὰ τοῦδε μὲν
πεπραγμέν' ἔσται, τἀμὰ δ' ἡμαρτημένα.

ΚΡΕΩΝ

τί δῆτα χρῄζεις; ἦ με γῆς ἔξω βαλεῖν;

ΟΙΔΙΠΟΥΣ

ἥκιστα· θνῄσκειν, οὐ φυγεῖν σε βούλομαι.
* * * * *

ΚΡΕΩΝ

ὅταν προδείξῃς οἷόν ἐστι τὸ φθονεῖν
* * * * *

ΟΙΔΙΠΟΥΣ

ὡς οὐχ ὑπείξων οὐδὲ πιστεύσων λέγεις;

ΚΡΕΩΝ

οὐ γὰρ φρονοῦντά σ' εὖ βλέπω.

ΟΙΔΙΠΟΥΣ

τὸ γοῦν ἐμόν.

ΚΡΕΩΝ

ἀλλ' ἐξ ἴσου δεῖ κἀμόν.

ΟΙΔΙΠΟΥΣ

ἀλλ' ἔφυς κακός.

623 post hunc versum et 624 lacunas statuit Bruhn (cf. 641)

CHORUS

He has spoken well, lord, in the view of a man who takes care not to fall; for those who think quickly do not think safely.

OEDIPUS

When the secret conspirator moves fast, I also must plan quickly; but if I quietly wait for him, his design will be accomplished, and I shall have lost.

CREON

What is it you want? To expel me from the land?

OEDIPUS

Not so! I want death for you, not exile!

[*at least two lines are missing*]

CREON

When you have first shown what envy is!

[*again there is a gap in the text*]

OEDIPUS

Do your words mean that you will not yield and will not believe me?

CREON

Yes, because I can see that you are not true to me.

OEDIPUS

I am true to myself.

CREON

But you should be true to me also.

OEDIPUS

But you are a traitor!

---

627 κἀμὸν] τοὐμὸν Herwerden

ΚΡΕΩΝ

εἰ δὲ ξυνίῃς μηδέν;

ΟΙΔΙΠΟΥΣ

ἀρκτέον γ᾽ ὅμως.

ΚΡΕΩΝ

οὔτοι κακῶς γ᾽ ἄρχοντος.

ΟΙΔΙΠΟΥΣ

ὦ πόλις πόλις.

ΚΡΕΩΝ

κἀμοὶ πόλεως μέτεστιν, οὐχὶ σοὶ μόνῳ.

ΧΟΡΟΣ

παύσασθ᾽, ἄνακτες· καιρίαν δ᾽ ὑμῖν ὁρῶ
τήνδ᾽ ἐκ δόμων στείχουσαν Ἰοκάστην, μεθ᾽ ἧς
τὸ νῦν παρεστὸς νεῖκος εὖ θέσθαι χρεών.

ΙΟΚΑΣΤΗ

τί τὴν ἄβουλον, ὦ ταλαίπωροι, στάσιν
γλώσσης ἐπήρασθ᾽; οὐδ᾽ ἐπαισχύνεσθε γῆς
οὕτω νοσούσης ἴδια κινοῦντες κακά;
οὐκ εἶ σύ τ᾽ οἴκους σύ τε, Κρέον, τὰς σὰς στέγας,
καὶ μὴ τὸ μηδὲν ἄλγος ἐς μέγ᾽ οἴσετε;

ΚΡΕΩΝ

ὅμαιμε, δεινά μ᾽ Οἰδίπους ὁ σὸς πόσις
δρᾶσαι δικαιοῖ †δυοῖν ἀποκρίνας† κακοῖν,
ἢ γῆς ἀπῶσαι πατρίδος, ἢ κτεῖναι λαβών.

CREON

But if you understand nothing?

OEDIPUS

None the less, I have to rule!

CREON

Not if you rule badly!

OEDIPUS

Think of the city, the city!

CREON

But I too have a share in the city, and not you alone.

CHORUS

Cease, my lords! In timely fashion I see Iocaste here coming from the house; with her aid you must settle your present quarrel.

Enter IOCASTE.

IOCASTE

Wretches, why have you struck up this foolish battle of abuse? Are you not ashamed to start up private troubles when the country is thus sick? Will you not go indoors, and you, Creon, to your house, and not make what ought not to pain you into something big?

CREON

Sister, your husband Oedipus threatens to do terrible things to me, one of two evils, either to drive me from my native land or to take me and kill me.

---

628 γ'] δ' O

634 τὴν] τήνδ' Doederlein

637 τὰς σὰς Meineke: κατὰ Lrpa: om. Zrt

640 δυοῖν ἀποκρίνας] θἄτερον δυοῖν Dindorf

ΟΙΔΙΠΟΥΣ

ξύμφημι· δρῶντα γάρ νιν, ὦ γύναι, κακῶς
εἴληφα τοὐμὸν σῶμα σὺν τέχνῃ κακῇ.

ΚΡΕΩΝ

μή νυν ὀναίμην, ἀλλ' ἀραῖος, εἴ σέ τι
δέδρακ', ὀλοίμην, ὧν ἐπαιτιᾷ με δρᾶν.

ΙΟΚΑΣΤΗ

ὦ πρὸς θεῶν πίστευσον, Οἰδίπους, τάδε,
μάλιστα μὲν τόνδ' ὅρκον αἰδεσθεὶς θεῶν,
ἔπειτα κἀμὲ τούσδε θ' οἳ πάρεισί σοι.

ΧΟΡΟΣ

πιθοῦ θελήσας φρονή- στρ.
σας τ', ἄναξ, λίσσομαι—

ΟΙΔΙΠΟΥΣ

τί σοι θέλεις δῆτ' εἰκάθω;

ΧΟΡΟΣ

τὸν οὔτε πρὶν νήπιον
νῦν τ' ἐν ὅρκῳ μέγαν καταίδεσαι.

ΟΙΔΙΠΟΥΣ

οἶσθ' οὖν ἃ χρῄζεις;

ΧΟΡΟΣ

οἶδα.

ΟΙΔΙΠΟΥΣ

φράζε δή· τί φῄς;

OEDIPUS

It is true, because I have found him out in trying to do violence against me by an evil scheme.

CREON

May I never prosper, but may I perish under a curse if I have done to you any of the things with which you charge me!

IOCASTE

I beg you, Oedipus, believe him! You should respect first of all the oath by the gods which he has sworn, and then me and these men whom you see here.

CHORUS

Let your will and thought cause you to comply, my lord, I beg you—

OEDIPUS

What is it that you wish me to concede?

CHORUS

Respect the man who was never foolish in the past and who now acquires greatness by his oath!

OEDIPUS

Then do you know what it is you wish for?

CHORUS

Yes!

OEDIPUS

Tell me, then! What are you saying!

ΧΟΡΟΣ

τὸν ἐναγῆ φίλον μήποτέ σ᾽ αἰτίᾳ
σὺν ἀφανεῖ λόγων ἄτιμον βαλεῖν.

ΟΙΔΙΠΟΥΣ

εὖ νυν ἐπίστω, ταῦθ᾽ ὅταν ζητῇς, ἐμοὶ
ζητῶν ὄλεθρον ἢ φυγὴν ἐκ τῆσδε γῆς.

ΧΟΡΟΣ

οὐ τὸν πάντων θεῶν θεὸν πρόμον
Ἅλιον· ἐπεὶ ἄθεος ἄφιλος ὅ τι πύματον
ὀλοίμαν, φρόνησιν εἰ τάνδ᾽ ἔχω.
ἀλλά μοι δυσμόρῳ γᾶ φθίνου-
σα τρύχει καρδίαν, τάδ᾽ εἰ κακοῖς
προσάψει τοῖς πάλαι τὰ πρὸς σφῷν.

ΟΙΔΙΠΟΥΣ

ὁ δ᾽ οὖν ἴτω, κεἰ χρή με παντελῶς θανεῖν,
ἢ γῆς ἄτιμον τῆσδ᾽ ἀπωσθῆναι βίᾳ.
τὸ γὰρ σόν, οὐ τὸ τοῦδ᾽, ἐποικτίρω στόμα
ἐλεινόν· οὗτος δ᾽ ἔνθ᾽ ἂν ᾖ στυγήσεται.

ΚΡΕΩΝ

στυγνὸς μὲν εἴκων δῆλος εἶ, βαρὺς δ᾽ ὅταν
θυμοῦ περάσῃς. αἱ δὲ τοιαῦται φύσεις
αὑταῖς δικαίως εἰσὶν ἄλγισται φέρειν.

ΟΙΔΙΠΟΥΣ

οὔκουν μ᾽ ἐάσεις κἀκτὸς εἶ;

CHORUS

That you should never assail with a doubtful charge your friend who is made holy by his oath, denying him the right to speak.

OEDIPUS

Know well that when you ask for this, you are asking for death or exile from this land for me!

CHORUS

No, by the foremost of the gods, the Sun! May I perish in the most awful fashion, given up by gods and friends, if I harbour this thought! But alas for me, the wasting away of the land tears my heart, if the earlier troubles are to have added to them this trouble sprung from you.

OEDIPUS

Well, let him go, even if I must altogether perish, or be driven from this land, deprived of honour. It is your pathetic words, not his, that rouse my pity; he, wherever he is, shall be loathed!

CREON

It is clear that you yield with hatred, and you are formidable when far gone in rage. Such natures are hardest to bear for themselves, and justly.

OEDIPUS

Will you not let me be and depart?

---

656 *μήποτέ σ'* Nauck: *μήποτ' ἐν* codd.

657 *λόγων* Krp: *λόγωι* pa: *λόγον* L *βαλεῖν* t et Suda: *ἐκβαλεῖν* codd.

666 *καρδίαν* Hermann: *ψυχὰν καὶ* codd. post *κακοῖς* add. *κακὰ* codd.: del. Brandscheid

ΚΡΕΩΝ

πορεύσομαι,
σοῦ μὲν τυχὼν ἀγνῶτος, ἐν δὲ τοῖσδε σῶς.

ΧΟΡΟΣ

γύναι, τί μέλλεις κομί- ἀντ.
ζειν δόμων τόνδ᾽ ἔσω;

ΙΟΚΑΣΤΗ

μαθοῦσά γ᾽ ἥτις ἡ τύχη.

ΧΟΡΟΣ

δόκησις ἀγνὼς λόγων
ἦλθε, δάπτει δὲ καὶ τὸ μὴ ᾿νδικον.

ΙΟΚΑΣΤΗ

ἀμφοῖν ἀπ᾽ αὐτοῖν

ΧΟΡΟΣ

ναίχι.

ΙΟΚΑΣΤΗ

καὶ τίς ἦν λόγος;

ΧΟΡΟΣ

ἅλις ἔμοιγ᾽, ἅλις, γᾶς προνοουμένῳ
φαίνεται, ἔνθ᾽ ἔληξεν, αὐτοῦ μένειν.

ΟΙΔΙΠΟΥΣ

ὁρᾷς ἵν᾽ ἥκεις, ἀγαθὸς ὢν γνώμην ἀνήρ,
τοὐμὸν παριεὶς καὶ καταμβλύνων κέαρ;

ΧΟΡΟΣ

ὦναξ, εἶπον μὲν οὐχ ἅπαξ μόνον,
ἴσθι δὲ παραφρόνιμον, ἄπορον ἐπὶ φρόνιμα

CREON

I will go; you I have found uncomprehending, but they have saved me.

Exit CREON.

CHORUS

Lady, why do you delay to conduct him inside?

IOCASTE

I will when I have learned what was the matter.

CHORUS

An ignorant supposition came up in their talk, but even something that is unjust may sting.

IOCASTE

It came from both?

CHORUS

Yes!

IOCASTE

And what was said?

CHORUS

It is enough, enough, it seems to me, in my concern for this land, that it should remain here where it left off.

OEDIPUS

Do you see what point you have come to, good as your judgment is, by neglecting my interest and blunting my passion?

CHORUS

Lord, I have said it not once only, but know that I should

---

677 *τοῖσδε σῶς* Ll.-J.: *τοῖσδ' ἴσως* rpa: *τοῖσδ' ἴσος* Lpat: *ἴσων* Blaydes 685 *προνοουμένωι* Ven. gr. 468, coni. Blaydes: *προπονουμένῳ* rp: *προπονουμένας* Lpat

πεφάνθαι μ' ἄν, εἴ σ' ἐνοσφιζόμαν,
ὅς γ' ἐμὰν γᾶν φίλαν ἐν πόνοις
ἀλύουσαν κατ' ὀρθὸν οὔρισας,
τανῦν δ' εὔπομπος αὖ γένοιο.

ΙΟΚΑΣΤΗ

πρὸς θεῶν δίδαξον κἄμ', ἄναξ, ὅτου ποτὲ
μῆνιν τοσήνδε πράγματος στήσας ἔχεις.

ΟΙΔΙΠΟΥΣ

ἐρῶ· σὲ γὰρ τῶνδ' ἐς πλέον, γύναι, σέβω·
Κρέοντος, οἷά μοι βεβουλευκὼς ἔχει.

ΙΟΚΑΣΤΗ

λέγ', εἰ σαφῶς τὸ νεῖκος ἐγκαλῶν ἐρεῖς.

ΟΙΔΙΠΟΥΣ

φονέα με φησὶ Λαΐου καθεστάναι.

ΙΟΚΑΣΤΗ

αὐτὸς ξυνειδώς, ἢ μαθὼν ἄλλου πάρα;

ΟΙΔΙΠΟΥΣ

μάντιν μὲν οὖν κακοῦργον ἐσπέμψας, ἐπεὶ
τό γ' εἰς ἑαυτὸν πᾶν ἐλευθεροῖ στόμα.

ΙΟΚΑΣΤΗ

σύ νυν, ἀφεὶς σεαυτὸν ὧν λέγεις πέρι,
ἐμοῦ 'πάκουσον καὶ μάθ' οὕνεκ' ἔστι σοι
βρότειον οὐδὲν μαντικῆς ἔχον τέχνης.
φανῶ δέ σοι σημεῖα τῶνδε σύντομα.

692 σ' ἐνοσφιζόμαν Hermann: σε νοσφίζομαι codd.
694 γ' p, coni. Turnebus: τ' codd. plerique

be seen as mad, resourceless as regards my thought, if I were to turn away from you, who when my beloved country was in a sea of troubles gave it a fair wind; now again may you waft it to safety!

IOCASTE

I beg you, my lord, explain to me also what matter has caused you to build up such great anger.

OEDIPUS

I will, for I have more respect for you, lady, than I have for these. It was Creon, such has been his plot against me!

IOCASTE

Tell me, if you can clearly describe the quarrel in your accusation.

OEDIPUS

He says that I was the murderer of Laius.

IOCASTE

From his own knowledge, or on information from another?

OEDIPUS

No, he sent in a villainous prophet, because as regards himself he keeps his tongue altogether clean.

IOCASTE

Do you now acquit yourself in the matter of which you speak; listen to me and learn that nothing that is mortal is possessed of the prophetic art! I shall show you in brief the proof of this.

---

695 οὔρισας Π1, r, Eustath.: οὔρησας Lpat
696 αὖ γένοιο Blaydes: εἰ δύναιο codd.
709 ἔχον suspectum

χρησμὸς γὰρ ἦλθε Λαΐῳ ποτ᾽, οὐκ ἐρῶ
Φοίβου γ᾽ ἀπ᾽ αὐτοῦ, τῶν δ᾽ ὑπηρετῶν ἄπο,
ὡς αὐτὸν ἥξοι μοῖρα πρὸς παιδὸς θανεῖν,
ὅστις γένοιτ᾽ ἐμοῦ τε κἀκείνου πάρα.
καὶ τὸν μέν, ὥσπερ γ᾽ ἡ φάτις, ξένοι ποτὲ
λῃσταὶ φονεύουσ᾽ ἐν τριπλαῖς ἁμαξιτοῖς·
παιδὸς δὲ βλάστας οὐ διέσχον ἡμέραι
τρεῖς, καί νιν ἄρθρα κεῖνος ἐνζεύξας ποδοῖν
ἔρριψεν ἄλλων χερσὶν εἰς ἄβατον ὄρος.
κἀνταῦθ᾽ Ἀπόλλων οὔτ᾽ ἐκεῖνον ἤνυσεν
φονέα γενέσθαι πατρὸς οὔτε Λάιον
τὸ δεινὸν οὑφοβεῖτο πρὸς παιδὸς παθεῖν.
τοιαῦτα φῆμαι μαντικαὶ διώρισαν,
ὧν ἐντρέπου σὺ μηδέν· ὧν γὰρ ἂν θεὸς
χρείαν ἐρευνᾷ ῥᾳδίως αὐτὸς φανεῖ.

ΟΙΔΙΠΟΥΣ

οἷόν μ᾽ ἀκούσαντ᾽ ἀρτίως ἔχει, γύναι,
ψυχῆς πλάνημα κἀνακίνησις φρενῶν.

ΙΟΚΑΣΤΗ

ποίας μερίμνης τοῦθ᾽ ὑποστραφεὶς λέγεις;

ΟΙΔΙΠΟΥΣ

ἔδοξ᾽ ἀκοῦσαι σοῦ τόδ᾽, ὡς ὁ Λάιος
κατασφαγείη πρὸς τριπλαῖς ἁμαξιτοῖς.

ΙΟΚΑΣΤΗ

ηὐδᾶτο γὰρ ταῦτ᾽, οὐδέ πω λήξαντ᾽ ἔχει.

ΟΙΔΙΠΟΥΣ

καὶ ποῦ 'σθ᾽ ὁ χῶρος οὗτος οὗ τόδ᾽ ἦν πάθος;

An oracle once came to Laius, I will not say from Phoebus himself, but from his servants, saying that it would be his fate to die at the hands of the son who should be the child of him and me. And he, as the story goes, was murdered one day by foreign robbers at the place where three roads meet; but the child's birth was not three days past when Laius fastened his ankles and had him cast out by the hands of others upon the trackless mountain. And so Apollo did not bring it about that he should become the murderer of his father, nor that Laius should suffer the disaster which he feared, death at his son's hands.

Thus did the voices of prophecy outline the future; pay them no regard, for when the god needs a thing and looks for it, he will easily reveal it by himself.

OEDIPUS

What a wandering of the spirit and a stirring of the mind is upon me, lady, since I heard your words just now!

IOCASTE

What is the worry that has made you turn about and speak these words?

OEDIPUS

I thought I heard you say that Laius was slaughtered at the place where three roads meet.

IOCASTE

Yes, that was the story, and it is still told.

OEDIPUS

And where is this place where the disaster happened?

---

719 εἰς post ἄβατον traiecit Musgrave

ΙΟΚΑΣΤΗ

Φωκὶς μὲν ἡ γῆ κλῄζεται, σχιστὴ δ᾽ ὁδὸς
ἐς ταὐτὸ Δελφῶν κἀπὸ Δαυλίας ἄγει.

ΟΙΔΙΠΟΥΣ

καὶ τίς χρόνος τοῖσδ᾽ ἐστὶν οὑξεληλυθώς;

ΙΟΚΑΣΤΗ

σχεδόν τι πρόσθεν ἢ σὺ τῆσδ᾽ ἔχων χθονὸς
ἀρχὴν ἐφαίνου τοῦτ᾽ ἐκηρύχθη πόλει.

ΟΙΔΙΠΟΥΣ

ὦ Ζεῦ, τί μου δρᾶσαι βεβούλευσαι πέρι;

ΙΟΚΑΣΤΗ

τί δ᾽ ἐστί σοι τοῦτ᾽, Οἰδίπους, ἐνθύμιον;

ΟΙΔΙΠΟΥΣ

μήπω μ᾽ ἐρώτα· τὸν δὲ Λάιον φύσιν
τίν᾽ εἶρπε φράζε, τίνα δ᾽ ἀκμὴν ἥβης ἔχων.

ΙΟΚΑΣΤΗ

μέλας, χνοάζων ἄρτι λευκανθὲς κάρα.
μορφῆς δὲ τῆς σῆς οὐκ ἀπεστάτει πολύ.

ΟΙΔΙΠΟΥΣ

οἴμοι τάλας· ἔοικ᾽ ἐμαυτὸν εἰς ἀρὰς
δεινὰς προβάλλων ἀρτίως οὐκ εἰδέναι.

ΙΟΚΑΣΤΗ

πῶς φής; ὀκνῶ τοι πρός σ᾽ ἀποσκοποῦσ᾽, ἄναξ.

ΟΙΔΙΠΟΥΣ

δεινῶς ἀθυμῶ μὴ βλέπων ὁ μάντις ᾖ.
δείξεις δὲ μᾶλλον, ἢν ἓν ἐξείπῃς ἔτι.

IOCASTE

The country is called Phocis, and the road divides; it goes to the same point from Delphi and from Daulis.

OEDIPUS

And how long is it since these things happened?

IOCASTE

This was proclaimed in the city a little before you became manifest as king.

OEDIPUS

O Zeus, how have you decided to act with regard to me?

IOCASTE

What is this, Oedipus, that weighs upon your mind?

OEDIPUS

Do not ask me yet; but tell me about Laius, what he looked like and what stage in manhood he had reached.

IOCASTE

He was dark, but just beginning to have grizzled hair, and his appearance was not far from yours.

OEDIPUS

Ah me! It seems that all unknowing I have exposed myself to a dread curse.

IOCASTE

How do you say? I am afraid as I gaze on you, my lord.

OEDIPUS

I have grievous misgivings that the prophet may have sight; and you will make it clearer, if you tell me one thing more.

---

741 εἶρπε Schneidewin: εἶχε codd. | ἔχων : γύναι Günther
742 μέλας rp: μέγας Lpat

ΙΟΚΑΣΤΗ

καὶ μὴν ὀκνῶ μέν, ἃ δ' ἂν ἔρῃ μαθοῦσ' ἐρῶ.

ΟΙΔΙΠΟΥΣ

πότερον ἐχώρει βαιός, ἢ πολλοὺς ἔχων
ἄνδρας λοχίτας, οἷ' ἀνὴρ ἀρχηγέτης;

ΙΟΚΑΣΤΗ

πέντ' ἦσαν οἱ ξύμπαντες, ἐν δ' αὐτοῖσιν ἦν
κῆρυξ· ἀπήνη δ' ἦγε Λάιον μία.

ΟΙΔΙΠΟΥΣ

αἰαῖ, τάδ' ἤδη διαφανῆ. τίς ἦν ποτε
ὁ τούσδε λέξας τοὺς λόγους ὑμῖν, γύναι;

ΙΟΚΑΣΤΗ

οἰκεύς τις, ὅσπερ ἵκετ' ἐκσωθεὶς μόνος.

ΟΙΔΙΠΟΥΣ

ἦ κἀν δόμοισι τυγχάνει τανῦν παρών;

ΙΟΚΑΣΤΗ

οὐ δῆτ'· ἀφ' οὗ γὰρ κεῖθεν ἦλθε καὶ κράτη
σέ τ' εἶδ' ἔχοντα Λάιόν τ' ὀλωλότα,
ἐξικέτευσε τῆς ἐμῆς χειρὸς θιγὼν
ἀγρούς σφε πέμψαι κἀπὶ ποιμνίων νομάς,
ὡς πλεῖστον εἴη τοῦδ' ἄποπτος ἄστεως.
κἄπεμψ' ἐγώ νιν· ἄξιος γάρ, οἷ' ἀνὴρ
δοῦλος, φέρειν ἦν τῆσδε καὶ μείζω χάριν.

ΟΙΔΙΠΟΥΣ

πῶς ἂν μόλοι δῆθ' ἡμὶν ἐν τάχει πάλιν;

IOCASTE

Well, I am afraid, but whatever you ask me I will listen and answer.

OEDIPUS

Did he go with a small retinue, or had he many guards, in the manner of a king?

IOCASTE

There were altogether five, and one of them a herald, and a single wagon carried Laius.

OEDIPUS

Alas, now all is crystal clear! Who was it that told you this story, lady?

IOCASTE

A slave, who was the only one to come back safe.

OEDIPUS

Does it happen that he is now in the house?

IOCASTE

No; for after he returned and saw that you were in power and Laius was dead, he clasped my hand in supplication, begging me to send him to the fields and to the pastures, so that he could be as far as possible from the city. And I sent him there; for as slaves go he would have deserved a greater favour than this.

OEDIPUS

Could he come back here quickly?

---

749 ἃ δ' ἂν codd. plerique: ἂν δ' Dresdensis D. 183 et Laud. gr. 54

763 οἷ' Hermann: ὅ γ' LP: ὅδ' Krpa: ὅδε γε at

ΙΟΚΑΣΤΗ

πάρεστιν. ἀλλὰ πρὸς τί τοῦτ᾽ ἐφίεσαι;

ΟΙΔΙΠΟΥΣ

δέδοικ᾽ ἐμαυτόν, ὦ γύναι, μὴ πόλλ᾽ ἄγαν
εἰρημέν᾽ ᾖ μοι δι᾽ ἅ νιν εἰσιδεῖν θέλω.

ΙΟΚΑΣΤΗ

ἀλλ᾽ ἵξεται μέν· ἀξία δέ που μαθεῖν
κἀγὼ τά γ᾽ ἐν σοὶ δυσφόρως ἔχοντ᾽, ἄναξ.

ΟΙΔΙΠΟΥΣ

κοὐ μὴ στερηθῇς γ᾽ ἐς τοσοῦτον ἐλπίδων
ἐμοῦ βεβῶτος. τῷ γὰρ ἂν καὶ κρείσσονι
λέξαιμ᾽ ἂν ἢ σοὶ διὰ τύχης τοιᾶσδ᾽ ἰών;
ἐμοὶ πατὴρ μὲν Πόλυβος ἦν Κορίνθιος,
μήτηρ δὲ Μερόπη Δωρίς. ἠγόμην δ᾽ ἀνὴρ
ἀστῶν μέγιστος τῶν ἐκεῖ, πρίν μοι τύχη
τοιάδ᾽ ἐπέστη, θαυμάσαι μὲν ἀξία,
σπουδῆς γε μέντοι τῆς ἐμῆς οὐκ ἀξία.
ἀνὴρ γὰρ ἐν δείπνοις μ᾽ ὑπερπλησθεὶς μέθης
καλεῖ παρ᾽ οἴνῳ πλαστὸς ὡς εἴην πατρί.
κἀγὼ βαρυνθεὶς τὴν μὲν οὖσαν ἡμέραν
μόλις κατέσχον, θἠτέρᾳ δ᾽ ἰὼν πέλας
μητρὸς πατρός τ᾽ ἤλεγχον· οἱ δὲ δυσφόρως
τοὔνειδος ἦγον τῷ μεθέντι τὸν λόγον.
κἀγὼ τὰ μὲν κείνοιν ἐτερπόμην, ὅμως δ᾽
ἔκνιζέ μ᾽ ἀεὶ τοῦθ᾽· ὑφεῖρπε γὰρ πολύ.
λάθρᾳ δὲ μητρὸς καὶ πατρὸς πορεύομαι
Πυθώδε, καί μ᾽ ὁ Φοῖβος ὧν μὲν ἱκόμην

IOCASTE

It can be done; but why do you make this demand?

OEDIPUS

I am afraid I may have said too much, and that is why I wish to see him.

IOCASTE

Why, he shall come; but I think I deserve to learn what worries you, my lord.

OEDIPUS

And you shall not be cheated of the knowledge, now that I have reached such a pitch of expectation! Who has a better right than you to hear the story, since I am living through such an experience?

My father was Polybus of Corinth, and my mother Merope, a Dorian; and I was brought up as the greatest of the citizens, till this happened to me, a thing to be wondered at, but not a thing for me to work for.

At dinner a man got drunk, and over the wine charged me with not being my father's child. I was riled, and for that day scarcely controlled myself; and on the next I went to my mother and my father and questioned them; and they made the man who had let slip the word pay dearly for the insult. So far as concerned them I was comforted, but still this continued to vex me, since it constantly recurred to me. Without the knowledge of my mother and my father I went to Pytho, and Phoebus sent

---

772 καὶ κρείσσονι Blaydes: καὶ μείζονι codd.

ἄτιμον ἐξέπεμψεν, ἄλλα δ' ἀθλίῳ
καὶ δεινὰ καὶ δύστηνα προὔφηνεν λέγων,
ὡς μητρὶ μὲν χρείη με μειχθῆναι, γένος δ'
ἄτλητον ἀνθρώποισι δηλώσοιμ' ὁρᾶν,
φονεὺς δ' ἐσοίμην τοῦ φυτεύσαντος πατρός.
　　κἀγὼ 'πακούσας ταῦτα τὴν Κορινθίαν
ἄστροις τὸ λοιπὸν τεκμαρούμενος χθόνα
ἔφευγον, ἔνθα μήποτ' ὀψοίμην κακῶν
χρησμῶν ὀνείδη τῶν ἐμῶν τελούμενα.
στείχων δ' ἱκνοῦμαι τούσδε τοὺς χώρους ἐν οἷς
σὺ τὸν τύραννον τοῦτον ὄλλυσθαι λέγεις.
καί σοι, γύναι, τἀληθὲς ἐξερῶ. τριπλῆς
ὅτ' ἦ κελεύθου τῆσδ' ὁδοιπορῶν πέλας,
ἐνταῦθά μοι κῆρυξ τε κἀπὶ πωλικῆς
ἀνὴρ ἀπήνης ἐμβεβώς, οἷον σὺ φής,
ξυνηντίαζον· κἀξ ὁδοῦ μ' ὅ θ' ἡγεμὼν
αὐτός θ' ὁ πρέσβυς πρὸς βίαν ἠλαυνέτην.
κἀγὼ τὸν ἐκτρέποντα, τὸν τροχηλάτην,
παίω δι' ὀργῆς· καί μ' ὁ πρέσβυς, ὡς ὁρᾷ,
ὄχους παραστείχοντα τηρήσας, μέσον
κάρα διπλοῖς κέντροισί μου καθίκετο.
οὐ μὴν ἴσην γ' ἔτεισεν, ἀλλὰ συντόμως
σκήπτρῳ τυπεὶς ἐκ τῆσδε χειρὸς ὕπτιος
μέσης ἀπήνης εὐθὺς ἐκκυλίνδεται·
κτείνω δὲ τοὺς ξύμπαντας. εἰ δὲ τῷ ξένῳ
τούτῳ προσήκει Λαΐῳ τι συγγενές,
τίς τοῦδέ γ' ἀνδρὸς νῦν ἂν ἀθλιώτερος,
τίς ἐχθροδαίμων μᾶλλον ἂν γένοιτ' ἀνήρ,

me away cheated of what I had come for, but came out with other things terrible and sad for my unhappy self, saying that I was destined to lie with my mother, and to show to mortals a brood they could not bear to look on, and I should be the murderer of the father who had begotten me.

When I heard this I left the land of Corinth, henceforth making out its position by the stars, and went where I could never see accomplished the shameful predictions of my cruel oracles. And on my way I came to the regions in which you say this king met his death. And I will tell you the truth, lady! When I was walking near this meeting of three roads, I was met by a herald and a man riding in a wagon, such as you describe; and the leader and the old man himself tried to drive me from the road by force. In anger I struck the driver, the man who was trying to turn me back; and when the old man saw it, he waited till I was passing his chariot, and struck me right on the head with his double-pointed goad. Yet he paid the penalty with interest; in a word, this hand struck him with a stick, and he rolled backwards right out of the wagon, and I killed them all. But if this foreigner had any tie with Laius, who now could be more miserable, and who more hateful to the gods, than I, whom no stranger and no citi-

---

789 ἀθλίῳ Herwerden: -ια codd.
790 προὔφηνεν Hermann: προὐφάνη codd.
795 τεκμαρούμενος Nauck: ἐκμετρούμενος codd.
800 om. L
807–8 sic interpunxit Kassel
808 ὄχους Doederlein: ὄχου codd.: ὄχον H. Stephanus
815 ἂν Bergk: ἐστ(ιν) codd.

ὃν μὴ ξένων ἔξεστι μηδ' ἀστῶν τινι
δόμοις δέχεσθαι, μηδὲ προσφωνεῖν τινα,
ὠθεῖν δ' ἀπ' οἴκων; καὶ τάδ' οὔτις ἄλλος ἦν
ἢ 'γὼ 'π' ἐμαυτῷ τάσδ' ἀρὰς ὁ προστιθείς.
λέχη δὲ τοῦ θανόντος ἐν χεροῖν ἐμαῖν
χραίνω, δι' ὧνπερ ὤλετ'. ἆρ' ἔφυν κακός;
ἆρ' οὐχὶ πᾶς ἄναγνος; εἴ με χρὴ φυγεῖν,
καί μοι φυγόντι μήστι τοὺς ἐμοὺς ἰδεῖν
μηδ' ἐμβατεῦσαι πατρίδος, ἢ γάμοις με δεῖ
μητρὸς ζυγῆναι καὶ πατέρα κατακτανεῖν
Πόλυβον, ὃς ἐξέθρεψε κἀξέφυσέ με.
ἆρ' οὐκ ἀπ' ὠμοῦ ταῦτα δαίμονός τις ἂν
κρίνων ἐπ' ἀνδρὶ τῷδ' ἂν ὀρθοίη λόγον;
μὴ δῆτα μὴ δῆτ', ὦ θεῶν ἁγνὸν σέβας,
ἴδοιμι ταύτην ἡμέραν, ἀλλ' ἐκ βροτῶν
βαίην ἄφαντος πρόσθεν ἢ τοιάνδ' ἰδεῖν
κηλῖδ' ἐμαυτῷ συμφορᾶς ἀφιγμένην.

ΧΟΡΟΣ

ἡμῖν μέν, ὦναξ, ταῦτ' ὀκνήρ'· ἕως δ' ἂν οὖν
πρὸς τοῦ παρόντος ἐκμάθῃς, ἔχ' ἐλπίδα.

ΟΙΔΙΠΟΥΣ

καὶ μὴν τοσοῦτόν γ' ἐστί μοι τῆς ἐλπίδος,
τὸν ἄνδρα τὸν βοτῆρα προσμεῖναι μόνον.

ΙΟΚΑΣΤΗ

πεφασμένου δὲ τίς ποθ' ἡ προθυμία;

zen may receive in his home, whom no man may address, but all must drive from their houses. And it was none other than I myself who laid upon myself these curses. And I am polluting the bed of the dead man with the hands by which he perished. Am I a criminal? am I not altogether unholy, if I must leave my country, and in my exile never see my dear ones, nor set foot upon my native land, or else be joined in marriage with my mother and slay my father Polybus, him who brought me up, him who begot me? Would one not be right who judged that this came upon me by the action of a cruel deity? Never, never, O sacred majesty of the gods, may I see that day, but may I vanish from among men before I see the stain of such a disaster come upon me!

CHORUS

For us, my lord, this is dreadful; but until you have learned from the man who was present, have hope!

OEDIPUS

Why, I have just so much of hope, simply to wait for the herdsman!

IOCASTE

But when he has appeared, what is your desire?

---

817 ὃν Schaefer: ᾧ codd. | τινι Dindorf: τινα codd.

825 ἐμβατεῦσαι Π 10: -εύειν codd.

827 ἐξέθρεψε κἀξέφυσέ Π 10, pZr: ἐξέφυσε κἀξέθρεψέ Lrpat

ΟΙΔΙΠΟΥΣ

ἐγὼ διδάξω σ᾽· ἢν γὰρ εὑρεθῇ λέγων
σοὶ ταὔτ᾽, ἔγωγ᾽ ἂν ἐκπεφευγοίην πάθος.

ΙΟΚΑΣΤΗ

ποῖον δέ μου περισσὸν ἤκουσας λόγον;

ΟΙΔΙΠΟΥΣ

λῃστὰς ἔφασκες αὐτὸν ἄνδρας ἐννέπειν
ὥς νιν κατακτείνειαν. εἰ μὲν οὖν ἔτι
λέξει τὸν αὐτὸν ἀριθμόν, οὐκ ἐγὼ ᾽κτανον·
οὐ γὰρ γένοιτ᾽ ἂν εἷς γε τοῖς πολλοῖς ἴσος·
εἰ δ᾽ ἄνδρ᾽ ἕν᾽ οἰόζωνον αὐδήσει σαφῶς,
τοῦτ᾽ ἐστὶν ἤδη τοὔργον εἰς ἐμὲ ῥέπον.

ΙΟΚΑΣΤΗ

ἀλλ᾽ ὡς φανέν γε τοὔπος ὧδ᾽ ἐπίστασο,
κοὐκ ἔστιν αὐτῷ τοῦτό γ᾽ ἐκβαλεῖν πάλιν·
πόλις γὰρ ἤκουσ᾽, οὐκ ἐγὼ μόνη, τάδε.
εἰ δ᾽ οὖν τι κἀκτρέποιτο τοῦ πρόσθεν λόγου,
οὔτοι ποτ᾽, ὦναξ, τόν γε Λαΐου φόνον
φανεῖ δικαίως ὀρθόν, ὅν γε Λοξίας
διεῖπε χρῆναι παιδὸς ἐξ ἐμοῦ θανεῖν.
καίτοι νιν οὐ κεῖνός γ᾽ ὁ δύστηνός ποτε
κατέκταν᾽, ἀλλ᾽ αὐτὸς πάροιθεν ὤλετο.
ὥστ᾽ οὐχὶ μαντείας γ᾽ ἂν οὔτε τῇδ᾽ ἐγὼ
βλέψαιμ᾽ ἂν οὕνεκ᾽ οὔτε τῇδ᾽ ἂν ὕστερον.

ΟΙΔΙΠΟΥΣ

καλῶς νομίζεις. ἀλλ᾽ ὅμως τὸν ἐργάτην
πέμψον τινὰ στελοῦντα μηδὲ τοῦτ᾽ ἀφῇς.

OEDIPUS

I will explain; if he is found to say what you said, I shall have escaped disaster.

IOCASTE

And what special saying did you hear from me?

OEDIPUS

You said that he told you that robbers had killed him; so if he still gives the same number, I was not the killer, for one is not the same as many. But if he speaks unmistakably of one solitary man, then at once the balance tilts towards me.

IOCASTE

Well, know that that is how the word was made known, and he cannot take back that word, for the whole city heard it, and not I alone. But even if he should turn back at all from what he said before, he will never prove that the killing of Laius was as predicted, of him who Loxias had prophesied would die at the hands of my son. Yet that poor child never killed him, but he himself perished before him; so that after that I would look neither this way nor that on account of a prophecy.

OEDIPUS

Your belief is sensible; but none the less, send someone to bring the slave, and do not fail to do so.

ΙΟΚΑΣΤΗ

πέμψω ταχύνασ᾽· ἀλλ᾽ ἴωμεν ἐς δόμους.
οὐδὲν γὰρ ἂν πράξαιμ᾽ ἂν ὧν οὐ σοὶ φίλον.

ΧΟΡΟΣ

εἴ μοι ξυνείη φέροντι μοῖρα τὰν — στρ. α´
εὔσεπτον ἁγνείαν λόγων
ἔργων τε πάντων, ὧν νόμοι πρόκεινται
ὑψίποδες, οὐρανίᾳ ᾽ν
αἰθέρι τεκνωθέντες, ὧν Ὄλυμπος
πατὴρ μόνος, οὐδέ νιν
θνατὰ φύσις ἀνέρων
ἔτικτεν, οὐδὲ μήποτε λά-
θα κατακοιμάσῃ·
μέγας ἐν τούτοις θεός, οὐδὲ γηράσκει.
ὕβρις φυτεύει τύραννον· ὕβρις, εἰ — ἀντ. α´
πολλῶν ὑπερπλησθῇ μάταν,
ἃ μὴ ᾽πίκαιρα μηδὲ συμφέροντα,
ἀκρότατα γεῖσ᾽ ἀναβᾶσ᾽
ἀπότομον ὤρουσεν εἰς ἀνάγκαν
ἔνθ᾽ οὐ ποδὶ χρησίμῳ
χρῆται. τὸ καλῶς δ᾽ ἔχον
πόλει πάλαισμα μήποτε λῦ-
σαι θεὸν αἰτοῦμαι.
θεὸν οὐ λήξω ποτὲ προστάταν ἴσχων.

866–67 *οὐρανίᾳ ᾽ν αἰθέρι* Enger: *οὐρανίαν δι᾽ αἰθέρα* fere codd.

873 *ὕβρις . . . τύραννον*] *ὕβριν . . . τυραννίς* Blaydes *τύραννον· ὕβρις*] *τύραννον ὕβριν·* Fraenkel

IOCASTE

I will make haste to send for him. But let us go into the house; for I would do nothing you did not desire.

Exeunt OEDIPUS *and* IOCASTE.

CHORUS

May such a destiny abide with me that I win praise for a reverent purity in all words and deeds sanctioned by laws that stand high, generated in lofty heaven, the laws whose only father is Olympus! The mortal nature of men did not beget them, neither shall they ever be lulled to sleep by forgetfulness. Great in these laws is the god, nor does he ever grow old.

Insolence has a child who is a tyrant; insolence, if vainly satiated with profusion that is not right or fitting, mounts to the topmost cornice and rushes to the edge of an abyss where its feet can do it no service. But I pray the god never to undo the wrestler's throw that brought good to the city; never shall I cease to hold the god for my protector.

---

876 *ἀκρότατα γεῖσ' ἀναβᾶσ'* G. Wolff: *ἀκροτάταν εἰσαναβᾶσ'* codd.

εἰ δέ τις ὑπέροπτα χερσὶν στρ. β´
ἢ λόγῳ πορεύεται,
Δίκας ἀφόβητος, οὐδὲ
δαιμόνων ἕδη σέβων,
κακά νιν ἕλοιτο μοῖρα,
δυσπότμου χάριν χλιδᾶς,
εἰ μὴ τὸ κέρδος κερδανεῖ δικαίως
καὶ τῶν ἀσέπτων ἕρξεται,
ἢ τῶν ἀθίκτων θίξεται ματᾴζων.
τίς ἔτι ποτ᾽ ἐν τοῖσδ᾽ ἀνὴρ †θυμῶν βέλη
ἕρξεται† ψυχᾶς ἀμύνων;
εἰ γὰρ αἱ τοιαίδε πράξεις τίμιαι,
τί δεῖ με χορεύειν;
οὐκέτι τὸν ἄθικτον εἶμι ἀντ. β´
γᾶς ἐπ᾽ ὀμφαλὸν σέβων,
οὐδ᾽ ἐς τὸν Ἀβαῖσι ναόν,
οὐδὲ τὰν Ὀλυμπίαν,
εἰ μὴ τάδε χειρόδεικτα
πᾶσιν ἁρμόσει βροτοῖς.
ἀλλ᾽, ὦ κρατύνων, εἴπερ ὄρθ᾽ ἀκούεις,
Ζεῦ, πάντ᾽ ἀνάσσων, μὴ λάθοι
σὲ τάν τε σὰν ἀθάνατον αἰὲν ἀρχάν.
φθίνοντα γὰρ <–∪–×> Λαΐου
θέσφατ᾽ ἐξαιροῦσιν ἤδη,
κοὐδαμοῦ τιμαῖς Ἀπόλλων ἐμφανής·
ἔρρει δὲ τὰ θεῖα.

But if a man moves arrogantly in deed or word, without fear of Justice, and without reverence for the seats of the gods, may an evil fate take him, for his ill-starred pride, if he will not win his advantage justly and keep himself from acts irreverent, or if he wantonly lays hands on things inviolate! In such a case, what man shall ward off the shafts of [. . .]? For if such actions are to win respect, why should we honour the gods with dances?

No longer shall I go in reverence to the inviolate navel of the earth, nor to the temple at Abae, nor to that of Olympia, if these oracles do not accord with truth, so that all mortals may point to them. But o ruler, if you are rightly thus called, Zeus, lord of all, may this not escape you and your ever deathless power! For already the oracles of Laius are fading and are being expunged, and nowhere is Apollo manifest in honour; but the power of the gods is perishing.

Enter IOCASTE, *carrying offerings which she will present to the statue of Apollo which is on the stage.*

---

891 *θίξεται* Blaydes: *ἕξεται* codd.

892 *θυμοῦ* pa: *θυμῷ* Lrpa: *θυμῶν* Schneidewin: *θεῶν* Hermann

894 *ἕρξεται* (vel *ἔρξεται*) codd. | *ἀμύνειν* : *ἀμύνων* Erfurdt: -*ειν* codd.

906 <*τοι παλαιὰ*> suppl. Hermann, alii alia: an <*καὶ πάλαι τὰ*>? *Λαΐου* Lrp: *Λαΐου παλαιὰ* a: *παλαιὰ Λαΐου* pa: *παλαιὰ* post *θέσφατα* (907) praebet K

ΙΟΚΑΣΤΗ

χώρας ἄνακτες, δόξα μοι παρεστάθη
ναοὺς ἱκέσθαι δαιμόνων, τάδ᾽ ἐν χεροῖν
στέφη λαβούσῃ κἀπιθυμιάματα.
ὑψοῦ γὰρ αἴρει θυμὸν Οἰδίπους ἄγαν
λύπαισι παντοίαισιν· οὐδ᾽ ὁποῖ᾽ ἀνὴρ
ἔννους τὰ καινὰ τοῖς πάλαι τεκμαίρεται,
ἀλλ᾽ ἐστὶ τοῦ λέγοντος, ἢν φόβους λέγῃ.
ὅτ᾽ οὖν παραινοῦσ᾽ οὐδὲν ἐς πλέον ποῶ,
πρὸς σ᾽, ὦ Λύκει᾽ Ἄπολλον, ἄγχιστος γὰρ εἶ,
ἱκέτις ἀφῖγμαι τοῖσδε σὺν κατεύγμασιν,
ὅπως λύσιν τιν᾽ ἡμὶν εὐαγῆ πόρῃς·
ὡς νῦν ὀκνοῦμεν πάντες ἐκπεπληγμένον
κεῖνον βλέποντες ὡς κυβερνήτην νεώς.

ΑΓΓΕΛΟΣ

ἆρ᾽ ἂν παρ᾽ ὑμῶν, ὦ ξένοι, μάθοιμ᾽ ὅπου
τὰ τοῦ τυράννου δώματ᾽ ἐστὶν Οἰδίπου;
μάλιστα δ᾽ αὐτὸν εἴπατ᾽ εἰ κάτισθ᾽ ὅπου.

ΧΟΡΟΣ

στέγαι μὲν αἵδε, καὐτὸς ἔνδον, ὦ ξένε·
γυνὴ δὲ μήτηρ θ᾽ ἥδε τῶν κείνου τέκνων.

ΑΓΓΕΛΟΣ

ἀλλ᾽ ὀλβία τε καὶ ξὺν ὀλβίοις ἀεὶ
γένοιτ᾽, ἐκείνου γ᾽ οὖσα παντελὴς δάμαρ.

928 θ᾽ Σ L et Syrianus in Hermogenem: om. codd.

IOCASTE

Lords of the land, the thought has come to me to go to the temples of the gods, bearing in my hands these garlands and this incense. For Oedipus is exciting his mind in excess with every kind of grief, and he is not interpreting new happenings by means of earlier ones like a rational man, but he is at the mercy of the speaker, if he speaks of terrors. So since I do no good by trying to counsel him, I come as a suppliant to you, Lycian Apollo, since you are our neighbour, with these accompaniments of prayer, that you may provide us with some cleansing solution. For now we are all afraid, when we see him, the captain of our ship, struck powerless.

Enter MESSENGER

MESSENGER

Might I learn from you, strangers, where is the house of King Oedipus? But best of all, tell me if you know where he is!

CHORUS

This is his dwelling, and he himself is in it, stranger, and this lady is his wife and the mother of his children.

MESSENGER

Why, may she ever be happy and with others who are happy, since she is his queen!

ΙΟΚΑΣΤΗ

αὔτως δὲ καὶ σύ γ᾽, ὦ ξέν᾽· ἄξιος γὰρ εἶ
τῆς εὐεπείας οὕνεκ᾽. ἀλλὰ φράζ᾽ ὅτου
χρῄζων ἀφῖξαι χὤτι σημῆναι θέλων.

ΑΓΓΕΛΟΣ

ἀγαθὰ δόμοις τε καὶ πόσει τῷ σῷ, γύναι.

ΙΟΚΑΣΤΗ

τὰ ποῖα ταῦτα; παρὰ τίνος δ᾽ ἀφιγμένος;

ΑΓΓΕΛΟΣ

ἐκ τῆς Κορίνθου. τὸ δ᾽ ἔπος οὑξερῶ—τάχα
ἥδοιο μέν, πῶς δ᾽ οὐκ ἄν; ἀσχάλλοις δ᾽ ἴσως.

ΙΟΚΑΣΤΗ

τί δ᾽ ἔστι; ποίαν δύναμιν ὧδ᾽ ἔχει διπλῆν;

ΑΓΓΕΛΟΣ

τύραννον αὐτὸν οὑπιχώριοι χθονὸς
τῆς Ἰσθμίας στήσουσιν, ὡς ηὐδᾶτ᾽ ἐκεῖ.

ΙΟΚΑΣΤΗ

τί δ᾽; οὐχ ὁ πρέσβυς Πόλυβος ἐγκρατὴς ἔτι;

ΑΓΓΕΛΟΣ

οὐ δῆτ᾽, ἐπεί νιν θάνατος ἐν δόμοις ἔχει.

ΙΟΚΑΣΤΗ

πῶς εἶπας; ἦ τέθνηκε<ν Οἰδίπου πατήρ>;

ΑΓΓΕΛΟΣ

εἰ μὴ λέγω τἀληθές, ἀξιῶ θανεῖν.

942 δόμοις p : τάφνις cett.
943 suppl. Nauck: τέθνηκε Πόλυβος Lrpa: alii alia

IOCASTE

The same to you, stranger, since you deserve it for your courtesy! But tell me with what wish or for what announcement you have come!

MESSENGER

I bring good news for your house and your husband, lady!

IOCASTE

What news is that? and from whom do you come?

MESSENGER

From Corinth; and the word I shall soon speak will bring you pleasure—of course—but perhaps also sorrow.

IOCASTE

What is it? How does it possess a double power?

MESSENGER

The natives of the Isthmian land are to establish him as king, as the story went there.

IOCASTE

How so? Is not the aged Polybus still in power?

MESSENGER

No, for death holds him in the tomb.

IOCASTE

What have you said? Is Oedipus' father dead?

MESSENGER

If I am not telling the truth, I say that I deserve to die.

ΙΟΚΑΣΤΗ

ὦ πρόσπολ᾽, οὐχὶ δεσπότῃ τάδ᾽ ὡς τάχος
μολοῦσα λέξεις; ὦ θεῶν μαντεύματα,
ἵν᾽ ἐστέ. τοῦτον Οἰδίπους πάλαι τρέμων
τὸν ἄνδρ᾽ ἔφευγε μὴ κτάνοι· καὶ νῦν ὅδε
πρὸς τῆς τύχης ὄλωλεν οὐδὲ τοῦδ᾽ ὕπο.

ΟΙΔΙΠΟΥΣ

ὦ φίλτατον γυναικὸς Ἰοκάστης κάρα,
τί μ᾽ ἐξεπέμψω δεῦρο τῶνδε δωμάτων;

ΙΟΚΑΣΤΗ

ἄκουε τἀνδρὸς τοῦδε, καὶ σκόπει κλύων
τὰ σέμν᾽ ἵν᾽ ἥκει τοῦ θεοῦ μαντεύματα.

ΟΙΔΙΠΟΥΣ

οὗτος δὲ τίς ποτ᾽ ἐστὶ καὶ τί μοι λέγει;

ΙΟΚΑΣΤΗ

ἐκ τῆς Κορίνθου, πατέρα τὸν σὸν ἀγγελῶν
ὡς οὐκέτ᾽ ὄντα Πόλυβον, ἀλλ᾽ ὀλωλότα.

ΟΙΔΙΠΟΥΣ

τί φής, ξέν᾽; αὐτός μοι σὺ σημήνας γενοῦ.

ΑΓΓΕΛΟΣ

εἰ τοῦτο πρῶτον δεῖ μ᾽ ἀπαγγεῖλαι σαφῶς,
εὖ ἴσθ᾽ ἐκεῖνον θανάσιμον βεβηκότα.

ΟΙΔΙΠΟΥΣ

πότερα δόλοισιν, ἢ νόσου ξυναλλαγῇ;

ΑΓΓΕΛΟΣ

σμικρὰ παλαιὰ σώματ᾽ εὐνάζει ῥοπή.

IOCASTE

Servant, go at once and tell this to the master! O prophecies of the gods, where are you? Oedipus long avoided this man for fear of killing him, and now he has died a natural death, not at his hands.

Enter OEDIPUS.

OEDIPUS

My dearest wife, Iocaste, why have you summoned me here from the house?

IOCASTE

Listen to this man, and then ask where the god's revered oracles stand!

OEDIPUS

And who is he and what does he say to me?

IOCASTE

From Corinth, to report that your father Polybus is no more—he is dead.

OEDIPUS

What are you saying, stranger? Tell me yourself!

MESSENGER

If I must first tell you this truly, know for certain that he is dead and gone!

OEDIPUS

Was it by treason, or through sickness?

MESSENGER

A small jolt brings aged persons to their rest.

---

957 *σημήνας* LrPa: *σημάντωρ* Kpat et *γρ* in L et G

ΟΙΔΙΠΟΥΣ

νόσοις ὁ τλήμων, ὡς ἔοικεν, ἔφθιτο.

ΑΓΓΕΛΟΣ

καὶ τῷ μακρῷ γε συμμετρούμενος χρόνῳ.

ΟΙΔΙΠΟΥΣ

φεῦ φεῦ, τί δῆτ' ἄν, ὦ γύναι, σκοποῖτό τις
τὴν Πυθόμαντιν ἑστίαν, ἢ τοὺς ἄνω
κλάζοντας ὄρνεις, ὧν ὑφ' ἡγητῶν ἐγὼ
κτανεῖν ἔμελλον πατέρα τὸν ἐμόν; ὁ δὲ θανὼν
κεύθει κάτω δὴ γῆς· ἐγὼ δ' ὅδ' ἐνθάδε
ἄψαυστος ἔγχους, εἴ τι μὴ τὠμῷ πόθῳ
κατέφθιθ'· οὕτω δ' ἂν θανὼν εἴη 'ξ ἐμοῦ.
τὰ δ' οὖν παρόντα συλλαβὼν θεσπίσματα
κεῖται παρ' Ἅιδῃ Πόλυβος ἄξι' οὐδενός.

ΙΟΚΑΣΤΗ

οὔκουν ἐγώ σοι ταῦτα προὔλεγον πάλαι;

ΟΙΔΙΠΟΥΣ

ηὔδας· ἐγὼ δὲ τῷ φόβῳ παρηγόμην.

ΙΟΚΑΣΤΗ

μή νυν ἔτ' αὐτῶν μηδὲν ἐς θυμὸν βάλῃς.

ΟΙΔΙΠΟΥΣ

καὶ πῶς τὸ μητρὸς λέκτρον οὐκ ὀκνεῖν με δεῖ;

ΙΟΚΑΣΤΗ

τί δ' ἂν φοβοῖτ' ἄνθρωπος, ᾧ τὰ τῆς τύχης
κρατεῖ, πρόνοια δ' ἐστὶν οὐδενὸς σαφής;
εἰκῇ κράτιστον ζῆν, ὅπως δύναιτό τις.
σὺ δ' ἐς τὰ μητρὸς μὴ φοβοῦ νυμφεύματα·

OEDIPUS

It is from sickness, it seems, that he died, alas!

MESSENGER

And from the long years that he had measured out.

OEDIPUS

Ah, ah, lady, why should one look to the prophetic hearth of Pytho, or to the birds that shriek above us, according to whose message I was to kill my father? But he is dead, and lies deep below the earth; and I am here, not having touched the weapon, unless he died from missing me; in that way I might have caused his death. But still, Polybus lies in Hades, and with him have gone the oracles that were with us, now worth nothing.

IOCASTE

Did I not foretell this to you long ago?

OEDIPUS

You told me; but I was led along by fear.

IOCASTE

Then let none of these things worry you any more!

OEDIPUS

And how can I not fear intercourse with my mother?

IOCASTE

But what should a man be afraid of when for him it is the event that rules, and there is no certain foreknowledge of anything? It is best to live anyhow, as one may; do not be

πολλοὶ γὰρ ἤδη κἀν ὀνείρασιν βροτῶν
μητρὶ ξυνηυνάσθησαν. ἀλλὰ ταῦθ᾽ ὅτῳ
παρ᾽ οὐδέν ἐστι, ῥᾷστα τὸν βίον φέρει.

ΟΙΔΙΠΟΥΣ

καλῶς ἅπαντα ταῦτ᾽ ἂν ἐξείρητό σοι,
εἰ μὴ ᾽κύρει ζῶσ᾽ ἡ τεκοῦσα· νῦν δ᾽ ἐπεὶ
ζῇ, πᾶσ᾽ ἀνάγκη, κεἰ καλῶς λέγεις, ὀκνεῖν.

ΙΟΚΑΣΤΗ

καὶ μὴν μέγας <γ᾽> ὀφθαλμὸς οἱ πατρὸς τάφοι.

ΟΙΔΙΠΟΥΣ

μέγας, ξυνίημ᾽· ἀλλὰ τῆς ζώσης φόβος.

ΑΓΓΕΛΟΣ

ποίας δὲ καὶ γυναικὸς ἐκφοβεῖσθ᾽ ὕπερ;

ΟΙΔΙΠΟΥΣ

Μερόπης, γεραιέ, Πόλυβος ἧς ᾤκει μέτα.

ΑΓΓΕΛΟΣ

τί δ᾽ ἔστ᾽ ἐκείνης ὑμὶν ἐς φόβον φέρον;

ΟΙΔΙΠΟΥΣ

θεήλατον μάντευμα δεινόν, ὦ ξένε.

ΑΓΓΕΛΟΣ

ἦ ῥητόν; ἢ οὐ θεμιστὸν ἄλλον εἰδέναι;

ΟΙΔΙΠΟΥΣ

μάλιστά γ᾽· εἶπε γάρ με Λοξίας ποτὲ
χρῆναι μιγῆναι μητρὶ τὴμαυτοῦ, τό τε
πατρῷον αἷμα χερσὶ ταῖς ἐμαῖς ἑλεῖν.

afraid of marriage with your mother! Many have lain with their mothers in dreams too. It is he to whom such things are nothing who puts up with life the best.

OEDIPUS

Everything you have said would be right, were not my mother still alive; but since she still lives, even though you are right, I must be afraid.

IOCASTE

Well, your father's funeral is a great source of light.

OEDIPUS

Yes, I understand; but I am afraid while she still lives.

MESSENGER

But who is the woman who makes you afraid?

OEDIPUS

Merope, old man, the wife of Polybus.

MESSENGER

What is it about her that causes you to be afraid?

OEDIPUS

A terrible prophecy from the gods, stranger.

MESSENGER

Can it be mentioned? or is it not lawful for another to know of it?

OEDIPUS

Yes! Loxias once said that I was fated to lie with my mother, and to spill my father's blood with my own hands.

---

981 κἀν] τοῖς γ' Dawe dubitanter: 'ν τοῖς Blaydes

987 ‹γ'› anon. (1746)

993 οὐ θεμιστὸν Johnson: οὐ θεμιτὸν codd.: οὐχὶ θεμιτὸν Brunck

ὧν οὕνεχ' ἡ Κόρινθος ἐξ ἐμοῦ πάλαι
μακρὰν ἀπῳκεῖτ'· εὐτυχῶς μέν, ἀλλ' ὅμως
τὰ τῶν τεκόντων ὄμμαθ' ἥδιστον βλέπειν.

ΑΓΓΕΛΟΣ

ἦ γὰρ τάδ' ὀκνῶν κεῖθεν ἦσθ' ἀπόπτολις;

ΟΙΔΙΠΟΥΣ

πατρός γε χρῄζων μὴ φονεὺς εἶναι, γέρον.

ΑΓΓΕΛΟΣ

τί δῆτ' ἐγὼ οὐχὶ τοῦδε τοῦ φόβου σ', ἄναξ,
ἐπείπερ εὔνους ἦλθον, ἐξελυσάμην;

ΟΙΔΙΠΟΥΣ

καὶ μὴν χάριν γ' ἂν ἀξίαν λάβοις ἐμοῦ.

ΑΓΓΕΛΟΣ

καὶ μὴν μάλιστα τοῦτ' ἀφικόμην, ὅπως
σοῦ πρὸς δόμους ἐλθόντος εὖ πράξαιμί τι.

ΟΙΔΙΠΟΥΣ

ἀλλ' οὔποτ' εἶμι τοῖς φυτεύσασίν γ' ὁμοῦ.

ΑΓΓΕΛΟΣ

ὦ παῖ, καλῶς εἶ δῆλος οὐκ εἰδὼς τί δρᾷς.

ΟΙΔΙΠΟΥΣ

πῶς, ὦ γεραιέ πρὸς θεῶν δίδασκέ με.

ΑΓΓΕΛΟΣ

εἰ τῶνδε φεύγεις οὕνεκ' εἰς οἴκους μολεῖν.

1001 γε p, coni. Hermann: τε cett.

This is why I have long lived far from Corinth; my fortune has been good, but none the less it is the greatest delight to see the faces of one's parents.

MESSENGER

Was it for fear of this that you had left?

OEDIPUS

Yes, and from the wish not to be my father's murderer, old man.

MESSENGER

Why, since I have come in friendship, do I not release you from this fear, my lord?

OEDIPUS

Indeed, you would receive a reward worthy of the service.

MESSENGER

Why, I came here most of all in the hope that when you came home I might acquire some benefit!

OEDIPUS

But I will never go to where my parents are.

MESSENGER

My son, it is clear that you do not know what you are doing.

OEDIPUS

How so, old man? Explain to me!

MESSENGER

If it is because of them that you avoid coming home.

ΟΙΔΙΠΟΥΣ

ταρβῶν γε μή μοι Φοῖβος ἐξέλθῃ σαφής.

ΑΓΓΕΛΟΣ

ἦ μὴ μίασμα τῶν φυτευσάντων λάβῃς;

ΟΙΔΙΠΟΥΣ

τοῦτ᾽ αὐτό, πρέσβυ, τοῦτό μ᾽ εἰσαεὶ φοβεῖ.

ΑΓΓΕΛΟΣ

ἆρ᾽ οἶσθα δῆτα πρὸς δίκης οὐδὲν τρέμων;

ΟΙΔΙΠΟΥΣ

πῶς δ᾽ οὐχί, παῖς γ᾽ εἰ τῶνδε γεννητῶν ἔφυν;

ΑΓΓΕΛΟΣ

ὁθούνεκ᾽ ἦν σοι Πόλυβος οὐδὲν ἐν γένει.

ΟΙΔΙΠΟΥΣ

πῶς εἶπας; οὐ γὰρ Πόλυβος ἐξέφυσέ με;

ΑΓΓΕΛΟΣ

οὐ μᾶλλον οὐδὲν τοῦδε τἀνδρός, ἀλλ᾽ ἴσον.

ΟΙΔΙΠΟΥΣ

καὶ πῶς ὁ φύσας ἐξ ἴσου τῷ μηδενί;

ΑΓΓΕΛΟΣ

ἀλλ᾽ οὔ σ᾽ ἐγείνατ᾽ οὔτ᾽ ἐκεῖνος οὔτ᾽ ἐγώ.

ΟΙΔΙΠΟΥΣ

ἀλλ᾽ ἀντὶ τοῦ δὴ παῖδά μ᾽ ὠνομάζετο;

ΑΓΓΕΛΟΣ

δῶρόν ποτ᾽, ἴσθι, τῶν ἐμῶν χειρῶν λαβών.

OEDIPUS

Yes, for fear that Phoebus may prove true.

MESSENGER

Is it so that you shall not acquire pollution through your parents?

OEDIPUS

Exactly that, old man, that is what always frightens me.

MESSENGER

Do you not know that you have no reason to be afraid?

OEDIPUS

But I must, if indeed these are my parents!

MESSENGER

Because Polybus was no relation to you!

OEDIPUS

What are you saying? Was not Polybus my father?

MESSENGER

No more than I was, but just as much!

OEDIPUS

And how can my father be as much my father as one who is nothing to me?

MESSENGER

Well, neither he nor I begot you.

OEDIPUS

But why did he call me his son?

MESSENGER

He received you once, I tell you, from my hands, as a gift.

ΟΙΔΙΠΟΥΣ

κᾆθ' ὧδ' ἀπ' ἄλλης χειρὸς ἔστερξεν μέγα;

ΑΓΓΕΛΟΣ

ἡ γὰρ πρὶν αὐτὸν ἐξέπεισ' ἀπαιδία.

ΟΙΔΙΠΟΥΣ

σὺ δ' ἐμπολήσας ἢ τυχών μ' αὐτῷ δίδως;

ΑΓΓΕΛΟΣ

εὑρὼν ναπαίαις ἐν Κιθαιρῶνος πτυχαῖς.

ΟΙΔΙΠΟΥΣ

ὡδοιπόρεις δὲ πρὸς τί τούσδε τοὺς τόπους;

ΑΓΓΕΛΟΣ

ἐνταῦθ' ὀρείοις ποιμνίοις ἐπεστάτουν.

ΟΙΔΙΠΟΥΣ

ποιμὴν γὰρ ἦσθα κἀπὶ θητείᾳ πλάνης;

ΑΓΓΕΛΟΣ

σοῦ δ', ὦ τέκνον, σωτήρ γε τῷ τότ' ἐν χρόνῳ.

ΟΙΔΙΠΟΥΣ

τί δ' ἄλγος ἴσχοντ' ἐν χεροῖν με λαμβάνεις;

ΑΓΓΕΛΟΣ

ποδῶν ἂν ἄρθρα μαρτυρήσειεν τὰ σά.

ΟΙΔΙΠΟΥΣ

οἴμοι, τί τοῦτ' ἀρχαῖον ἐννέπεις κακόν;

ΑΓΓΕΛΟΣ

λύω σ' ἔχοντα διατόρους ποδοῖν ἀκμάς.

1025 τυχών Bothe: τεκών codd. 1030 δ' G: γ' cett.

OEDIPUS

And then he cherished me so greatly, though I had come to him from another's hand?

MESSENGER

Yes, his previous lack of any child brought him to that.

OEDIPUS

Did you buy me or find me before you gave me to him?

MESSENGER

I found you in the wooded glens of Cithaeron.

OEDIPUS

And why were you travelling in those regions?

MESSENGER

I was there in charge of the flocks grazing on the mountain.

OEDIPUS

So were you a shepherd, wandering about in your servitude?

MESSENGER

Yes, and I saved you, my son, at that time.

OEDIPUS

What trouble was I suffering from when you took me in your arms?

MESSENGER

Your ankles would bear witness to it.

OEDIPUS

Ah, why do you speak of that ancient grief?

MESSENGER

When I released you, your ankles had been pierced.

ΟΙΔΙΠΟΥΣ

δεινόν γ᾿ ὄνειδος σπαργάνων ἀνειλόμην.

ΑΓΓΕΛΟΣ

ὥστ᾿ ὠνομάσθης ἐκ τύχης ταύτης ὃς εἶ.

ΟΙΔΙΠΟΥΣ

ὦ πρὸς θεῶν, πρὸς μητρός, ἢ πατρός; φράσον.

ΑΓΓΕΛΟΣ

οὐκ οἶδ᾿· ὁ δοὺς δὲ ταῦτ᾿ ἐμοῦ λῷον φρονεῖ.

ΟΙΔΙΠΟΥΣ

ἦ γὰρ παρ᾿ ἄλλου μ᾿ ἔλαβες οὐδ᾿ αὐτὸς τυχών;

ΑΓΓΕΛΟΣ

οὔκ, ἀλλὰ ποιμὴν ἄλλος ἐκδίδωσί μοι.

ΟΙΔΙΠΟΥΣ

τίς οὗτος; ἦ κάτοισθα δηλῶσαι λόγῳ;

ΑΓΓΕΛΟΣ

τῶν Λαΐου δήπου τις ὠνομάζετο.

ΟΙΔΙΠΟΥΣ

ἦ τοῦ τυράννου τῆσδε γῆς πάλαι ποτέ;

ΑΓΓΕΛΟΣ

μάλιστα· τούτου τἀνδρὸς οὗτος ἦν βοτήρ.

ΟΙΔΙΠΟΥΣ

ἦ κἄστ᾿ ἔτι ζῶν οὗτος, ὥστ᾿ ἰδεῖν ἐμέ;

OEDIPUS

Yes, it was a dreadful brand of shame that I had from my cradle.

MESSENGER

So that it was from that occurrence that you got the name you bear.

OEDIPUS

By heaven, did my father or my mother name me? Tell me that!

MESSENGER

I do not know; the man who gave you to me knows it all better than I did.

OEDIPUS

Then did you not find me, but received me from another man?

MESSENGER

Yes, another shepherd gave you to me.

OEDIPUS

Who was he? Do you know how to tell this truly?

MESSENGER

I think he was said to be one of Laius' men.

OEDIPUS

The man who long ago was ruler of this land?

MESSENGER

Yes; that was the man whose shepherd he was.

OEDIPUS

Is he still alive, so that I could see him?

ΑΓΓΕΛΟΣ

ὑμεῖς γ᾽ ἄριστ᾽ εἰδεῖτ᾽ ἂν οὑπιχώριοι.

ΟΙΔΙΠΟΥΣ

ἔστιν τις ὑμῶν τῶν παρεστώτων πέλας,
ὅστις κάτοιδε τὸν βοτῆρ᾽, ὃν ἐννέπει,
εἴτ᾽ οὖν ἐπ᾽ ἀγρῶν εἴτε κἀνθάδ᾽ εἰσιδών;
σημήναθ᾽, ὡς ὁ καιρὸς ηὑρῆσθαι τάδε.

ΧΟΡΟΣ

οἶμαι μὲν οὐδέν᾽ ἄλλον ἢ τὸν ἐξ ἀγρῶν,
ὃν κἀμάτευες πρόσθεν εἰσιδεῖν· ἀτὰρ
ἥδ᾽ ἂν τάδ᾽ οὐχ ἥκιστ᾽ ἂν Ἰοκάστη λέγοι.

ΟΙΔΙΠΟΥΣ

γύναι, νοεῖς ἐκεῖνον, ὅντιν᾽ ἀρτίως
μολεῖν ἐφιέμεσθα; τόνδ᾽ οὗτος λέγει;

ΙΟΚΑΣΤΗ

τί δ᾽ ὅντιν᾽ εἶπε; μηδὲν ἐντραπῇς. μάτην
ῥηθέντα βούλου μηδὲ μεμνῆσθαι τάδε.

ΟΙΔΙΠΟΥΣ

οὐκ ἂν γένοιτο τοῦθ᾽, ὅπως ἐγὼ λαβὼν
σημεῖα τοιαῦτ᾽ οὐ φανῶ τοὐμὸν γένος.

ΙΟΚΑΣΤΗ

μὴ πρὸς θεῶν, εἴπερ τι τοῦ σαυτοῦ βίου
κήδῃ, ματεύσῃς τοῦθ᾽· ἅλις νοσοῦσ᾽ ἐγώ.

MESSENGER

You who are the people of the country would know that best.

OEDIPUS

Is there one among you who are standing by who knows the shepherd of whom he speaks, whether he has seen him in the fields or here? Tell me, since it is time these things were found out!

CHORUS

I think he is none other than the man from the fields whom you were eager to see before; but Iocaste here could tell that best.

OEDIPUS

Lady, you know the man we lately sent for; is he the one this man speaks of?

IOCASTE

Why ask of whom he spoke? Take no thought of it! Let these words go for nothing and not be remembered!

OEDIPUS

It cannot be that when I have obtained such indications I shall not bring to light my birth!

IOCASTE

I beg you, do not search this out, if you care for your own life! My anguish is enough!

1056–57 *μάτην . . . τάδε* A. Y. Campbell: *τὰ δὲ . . . μάτην* codd.

ΟΙΔΙΠΟΥΣ

θάρσει· σὺ μὲν γὰρ οὐδ᾽ ἐὰν τρίτης ἐγὼ
μητρὸς φανῶ τρίδουλος, ἐκφανῇ κακή.

ΙΟΚΑΣΤΗ

ὅμως πιθοῦ μοι, λίσσομαι· μὴ δρᾶ τάδε.

ΟΙΔΙΠΟΥΣ

οὐκ ἂν πιθοίμην μὴ οὐ τάδ᾽ ἐκμαθεῖν σαφῶς.

ΙΟΚΑΣΤΗ

καὶ μὴν φρονοῦσά γ᾽ εὖ τὰ λῷστά σοι λέγω.

ΟΙΔΙΠΟΥΣ

τὰ λῷστα τοίνυν ταῦτά μ᾽ ἀλγύνει πάλαι.

ΙΟΚΑΣΤΗ

ὦ δύσποτμ᾽, εἴθε μήποτε γνοίης ὃς εἶ.

ΟΙΔΙΠΟΥΣ

ἄξει τις ἐλθὼν δεῦρο τὸν βοτῆρά μοι;
ταύτην δ᾽ ἐᾶτε πλουσίῳ χαίρειν γένει.

ΙΟΚΑΣΤΗ

ἰοὺ ἰού, δύστηνε· τοῦτο γάρ σ᾽ ἔχω
μόνον προσειπεῖν, ἄλλο δ᾽ οὔποθ᾽ ὕστερον.

ΧΟΡΟΣ

τί ποτε βέβηκεν, Οἰδίπους, ὑπ᾽ ἀγρίας
ᾄξασα λύπης ἡ γυνή; δέδοιχ᾽ ὅπως
μὴ ᾽κ τῆς σιωπῆς τῆσδ᾽ ἀναρρήξει κακά.

1062 ἐὰν Hermann: ἂν ἐκ codd.

OEDIPUS

Do not worry! Even if I prove to be the offspring of three generations of slaves, you will not be shown to be low-born!

IOCASTE

All the same do as I wish, I beg you! Do not do this!

OEDIPUS

You will never persuade me not to find out the truth!

IOCASTE

Yet it is in loyalty that I am telling you what is best for you!

OEDIPUS

It is that "best" that has long been causing me distress!

IOCASTE

Ill-fated one, may you never find out who you are!

OEDIPUS

Will someone go and bring the shepherd here? and leave her to take pride in her noble family!

IOCASTE

Ah, ah, unhappy one! That is all that I can say to you, and nothing any more!

Exit IOCASTE.

CHORUS

Why has the lady sped away, Oedipus, in bitter pain? I am afraid evil may burst forth after this silence.

ΟΙΔΙΠΟΥΣ

ὁποῖα χρῄζει ῥηγνύτω· τοὐμὸν δ᾽ ἐγώ,
κεἰ σμικρόν ἐστι, σπέρμ᾽ ἰδεῖν βουλήσομαι.
αὕτη δ᾽ ἴσως, φρονεῖ γὰρ ὡς γυνὴ μέγα,
τὴν δυσγένειαν τὴν ἐμὴν αἰσχύνεται.
ἐγὼ δ᾽ ἐμαυτὸν παῖδα τῆς Τύχης νέμων
τῆς εὖ διδούσης οὐκ ἀτιμασθήσομαι.
τῆς γὰρ πέφυκα μητρός· οἱ δὲ συγγενεῖς
μῆνές με μικρὸν καὶ μέγαν διώρισαν.
τοιόσδε δ᾽ ἐκφὺς οὐκ ἂν ἐξέλθοιμ᾽ ἔτι
ποτ᾽ ἄλλος, ὥστε μὴ ᾽κμαθεῖν τοὐμὸν γένος.

ΧΟΡΟΣ

εἴπερ ἐγὼ μάντις εἰ- *στρ.*
μι καὶ κατὰ γνώμαν ἴδρις,
οὐ τὸν Ὄλυμπον ἀπείρων,
ὦ Κιθαιρών, οὐκ ἔσῃ τὰν αὔριον
πανσέληνον μὴ οὐ σέ γε καὶ πατριώταν Οἰδίπου
καὶ τροφὸν καὶ ματέρ᾽ αὔξειν,
καὶ χορεύεσθαι πρὸς ἡ-
μῶν ὡς ἐπίηρα φέροντα
τοῖς ἐμοῖς τυράννοις.
ἰήιε Φοῖβε, σοὶ δὲ
ταῦτ᾽ ἀρέστ᾽ εἴη.
τίς σε, τέκνον, τίς σ᾽ ἔτι- *ἀντ.*
κτε τᾶν μακραιώνων ἄρα
Πανὸς ὀρεσσιβάτα πα-
τρὸς πελασθεῖσ᾽; ἢ σέ γ᾽ εὐνάτειρά τις

OEDIPUS

May whatever will burst forth! Even if it is lowly, I desire to learn my origin; but she, for she is proud in woman's fashion, is perhaps ashamed of my low birth. But I regard myself as child of the event that brought good fortune, and shall not be dishonoured. *She* is my mother; and the months that are my kin have determined my smallness and my greatness. With such a parent, I could never turn out another kind of person, so as not to learn what was my birth.

OEDIPUS remains on stage during the Third Stasimon.

CHORUS

If I am a prophet and wise in my judgment, O Cithaeron, you shall not fail to know that tomorrow's full moon exalts you as the fellow-native and nurse and mother of Oedipus, and that you are honoured by us with dances, as doing kindness to our princes. O Phoebus to whom men cry out, may these things prove agreeable to you!

Who, who among those who live long bore you, with Pan who roves the mountains as your father? Or was it

---

1085 ποτ' ἄλλος] ἄτιμος Nauck: ἀλλοῖος Dindorf

1090 καὶ codd.: τὸν Wilamowitz

1099 τᾶν Heimsoeth: τῶν codd.

1101 πατρὸς πελασθεῖσ' Lachmann: προσπελασθεῖσ' codd. | σέ γ' εὐνάτειρά τις Arndt: σέ γε θυγάτηρ Lp: σέ γέ τις θυγάτηρ rpat

Λοξίου; τῷ γὰρ πλάκες ἀγρόνομοι πᾶσαι
φίλαι·
εἴθ' ὁ Κυλλάνας *ἀνάσσων,*
εἴθ' ὁ Βακχεῖος *θεὸς*
ναίων ἐπ' ἄκρων ὀρέων <*σ'*> *εὕ-*
ρημα δέξατ' ἔκ του
Νυμφᾶν *ἑλικωπίδων, αἷς*
πλεῖστα συμπαίζει.

ΟΙΔΙΠΟΥΣ

εἰ χρή τι κἀμὲ μὴ συναλλάξαντά πω,
πρέσβεις, σταθμᾶσθαι, τὸν βοτῆρ' ὁρᾶν δοκῶ,
ὅνπερ πάλαι ζητοῦμεν. ἔν τε γὰρ μακρῷ
γήρᾳ ξυνᾴδει τῷδε τἀνδρὶ σύμμετρος,
ἄλλως τε τοὺς ἄγοντας ὥσπερ οἰκέτας
ἔγνωκ' ἐμαυτοῦ· τῇ δ' ἐπιστήμῃ σύ μου
προὔχοις τάχ' ἄν που, τὸν βοτῆρ' ἰδὼν πάρος.

ΧΟΡΟΣ

ἔγνωκα γάρ, σάφ' ἴσθι· Λαΐου *γὰρ ἦν*
εἴπερ τις ἄλλος πιστὸς ὡς νομεὺς ἀνήρ.

ΟΙΔΙΠΟΥΣ

σὲ πρῶτ' ἐρωτῶ, τὸν Κορίνθιον *ξένον,*
ἦ τόνδε φράζεις;

ΑΓΓΕΛΟΣ

τοῦτον, ὅνπερ εἰσορᾷς.

some bedfellow of Loxias? For the mountain pastures are all dear to him. Or was it the lord of Cyllene, or the Bacchic god dwelling on the mountain tops that received you as a lucky find from one of the black-eyed Nymphs, with whom he often plays?

OEDIPUS

If I, who have had no dealings with him, am able to judge, aged sirs, I think I see the shepherd whom we have long been seeking; for in old age he matches this man; yes, and I recognise those who are bringing him as servants of my own. But in point of knowledge you have the advantage of me, since you have seen the shepherd before.

CHORUS

Yes, I recognise him, be assured! He was as trusty a servant of Laius as any, although but a shepherd.

Enter SHEPHERD

OEDIPUS

I ask you first, stranger from Corinth: is this the man you mean?

MESSENGER

Yes, the man you see.

1103 *ἀγρόνομοι* Zrt: *-νόμοι* cett.: an *ἀγρονόμων*?

1106 suppl. Dindorf

1108 *ἑλικωπίδων* Wilamowitz: *Ἑλικωνιάδων* codd.: *Ἑλικωνίδων* A[ac], coni. Porson

ΟΙΔΙΠΟΥΣ

οὗτος σύ, πρέσβυ, δεῦρό μοι φώνει βλέπων
ὅσ᾽ ἄν σ᾽ ἐρωτῶ. Λαΐου ποτ᾽ ἦσθα σύ;

ΘΕΡΑΠΩΝ

ἦ, δοῦλος οὐκ ὠνητός, ἀλλ᾽ οἴκοι τραφείς.

ΟΙΔΙΠΟΥΣ

ἔργον μεριμνῶν ποῖον ἢ βίον τίνα;

ΘΕΡΑΠΩΝ

ποίμναις τὰ πλεῖστα τοῦ βίου συνειπόμην.

ΟΙΔΙΠΟΥΣ

χώροις μάλιστα πρὸς τίσι ξύναυλος ὤν;

ΘΕΡΑΠΩΝ

ἦν μὲν Κιθαιρών, ἦν δὲ πρόσχωρος τόπος.

ΟΙΔΙΠΟΥΣ

τὸν ἄνδρα τόνδ᾽ οὖν οἶσθα τῇδέ που μαθών;

ΘΕΡΑΠΩΝ

τί χρῆμα δρῶντα; ποῖον ἄνδρα καὶ λέγεις;

ΟΙΔΙΠΟΥΣ

τόνδ᾽ ὃς πάρεστιν· ἦ ξυνήλλαξας τί πω;

ΘΕΡΑΠΩΝ

οὐχ ὥστε γ᾽ εἰπεῖν ἐν τάχει μνήμης ὕπο.

ΑΓΓΕΛΟΣ

κοὐδέν γε θαῦμα, δέσποτ᾽. ἀλλ᾽ ἐγὼ σαφῶς
ἀγνῶτ᾽ ἀναμνήσω νιν. εὖ γὰρ οἶδ᾽ ὅτι

OEDIPUS

You there, old man, look at me and answer my questions! Did you once belong to Laius?

SHEPHERD

Yes, I was a slave not bought, but brought up in the house.

OEDIPUS

What work, or what way of life, was your care?

SHEPHERD

For most of my life I have been with the herds.

OEDIPUS

In what places for the most part did you bivouac?

SHEPHERD

There was Cithaeron, and there was the region near it.

OEDIPUS

Then do you know this man from having met him there?

SHEPHERD

Met him doing what? What man do you mean?

OEDIPUS

This man here; have you ever had to do with him?

SHEPHERD

Not so that I could speak at once from memory.

MESSENGER

No wonder, my lord! But though he does not know me, I will help him to remember clearly; because I know well

κάτοιδεν ἦμος τὸν Κιθαιρῶνος τόπον
ὁ μὲν διπλοῖσι ποιμνίοις, ἐγὼ δ᾽ ἑνὶ
* * * * *
ἐπλησίαζον τῷδε τἀνδρὶ τρεῖς ὅλους
ἐξ ἦρος εἰς ἀρκτοῦρον ἑκμήνους χρόνους·
χειμῶνι δ᾽ ἤδη τἀμά τ᾽ εἰς ἔπαυλ᾽ ἐγὼ
ἤλαυνον οὗτός τ᾽ ἐς τὰ Λαΐου σταθμά.
λέγω τι τούτων, ἢ οὐ λέγω πεπραγμένον;

ΘΕΡΑΠΩΝ

λέγεις ἀληθῆ, καίπερ ἐκ μακροῦ χρόνου.

ΑΓΓΕΛΟΣ

φέρ᾽ εἰπέ νυν, τότ᾽ οἶσθα παῖδά μοί τινα
δούς, ὡς ἐμαυτῷ θρέμμα θρεψαίμην ἐγώ;

ΘΕΡΑΠΩΝ

τί δ᾽ ἔστι; πρὸς τί τοῦτο τοὔπος ἱστορεῖς;

ΑΓΓΕΛΟΣ

ὅδ᾽ ἐστίν, ὦ τᾶν, κεῖνος ὃς τότ᾽ ἦν νέος.

ΘΕΡΑΠΩΝ

οὐκ εἰς ὄλεθρον; οὐ σιωπήσας ἔσῃ;

ΟΙΔΙΠΟΥΣ

ἆ, μὴ κόλαζε, πρέσβυ, τόνδ᾽, ἐπεὶ τὰ σὰ
δεῖται κολαστοῦ μᾶλλον ἢ τὰ τοῦδ᾽ ἔπη.

that he is aware that when <we were both staying in> the region round Cithaeron, he with two herds and I with one, I was in this man's company for three whole periods of six months each, from spring to the rising of Arcturus; and when winter came I would drive my flock back to their byres and he his to the steadings of Laius. Is what I am saying true, or not?

SHEPHERD

What you say is true, though it is long ago.

MESSENGER

Tell me now, do you remember giving me a child, so that I could bring it up as my own?

SHEPHERD

What? Why are you asking me this question?

MESSENGER

This man, sir, is he who was once that child.

SHEPHERD

A plague on you! Will you not be silent?

OEDIPUS

No, do not strike him, old man! Your words deserve a blow more than his do.

1135 post hunc v. lacunam statuit Reiske: ex. gr. <*ἐπιστατοῦντες εἴχομεν· τότ' οὖν ἐγὼ*> Ll.-J.
1137 *ἐκμήνους* Eustath.: *ἐμμήνους* codd.

ΘΕΡΑΠΩΝ

τί δ', ὦ φέριστε δεσποτῶν, ἁμαρτάνω;

ΟΙΔΙΠΟΥΣ

οὐκ ἐννέπων τὸν παῖδ' ὃν οὗτος ἱστορεῖ.

ΘΕΡΑΠΩΝ

λέγει γὰρ εἰδὼς οὐδέν, ἀλλ' ἄλλως πονεῖ.

ΟΙΔΙΠΟΥΣ

σὺ πρὸς χάριν μὲν οὐκ ἐρεῖς, κλαίων δ' ἐρεῖς.

ΘΕΡΑΠΩΝ

μὴ δῆτα, πρὸς θεῶν, τὸν γέροντά μ' αἰκίσῃ.

ΟΙΔΙΠΟΥΣ

οὐχ ὡς τάχος τις τοῦδ' ἀποστρέψει χέρας;

ΘΕΡΑΠΩΝ

δύστηνος, ἀντὶ τοῦ; τί προσχρῄζεις μαθεῖν;

ΟΙΔΙΠΟΥΣ

τὸν παῖδ' ἔδωκας τῷδ' ὃν οὗτος ἱστορεῖ;

ΘΕΡΑΠΩΝ

ἔδωκ'· ὀλέσθαι δ' ὤφελον τῇδ' ἡμέρᾳ.

ΟΙΔΙΠΟΥΣ

ἀλλ' ἐς τόδ' ἥξεις μὴ λέγων γε τοὔνδικον.

ΘΕΡΑΠΩΝ

πολλῷ γε μᾶλλον, ἢν φράσω, διόλλυμαι.

ΟΙΔΙΠΟΥΣ

ἁνὴρ ὅδ', ὡς ἔοικεν, εἰς τριβὰς ἐλᾷ.

SHEPHERD

But, noblest of masters, what is my offence?

OEDIPUS

You are not telling about the child about whom he is asking!

SHEPHERD

Because he speaks from ignorance, and is wasting his labour!

OEDIPUS

If kindness will not get you to speak, pain will!

SHEPHERD

I am old; do not torture me, I beg you!

OEDIPUS

Will not one of you at once tie his hands behind his back?

SHEPHERD

Ah, misery, why? What do you wish to learn?

OEDIPUS

Did you give to this man the child he is asking about?

SHEPHERD

I did; I wish I had perished on that day!

OEDIPUS

It will come to that, if you do not tell the truth!

SHEPHERD

My ruin is far more certain if I tell!

OEDIPUS

It seems that this man is playing for time.

1155 *προσχρήζεις* Blaydes: *-ων* codd.

ΘΕΡΑΠΩΝ

οὐ δῆτ᾽ ἔγωγ᾽, ἀλλ᾽ εἶπον ὡς δοίην πάλαι.

ΟΙΔΙΠΟΥΣ

πόθεν λαβών; οἰκεῖον, ἢ ᾽ξ ἄλλου τινός;

ΘΕΡΑΠΩΝ

ἐμὸν μὲν οὐκ ἔγωγ᾽, ἐδεξάμην δέ του.

ΟΙΔΙΠΟΥΣ

τίνος πολιτῶν τῶνδε κἀκ ποίας στέγης;

ΘΕΡΑΠΩΝ

μὴ πρὸς θεῶν, μή, δέσποθ᾽, ἱστόρει πλέον.

ΟΙΔΙΠΟΥΣ

ὄλωλας, εἴ σε ταῦτ᾽ ἐρήσομαι πάλιν.

ΘΕΡΑΠΩΝ

τῶν Λαΐου τοίνυν τις ἦν †γεννημάτων†.

ΟΙΔΙΠΟΥΣ

ἦ δοῦλος, ἢ κείνου τις ἐγγενὴς γεγώς;

ΘΕΡΑΠΩΝ

οἴμοι, πρὸς αὐτῷ γ᾽ εἰμὶ τῷ δεινῷ λέγειν.

ΟΙΔΙΠΟΥΣ

κἄγωγ᾽ ἀκούειν· ἀλλ᾽ ὅμως ἀκουστέον.

ΘΕΡΑΠΩΝ

κείνου γέ τοι δὴ παῖς ἐκλῄζεθ᾽· ἡ δ᾽ ἔσω
κάλλιστ᾽ ἂν εἴποι σὴ γυνὴ τάδ᾽ ὡς ἔχει.

SHEPHERD

No, I said some time ago that I gave him the child.

OEDIPUS

Where did you get it from? Was it your own, or someone else's?

SHEPHERD

It was not my own; I received it from another person.

OEDIPUS

From which of these citizens, and from which house?

SHEPHERD

Master, I implore you, question me no more!

OEDIPUS

You are dead, if I have to ask you this once more!

SHEPHERD

It was someone from the house of Laius.

OEDIPUS

Was it a slave, or one of his family?

SHEPHERD

Ah, I have come to the danger point in telling my story!

OEDIPUS

And I in listening to it! But all the same I have to listen.

SHEPHERD

It was said to be his child; but your wife indoors could best tell you how it was.

1167 γεννημάτων] ἐκ δωμάτων Herwerden

ΟΙΔΙΠΟΥΣ

ἦ γὰρ δίδωσιν ἥδε σοι;

ΘΕΡΑΠΩΝ

μάλιστ᾽, ἄναξ.

ΟΙΔΙΠΟΥΣ

ὡς πρὸς τί χρείας;

ΘΕΡΑΠΩΝ

ὡς ἀναλώσαιμί νιν.

ΟΙΔΙΠΟΥΣ

τεκοῦσα τλήμων;

ΘΕΡΑΠΩΝ

θεσφάτων γ᾽ ὄκνῳ κακῶν.

ΟΙΔΙΠΟΥΣ

ποίων;

ΘΕΡΑΠΩΝ

κτενεῖν νιν τοὺς τεκόντας ἦν λόγος.

ΟΙΔΙΠΟΥΣ

πῶς δῆτ᾽ ἀφῆκας τῷ γέροντι τῷδε σύ;

ΘΕΡΑΠΩΝ

κατοικτίσας, ὦ δέσποθ᾽, ὡς ἄλλην χθόνα
δοκῶν ἀποίσειν, αὐτὸς ἔνθεν ἦν· ὁ δὲ
κάκ᾽ ἐς μέγιστ᾽ ἔσωσεν. εἰ γὰρ αὐτὸς εἶ
ὅν φησιν οὗτος, ἴσθι δύσποτμος γεγώς.

1180 αὐτὸς Heimsoeth: οὗτος codd.

OEDIPUS

Was it she who gave it you?

SHEPHERD

Yes, my lord.

OEDIPUS

For what purpose?

SHEPHERD

So that I could make away with it.

OEDIPUS

Poor thing, was she its mother?

SHEPHERD

Yes, it was for fear of evil prophecies.

OEDIPUS

What prophecies?

SHEPHERD

It was said that it would kill its parents.

OEDIPUS

How then did you come to make it over to this man?

SHEPHERD

I felt sorry for it, my lord, and thought he would take it to another country, where he came from; but he preserved it for a great disaster; because if you are who he says you are, know that you were born to misery!

ΟΙΔΙΠΟΥΣ

ἰοὺ ἰού· τὰ πάντ᾽ ἂν ἐξήκοι σαφῆ.
ὦ φῶς, τελευταῖόν σε προσβλέψαιμι νῦν,
ὅστις πέφασμαι φύς τ᾽ ἀφ᾽ ὧν οὐ χρῆν, ξὺν οἷς τ᾽
οὐ χρῆν ὁμιλῶν, οὕς τέ μ᾽ οὐκ ἔδει κτανών.

ΧΟΡΟΣ

ἰὼ γενεαὶ βροτῶν, στρ. α΄
ὡς ὑμᾶς ἴσα καὶ τὸ μη-
δὲν ζώσας ἐναριθμῶ.
τίς γάρ, τίς ἀνὴρ πλέον
τᾶς εὐδαιμονίας φέρει
ἢ τοσοῦτον ὅσον δοκεῖν
καὶ δόξαντ᾽ ἀποκλῖναι;
τὸν σόν τοι παράδειγμ᾽ ἔχων,
τὸν σὸν δαίμονα, τὸν σόν, ὦ
τλᾶμον Οἰδιπόδα, βροτῶν
οὐδὲν μακαρίζω·
ὅστις καθ᾽ ὑπερβολὰν ἀντ. α΄
τοξεύσας ἐκράτησας οὐ
πάντ᾽ εὐδαίμονος ὄλβου,
ὦ Ζεῦ, κατὰ μὲν φθίσας
τὰν γαμψώνυχα παρθένον
χρησμῳδόν, θανάτων δ᾽ ἐμᾷ
χώρᾳ πύργος ἀνέστας·
ἐξ οὗ καὶ βασιλεὺς καλῇ
ἐμὸς καὶ τὰ μέγιστ᾽ ἐτι-

OEDIPUS

Oh, oh! All is now clear! O light, may I now look on you for the last time, I who am revealed as cursed in my birth, cursed in my marriage, cursed in my killing!

Exit OEDIPUS; *the* MESSENGER *and the* SHEPHERD *also leave.*

CHORUS

Ah, generations of men, how close to nothingness I estimate your life to be! What man, what man wins more of happiness than enough to seem, and after seeming to decline? With your fate as my example, your fate, unhappy Oedipus, I say that nothing pertaining to mankind is enviable.

You it was whose arrow unbelievably found its mark and you won a success not in all ways sanctioned by the gods—O Zeus—when you destroyed the prophesying maiden with hooked talons,[a] and for my country stood like a wall keeping off death. Because of that are you

[a] The Sphinx.

1189–90 an πλέον et φέρει permutanda sunt?

1193 τὸν Camerarius: τὸ codd.

1197 ἐκράτησας οὐ Reisig: ἐκράτησας τοῦ codd.: ἐκράτησε τοῦ Ambrosianus L.39 sup., coni. Hermann

1201 ἀνέστας rpat: ἀνέστα LPa

1202–3 καλῇ ἐμὸς] ἐμὸς καλῇ Elmsley: καλῇ τ' ἐμὸς Blaydes

μάθης, ταῖς μεγάλαισιν ἐν
Θήβαισιν ἀνάσσων.
τανῦν δ᾽ ἀκούειν τίς ἀθλιώτερος, στρ. β′
†τίς ἐν πόνοις τίς ἄταις ἀγρίαις†
ξύνοικος ἀλλαγᾷ βίου;
ἰὼ κλεινὸν Οἰδίπου κάρα,
ᾧ μέγας λιμὴν
αὑτὸς ἤρκεσεν
παιδὶ καὶ πατρὶ
θαλαμηπόλῳ πεσεῖν,
πῶς ποτε πῶς ποθ᾽ αἱ πατρῷ-
αί σ᾽ ἄλοκες φέρειν, τάλας,
σῖγ᾽ ἐδυνάθησαν ἐς τοσόνδε;
ἐφηῦρέ σ᾽ ἄκονθ᾽ ὁ πάνθ᾽ ὁρῶν χρόνος, ἀντ. β′
δικάζει τὸν ἄγαμον γάμον πάλαι
τεκνοῦντα καὶ τεκνούμενον.
ἰὼ Λαΐειον <ὦ> τέκνον,
εἴθε σ᾽ εἴθε σε
μήποτ᾽ εἰδόμαν·
ὡς ὀδύρομαι
περίαλλ᾽ ἰὰν χέων
ἐκ στομάτων. τὸ δ᾽ ὀρθὸν εἰ-
πεῖν, ἀνέπνευσά τ᾽ ἐκ σέθεν
καὶ κατεκοίμησα τοὐμὸν ὄμμα.

ΕΞΑΓΓΕΛΟΣ

ὦ γῆς μέγιστα τῆσδ᾽ ἀεὶ τιμώμενοι,
οἷ᾽ ἔργ᾽ ἀκούσεσθ᾽, οἷα δ᾽ εἰσόψεσθ᾽, ὅσον δ᾽

called king, and you received the greatest honours, ruling in mighty Thebes.

But now whose story is sadder to hear, who dwells amid more cruel torments, more cruel labours through the reversal of his life? Ah, famous Oedipus, whom the same wide harbour served as child and as father on your bridal bed! How, how could the field your father sowed put up with you so long in silence?

Time the all-seeing has found you out against your will; long since has it condemned the monstrous marriage that produced offspring for you and offspring for itself.[a] Ah, son of Laius, would that I had never set eyes on you! For I grievously lament, pouring from my lips a dirge. To tell the truth, you restored me to life and you lulled my eyes in death.

Enter SECOND MESSENGER.

SECOND MESSENGER

You who are ever held in greatest honour in this land, what actions shall you hear of, what actions shall you see,

[a] See *Sophoclea* 107f.

1205 τίς ἄταις ἀγρίαις, τίς ἐν πόνοις Hermann: alii alia
1209 πατρὶ] πόσει Wunder
1216 suppl. Erfurdt
1218 ὡς ὀδύρομαι Kamerbeek: ὀδύρομαι γὰρ ὡς codd.
1219 ἰὰν χέων Burges: ἰαχέων codd.

ἀρεῖσθε πένθος, εἴπερ εὐγενῶς ἔτι
τῶν Λαβδακείων ἐντρέπεσθε δωμάτων.
οἶμαι γὰρ οὔτ᾽ ἂν Ἴστρον οὔτε Φᾶσιν ἂν
νίψαι καθαρμῷ τήνδε τὴν στέγην, ὅσα
κεύθει, τὰ δ᾽ αὐτίκ᾽ ἐς τὸ φῶς φανεῖ κακὰ
ἑκόντα κοὐκ ἄκοντα. τῶν δὲ πημονῶν
μάλιστα λυποῦσ᾽ αἳ φανῶσ᾽ αὐθαίρετοι.

ΧΟΡΟΣ

λείπει μὲν οὐδ᾽ ἃ πρόσθεν ᾔδεμεν τὸ μὴ οὐ
βαρύστον᾽ εἶναι· πρὸς δ᾽ ἐκείνοισιν τί φής;

ΕΞΑΓΓΕΛΟΣ

ὁ μὲν τάχιστος τῶν λόγων εἰπεῖν τε καὶ
μαθεῖν, τέθνηκε θεῖον Ἰοκάστης κάρα.

ΧΟΡΟΣ

ὦ δυστάλαινα, πρὸς τίνος ποτ᾽ αἰτίας;

ΕΞΑΓΓΕΛΟΣ

αὐτὴ πρὸς αὑτῆς. τῶν δὲ πραχθέντων τὰ μὲν
ἄλγιστ᾽ ἄπεστιν· ἡ γὰρ ὄψις οὐ πάρα.
ὅμως δ᾽, ὅσον γε κἀν ἐμοὶ μνήμης ἔνι,
πεύσῃ τὰ κείνης ἀθλίας παθήματα.
ὅπως γὰρ ὀργῇ χρωμένη παρῆλθ᾽ ἔσω
θυρῶνος, ἵετ᾽ εὐθὺ πρὸς τὰ νυμφικὰ
λέχη, κόμην σπῶσ᾽ ἀμφιδεξίοις ἀκμαῖς·
πύλας δ᾽, ὅπως εἰσῆλθ᾽, ἐπιρράξασ᾽ ἔσω,
καλεῖ τὸν ἤδη Λάιον πάλαι νεκρόν,
μνήμην παλαιῶν σπερμάτων ἔχουσ᾽, ὑφ᾽ ὧν

and what mourning shall you endure, if you have still loyal regard for the house of Laius! For I think that neither Ister nor Phasis[a] could wash clean this house, such horrors does it conceal, and some it shall soon expose to the light, horrors willed and not unwilled. And the griefs that give most pain are those we bring upon ourselves.

CHORUS

Even the things we knew before do not fall short of being grievous; what can you add to them?

SECOND MESSENGER

The news I must first speak and you must first learn is that the august Iocaste is dead.

CHORUS

Oh sorrow! What was the cause?

SECOND MESSENGER

It was by her own hand. The most painful part of what has happened you are spared, because you did not see it; but so far as my memory can serve me, you shall hear of the sufferings of that poor woman.

When in her passion she passed through the door, she sped directly to her bridal bed, tearing her hair with fingers of both hands. And when she entered she slammed shut both panels of the door, calling on Laius, now long a corpse, remembering their love-making long ago, which

[a] The Danube and the Rioni (in the Caucasus).

1225 εὐγενῶς Hartung: ἐγγενῶς codd.

θάνοι μὲν αὐτός, τὴν δὲ τίκτουσαν λίποι
τοῖς οἷσιν αὐτοῦ δύστεκνον παιδουργίαν.
γοᾶτο δ' εὐνάς, ἔνθα δύστηνος διπλῆ
ἐξ ἀνδρὸς ἄνδρα καὶ τέκν' ἐκ τέκνων τέκοι.
χὤπως μὲν ἐκ τῶνδ' οὐκέτ' οἶδ' ἀπόλλυται·
βοῶν γὰρ εἰσέπαισεν Οἰδίπους, ὑφ' οὗ
οὐκ ἦν τὸ κείνης ἐκθεάσασθαι κακόν,
ἀλλ' εἰς ἐκεῖνον περιπολοῦντ' ἐλεύσσομεν.
φοιτᾷ γὰρ ἡμᾶς ἔγχος ἐξαιτῶν πορεῖν,
γυναῖκά τ' οὐ γυναῖκα, μητρῴαν δ' ὅπου
κίχοι διπλῆν ἄρουραν οὗ τε καὶ τέκνων.
λυσσῶντι δ' αὐτῷ δαιμόνων δείκνυσί τις·
οὐδεὶς γὰρ ἀνδρῶν, οἳ παρῆμεν ἐγγύθεν.
δεινὸν δ' ἀΰσας ὡς ὑφ' ἡγητοῦ τινος
πύλαις διπλαῖς ἐνήλατ', ἐκ δὲ πυθμένων
ἔκλινε κοῖλα κλῇθρα κἀμπίπτει στέγῃ.
οὗ δὴ κρεμαστὴν τὴν γυναῖκ' εἰσείδομεν,
πλεκταῖσιν αἰώραισιν ἐμπεπλεγμένην.
ὁ δ' ὡς ὁρᾷ νιν, δεινὰ βρυχηθεὶς τάλας,
χαλᾷ κρεμαστὴν ἀρτάνην. ἐπεὶ δὲ γῇ
ἔκειτο τλήμων, δεινά γ' ἦν τἀνθένδ' ὁρᾶν.
ἀποσπάσας γὰρ εἱμάτων χρυσηλάτους
περόνας ἀπ' αὐτῆς, αἷσιν ἐξεστέλλετο,
ἄρας ἔπαισεν ἄρθρα τῶν αὑτοῦ κύκλων,
αὐδῶν τοιαῦθ', ὁθούνεκ' οὐκ ὄψοιντό νιν
οὔθ' οἷ' ἔπασχεν οὔθ' ὁποῖ' ἔδρα κακά,
ἀλλ' ἐν σκότῳ τὸ λοιπὸν οὓς μὲν οὐκ ἔδει
ὀψοίαθ', οὓς δ' ἔχρῃζεν οὐ γνωσοίατο.

had brought him death, leaving her to bring forth a progeny accursed by one that was his own; and she wept over the bed where in double misery she had brought forth a husband by her husband and children by her child. And how after that she perished is more than I know; for Oedipus burst in crying out loud, so that we could not watch her calamity to its end, but were gazing upon him as he moved around. For he ranged about asking us to hand him a sword, and asking where he should find not his wife, but the field that had yielded two harvests, himself and his children. And in his fury some god showed her to him; it was none of us men who stood nearby. And with a dreadful cry, as though someone were guiding him he rushed at the double doors, forced the bolts inwards from their sockets and fell into the room. There we saw the woman hanging, her neck tied in a twisted noose. And when he saw her, with a fearful roar, poor man, he untied the knot from which she hung; and when the unhappy woman lay upon the ground, what we saw next was terrible. For he broke off the golden pins from her raiment, with which she was adorned, and lifting up his eyes struck them, uttering such words as these: that they should not see his dread sufferings or his dread actions, but in the future they should see in darkness those they never should have seen, and fail to recognise those he wished to know. Repeating such words as these he

---

1249 διπλῇ P: -ᾶς K: -ᾶ O s.l.: -οῦς cett.

1264 *πλεκταῖσιν* Ambrosiani G.56, L.39: *πλεκταῖς* cett. | *αἰώραισιν* Ambros. G.56: *αἰώραις* G. s.l., pat: *ἐώραις* Lrpa post *ἐμπεπλεγμένην* add. ὁ δὲ codd., quod aut delendum aut in initio v. 1265 legendum censuit Blaydes

1265 ὁ δ' ὡς Blaydes: ὅπως pat: ὅπως δ' Lrp

τοιαῦτ᾽ ἐφυμνῶν πολλάκις τε κοὐχ ἅπαξ
ἤρασσ᾽ ἐπαίρων βλέφαρα. φοίνιαι δ᾽ ὁμοῦ
γλῆναι γένει᾽ ἔτεγγον, οὐδ᾽ ἀνίεσαν.
[φόνου μυδώσας σταγόνας, ἀλλ᾽ ὁμοῦ μέλας
ὄμβρος †χαλάζης αἵματος† ἐτέγγετο.]
†τάδ᾽ ἐκ δυοῖν ἔρρωγεν οὐ μόνου κακά†
ἀλλ᾽ ἀνδρὶ καὶ γυναικὶ συμμιγῆ κακά.
ὁ πρὶν παλαιὸς δ᾽ ὄλβος ἦν πάροιθε μὲν
ὄλβος δικαίως, νῦν δὲ τῇδε θἠμέρᾳ
στεναγμός, ἄτη, θάνατος, αἰσχύνη, κακῶν
ὅσ᾽ ἐστὶ πάντων ὀνόματ᾽, οὐδέν ἐστ᾽ ἀπόν.

ΧΟΡΟΣ

νῦν δ᾽ ἔσθ᾽ ὁ τλήμων ἔν τινι σχολῇ κακοῦ;

ΕΞΑΓΓΕΛΟΣ

βοᾷ διοίγειν κλῇθρα καὶ δηλοῦν τινα
τοῖς πᾶσι Καδμείοισι τὸν πατροκτόνον,
τὸν μητρός, αὐδῶν ἀνόσι᾽ οὐδὲ ῥητά μοι,
ὡς ἐκ χθονὸς ῥίψων ἑαυτόν, οὐδ᾽ ἔτι
μενῶν δόμοις ἀραῖος, ὡς ἠράσατο.
ῥώμης γε μέντοι καὶ προηγητοῦ τινος
δεῖται· τὸ γὰρ νόσημα μεῖζον ἢ φέρειν.
δείξει δὲ καὶ σοί. κλῇθρα γὰρ πυλῶν τάδε
διοίγεται· θέαμα δ᾽ εἰσόψῃ τάχα
τοιοῦτον οἷον καὶ στυγοῦντ᾽ ἐποικτίσαι.

lifted up his eyes and not once but many times struck them; the bleeding eyeballs soaked his cheeks, and did not cease to drip [sending forth sluggish drops of gore, but all at once a dark shower of blood came down like hail].

These horrors burst forth not from one person, but brought commingled grief to man and woman. Their earlier happiness was truly happiness; but now in this day lamentation, ruin, death, shame, all ills that can be named, none of them is absent.

CHORUS

And now does the wretched man have any respite from pain?

SECOND MESSENGER

He is crying for someone to unbar the gates and show to all the Cadmeians his father's killer, his mother's—he spoke unholy words, which I cannot utter—meaning to cast himself out of this land, and not to linger in the house under the curse, that curse that was his own. But he is in need of the strength of some guide; for his sickness is too great for him to bear it. But he will display it to you also; for the bars of the gates are being opened, and you shall soon see such a sight as would drive to pity even one who hates him.

Enter OEDIPUS, *now blind.*

1278–79 del. West

1280–81 del. Dindorf

1280 ἐκ] ἐς Pearson *οὐ μόνου κακά*] *οὐ μόνου κάτα* Otto: *οὐχ ἑνὸς μόνου* Porson

ΧΟΡΟΣ

ὦ δεινὸν ἰδεῖν πάθος ἀνθρώποις,
ὦ δεινότατον πάντων ὅσ' ἐγὼ
προσέκυρσ' ἤδη. τίς σ', ὦ τλῆμον,
προσέβη μανία; τίς ὁ πηδήσας
μείζονα δαίμων τῶν μηκίστων
πρὸς σῇ δυσδαίμονι μοίρᾳ;
φεῦ φεῦ δύστην', ἀλλ' οὐδ' ἐσιδεῖν
δύναμαί σ', ἐθέλων πόλλ' ἀνερέσθαι,
πολλὰ πυθέσθαι, πολλὰ δ' ἀθρῆσαι·
τοίαν φρίκην παρέχεις μοι.

ΟΙΔΙΠΟΥΣ

αἰαῖ αἰαῖ, δύστανος ἐγώ,
ποῖ γᾶς φέρομαι τλάμων; πᾷ μοι
φθογγὰ διαπωτᾶται φοράδαν;
ἰὼ δαῖμον, ἵν' ἐξήλου.

ΧΟΡΟΣ

ἐς δεινόν, οὐδ' ἀκουστόν, οὐδ' ἐπόψιμον.

ΟΙΔΙΠΟΥΣ

ἰὼ σκότου στρ. α'
νέφος ἐμὸν ἀπότροπον, ἐπιπλόμενον ἄφατον,
ἀδάματόν τε καὶ δυσούριστον <ὄν>.
οἴμοι,
οἴμοι μάλ' αὖθις· οἷον εἰσέδυ μ' ἅμα
κέντρων τε τῶνδ' οἴστρημα καὶ μνήμη κακῶν.

CHORUS

O grief terrible for men to see, O grief most terrible of any I have yet encountered! What madness has come upon you, unhappy one? Who is the god that with a leap longer than the longest has sprung upon your miserable fate? Ah, ah, unhappy one, I cannot even bear to look on you, though I wish to ask you many questions and to learn many answers and perceive many things; such is the horror you inspire in me!

OEDIPUS

Alas, alas, miserable am I! Where am I being carried in my sorrow? Where is my voice borne on the wings of the air? Ah, god, how far have you leaped?

CHORUS

To something terrible, not to be heard or looked upon.

OEDIPUS

Ah, cloud of darkness abominable, coming over me unspeakably, irresistible, sped by an evil wind! Alas, alas once more! How the sting of these goads has sunk into me together with the remembrance of my troubles!

1310 διαπωτᾶται Musgrave, et fort. Π 10: -πέταται Lpa: -πέπταται rpXrt

1315 ἀδάματον Hermann: -αστον codd. | <ὂν> suppl. Hermann

ΧΟΡΟΣ

καὶ θαῦμά γ' οὐδὲν ἐν τοσοῖσδε πήμασιν
διπλᾶ σε πενθεῖν καὶ διπλᾶ θροεῖν κακά.

ΟΙΔΙΠΟΥΣ

ἰὼ φίλος, ἀντ. α´
σὺ μὲν ἐμὸς ἐπίπολος ἔτι μόνιμος· ἔτι γὰρ
ὑπομένεις με τὸν τυφλὸν κηδεύων.
φεῦ φεῦ·
οὐ γάρ με λήθεις, ἀλλὰ γιγνώσκω σαφῶς,
καίπερ σκοτεινός, τήν γε σὴν αὐδὴν ὅμως.

ΧΟΡΟΣ

ὦ δεινὰ δράσας, πῶς ἔτλης τοιαῦτα σὰς
ὄψεις μαρᾶναι; τίς σ' ἐπῆρε δαιμόνων;

ΟΙΔΙΠΟΥΣ

Ἀπόλλων τάδ' ἦν, Ἀπόλλων, φίλοι, στρ. β´
ὁ κακὰ κακὰ τελῶν ἐμὰ τάδ' ἐμὰ πάθεα.
ἔπαισε δ' αὐτόχειρ νιν οὔ-
τις, ἀλλ' ἐγὼ τλάμων.
τί γὰρ ἔδει μ' ὁρᾶν,
ὅτῳ γ' ὁρῶντι μηδὲν ἦν ἰδεῖν γλυκύ;

ΧΟΡΟΣ

ἦν τᾷδ' ὅπωσπερ καὶ σὺ φής.

ΟΙΔΙΠΟΥΣ

τί δῆτ' ἐμοὶ βλεπτὸν ἢ
στερκτόν, ἢ προσήγορον
ἔτ' ἔστ' ἀκούειν ἡδονᾷ, φίλοι;
ἀπάγετ' ἐκτόπιον ὅτι τάχιστά με,
ἀπάγετ', ὦ φίλοι, τὸν μέγ' ὀλέθριον,

CHORUS

It is no wonder that in such sorrows you should doubly lament and doubly cry out upon your woes!

OEDIPUS

Ah, my friend, you are still remaining to protect me; you still stay behind to care for the blind man! Alas, alas! Your presence is not hid from me, but I recognise your voice, though I am in the dark.

CHORUS

Doer of dreadful deeds, how did you bring yourself so to quench your sight? Which of the gods set you on?

OEDIPUS

It was Apollo, Apollo, my friends, who accomplished these cruel, cruel sufferings of mine! And no other hand struck my eyes, but my own miserable hand! For why did I have to see, when there was nothing I could see with pleasure?

CHORUS

It was just as you say.

OEDIPUS

What was I to look upon or cherish, or what greeting could I hear with pleasure, friends? Take me away as soon as you can, take me, my friends, the utterly lost, the

---

1320 θροεῖν Nauck: φορεῖν codd. plerique
1323 με τὸν Erfurdt: ἐμὲ τὸν Lrpa
1336 τᾷδ' Nauck: τάδ' Lp: ταῦθ' rpat
1337 ᾗ : ἦν Wilamowitz
1343 μέγ' ὀλέθριον Erfurdt: ὀλέθριον μέγα pXrt: ὀλέθριον μέγαν Lrpa

τὸν καταρατότατον, ἔτι δὲ καὶ θεοῖς
ἐχθρότατον βροτῶν.

ΧΟΡΟΣ

δείλαιε τοῦ νοῦ τῆς τε συμφορᾶς ἴσον,
ὥς σ᾽ ἠθέλησα μηδαμὰ γνῶναί ποτ᾽ ἄν.

ΟΙΔΙΠΟΥΣ

ὄλοιθ᾽ ὅστις ἦν ὃς ἀγρίας πέδας ἀντ. β´
νομὰς ἐπιποδίας ἔλαβέ μ᾽ ἀπό τε φόνου <μ᾽>
ἔρυτο κἀνέσωσεν, οὐ-
δὲν ἐς χάριν πράσσων.
τότε γὰρ ἂν θανὼν
οὐκ ἦ φίλοισιν οὐδ᾽ ἐμοὶ τοσόνδ᾽ ἄχος.

ΧΟΡΟΣ

θέλοντι κἀμοὶ τοῦτ᾽ ἂν ἦν.

ΟΙΔΙΠΟΥΣ

οὔκουν πατρός γ᾽ ἂν φονεὺς
ἦλθον, οὐδὲ νυμφίος
βροτοῖς ἐκλήθην ὧν ἔφυν ἄπο.
νῦν δ᾽ ἄθεος μέν εἰμ᾽, ἀνοσίων δὲ παῖς,
ὁμογενὴς δ᾽ ἀφ᾽ ὧν αὐτὸς ἔφυν τάλας.
εἰ δέ τι πρεσβύτερον ἔτι κακοῦ κακόν,
τοῦτ᾽ ἔλαχ᾽ Οἰδίπους.

ΧΟΡΟΣ

οὐκ οἶδ᾽ ὅπως σε φῶ βεβουλεῦσθαι καλῶς.
κρείσσων γὰρ ἦσθα μηκέτ᾽ ὢν ἢ ζῶν τυφλός.

1348 μηδαμὰ γνῶναί Dobree: μηδ᾽ ἀναγνῶναί codd.
1349 ὃς t: ὃς ἀπ᾽ fere codd.

thrice accursed, and moreover the one among mortals most hated by the gods!

CHORUS

Wretched in your mind and wretched in your fortune, how I wish I had never come to know you!

OEDIPUS

A curse upon the shepherd who released me from the cruel fetters of my feet, and saved me from death, and preserved me, doing me no kindness! For if I had died then, I would not have been so great a grief to my friends or to myself.

CHORUS

I too wish that it had been so.

OEDIPUS

I would not have come to be my father's killer, nor would I have been called by men the bridegroom of her that gave me birth. But now I am abandoned by the gods, the child of unholy parents, a sharer in my father's marriage-bed, and if there is any evil even beyond evil, that is the portion of Oedipus.

CHORUS

I do not know how I can say that you were well advised; for you would have been better dead than living but blind.

1350 νομὰς Hartung: νομάδος codd. | ἔλαβέ μ' Ven. gr. 468: ἔλυσέ μ' Krp: ἔλυσεν a | <μ'> suppl. Kennedy

1360 ἄθεος Erfurdt et Elmsley: ἄθλιος codd.

1365 ἔτι Hermann: ἔφυ rpat

1368 ἦσθ' <ἂν> Porson et Purgold

ΟΙΔΙΠΟΥΣ

ὡς μὲν τάδ᾽ οὐχ ὧδ᾽ ἔστ᾽ ἄριστ᾽ εἰργασμένα,
μή μ᾽ ἐκδίδασκε, μηδὲ συμβούλευ᾽ ἔτι.
ἐγὼ γὰρ οὐκ οἶδ᾽ ὄμμασιν ποίοις βλέπων
πατέρα ποτ᾽ ἂν προσεῖδον εἰς Ἅιδου μολών,
οὐδ᾽ αὖ τάλαιναν μητέρ᾽, οἷν ἐμοὶ δυοῖν
ἔργ᾽ ἐστὶ κρείσσον᾽ ἀγχόνης εἰργασμένα.
ἀλλ᾽ ἡ τέκνων δῆτ᾽ ὄψις ἦν ἐφίμερος,
βλαστοῦσ᾽ ὅπως ἔβλαστε, προσλεύσσειν ἐμοί;
οὐ δῆτα τοῖς γ᾽ ἐμοῖσιν ὀφθαλμοῖς ποτε·
οὐδ᾽ ἄστυ γ᾽, οὐδὲ πύργος, οὐδὲ δαιμόνων
ἀγάλμαθ᾽ ἱερά θ᾽, ὧν ὁ παντλήμων ἐγὼ
κάλλιστ᾽ ἀνὴρ εἷς ἔν γε ταῖς Θήβαις τραφεὶς
ἀπεστέρησ᾽ ἐμαυτόν, αὐτὸς ἐννέπων
ὠθεῖν ἅπαντας τὸν ἀσεβῆ, τὸν ἐκ θεῶν
φανέντ᾽ ἄναγνον καὶ γένους τοῦ Λαΐου.
τοιάνδ᾽ ἐγὼ κηλῖδα μηνύσας ἐμὴν
ὀρθοῖς ἔμελλον ὄμμασιν τούτους ὁρᾶν;
ἥκιστά γ᾽· ἀλλ᾽ εἰ τῆς ἀκουούσης ἔτ᾽ ἦν
πηγῆς δι᾽ ὤτων φραγμός, οὐκ ἂν ἐσχόμην
τὸ μὴ ἀποκλῇσαι τοὐμὸν ἄθλιον δέμας,
ἵν᾽ ἦ τυφλός τε καὶ κλύων μηδέν· τὸ γὰρ
τὴν φροντίδ᾽ ἔξω τῶν κακῶν οἰκεῖν γλυκύ.
ἰὼ Κιθαιρών, τί μ᾽ ἐδέχου; τί μ᾽ οὐ λαβὼν
ἔκτεινας εὐθύς, ὡς ἔδειξα μήποτε
ἐμαυτὸν ἀνθρώποισιν ἔνθεν ἦ γεγώς;

1379 ἱερά θ᾽, ὧν Nauck: ἱερά, τῶν codd.

OEDIPUS

Do not try to show me that what has been done was not done for the best, and give me no more counsel! For I do not know with what eyes I could have looked upon my father when I went to Hades, or upon my unhappy mother, since upon them both I have done deeds that hanging could not atone for.

Then, could I desire to look upon my children, since their origins were what they were? Never could these eyes have harboured such desire! Nor to look upon the city, or the wall, or the statues of the gods or the temples, from which I, who had enjoyed the greatest luxury in Thebes, had in my misery cut myself off, commanding with my own lips that all should drive from their houses the impious one, the one whom the gods had shown to be impure and of the race of Laius.

When I had proclaimed that such a stain lay upon me, was I to look upon these with steady eyes? Never! Why, if there had been a means of blocking the stream of hearing through my ears, I would not have hesitated to shut off my wretched self, making myself blind and deaf. It is a joy to live with one's thoughts beyond the reach of sorrow.

Ah, Cithaeron, why did you receive me? Why did you not take me and kill me at once, so that I could never have revealed to mortals what was my origin? O Polybus and

ὦ Πόλυβε καὶ Κόρινθε καὶ τὰ πάτρια
λόγῳ παλαιὰ δώμαθ', οἷον ἆρά με
κάλλος κακῶν ὕπουλον ἐξεθρέψατε.
νῦν γὰρ κακός τ' ὢν κἀκ κακῶν εὑρίσκομαι.
ὦ τρεῖς κέλευθοι καὶ κεκρυμμένη νάπη
δρυμός τε καὶ στενωπὸς ἐν τριπλαῖς ὁδοῖς,
αἳ τοὐμὸν αἷμα τῶν ἐμῶν χειρῶν ἄπο
ἐπίετε πατρός, ἆρά μου μέμνησθ' ἔτι
οἷ' ἔργα δράσας ὑμὶν εἶτα δεῦρ' ἰὼν
ὁποῖ' ἔπρασσον αὖθις; ὦ γάμοι γάμοι,
ἐφύσαθ' ἡμᾶς, καὶ φυτεύσαντες πάλιν
ἀνεῖτε ταὐτὸν σπέρμα, κἀπεδείξατε
πατέρας ἀδελφούς, παῖδας αἷμ' ἐμφύλιον,
νύμφας γυναῖκας μητέρας τε, χὠπόσα
αἴσχιστ' ἐν ἀνθρώποισιν ἔργα γίγνεται.
ἀλλ', οὐ γὰρ αὐδᾶν ἔσθ' ἃ μηδὲ δρᾶν καλόν,
ὅπως τάχιστα πρὸς θεῶν ἔξω μέ που
καλύψατ', ἢ φονεύσατ', ἢ θαλάσσιον
ἐκρίψατ', ἔνθα μήποτ' εἰσόψεσθ' ἔτι.
ἴτ', ἀξιώσατ' ἀνδρὸς ἀθλίου θιγεῖν·
πίθεσθε, μὴ δείσητε· τἀμὰ γὰρ κακὰ
οὐδεὶς οἷός τε πλὴν ἐμοῦ φέρειν βροτῶν.

ΧΟΡΟΣ

ἀλλ' ὧν ἐπαιτεῖς ἐς δέον πάρεσθ' ὅδε
Κρέων τὸ πράσσειν καὶ τὸ βουλεύειν, ἐπεὶ
χώρας λέλειπται μοῦνος ἀντὶ σοῦ φύλαξ.

1406 sic interpunxit Macleod
1411–12 καλύψατ' et ἐκρίψατ' permutavit Burges

Corinth and what was called the ancient home of my fathers, how beautiful was the veneer with which the care you gave me veiled my secret sickness! For now I am discovered to be evil and sprung from evil ancestors. O three roads, hidden glade, coppice and narrow path where three ways meet, ways that drank my own, my father's blood shed by my hands, do you still remember what deeds you saw me do and what deeds I did when I came here? Marriage, marriage, you gave me birth, and after you had done so you brought up the selfsame seed, and displayed fathers who were brothers, children who were fruit of incest, brides who were both wives and mothers to their spouses, and all things that are most atrocious among men.

But since it is hateful to speak of hateful deeds, as soon as possible, I beg you, hide me somewhere abroad, or kill me, or hurl me into the sea, where you shall never again see me! Come, condescend to touch a man accursed! Do as I say, do not be afraid! For there is no human being who can bear my woes but I.

Enter CREON.

CHORUS

But here is Creon ready for the actions and the counsels you demand, since he is left as the sole guardian of the land in your place.

ΟΙΔΙΠΟΥΣ

οἴμοι, τί δῆτα λέξομεν πρὸς τόνδ᾿ ἔπος;
τίς μοι φανεῖται πίστις ἔνδικος; τὰ γὰρ
πάρος πρὸς αὐτὸν πάντ᾿ ἐφηύρημαι κακός.

ΚΡΕΩΝ

οὐχ ὡς γελαστής, Οἰδίπους, ἐλήλυθα,
οὐδ᾿ ὡς ὀνειδιῶν τι τῶν πάρος κακῶν.
ἀλλ᾿ εἰ τὰ θνητῶν μὴ καταισχύνεσθ᾿ ἔτι
γένεθλα, τὴν γοῦν πάντα βόσκουσαν φλόγα
αἰδεῖσθ᾿ ἄνακτος Ἡλίου, τοιόνδ᾿ ἄγος
ἀκάλυπτον οὕτω δεικνύναι, τὸ μήτε γῆ
μήτ᾿ ὄμβρος ἱερὸς μήτε φῶς προσδέξεται.
ἀλλ᾿ ὡς τάχιστ᾿ ἐς οἶκον ἐσκομίζετε·
τοῖς ἐν γένει γὰρ τἀγγενῆ μόνοις θ᾿ ὁρᾶν
μόνοις τ᾿ ἀκούειν εὐσεβῶς ἔχει κακά.

ΟΙΔΙΠΟΥΣ

πρὸς θεῶν, ἐπείπερ ἐλπίδος μ᾿ ἀπέσπασας,
ἄριστος ἐλθὼν πρὸς κάκιστον ἄνδρ᾿ ἐμέ,
πιθοῦ τί μοι· πρὸς σοῦ γάρ, οὐδ᾿ ἐμοῦ, φράσω.

ΚΡΕΩΝ

καὶ τοῦ με χρείας ὧδε λιπαρεῖς τυχεῖν;

ΟΙΔΙΠΟΥΣ

ῥῖψόν με γῆς ἐκ τῆσδ᾿ ὅσον τάχισθ᾿, ὅπου
θνητῶν φανοῦμαι μηδενὸς προσήγορος.

OEDIPUS

Alas, what words can I address to him? What just claim to confidence shall I produce? For in all my past dealings with him I am found to have done wrong.

CREON

I have not come to mock you, Oedipus, or to reproach you with any wrong that lies in the past. (*To the attendants.*) But if you have no shame before the face of men, revere at least the fire of the Sun that feeds all things, and do not expose openly such a pollution, one which neither the earth nor the sacred rain nor the light shall welcome! Take him at once into the house! Piety demands that kinsmen alone should see and alone should hear the sorrows of their kin.

OEDIPUS

I beg you, since beyond all expectation you have come in all your goodness to my badness, grant me a favour! It is for your sake I ask it, not my own.

CREON

And what is the favour that you thus demand of me?

OEDIPUS

Cast me out of this land as soon as possible, to a place where I cannot be addressed by any mortal being!

1430 μόνοις θ' Pflugk (μόνοις iam Dobree): μάλισθ' codd.

ΚΡΕΩΝ

ἔδρασ' ἂν εὖ τοῦτ' ἴσθ' ἄν, εἰ μὴ τοῦ θεοῦ
πρώτιστ' ἔχρῃζον ἐκμαθεῖν τί πρακτέον.

ΟΙΔΙΠΟΥΣ

ἀλλ' ἥ γ' ἐκείνου πᾶσ' ἐδηλώθη φάτις,
τὸν πατροφόντην, τὸν ἀσεβῆ μ' ἀπολλύναι.

ΚΡΕΩΝ

οὕτως ἐλέχθη ταῦθ'· ὅμως δ' ἵν' ἕσταμεν
χρείας ἄμεινον ἐκμαθεῖν τί δραστέον.

ΟΙΔΙΠΟΥΣ

οὕτως ἄρ' ἀνδρὸς ἀθλίου πεύσεσθ' ὕπερ;

ΚΡΕΩΝ

καὶ γὰρ σὺ νῦν γ' ἂν τῷ θεῷ πίστιν φέροις.

ΟΙΔΙΠΟΥΣ

καὶ σοί γ' ἐπισκήπτω τε καὶ προτρέψομαι,
τῆς μὲν κατ' οἴκους αὐτὸς ὃν θέλεις τάφον
θοῦ—καὶ γὰρ ὀρθῶς τῶν γε σῶν τελεῖς ὕπερ—,
ἐμοῦ δὲ μήποτ' ἀξιωθήτω τόδε
πατρῷον ἄστυ ζῶντος οἰκητοῦ τυχεῖν,
ἀλλ' ἔα με ναίειν ὄρεσιν, ἔνθα κλῄζεται
οὑμὸς Κιθαιρὼν οὗτος, ὃν μήτηρ τέ μοι
πατήρ τ' ἐθέσθην ζῶντε κύριον τάφον,
ἵν' ἐξ ἐκείνων, οἵ μ' ἀπωλλύτην, θάνω.
καίτοι τοσοῦτόν γ' οἶδα, μήτε μ' ἂν νόσον
μήτ' ἄλλο πέρσαι μηδέν· οὐ γὰρ ἄν ποτε
θνῄσκων ἐσώθην, μὴ 'πί τῳ δεινῷ κακῷ.

CREON

I would have done so, be assured, only I wished first to learn from the god what I should do.

OEDIPUS

But his pronouncement is all too clear, that I, the parricide, the impious one, should be allowed to perish!

CREON

Such things were said; but in the emergency in which we are it is better to find out how we should act.

OEDIPUS

Will you then inquire about my wretched person?

CREON

Yes, this time you will believe the god!

OEDIPUS

Yes, and I charge you and shall urge you; bury yourself, as you will, her who is in the house; for it is right that you should discharge the duty for one who is your own. But as for me, do not require the city of my father to have me living in it, but let me live in the mountains, where there is that mountain of my own that is called Cithaeron, which my mother and my father, while they lived, appointed to be my tomb, so that I may get my death from them who tried to kill me.

So much, at least, I know, that no sickness or other factor would have killed me; for I should never have been saved from death but for some dreadful evil. But let my

---

1445 γ' ἂν Kr: τἂν Lpat

1446 προτρέψομαι rat: προσ- LpZr

ἀλλ' ἡ μὲν ἡμῶν μοῖρ', ὅποιπερ εἶσ', ἴτω·
παίδων δὲ τῶν μὲν ἀρσένων μή μοι, Κρέον,
προσθῇ μέριμναν· ἄνδρες εἰσίν, ὥστε μὴ
σπάνιν ποτὲ σχεῖν, ἔνθ' ἂν ὦσι, τοῦ βίου·
ταῖν δ' ἀθλίαιν οἰκτραῖν τε παρθένοιν ἐμαῖν,
αἶν οὔποθ' †ἡμὴ† χωρὶς ἐστάθη βορᾶς
τράπεζ' ἄνευ τοῦδ' ἀνδρός, ἀλλ' ὅσων ἐγὼ
ψαύοιμι, πάντων τώδ' ἀεὶ μετειχέτην,
ταῖν μοι μέλεσθαι· καὶ μάλιστα μὲν χεροῖν
ψαῦσαί μ' ἔασον κἀποκλαύσασθαι κακά.
ἴθ' ὦναξ,
ἴθ' ὦ γονῇ γενναῖε. χερσί τἂν θιγὼν
δοκοῖμ' ἔχειν σφας, ὥσπερ ἡνίκ' ἔβλεπον.
τί φημι;
οὐ δὴ κλύω που πρὸς θεῶν τοῖν μοι φίλοιν
δακρυρροούντοιν, καί μ' ἐποικτίρας Κρέων
ἔπεμψέ μοι τὰ φίλτατ' ἐκγόνοιν ἐμοῖν;
λέγω τι;

ΚΡΕΩΝ

λέγεις· ἐγὼ γάρ εἰμ' ὁ πορσύνας τάδε,
γνοὺς τὴν παροῦσαν τέρψιν ἥ σ' εἶχεν πάλαι.

ΟΙΔΙΠΟΥΣ

ἀλλ' εὐτυχοίης, καί σε τῆσδε τῆς ὁδοῦ
δαίμων ἄμεινον ἢ 'μὲ φρουρήσας τύχοι.
ὦ τέκνα, ποῦ ποτ' ἐστέ; δεῦρ' ἴτ', ἔλθετε
ὡς τὰς ἀδελφὰς τάσδε τὰς ἐμὰς χέρας,
αἳ τοῦ φυτουργοῦ πατρὸς ὑμὶν ὧδ' ὁρᾶν

fate go wherever it will go; but as to my children, do not take thought for the males, for they are men, and wherever they are will never fail to get a living. But of my two girls, poor pitiable ones, for whom the table where I ate was never set apart so that they were without me, but they always shared in what I put a hand to—care for them! And if you can, let me touch them and lament over my sorrows! Come, my lord, come, you whom your birth made noble! If I can lay my hands on them I can seem to have them with me, as when I could see.

Enter the daughters of OEDIPUS.

What am I saying? Do I not hear, I ask, my dear ones weeping? Creon has taken pity on me and has sent me my two dearest children. Am I right?

CREON

You are; I have contrived this, knowing the joy you now feel, which possessed you in the past also.

OEDIPUS

May you have good fortune, and may a god guide you on this path better than I was guided! Children, where are you? Come here! Come to these hands that are your brother's, which have done the duty of the eyes of the

---

1463–64 obscuri

1463 *οὔποθ' ἡμὴ*] *οὔποτ' ἀμῆς* Kennedy

1465 *τώδ'* Schneidewin: *τῶνδ'* codd.

1466 *ταῖν* Zr (coni. Heath): *αἶν* codd.

1477 *ἥ σ' εἶχεν* Lac: *ἥ σ' ἔχει* Zg: *ἣν εἶχες* Lpc ra

τὰ πρόσθε λαμπρὰ προὐξένησαν ὄμματα·
ὃς ὑμίν, ὦ τέκν', οὔθ' ὁρῶν οὔθ' ἱστορῶν
πατὴρ ἐφάνθην ἔνθεν αὐτὸς ἠρόθην.
καὶ σφὼ δακρύω· προσβλέπειν γὰρ οὐ σθένω·
νοούμενος τὰ πικρὰ τοῦ λοιποῦ βίου,
οἷον βιῶναι σφὼ πρὸς ἀνθρώπων χρεών.
ποίας γὰρ ἀστῶν ἥξετ' εἰς ὁμιλίας,
ποίας δ' ἑορτάς, ἔνθεν οὐ κεκλαυμέναι
πρὸς οἶκον ἵξεσθ' ἀντὶ τῆς θεωρίας;
ἀλλ' ἡνίκ' ἂν δὴ πρὸς γάμων ἥκητ' ἀκμάς,
τίς οὗτος ἔσται, τίς παραρρίψει, τέκνα,
τοιαῦτ' ὀνείδη λαμβάνειν, ἃ †τοῖς ἐμοῖς†
γονεῦσιν ἔσται σφῷν θ' ὁμοῦ δηλήματα;
τί γὰρ κακῶν ἄπεστι; τὸν πατέρα πατὴρ
ὑμῶν ἔπεφνε· τὴν τεκοῦσαν ἤροσεν,
ὅθεν περ αὐτὸς ἐσπάρη, κἀκ τῶν ἴσων
ἐκτήσαθ' ὑμᾶς, ὧνπερ αὐτὸς ἐξέφυ.
τοιαῦτ' ὀνειδιεῖσθε. κᾆτα τίς γαμεῖ;
οὐκ ἔστιν οὐδείς, ὦ τέκν', ἀλλὰ δηλαδὴ
χέρσους φθαρῆναι κἀγάμους ὑμᾶς χρεών.
ὦ παῖ Μενοικέως, ἀλλ' ἐπεὶ μόνος πατὴρ
ταύταιν λέλειψαι, νὼ γάρ, ὣ 'φυτεύσαμεν,
ὀλώλαμεν δύ' ὄντε, μή σφε, πάτερ, ἴδῃς
πτωχὰς ἀνάνδρους ἐγγενεῖς ἀλωμένας,
μηδ' ἐξισώσῃς τάσδε τοῖς ἐμοῖς κακοῖς.
ἀλλ' οἴκτισόν σφας, ὧδε τηλικάσδ' ὁρῶν
πάντων ἐρήμους, πλὴν ὅσον τὸ σὸν μέρος.
ξύννευσον, ὦ γενναῖε, σῇ ψαύσας χερί.

father who begat you, once so bright; he who unseeing, unknowing became your father by her from whom he himself was got.

And I weep for you, for I have no power to look upon you, as I think upon the bitterness of the life that awaits you, the life that will be dealt out to you by men. For to what assemblies, to what feasts of the citizens will you go, from which you will not return in tears instead of taking pleasure in the show? But when you come to the age of marriage, who shall he be, who shall take up the hazard of incurring such reproaches as will attach disastrously to your parents and to you? Why, what misery is absent? Your father killed his father; he had issue of his mother, from whom he himself had sprung, and begot you from the source of his own being. Such are the taunts you will encounter; and then who shall marry you? There is no one, my children, but it is clear that you are destined to perish barren, without husbands.

Son of Menoeceus, since you are left as the only father for these girls, since we two who were their parents have perished, do not look on, father, while these that are your kin wander in beggary without husbands, and do not degrade them to the level of my sorrows! Take pity on them, seeing them at their age bereft of everything, except so far as you provide. Nod your assent, noble one, and touch them with your hand! To you, children, if you

---

1485 πατὴρ] ἀροτὴρ Herwerden

1487 πικρὰ . . . λοιποῦ Kp: λοιπὰ . . . πικροῦ Lrpat

1494 τοῖς ἐμοῖς] τοῖσί τε Herwerden: alii alia

1505 πάτερ, ἴδῃς Jackson: παρίδῃς codd.

σφῷν δ', ὦ τέκν', εἰ μὲν εἰχέτην ἤδη φρένας,
πόλλ' ἂν παρῄνουν· νῦν δὲ τοῦτ' εὔχεσθέ μοι,
οὗ καιρὸς ἐᾷ ζῆν, τοῦ βίου δὲ λῴονος
ὑμᾶς κυρῆσαι τοῦ φυτεύσαντος πατρός.

ΚΡΕΩΝ

ἅλις ἵν' ἐξήκεις δακρύων· ἀλλ' ἴθι στέγης ἔσω.

ΟΙΔΙΠΟΥΣ

πειστέον, κεἰ μηδὲν ἡδύ.

ΚΡΕΩΝ

πάντα γὰρ καιρῷ καλά.

ΟΙΔΙΠΟΥΣ

οἶσθ' ἐφ' οἷς οὖν εἶμι;

ΚΡΕΩΝ

λέξεις, καὶ τότ' εἴσομαι κλυών.

ΟΙΔΙΠΟΥΣ

γῆς μ' ὅπως πέμψεις ἄποικον.

ΚΡΕΩΝ

τοῦ θεοῦ μ' αἰτεῖς δόσιν.

ΟΙΔΙΠΟΥΣ

ἀλλὰ θεοῖς γ' ἔχθιστος ἥκω.

ΚΡΕΩΝ

τοιγαροῦν τεύξῃ τάχα.

ΟΙΔΙΠΟΥΣ

φὴς τάδ' οὖν;

ΚΡΕΩΝ

ἃ μὴ φρονῶ γὰρ οὐ φιλῶ λέγειν μάτην.

had already understanding, I would give much advice; but as things are, pray for this for me, that you may live where opportunity allows, and that you may have a better life than that of the father who begot you.

CREON

You have wept long enough; go inside the house!

OEDIPUS

I shall obey, though it gives me no pleasure.

CREON

All things are good that are in season.

OEDIPUS

Do you know, then, on what conditions I will go?

CREON

You will tell me, and when I have heard you I shall know.

OEDIPUS

That you shall send me out of the country.

CREON

What you ask of me is in the gift of the god.

OEDIPUS

But the gods detest me!

CREON

For that reason you shall soon receive it!

OEDIPUS

Do you say so?

CREON

Yes, for I am not accustomed to say frivolously things I do not mean.

1513 ἐᾷ Dindorf: ἀεὶ codd. 1513–30 del. Teuffel

ΟΙΔΙΠΟΥΣ

ἄπαγέ νύν μ᾽ ἐντεῦθεν ἤδη.

ΚΡΕΩΝ

στεῖχέ νυν, τέκνων δ᾽ ἀφοῦ.

ΟΙΔΙΠΟΥΣ

μηδαμῶς ταύτας γ᾽ ἕλῃ μου.

ΚΡΕΩΝ

πάντα μὴ βούλου κρατεῖν·
καὶ γὰρ ἁκράτησας οὔ σοι τῷ βίῳ ξυνέσπετο.

ΧΟΡΟΣ

ὦ πάτρας Θήβης ἔνοικοι, λεύσσετ᾽, Οἰδίπους ὅδε,
ὃς τὰ κλείν᾽ αἰνίγματ᾽ ᾔδει καὶ κράτιστος ἦν ἀνήρ,
οὗ τίς οὐ ζήλῳ πολιτῶν ταῖς τύχαις ἐπέβλεπεν,
εἰς ὅσον κλύδωνα δεινῆς συμφορᾶς ἐλήλυθεν.
ὥστε θνητὸν ὄντ᾽ ἐκείνην τὴν τελευταίαν ἔδει
ἡμέραν ἐπισκοποῦντα μηδέν᾽ ὀλβίζειν, πρὶν ἂν
τέρμα τοῦ βίου περάσῃ μηδὲν ἀλγεινὸν παθών.

1524–30 del. Ritter

1526 οὗ τίς Martin: ὅστις codd. | ταῖς Canter: καὶ codd. | ἐπέβλεπεν Musgrave: ἐπιβλέπων codd.

1528 ἔδει Stanley: ἰδεῖν codd.

OEDIPUS

So now take me away from here!

CREON

Go now, and let go of your children!

OEDIPUS

By no means take these away from me!

CREON

Do not wish to have control in everything! Power to control did not accompany you through all your life.

Exeunt OEDIPUS *and* CREON.

CHORUS

Dwellers in our native land of Thebes, see to what a storm of cruel disaster has come Oedipus here, who knew the answer to the famous riddle and was a mighty man, on whose fortune every one among the citizens used to look with envy! So that one should wait to see the final day and should call none among mortals fortunate, till he has crossed the bourne of life without suffering grief.